TEACHING STRATEGIES

TEACHING STRATEGIES

A Guide to Better Instruction

————◆————

THIRD EDITION

Donald C. Orlich
Washington State University

Donald P. Kauchak
University of Utah

Robert J. Harder
Washington State University

R. A. Pendergrass
*Superintendent of Schools,
Bakersfield, MO*

Richard C. Callahan
Shipley Associates

Andrew J. Keogh
North Dakota State University

Harry Gibson
St. Martin's College

D. C. HEATH AND COMPANY
Lexington, Massachusetts   Toronto

Copyright © 1990 by D. C. Heath and Company.
Previous editions copyright © 1985, 1980 by D. C. Heath and Company.

Published simultaneously in Canada.

Printed in the United States of America.

International Standard Book Number: 0-669-20160-X

Library of Congress Catalog Card Number: 89-84051

10   9   8   7   6   5   4   3   2   1

Preface

Teaching Strategies: A Guide to Better Instruction, Third Edition, provides proven teaching methods, coupled with effective instructional theory, to interested educators at all levels. We develop the premise that the teacher is an educational leader and decision-maker who both directly affects the students and influences the presentation of subject matter. This assertion is substantiated in every chapter of the guide.

This text offers a broad spectrum of instructional methodologies, techniques, and approaches that are workable in today's classroom. Practitioners and novices have found this book valuable as a basis for identifying sound educational practices and as a guide for making systematic, logical, and humane instructional choices. *Teaching Strategies* is designed for courses dealing with educational methods or techniques, but it may be profitably used as a reference book for a variety of other purposes. For example, in–service teachers have found the book a valuable and easy-to-use resource. This third edition reflects our attempt to translate the exciting findings of educational researchers into applicable classroom strategies.

Each chapter focuses on a major theme, which is explored in great depth, including significant research studies. In Chapter 1, we provide a brief introduction to schooling and broad educational goals. We also introduce our major concepts of instructional decision-making and teacher responsibility. Unique to this text is an analysis of the emerging field of school culture and the impact of the environment on teacher incentives. Chapters 2 through 5 present the basic "tools" for effective and systematic teaching. The major topics include specifying instructional objectives, sequencing learning activities, applying the various taxonomies, preparing lesson plans, and conducting micro-teaching. We offer the profession the most novel interpretative model yet created for applying the cognitive taxonomy. You are invited to test this analogue and communicate your findings. The treatment of lesson planning (lesson design) may be the most comprehensive presented in a text of this type. Collectively, the first five chapters present the basics for instructional planning and stress the future teacher's comprehension of the fundamentals. We have analyzed and synthesized instructional and educational trends so that you gain a broad perspective of the field. We want you to develop your own individual framework for instruction, based on proven educational practices and current professional theories.

The last five chapters present instruction as a dynamic process operating within a social context (the classroom)—with the realities of interaction between teacher and student our foremost concern. Making this interaction more productive is our key objective. Chapter 6 is one of the most detailed discussions on posing questions found in any methods textbook. In revising this chapter we have altered some of our previous techniques, incorporating feedback from users of the second edition, several teachers in the field, and professors who had adopted the text. Chapter 7, "Decisions About Discussions," provides the background for successful discussion techniques and synthesizes the essential principles from social psychology for easy application by classroom teachers. We have revised this chapter to illustrate contemporary techniques and to explain the application of the powerful cooperative learning model. In Chapter 8 the topics of inquiry and simulations illustrate some of the higher-level interactive techniques for teachers at all levels. Chapter 9 is entirely new and focuses on a generic model by which to teach thinking skills. We urge teachers at every level to learn to apply effective thinking strategies. Finally, Chapter 10 views classroom management from several research and theoretical perspectives, again stressing an underlying tenet of the book—the teacher as a decision-maker. Our candid treatment of teacher biases—grounded in equity, gender, and racial issues—is certainly unmatched.

In addition, we present several techniques that will help both new and experienced teachers stimulate the development of critical thinking skills. These thought-producing techniques include the appropriate use of hierarchy charts, specialized grids to apply the taxonomies, "wait time," question mapping, probing, student-directed discussions, inquiry, simulations, and so forth. We deliberately specify student's entry-level skills to ensure the successful use of this information in highly interactive and complex instructional environments.

At the beginning of each chapter, a set of intended learner outcomes focuses the users' study efforts. As the themes develop, we subtly interject "affective" desires for the user—to illustrate the relationship between affective and cognitive objectives. At appropriate points, *Formative Evaluations* are introduced, enabling students to judge their success in meeting the intended objectives. Our formative evaluations also provide users with models preparing them to use similar instruments in future classroom use.

Overall, the topics in this text reflect a wide range of teaching and instructional strategies, presented as a unified—albeit eclectic—system. All topics have been used, critiqued, and reviewed several times by our own pre–service students and by fellow teachers. All techniques are presented as realistic and practical classroom methods—not simply theoretical ones. Examples of all strategies are provided in a variety of instructional contexts to illustrate abstract concepts. The techniques also work in multicultural settings; several professors who teach in such settings have commended the second edition for its usefulness in this context. Our rather conservative treatment of computer-aided instruction is based on up-to-date research findings indicating that computers free teachers for higher-level instruction. Yet there is no compelling evidence that classroom computers are being used to their optimum. If you use a microcomputer in the classroom, then our text provides you with the competencies to restructure your classroom learning environment so that the computer, in fact, changes your role as a facilitator of learning.

As a whole, the topics in this textbook are those most often taught in basic methods of instruction courses. These topics appear on state or national lists of generic teacher competencies required by all those entering the profession. We deliberately avoided duplicating topics taught in separate courses at most universities and colleges.

This book is written with the sincere desire to improve classroom teaching and to make a genuine contribution to the profession by providing a rationale and applying it. We are indebted to Mollie B. Bailey, Jack Cousins, Elaine McNally Jarchaw, and Geoffrey L. Hughes for their critiques and suggestions on the first edition and to Susan Reimer-Sachs for her insightful critique for the second edition. We thank Shirley Yamashita for her positive feedback that helped to shape the third edition. We express our appreciation to Dr. Dorothy I. Hellene for her contributions to the first edition. And to our colleague, Dr. Constance H. Kravas, we appreciate her efforts that are reflected in the first two editions. We acknowledge Judith Leet for her contributions to the second edition and Sandra Tyacke for the many manuscript preparations. We are grateful to Herb Cohen, Arizona State University; Carol Sharp, Glassboro State College; Natalie S. Barman, Park Tudor School; Bonita Franks, Bloomsburg University of Pennsylvania; and Truman Whitfield, Murray State University for all their comments and suggestions. We especially acknowledge the many professors, teachers, and administrators who provided their suggestions and evaluations. We thank our students for their patience and recommendations as materials were developed, field-tested, and revised. Finally, we point out that this edition has a newly designed and innovative manual for the instructor. Those who are pressed for time will appreciate the entire package of materials that accompany this edition.

Donald C. Orlich

Contents

1

Teaching as Decision-Making

*A*s the twentieth century wanes, the schools of America are yet its single largest industry. The combined expenditure for all K–12 schooling is over $190 billion. Add to that an estimated $115 billion for higher education and the magnitude of our industry is staggering. Few teachers ever recognize that, as members of this "industry," they must have a broad understanding of teaching. Too few teachers or administrators acknowledge the need to be able to analyze *how* they teach in terms of *what* and *whom* they are teaching. This book views such an approach as an important ideal, and the authors present this chapter as a rationale that gives a theoretical and practical structure to guide action in the classroom. Our intent is to provide a general instructional guide for all teachers.

Objectives   After completing this chapter, you should be able to:

- Illustrate a rationale for teaching
- Discuss decision-making as a technology of teaching
- Illustrate the impact of the school culture on the individual teacher
- Present the rewards structure of the schools
- Present an overview of curricular and instructional decision areas
- List general areas where teachers must make decisions
- Summarize the concept of "effective schools"
- Synthesize issues that affect schooling
- Introduce the concept of formative evaluation

THE TEACHER AS DECISION-MAKER

The art and science of effective teaching may be defined from many points of view. There are those who sincerely believe that "good teachers are born, not made." If this were the case, good teachers could simply be identified without the expense of schooling. But as yet, no one has been able to identify those "natural" tendencies that produce good teachers. At the opposite pole, there are those who claim that teaching is nothing more than the simple application of the correct reinforcers so that appropriate learner behaviors are elicited. The only problem with this position is that no one has discovered all of the positive reinforcers to be used each day with millions of children and by hundreds of thousands of teachers.

These two positions can be viewed as two extremes of a broad continuum. Teaching as an "art" relies heavily on intuition as a basis for action, whereas teaching as a "science" depends primarily on a behaviorally oriented model. In the former approach, teaching is conducted by a more subjective, spontaneous method; in the latter, the process of education tends to be perceived as a very simple stimulus-response interaction—a reductionist position—with every skill subdivided into component tasks or procedures. On the one hand, it is very possible that there are natural traits in some people that predispose them to being better teachers; on the other, it is also essential that all teachers master a set of tested teaching skills to be successful. Thus, it is difficult to subscribe totally to either perspective because both tend to be closed prescriptive systems; both, however, influence what happens in the classroom.

Teaching as Interaction and Decision-Making

We propose an alternate theory. The act of teaching is always a dynamic interaction of individuals (teachers and teachers, teachers and learners, learners and learners), in which all concerned are constantly making decisions. We believe that teaching must be deliberate and planned.

For example, teachers may decide to give one mass assignment to all students from a single textbook or to give multiple assignments from a variety of sources so that the students can select the ones of their choice. A decision may also be made to use multiple objectives, with accompanying learning materials that have been tailored to fit the instructional needs of various individuals or groups in the class. Teachers may then choose among a wide variety of options concerning how they will proceed. Will there be a lecture, a short quiz followed by a recitation period, a film, a filmstrip, or an audio tape? Decisions, decisions, decisions!

Phillip W. Jackson (1968) suggests that elementary teachers engage in as many as 1,000 personal interactions each day. His findings are similar to Paul V. Gump's observations (1967) that there are as many as 1,300 teacher acts in a single day of teaching. Most of these interactions involve minor as well as major decisions.

Not all the decisions are made as the result of systematic and organized planning. Sometimes the choices are made intuitively. The use of intuition in teaching is quite prevalent. Many choices must be made intuitively because the rapid pace of classroom learning demands instant decision-making. In these instances, teachers depend on experience and quick thinking to provide the most appropriate instructional technique. We may assume that the intuition of the experienced teacher is likely to be superior to that of the novice. Intuition is like an opinion in that its usefulness is dependent on the experiential background on which it is based. Yet, in many cases, teachers depend on intuition when systematic and organized planning would be more appropriate. For example, a teacher may believe that a new activity ought to be offered in the school setting, so a particular course of action is taken. Sometimes these "hunches" prove to be right, with beneficial results for the students; but sometimes they are not effective or are inappropriate for the needs of the learners.

Intuition as a sole guide to instructional behavior represents a very limited view of the teaching process. Like the proposition that "good teachers are born, not made," the use of intuition alone restricts teachers from considering teaching as both science and art. It negates the development of a systematic planning pattern from which rational and consistent decisions can be made. It implies that intuition is the beginning and end of instructional effectiveness, rather than one aspect of the teaching process.

Too often, the teacher who relies exclusively on intuition determines objectives and selects procedures that are more reflective of instructor needs than of student needs. Thus, a teacher who feels like lecturing delivers a lecture. If a teacher feels like showing a film, a film it is! Few of us would tolerate this mode of operation in arenas outside the realm of education. Consider for a minute how much confidence you would place in a bus driver who repeatedly changed the bus route because of a belief that such changes were inherently good and relieved both the driver and the riders of boredom.

Of course, we also propose that through meaningful experiences, a teacher may know instinctively how to handle or react to a specific situation. For example, students are almost always restive before vacation periods; thus, a teacher should not try to introduce a new topic on the Friday before a one-week vacation. Teachers can shift from an intuitive mode of operation to a more critical one simply by being *aware* that they are constantly making decisions affecting the intellectual, attitudinal, and psychomotor skills of learners. To this end, we agree with Louis J. Rubin (1984) and his concept of "teaching artistry." You develop artistry by being aware of what you do as a teacher and of how that affects what your charges do. Artistry of teaching implies that the teacher has developed a sophisticated set of skills. It further assumes that the best teachers use instructional strategies in ways that imprint their style on every child or adolescent in the class. The development of a humanistic and caring teaching style is a vision of this book.

Implicit within the concept of decision-making is the notion of *responsibility*. Teachers cannot pass the buck. If teachers make decisions, they must be willing to take the responsibility for both the implementation and the possible consequences of their decisions. For example, if teachers deliberately bias a discussion to fit their opinions, religious dogmas, or political tenets, then they are being agents of indoctrination. Some teachers we have known refuse to acknowledge that they are, in fact, being doctrinaire; they claim that "this is good for the students." Of course, they would *not* consider it "good" if the students were to be swayed toward the opposite doctrine.

We illustrate this potential problem area because, in our opinion, many teachers do not recognize their responsibility for making decisions. There is often a tendency to blame the "administration" or the "school board." To be sure, administrative regulations and school-board policies do govern selected instructional procedures and even content. But most classroom instructional decisions are, in fact, made by the teacher. (We will discuss these and other curricular matters later in Chapter 1.) Our plea is that the teacher will take the responsibility for making these decisions, and that most decisions will be made on a logical, systematic basis—and not on impulse.

One way to raise one's level of cognitive consciousness (awareness) is to begin thinking with the "if-then" logic. *If* teachers desire to encourage the students to learn through inquiry techniques, *then* they must provide the students with the initial learning skills with which to inquire. Furthermore, they must supply the learning materials in a sequential, systematic fashion so that the students may apply the concepts being learned to real situations.

The if-then logical paradigm provides the teacher with a cognitive map similar to that used in generating rules and principles. The teacher starts thinking about causes and effects of actions and statements and about relationships between classroom activities and students. The teacher learns to obtain as much information as possible about both students and subject matter prior to the lesson and then develops a plan for success. This technology of instruction is based on the conclusions developed about the interaction between the subject matter, the student, and the teacher.

Finding the Panacea

If there is one truism in teaching, it is that there is no *one way* to teach anything or anyone. With alarming frequency, educational authorities or critics announce that they have discovered *the* answer to teaching problems. The literature is full of such examples. Read about the advocates for behavioral objectives, team teaching, individually guided instruction, educational television, phonics or other reading techniques, new math, activity-oriented science, and new social studies. Many of these approaches are based on sound analysis and investigation of the teaching-learning act. Typically, each approach is related to a specific kind of teaching activity, a specific philosophy of education, or a specific perspective of the structure of the basic discipline for which the program is developed.

Unfortunately, many advocates, in their eagerness to "spread the word" about particular approaches or methodologies, myopically attempt to convince other educators that *their* method is, at long last, the right one. Such pronouncements, no matter how well intentioned, tend to be naive. The chances are likely that many teachers will not use *the* method; indeed, teachers who have never heard about *it* will be successful simply by using more eclectic methods combined with wisdom, logic, and a sound knowledge of educational psychology.

For example, during the late 1960s and the entire 1970s, standardized test scores for students above grade 3 tended to decline. By 1984, some scores began to stabilize and even to increase somewhat. To improve education (and test scores), nearly four-fifths of the state legislatures passed "accountability" laws. Nobody could really define *accountability,* but the term sounded impressive. In general, the accountability movement became a simple extension of testing and evaluating. The typical grades at which statewide tests were administered tended to be grades 4, 8, and 11. Other state legislatures or state boards of education established "minimum competency levels" for high school graduation as a measure of accountability. Almost no one listened to critics who asked, "Why are standardized test scores acceptable and satisfactory in grades 1, 2, and 3 but not in others?" Few legislators, school-board members, administrators, or teachers asked the question, "Of what use are test scores to a child six or eight months after the testing period?" We must, however, add a warning statement issued nationally by the president of the Educational Testing Service (ETS) in 1983: Gregory R. Anrig, addressing the ETS annual invitational conference, warned that the "quick fix" of using standardized tests to improve education was, in fact, a *test abuse*. An analysis of the history of the 1980s showed that policy-makers ignored Anrig's stern warning.

It appears that much of the methodology of educators tends to be based on simplistic thinking. During the 1950s and 1960s, furious conflicts developed about the way to teach reading—by sight, phonic, phonetic, psycholinguistic, or eclectic methods. Experts know that a variety of techniques is important to develop a broad set of reading skills. Using any one method exclusively will not bring instant reading success to all children but will strengthen certain skills over others. The literature shows that one program after another is proposed as a cure-all but eventually proves to be not entirely effective when used alone.

We thus caution you from the beginning: we will never say that we have *the* method. We will present a series of options that are all usable and that will all yield humanely conceived educational results. In other words, we are following our own theory. If teaching is a decision-making activity, then there ought to be divergent means by which to accomplish any instructional objective. That is what this book is about: to learn when to use a technique and what you can expect from using it. The context in which any method is used predicates its success; this is the notion of relevance.

Content and Process as Decisions

As you plan the teaching of a subject, you must remember that just as important as the *content* of the lesson are the *processes* that the students need to master the content. The Cunard Steamship Lines once advertised that getting there was half the fun! With teaching, the same logic is applicable. The students must know how to accomplish what you want. Let us examine a few situations.

If a teacher wants to teach about mathematical ratios (the content) and how to apply them, then the students must master various skills and processes. They must be able to understand the meaning of division, to comprehend the concept of whole numbers, to conceptualize the notion of proportions, and to perform a few other basic arithmetic operations. In certain cases, the processes associated with content are at times indistinguishable from the content; that is, both the thought processes and the resultant knowledge, skills, or information *are* the content. In this sense, there is "procedural content," and there is "cognitive content." The "modern math" movement was an attempt to build systematically on mathematical cognitive processes. The only trouble was that some professors of mathematics who wrote books on modern math forgot that it takes practice, drill, and application to learn a concept. Instead of providing the necessary procedural exercises, the mathematicians provided concept after concept without supplying concrete learning experiences. In short, the lack of procedural techniques—knowing how to know—tended to be ignored in favor of highly sophisticated math topics beyond the comprehension of most young people. Now, a decade or two after the "math revolution," there is a counterrevolution. Teachers and publishing companies are returning to the teaching of a broader spectrum of math rather than exposing the students to random sets of math concepts. And, in some cases, the content of math textbooks today looks remarkably similar to that of 1950!

When prospective teachers are asked "As you anticipate teaching, what concerns you most?" many, if not most, secondary education majors identify "knowledge of subject matter" as their chief problem. But while prospective secondary school teachers tend to be "subject-oriented," elementary school teachers tend to be "child-oriented." Their primary objective is to help the child to grow and mature both mentally and physically—not just to teach mathematics, physics, or English literature. This means that the early school experiences of children will be oriented toward helping them to adjust from their home environment to the institutional dimensions of school. However, the elementary school teacher's approach, in which the child comes first and the subject content second, may create some conflict within any school system.

In the middle schools, there is a transition period in which the emphasis shifts from a human-growth orientation to a subject orientation. It is critically important for middle school educators to understand that children (young adolescents) in these institutions are just beginning to emerge from Jean Piaget's *concrete operations* stage and are entering the initial *formal operations* stage. To teach this large group effectively, teachers must combine "hands-on" activities and "thinking" activities for all major concepts or lessons. Techniques such as preparing time lines, conducting experiments, preparing charts and graphs, classifying, and sequencing all help the learners. Lecturing and abstract discussions simply *do not* enhance learning for these children. But in nearly all high schools, teachers tend to be very academically inclined. The subject matter is first, last, and always the focus, although not to the exclusion of all personal considerations.

Who decided on these emphases? To say that "society" did would be a bit irresponsible. We argue that the teachers determined these priorities in response to the subtle pressures placed on them by institutions of higher education and perhaps even by society at large. Nearly one-half century ago, anthropologist Clyde Kluckhohn (1949) concluded that the schools of any society mirror that society. The wishes and beliefs of a society are subtly translated into the values, curricula, and instructions of the schools. This was exemplified when many secondary school educators wanted to "humanize" the secondary schools and to make them more process-oriented. But when newspaper writers, school-board members, legislators, and parents begin to pressure high school teachers to improve test scores, to raise academic standards, and to add content, those same teachers become acutely aware of content.

It is hard for all of us in education to realize that processes must be taught with content, and it is even more difficult to understand the motives of any teacher who says, "Well, if they didn't have the knowledge or techniques before they got into my class, that's too bad. . . ." If students do not have the so-called prerequisite skills, then you as a teacher must provide them! If you do not, then your students will suffer failure. If you provide the basics, then your students will be successful. The decision is yours.

UNDERSTANDING THE SCHOOL'S CULTURE

We just said that the decision is yours. But it's not yours alone. In elementary, middle, and secondary schools, there is a unique quality about the workplace that has only recently been labeled "the culture of the school." This emergent theoretical concept has taken on importance, for the massive attempts to implement meaningful changes in the schools during the 1970s and 1980s were not successful. There are several reasons for the failures. Many of the reforms were *cosmetic,* having no profound impact on student learning or teacher instructional strategies. Another reason suggests that the reforms were *intrinsically inferior.* Armchair theorists suggest very simplistic solutions to complex educational and social problems. As one colleague observed, "We have many solutions seeking problems."

William Chance (1986) examined legislative school reform efforts in seven states. His study shows dramatically how politicians (with some help from educators) had field days prescribing laws and prescriptions for the *sick institution.* The "political medicine" increased graduation requirements, raised competency standards for teachers, and instituted student testing. The underlying premise for the reforms was to make our nation more economically competitive in world markets.

During the 1980s virtually every state legislature passed laws that had great impact upon schools, teachers, teacher education, teacher licensing, school financing, and curriculum design. Linda Darling-Hammond and Barnett Berry (1988) estimated that over a thousand pieces of legislation were enacted—all to reform the schools and those who worked in them. The writers characterized state-mandated reforms as a series of waves. Initially, the wave was for efficiency, followed by a wave of teacherproof curricula, followed by a wave of "back to the basics" (as if we ever left them). We predict that the wave of the 1990s will be a renewed emphasis on teacher enhancement and professionalism.

Let us return to the original topic: culture of the schools. Actually there are cultures. Students of this movement include Seymour B. Sarason (1982), Ann Lieberman and Lynne Miller (1984), and John I. Goodlad (1987).

Concepts for Consideration

The primary concept associated with the school culture movement is that of *system.* A system is an entity comprised of many elements or components that interact in a positive manner so that the system functions effectively. A school district is an example of a system. It is a human creation—a collection of people, buildings, machinery, materials, rules, conventions, and a host of numerous parts and players. The system has subsystems: A school district has attendance areas, different types of schools, bus routes, and the like. A subsystem such as a high school has several smaller subsystems; for example, athletic teams, specific academic programs, vocational units, service groups, union and nonunion employees, student groups, faculty groups, and clubs.

Systems are important because they function as a whole, and they interact in a manner that stimulates or retards more interaction. The "effective schools movement" and "school-site" education advocates understand that the system, or in this case the subsystem, must function at a very high rate of efficiency; otherwise, the elements begin to deteriorate.

Lieberman and Miller (1984) summarized several points about the school culture. First, the school culture is characterized by great uncertainty. The explicit values of the schools are not easily identified or agreed upon. The work in a school is not a product, but the schools are continuously compared to the industrial product-oriented model.

Second, the ethos of schools differs greatly in any one district and between districts; hence, there is no simple prescription that will improve all the schools. As Arthur E. Wise (1988) noted, the more prescriptive the state legislatures become in making specific laws to fix conceived ills, the more problems arise as a direct effect of those same laws, which are rarely well thought out. Local conditions should have more to do with school improvement efforts than those imposed from outside.

Third, norms and values are different school by school. Teachers learn their roles through experience, regardless of the amount and content of formal education. Although norms and values differ significantly for elementary and secondary teachers, teaching is for all of them an isolated activity. Teachers interact intensively with children or adolescents all day with little professional contact with colleagues.

Fourth, instructional methods and practices are complex acts, having weak research bases. Teachers continuously show "the research" to be wrong by having good results and by never using "the" researched method. Perhaps that is what makes teaching and instructing so susceptible to charlatans—the knowledge base related to student learning is weak, while teaching artistry is not quantifiable (see Orlich, 1985).

The interaction of a system is critical for its *organizational health*. If the business office ignores teacher or principal requests for selected quality instructional materials, then that office may have a negative impact on student learning outcomes. If the principal is a weak instructional leader, then that specific school will probably show poor morale and poor student achievements. If the central office forces teachers to teach to some "company line," then the teachers will tend to do so halfheartedly and will subvert the policy, no matter how good its intent.

School cultures just do not happen—they develop over time. To determine some of the elements of any school culture, we can complete the profiling processes suggested by Robert E. Blum and Jocelyn A. Butler (1985). These include collecting and analyzing several data sets, such as (1) student achievement tests, (2) student progress in selected areas over a certain time, (3) promotion and retention in classes, (4) graduate competency measures, (5) student attitudes toward school, and (6) student social behavioral indicators. A set of profiles would illustrate schoolwide strengths and weaknesses; from them relevant changes could be made. John I. Goodlad's processes used in *A Place Called School* (1984) would produce data to identify critical elements. A major problem that faces a school culture is a predominance of educational psychology in teacher training to the neglect of the study of culture, norms, and interactions. These are found in sociology and anthropology, domains that are notoriously missing in virtually all teacher preparation programs or even graduate programs.

Some Specific Aspects of the Schools' Culture

Seymour B. Sarason (1982) observed that public schools have many ambiguities that affect how teachers and children perform in the workplace. For example, the specific objectives of the school are unclear. We agree in broad principle that the school should provide instruction in academic basics, health, citizenship, acculturation, values, vocational choices, leisure time, thinking skills, life survival skills, economic indoctrination, and competition. But the teaching of sex education is not at all clearly defined. One state forbids the mention of venereal diseases, while another passes a state law mandating instruction in AIDS prevention spanning kindergarten through grade 12. A values conflict, you say. Conflict indeed!

This leads to a second major point: educators are vulnerable to the external environment. Dan Lortie (as cited by Lee S. Shulman, 1987) quipped that teachers enter the profession after having spent seventeen years in an "apprenticeship of observation." Entering teachers have already been in school for at least sixteen or seventeen years and have been part of a tremendous amount of instruction. One cliché often heard in schooling is that "you teach the way you were taught," university courses in education notwithstanding.

Third, teachers work in seclusion, not sharing their work with other professionals or with the outside world. By being placed in semiseclusion, teachers tend to develop personalized teaching styles that may not be beneficial to student learning. Over the academic year principals or supervisors might spend a total of one or two hours "observing" and "evaluating" a teacher, with greater time for a novice and less for a veteran; but the vast amount of service that any teacher performs goes uncritiqued or unnoticed by fellow professionals.

Fourth, schools tend to develop their own independent culture, apart from other schools in the same district. Their norms and values may be generated from the inside. From this situation comes that horridly unprofessional comment often made to novice teachers: "Forget all that university theory. You're in the real world now." That comment reflects an anti-intellectual attitude and is a destructive blow to education as a fledgling science. There will be subtle or even intentional pressures placed on you to conform. It would be very easy to say, "Yes, I'll just lecture or go along with the gang." But, instead, you will have at your disposal a broad range of teaching strategies that the average or below-average teacher does not use. This book is designed to help you develop into the best of teachers. Study this and the remaining chapters so that you influence your environment instead of becoming its victim. In that way the ethos of your school can evolve; you can establish new norms that

Table 1-1   *Metaphors Used to Describe the School Culture*

Metaphor	General Statement
Building	Shaky leadership.
	Students have weak foundations.
War	Let's attack the problem.
	That solution is not defensible.
Flower Garden	Our children are growing so nicely.
	We must nuture the writing program.
Journey	We never got on the road.
	We're just spinning our wheels.
Hospital	We just do not operate effectively.
	The lunchroom is a blight.
Machine	We can fine-tune the program.
	Things are running smoothly around here.
Chemical Plant	We are diluting our efforts.
	Our test data were contaminated.
Target	That child is certainly misguided.
	Let's set our sights higher.
Containers	The textbook lacks substance.
	Where is the content?
Railway	Now, we're on the right track.
	The schools never "highball."
School	Our students are good learners.
	You come out of that class understanding history.

stress problem-solving, incorporation of "active" teaching, and positive student expectations.

Fifth, the general school culture is *technically weak*. Granted, we have performance objectives, overhead projectors, criterion-referenced tests, direct instruction, behavior modification, and even computer-aided instruction. Still, in general, the school culture is not sophisticated in a "high tech" sense. Although specific test or assessment data are used to make some decisions, we tend *not* to rely on technical analyses when teaching. Lee S. Shulman (1987) concluded that the knowledge base in teaching consists mostly of practical knowledge or "maxims." Thus, teaching is an imprecise art or science that allows teachers to select what knowledge they choose to use. We do not yet have computer or other technological equipment that assures us of better teaching and learning. Although futurists proclaim "A day when . . . ," that day may not be seen in the twentieth century.

The metaphors we use to describe the school reflect how we personally view the culture. The impact of these metaphors on our thoughts has been illustrated by Ernest R. House (1983). See Table 1-1 for several examples. The way we communicate about schooling affects our motives and personal convictions (see Marshall, 1988).

Metaphors of industrial production are commonplace when we speak about *our products, the bottom line,* and *delivery systems.* If the school is impersonal, then just listen to how children and programs are described; that is, what metaphors are used. The school can be described as a building, war, flower garden, target, container, railway, or even a school. Our actions are shaped by our perceptions of the culture.

Finally, the use of time is determined by a school's culture. There may be state laws or regulations governing the allocated school time; yet, it is a truism that in the school culture there is never enough time to meet all the demands.

You must recognize that the schools face the *quadrilateral dilemma.* The schools act as one component of that grand system linking the home, church, and government. The classic triangle—home, church, school—began in the New World in 1647 in the Massachusetts Bay Colony, with passage of the "Olde Deluder Satan Act." From that time until the latter half of the twentieth century, these three institutions reinforced each others' efforts to acculturate youth. The church provided the morals, religion, ethics, values, and philosophy. The home provided the human support group, nurturing, self-esteem, confidence, and care. While protecting all those cultural ideals, the school extended them. (If you got in trouble at school, you were really in trouble at home.) Each institution was an extension of the other.

Then great changes came. The home evolved into a two-worker household or to that modern social phenomenon, the single-parent household. The influence of the church lessened. Slowly moving into social engineering, the federal government shifted social, child-rearing, and nurturing tasks to the schools. Suddenly the school had a whole host of responsibilities that were not its function within the classic triangle.

All this means that some of the time in school is devoted to its social aspects, not really to its educational ones, which were once rather narrowly defined. That culture was imparted on the schools by the larger environment. But people still enter teaching. Why? Let us discuss that next.

Incentives and School Culture

Richard F. Barter (1984) observed that the school culture has an impact on the individuals in it: students and staff. In his study focusing on classroom teachers, he concluded that the quality of a school's instructional program is directly related to teacher-student interactions. As we noted previously, the number of teacher-student interactions is over a thousand per day! These interactions can lead to teacher stress. Barter cautioned that studies have shown that teachers are second only to air traffic controllers in the level of job stress. Thus, the culture of the school establishes an environment that increases or reduces the stress level for teachers —and certainly for students, too.

If there are uncertainties associated with teaching, isolation from other professionals, and a limited sharing of information, then what kind of incentives can enhance your job? Douglas E. Mitchell, Flora Ida Ortiz, and Tedi K. Mitchell (1987) examined this topic in great detail. They found that, in general, teachers acknowledge four incentives (job satisfiers).

First, there is the thrill of victory; that is, observing the success and achievement of one's students. This incentive (often called an *intrinsic motivator*) is probably the most powerful for all teachers. Teachers bask in the success of their charges. Student success reflects on the teacher's efficacy. It is great to be with "winners." That motto is especially true for second grade teachers who observe their pupils successfully mastering addition. The thrill (incentive) is no less rewarding for them than for their high school mathematics counterpart whose student wins the "Math Counts" contest and a tidy collegiate scholarship.

Inviting Student Success is the title of a book by William Watson Purkey and John M. Novak (1984). Calling that invitation our most powerful incentive, they place teachers into four categories*:

1. intentionally disinviting
2. unintentionally disinviting
3. unintentionally inviting
4. intentionally inviting

The fourth-named teacher, the one who is *intentionally inviting*, is the one who strives for student success. These teachers self-reinforce their own most powerful incentive. (Recall how earlier we asserted that "teaching must be deliberate and planned." Purkey and Novak's first and fourth categories reflect that assertion.)

The second job incentive is being recognized as an excellent teacher. Mitchell and associates (1987) labeled this characteristic as student warmth, enthusiasm, and appreciation for a teacher's efforts. Again, this is a strong intrinsic motivator. You know yourself how you felt when your teacher helped you to complete a tough assignment, or when you accomplished something and shared that feat with the responsible teacher. Yes, those are real *glows* in a teacher's eyes!

Again, as Mitchell and colleagues concluded, if the relationships between teachers and students are tense or aversive, then the work becomes physically and emotionally wearing. No amount of pay can keep a teacher *intentionally inviting* in such an environment. Unfortunately for the profession and the students, these negative traits are often the initial circumstances that lead to *intentionally disinviting* teachers.

Our colleagues' respect is the third incentive that we all appreciate. The Phi Delta Kappa educational honorary once had a motto that "the esteem of our colleagues is the foundation of power." The application of that slogan helps to make a teacher feel a sense of efficacy. Efficacy is the internal feeling that *you* can get the task done. It is similar to the motto of the Seabees of World War II: "The difficult we do immediately. The impossible may take a little longer." (Now that is an expression of efficacy!) Patricia Ashton (1985) discussed the sense of efficacy held by effective

---

*From William Watson Purkey and John M. Novak. (1984). *Inviting School Success,* 2nd ed. Belmont, Calif.: Wadsworth Publishing Co. Used with permission.

teachers: They believe that they control their own classroom destinies, and they show behaviors related to self-actualization (Abraham Maslow's highest need).

You gain respect from your colleagues when your classes achieve better than is expected, when students are successful in your class, and when the *tough* cases are *not tough* for you. These acknowledgments come from using a broad spectrum of teaching strategies that we illustrate in ensuing chapters. Efficacy, in the last analysis, is being able to see yourself doing the job, no matter how difficult or demanding.

A fourth incentive is working with other professionals. As we pointed out earlier, you will be isolated from other professionals for most of your typical working day. (We carefully inserted *typical* because some organizational structures—for example, teaming, cooperative teaching, or open schools—require greater interaction between professionals and other adults in school.) It is a positive experience and part of a being a professional to work on school problems, curriculum projects, or instructional designs with your colleagues. These activities allow you to participate in the decision-making of the school. Working in a collegial manner with your fellow professionals to improve the environment for learning is one aspect of teacher empowerment. The concept of efficacy is moved up one level to collective action, rather than just individual excellence.

What about money as an incentive? All the writers previously cited have concluded that teacher salary is *not* a motivator to do a better job of teaching. Jere L. Engleking (1986) worked with one of your authors in a research project and found that, of 442 classroom teachers surveyed, only 11 identified salary as a job satisfier! Surprised? You should not be. You and hundreds of thousands like you have selected teaching as a profession because you are intrinsically motivated. To be sure, salary is very important for achieving an acceptable standard of living. By itself, as a motivational factor, though, salary is not a key incentive.

Your Expectations as an Invitation to Learning

Knowing about the school's culture and explicitly identifying incentives gives you an advantage in teaching. This knowledge implies that you desire to be *intentionally inviting* as an instructor. It also implies that you will communicate your expectations to all your students in a very explicit manner. But how do teachers really communicate their intentions?

As we all know, there are high achievers and low achievers in all classrooms, homogeneous grouping included. How do your professional colleagues treat these two differing groups? Do they get equal warmth and feedback? Do they all get *intentionally invited* to succeed? A review of teacher behaviors and treatments toward high and low student achievers by Thomas L. Good and Jere E. Brophy (1987) indicated that there are seventeen major differences in the ways that our colleagues treat high and low achievers:

1. Waiting less time for low achievers to answer a question.
2. Giving low achievers answers or calling on someone else rather than trying to improve their responses by giving clues or repeating or rephrasing questions.
3. Inappropriate reinforcement: rewarding inappropriate behavior or incorrect answers by low achievers.
4. Criticizing low achievers more often for failure.
5. Praising low achievers less frequently than high achievers for success.
6. Failing to give feedback to the public responses of low achievers.
7. Generally paying less attention to low achievers or interacting with them less frequently.
8. Calling on low achievers less often to respond to questions or asking them easier, nonanalytic questions.
9. Seating low achievers farther away from the teacher.
10. Demanding less from low achievers . . . offers of gratuitous, unsolicited help . . . instead of behaviors designed to help low achievers meet success criteria.
11. Interacting with low achievers more privately than publicly, and monitoring and structuring their activities more closely.
12. Differential administration of grading tests or assignments, in which high achievers but not low achievers are given the benefit of the doubt in borderline cases.
13. Less friendly interaction with low achievers, including less smiling and fewer nonverbal indicators of support and less warm or more anxious voice tones.
14. Briefer and less informative feedback to questions of low achievers.
15. Less eye contact and other nonverbal communication of attention and responsiveness (forward lean, positive head nodding) in interaction with low achievers.
16. Less use of effective but time-consuming instructional methods with low achievers when time is limited.
17. Less acceptance and use of low-achieving students' ideas.*

Obviously, not every teacher demonstrates all the above traits, and in some cases the student treatments would be appropriate for a specific context. Collectively though, these teacher behaviors communicate negative expectancies to the students. They illustrate behaviors of teachers who are *unintentionally disinviting;* that is, some teachers are simply unaware of their role in the school culture and are not aware of more humane teaching methods—as we espouse in this book.

Let us address two different groups: new teachers and those with experience. Paul Burden (1990) studied persons new to teaching (in spite of that seventeen-year apprenticeship). He concluded that as a group new teachers illustrate seven traits:

1. Limited knowledge of teaching activities.
2. Limited knowledge about the teaching environment.
3. Conformity to an image of the teacher as authority.

---

*Excerpt from Thomas L. Good and Jere E. Brophy, *Looking in Classrooms* (New York: Harper & Row, Publishers, 1987), pp. 128–129. Copyright © 1987 by Harper & Row, Publishers. Reprinted with permission of the publisher.

4. Subject-centered approach to curriculum and teaching.
5. Limited professional insights and perceptions.
6. Feelings of uncertainty, confusion, and insecurity.
7. Unwillingness to try new teaching methods.

If those traits tend to describe you, then you might be *unintentionally disinviting*. Thus, as you study this book, keep referring to this section. It will help you to master the many teaching techniques that are available to you to be *intentionally inviting*.

To those of you who have some teaching experience but still can relate to Good and Brophy's seventeen negative traits, plus some of Paul Burden's seven, then you, too, have something to learn. We know that it takes much effort to change a teaching behavior. Success in the classroom with a new technique changes teacher attitudes. The attitudinal changes follow success in teaching behaviors (Guskey, 1986). And we know that classroom (student) success is the key motivator to teach and act *intentionally inviting*.

Let us return to our major thesis: Effective teaching is deliberate. Effective teachers use the technology of being rational decision-makers. You, as teacher, make decisions relating to student expectations, teaching strategies, lengths of assignments, organization of materials, who will be asked to recite, who will be included in special learning groups, how you will encourage slower learners or low achievers. Yes, you are in control of these decisions and hundreds more. The manner in which *you* invite school success is entirely your personal decision.

We have "tipped you off" about the school culture and about its apparent impact on those in it. It is up to you to decide how you will incorporate that knowledge into your value system. Donald R. Cruickshank (1987) refers to this reality as "reflective teaching." You know what you are doing as a teacher and why. Our goal is to provide you with a repertoire of teaching strategies that will result in rewarding you with that greatest of all rewards: watching another *human* succeed.

EXAMINING THE CULTURE UP-CLOSE

A Place Called School is a comprehensive study in which John I. Goodlad and his research team (1984) reported on a series of "feeder" schools: elementary, junior high, and senior high schools. He provided detailed case studies and generalizations about the sample of "triples" being studied. He then addressed a series of issues that impinge on the school: teacher preparation, instruction, curriculum, leadership, research, and entry ages of students.

School reform, observed Goodlad, requires great amounts of locally generated data about what is actually taking place in the schools. A part of that commonplace is a consistent pattern of findings. For example, students' satisfaction as to how well they are doing academically declines as they move from elementary to junior high to senior high school. Collectively, the best things that students like about their schools (in order) are their friends, sports, other students, nothing, classes, and teachers.

In 1970 Charles E. Silberman labeled the schools of America as exhibiting a "mindlessness," and Goodlad in 1984 described the classrooms as showing a "flatness." Goodlad found that most teachers spend the bulk of their time handling routines, with whole-group instruction being the predominant form of teaching. Other routines were teachers working alone; teachers controlling the content; little praise, feedback, or teacher correctives to aid instruction; a narrow range of student activities; passive students; and not enough time for students to complete or understand their assignments. This snapshot of classroom instruction is not exactly exciting, dynamic, or innovative.

Of importance to us is Goodlad's description of the instructional techniques. As potentials there are lecturing, writing, listening, discussing, preparing for assignments, practicing a performance, taking tests, watching a demonstration, or participating in a simulation or a role-playing episode; and using inquiry, problem-solving, or creating a product as a collective set of teaching techniques. At any one time a teacher has a wide array of methods by which to approach an instructional objective or activity. But Goodlad and his associates found that only elementary teachers tended to use many (but not all) of these, whereas the observed high school teachers primarily used lectures, written work assignments, testing, and quizzing. Teacher domination of the class was strikingly reinforced by the fact that teachers outtalked the entire class by a ratio of three to one! Such teachers surely are not using interactive or discussion techniques, described later in *Teaching Strategies: A Guide to Better Instruction.*

Table 1-2 illustrates the consistent patterns of instruction that Goodlad and his team found in the groups of public schools. Examine that table. Ask yourself this question, "Is this the kind of classroom environment that I want to create?" More importantly, after you have completed studying this entire book, reexamine Table 1-2 and ask yourself, "What techniques are missing that I now know?"

A longitudinal study of eleven seventh-grade life science teachers, by Alexis L. Mitman, Virginia A. Marchman, and John R. Mergendoller (1985 and Mergendoller et al., 1988), tended to show the same flatness in instruction. With this cohort of eleven teachers, recitation, seat work, transitions (interruptions and noncommitted time) accounted for 71 percent of the class time. Laboratory experiences accounted for 10 percent of the students' time. Demonstrations, films, and television accounted for 6 percent of the instructional time. *No* group discussions (that is correct, none) were observed (see our Chapter 7). Think of this: science classes where only low-level recitations were used, with no opportunity to discuss the impact of life science on students' lives or on their society. This is not what your authors endorse, nor does most of the science community (see Chapter 8).

Other Implications for Teachers

We have been discussing the impact of the school culture on those in it and have presented some conclusive evidence that teachers may not be using the most reflective or interactive instructional techniques. Examining this situation from 1983 to

Table 1-2   *Participation in Activities at Different Grade Levels*

Early Elementary Activity	%	Upper Elementary Activity	%
Written Work	28.3	Written Work	30.4
Listening to Explanations/Lectures	18.2	Listening to Explanations/Lectures	20.1
Preparation for Assignments	12.7	Preparation for Assignments	11.5
Practice/Performance—Physical	7.3	Discussion	7.7
Use of AV Equipment	6.8	Reading	5.5
Reading	6.0	Practice/Performance—Physical	5.3
Student Non-task Behavior—		Use of AV Equipment	4.9
No Assignment	5.7	Student Non-task Behavior—	
Discussion	5.3	No Assignment	4.8
Practice/Performance—Verbal	5.2	Practice/Performance—Verbal	4.4
Taking Tests	2.2	Taking Tests	3.3
Watching Demonstrations	1.5	Watching Demonstrations	1.0
Being Disciplined	0.5	Simulation/Role Play	0.4
Simulation/Role Play	0.2	Being Disciplined	0.3

Junior High Activity	%	Senior High Activity	%
Listening to Explanations/Lectures	21.9	Listening to Explanations/Lectures	25.3
Written Work	20.7	Practice/Performance—Physical	17.5
Preparation for Assignments	15.9	Written Work	15.1
Practice/Performance—Physical	14.7	Preparation for Assignments	12.8
Taking Tests	5.5	Student Non-task Behavior—	
Discussion	4.2	No Assignment	6.9
Practice/Performance—Verbal	4.2	Taking Tests	5.8
Use of AV Equipment	4.1	Discussion	5.1
Student Non-task Behavior—		Practice/Performance—Verbal	4.5
No Assignment	3.6	Use of AV Equipment	2.8
Reading	2.8	Reading	1.9
Watching Demonstrations	1.5	Watching Demonstrations	1.6
Simulation/Role Play	0.2	Simulation/Role Play	0.1
Being Disciplined	0.2	Being Disciplined	0.1

Source: John I. Goodlad, *A Place Called School* (New York: McGraw-Hill, 1984), Table 4-3, p. 107. Used with permission of the author and publisher.

1986, Larry Cuban (1986) labeled the phenomenon as *persistent instruction and classroom consistency.*

Cuban observed that school organizational configurations have had a negative impact on interactive teaching. (We describe these in Chapters 6 through 9.) Organizational elements are graded schools, self-contained classrooms, specific periods of instruction, and standardized tests, to list a few. These organizational elements logically led to classroom domination by the teacher, direct instruction, large-group instruction, overreliance on textbooks, seat work, uncreative assignments, recitations, and quizzes. These are the teacher-controlled elements so precisely described by Goodlad (1984) and Mitman et al. (1985) and Mergendoller et al. (1988). Recall that John I. Goodlad described this condition as "flatness." We might add: B-O-R-I-N-G!

Major Reforms to "Fix" the Culture

"But," you will surely think, "are there not major curriculum reform efforts that can change all of this?" Good question: It needs more than a *yes* or *no* response.

We tend to analyze school problems or crises by way of committee reports. To illustrate the plethora of rush reports, William Chance (1986) reported that more than 275 educational task forces were organized in just the United States. At least 18 published books or book-length national reports are available to fix the schools—and that does not count the reports from those 275 task forces! Chance wrote that as a result of these reforms, at least 43 states have increased high school graduation standards, college admissions standards have been increased by 17 states, statewide student assessment tests are used in 37 states. Teacher tests are used in 29 states, and 28 states have made changes in teacher certification requirements (Chance, p. 113).

A Nation at Risk: The Imperative for Educational Reform (1983), a study sponsored by the U.S. Department of Education, presented the strongest criticism of the schools. It stated: "If an unfriendly foreign power had attempted to impose on America the mediocre instructional performance that exists today, we might well have viewed it as an act of war." Although such rhetoric is nonsense, the report has been almost uncritically accepted by school boards, state boards of education, and others who know little of research or of our educational history to "tighten up standards."

A Nation at Risk recommended (1) a tougher set of academic basics for high school graduation, (2) higher standards for universities, (3) a longer school year or school day, (4) merit pay for top teachers, and (5) more citizen participation.

By the way, C. H. Edson (1983) concluded that *A Nation at Risk* very closely resembles the famous report issued by the Committee of Ten in 1893. Both groups were dominated by nonpublic school personnel. Both reports had recommendations that were intuitive-based, rather than based on empirical or evaluation data. Both groups recommended longer school terms. Both reports endorsed a philosophy of social Darwinism—survival of the academic fittest. One difference between the reports is that the Committee of Ten established the concept of academic, general, and vocational education for the high school, whereas *A Nation at Risk* implied that the high school should become an academically elite institution. Few reformers heeded James B. Conant's advice from 1959 that schools in America can be improved—but only school by school.

A Celebration of Teaching: High Schools in the 1980s (1983) is a national study written by Theodore R. Sizer. Providing a case study of fifteen public and private high schools, he then listed a series of elements for an "essential school." Sizer strongly advocated (1) incentives for learning, (2) emphasis on encouraging quality, (3) more student responsibility, (4) awarding of high school diplomas only when mastery of defined skills is achieved, and (5) inculcation of ethical values. Several of the elements Sizer advocated could be implemented in any high school. His study might be called the 1983 Conant Report. As we implied, much reform energy is derived from the powers of the state with its legalistic prescriptions to fix the local schools. But how do other major groups want to reform the schools?

In 1986 the Task Force on Teaching as Profession of the Carnegie Forum on Education and the Economy published *A Nation Prepared: Teachers for the 21st Century*. Eight major reforms were proposed. The first was to create a national board to license teachers. The second was to have teachers determine what will be taught in the schools, in light of state or local goals. The third reform proposal was that the teaching profession have ranks or, at least, "lead teachers" or differentiated staffing. Fourth, a bachelor's degree in arts and science should be the prerequisite for any education courses or certification courses. Fifth, a new degree, the Master of Teaching, should be established. Sixth, the nation should be encouraged to prepare more minority teachers. The seventh suggestion was to establish a merit-pay incentive program whereby student performance on tests would be the basic criterion for judging teacher performance. The eighth suggestion from the group called for an increase in teacher salaries to an average ranging from $20,000 to $56,000 per year, and even suggested a high of $72,000 for annual contracts of lead teachers.

The Holmes Group, a select group of research universities, have banded together to reform education. Their basic report is *Tomorrow's Teachers: A Report of the Holmes Group* (1986). The goals of the group are to make a usable teacher education test, to establish a network of cooperating universities, and to improve the school as a workplace. Obviously, these are noble goals.

It is yet too early to determine the impact that all these reform groups will have on *classroom instruction*. One point appears to be certain: teaching and student learning will be the focus of the last decade of the twentieth century.

State and Local Impact on Goals

Obviously, state laws and local regulations have an impact on the schools. State legislatures, state boards of education, and local boards of education all have the legal right to require that the schools teach certain subjects, skills, or ideals. Arizona, for example, requires a course on the free enterprise system of economics. Virginia and several other states require a state history course for high school graduation. Nearly every state has a legislated physical education curriculum. As national goals become converted to laws and then to curricula—as reflected in books, tapes, films, teacher guides, and the like—there is also a tendency for the state to establish the content and the processes that will help teach the content.

However, even with laws to the contrary, teachers ultimately make the decisions regarding how to teach and what to teach. Teachers must begin to sift through the goals, establish priorities, and select those goals that they think are important. The most valuable goals will then take precedence in the classroom. But, remember, it is not the goal that is taught. The goal is simply the framework within which content, skills, processes, attitudes, and the like are taught.

We believe that goals are not subdivided like apple pies. Goals become abstractions that inspire action. Goals are almost never attained. Rather, objectives are stated as action elements stemming from goals. Objectives then become the means by which we seek to achieve our goals, a topic that is expanded in Chapter 2.

However, we must provide one caveat. The people of the United States have many nationalities, races, classes, occupations, philosophies, religions, attitudes, outlooks, and values. The diversity of our nation has led to a pluralistic society, which, in turn, leads to a conflict of goals. Observe that in the typical school system there are social, moral, intellectual, political, and vocational goals. Some teachers tend to stress the goal regarding the improvement of our society. Others try to emphasize the goal to develop critical thinking. Still others attempt to develop individual students so that they may maximize their fullest potential. All these accepted goals have led to eclecticism as a means of operating; that is, we tend to mix parts of goals. The problem with eclecticism is that ultimately it leads to conflicts within goals. One cannot teach critical thinking and at the same time stress that "teacher knows best." If a teacher is *unknowingly eclectic,* then that teacher is probably inconsistent in teaching practices. If you are cognitively aware of your eclecticism, you at least should attempt to avoid placing your own students in those situations that promote personal conflicts. In our society there probably always will be confusion and disagreement over some goals. As a teacher you may or may not be able to resolve either the confusion or the disagreement, which is all part of being pluralistic.

CONTEMPORARY REFLECTIONS ON INSTRUCTION

During the 1980s the many "publics" of public education became concerned that the public schools were declining in quality at an unprecedented rate. The decline, of course, referred to the decline in standardized test scores.

To investigate the cause of these declines in high school students' test scores, many studies were conducted. They yielded only one useful finding: if students did not attend school regularly or did not take basic academic courses in science, English, and mathematics, they scored poorly. Annegret Harnischfeger and David E. Wiley (1975) prepared one of the more objective studies about the decline of test scores and concluded that no single variable could be identified to account for these declines.

By the late 1970s, several researchers began to identify public high schools whose graduates had test scores higher than the national average or that were showing growth rather than decline. The totality of this trend became labeled the "effective schools movement."

Effective Schools Movement

Roots of the Movement

One of the leading proponents of the effective schools movement was the late Ronald Edmonds—a prominent and well-respected researcher. Edmonds died in 1983 before he could successfully challenge the predominant social sciences theory that familial effects outweighed any school effects on learning. In short, Edmonds began to collect evidence to repudiate the work of James Coleman and his associates (1966) and of Christopher Jencks and others (1972). The Coleman and Jencks studies tended to establish *correlational* data that the higher the family's socioeconomic status, the better the school achievement of its children. Coleman and Jencks did provide an easy-to-use alibi for teachers and administrators, especially those in urban or predominantly minority schools: we cannot expect much from minority or poor students since social background and luck are far more important than the influence of school. Thus, the hypothesis of a sociologist and an economist was used by public educators as an excuse for not improving the schools in an active, rigorous manner.

You may well ask yourself why teachers and administrators do not rectify such poor instructional expectations. We again conclude that many public school educators have uncritically accepted the *familial effects* theory: teachers cannot be held accountable for some students' failure to learn when they know that the students come from poor home environments. Just as Ron Edmonds (1979) has cautioned all educators, a theory that is not applicable in all cases may be used as an alibi because it is convenient. Yet, quoting from Thomas Good, "Our research on mathematics instruction, especially at the elementary school level, has convinced us that teachers do make a *difference* in student learning" (1983, p. 60; see also Good and Grouws, 1987).

Emphasizing the research findings from instructionally related studies, Jere Brophy (1982) found eight teacher characteristics associated with effective schools: (1) establishing teacher expectations, (2) providing opportunities for children to learn, (3) using coherent classroom management and organization, (4) pacing the curriculum, (5) teaching actively rather than passively, (6) teaching to mastery, (7) identifying grade-level differences, and (8) providing a supportive learning environment.

Additionally, Andrew C. Porter and Jere Brophy (1988) synthesized research studies on "good teaching." Many of their conclusions substantiate those already listed, so we will mention only those highlights that are not repetitive. Effective teachers also (1) adapt instruction and anticipate student misconceptions, (2) teach student metacognitive strategies (those that help learners understand how they learn and how concepts relate to understanding), (3) address all levels of cognitive objectives, (4) integrate instruction with other subject areas, (5) are reflective about their actual teaching practice, and (6) are *active* teachers as opposed to being passive.

And Mitchell, Oritz, and Mitchell (1987) show some evidence that the technical core of teaching is *the lesson*. They found that teacher-led verbal lessons and those that focus on children performing an activity are the most effective for student performance. They note that drill work and testing are not as effective in enhancing student achievement. These elements will be expanded in Chapter 6.

We have outlined a busy agenda for effective teaching. You as the teacher can have a positive impact on that school culture. You can make your colleagues aware of options to make teaching more active. You can work cooperatively with other teachers who agree that active and reflective teaching are powerful strategies. You can discuss professional issues in the teachers' lounge. You can model the elements of active instruction in your own teaching. Cultures are not static. They evolve. Teachers change only if they see changes in student behavior and increased student achievement.

Describing Effective Schools

The most important question for teachers to address is how to provide *effective schools.* In the previous sentence, we deliberately emphasized the institutions—the *schools,* not individuals—the teachers or principals. For we feel strongly that it takes all the resources of the institution to make learning efficient, excellent, and effective. There are several so-called school effectiveness projects in the United States and Canada, but we will select one project synthesizing the entire movement that was initiated by the Northwest Regional Educational Laboratory (NWREL). After a review of school effectiveness studies, the NWREL staff identified five major elements that lead to effective school practices. The five elements are

1. leadership
2. school environment
3. curriculum
4. classroom instruction and management
5. assessment and evaluation

Because the focus of this text is on instruction and management, we will discuss only that major element; it must be noted, however, that the principal is the key person for any effective school. With a strong instructional leader who plans, organizes, staffs, coordinates, and directs the school improvement effort, almost any school can be transformed rapidly from an ineffective to an effective place for learning. The interaction of all the adults and students in the school helps to shape the environment.

Effective Classroom Instruction and Curriculum

There are at least eleven separate elements that collectively improve schooling, as noted by the effective schools movement.

Expectations for Behavior   It is no surprise that the first criterion relates to expectations for student behavior. In an effective school environment, all staff members expect all students to learn. All adults hold high expectations that are clearly defined for the learners. *Everyone* accepts the idea that school is a place for learning. Every activity relates to learning.

Student Behavior   A written code of conduct specifies acceptable student behavior, and all faculty and staff members are familiar with the code. The code is written and given to all students, usually in the form of book covers, notebook inserts, or composition holders. Behavioral expectations are uniformly enforced with disciplinary actions quickly following any infractions.

Class Routines and Procedures   Teachers are taught how to handle administrative matters quickly and efficiently. Everyone keeps class interruptions to a minimum; learning time is considered "sacred." Classes start promptly with few wasteful transitions.

Standards   Teachers, administrators, and parents agree on reasonable standards for their students and always let them know what is expected.

Grouping   Whole-group instruction tends to be most effective for learning basic skills. Small groups are formed to aid students in learning these skills thoroughly; however, all groups are heterogeneous and tend to be temporary. In elementary and middle schools, the schedules are arranged so that similar subjects are being taught at the same time. Students who lack entry-level skills or need more review may be shifted to a different group. Groups exist solely to help a student learn better.

Stage Setting   The teachers help the students get ready to learn. The teachers provide objectives, they repeat the learning objectives, and they continually determine what entry-level skills are needed by all students and bring them all up to that level.

Instruction and Direction   Teachers always give background information and clear directions—oral and written. During the conduct of classroom recitations or activities, teachers make sure that every student is involved in the instruction. One technique is to use "mass" responses for some questions or activities—one of the techniques used with "direct instruction" or "teacher-directed instruction."

Learning Time   Everyone concentrates on using class time for learning; little time is used for nonlearning activities. (If each teacher wastes ten minutes per day, this would waste more than ten days of school time a year—and would also be a hefty waste of taxpayers' money.)

Reteaching   You may hear a standing joke that there are "six R's": remedial reading, remedial. . . . There are no remedial classes in schools where the staff adopts an effective schooling plan. Teachers reteach all priority content until all students learn it. This is usually called *mastery learning.* Content is reviewed continually, especially key concepts. Learning activities are plentiful.

Teacher-Student Interactions Do not assume that the classrooms in effective schools are cold and impersonal just because they are businesslike. The teachers are enthusiastic supporters of their students and pay attention to student interests, problems, and accomplishments—both in and out of the classrooms. Teachers make sure that the students know that they really care.

Student Rewards and Incentives All student rewards are made in terms of specific student achievements. Exemplary student work and projects that show high standards are proudly displayed for all to see, including shop projects, English papers, art works, mathematics solutions, and social studies outlines. The incentive to continue to strive for excellence is continually reinforced. The most impressive results from this effort have been reported from ghetto schools in which school effectiveness projects have been instituted.

After considering these eleven points, we may conclude, yes, it takes a great effort to change a mediocre school into an effective one. Yes, the teachers go home tired after a day's work because they are teaching all-out all day. Yes, the teachers have great satisfaction each day because they have been able to teach creatively and with enthusiasm—the name of the game for effective schools and effective teachers.

A Few Emerging Instructional Problems for Teachers

The preceding discussion examines some of the major institutional problems. But what of the teacher? Following is a list of questions on trends that will affect the teacher in the future.

1. *The computer.* To what extent has the microcomputer changed the roles of the teacher and the learner?
2. *Textbook selection and production.* How can pressures be asserted on the few publishing companies to produce high quality textbooks?
3. *The basics.* How will each teacher actually implement the basics in his or her individual classroom?
4. *Controversial issues.* Will the classrooms of America be more or less "open" for discussion of controversial issues?
5. *School prayer.* Will the public schools continue to be a battleground for public school prayer advocates?
6. *Creationism.* To what extent will creationist forces continue their efforts to impose their religious views on the teaching of empirical science?
7. *Educational psychology.* To what extent will the repudiated elements of *faculty psychology* continue to be a force in teaching?

8. *The future.* How can the teacher honestly prepare children for a future when there is little agreement on what the future will be?
9. *School culture.* How can teachers work collaboratively to modify existent nonactive teachers to be more active?
10. *Teacher empowerment.* To what extent will the teacher empowerment ideal allow teachers greater control over decisions relating to instruction, curriculum design, and instructional materials?
11. *Teacher preparation.* How will the content, quality, and quantity of teacher preparation programs affect instruction?
12. *School restructuring.* With the plethora of social and educational ills facing education, will we witness a move to restructure the schools as we have observed in the business sector? That is, will there be mergers of schools with ineffective ones being eliminated?

AN OVERVIEW OF OUR TEXT

As you read this text, keep in mind that you, as teacher, will make decisions as an individual practitioner or collectively through some type of group consensus. Here, then, is an overview of selected areas that affect the teacher's decisions and *how* instruction takes place—that is, the methods the teacher will ultimately choose to use.

Goals to Be Emphasized

It is all well and good to realize that our society and specific states have generated lists of goals for the schools. Yet it is imperative to understand that it is the individual teacher who selects and identifies those goals that will be emphasized and those that will be minimized or even eliminated. You, as teacher, make the decisions about aims, outcomes, or purposes. Through your social and cultural values, you determine and interpret the specific objectives that will be emphasized in your classes. We submit that you are the one who is responsible for translating general or ideal goals into operationally accomplished objectives.

Deciding on what will be taught is influenced by a whole series of considerations that we often tend to discount. These include (1) the geographic location of the school, (2) the types of persons who are hired to teach, (3) the social class orientation of the instructor and the instructional materials, (4) the "neutral" or "noncontroversial" positions subscribed to by teachers when instructing or when avoiding controversial issues, (5) the actual instructional materials available to the teacher, and (6) the cultural, intellectual, emotional, and social attributes of the students. As teacher, you must keep all these in mind as you decide to teach a particular subject.

Objectives to Be Taught

The cognitive dimension of the schools rests on instructional objectives, which are either specified or implied. The teacher decides on the instructional focus—for example, content, concepts, and generalizations. After making these decisions, the teacher then states, in writing or orally, what specific lessons or outcomes are desired.

In Chapter 2 we illustrate this process by providing instructional experiences in specifying written learner-oriented objectives. Again, we add the cautionary note: You, as the teacher, should decide the specific instructional objectives deliberately by analyzing your students' needs. This task requires a sequencing of the objectives, a subject addressed in Chapter 3.

Levels of Instruction

One major decision that every teacher can control almost totally is the level of instruction. How much effort, time, and resources should be spent on what we might call "lower intellectual learnings"? How do you structure "thinking" abilities? As teacher, you must make these fundamental decisions in a systematic fashion.

If history is taught predominantly as the memorization of the "fifty great names," then the instructor has chosen to teach history at the lowest possible intellectual level. Concomitantly, that same history teacher may choose to provide a low-level historical perspective *and* then begin to evaluate the more advanced generalizations or theses of historians.

Chapter 4 is devoted to models that can help you to decide on the levels of instruction that you will use in selecting experiences.

Deciding How to Plan a Lesson

Chapter 5, "Decisions About Lesson Planning," introduces the concept of lesson planning. Teachers now incorporate several specific activities into the instructional whole. When preparing a lesson plan, they "screen" many elements of the lesson and make decisions that directly affect the classroom environment. They survey resources, both print and nonprint materials, and they assess possible instructional designs and methods. Interactions between individuals and groups must be planned. Estimates on student pacing must be considered, and motivational and evaluational techniques must be specified. All these decisions tend to fall into a "noninteractive" dimension of teaching. The teacher is not yet interacting with the real people of the school—the students. The remaining decisions focus on interaction. The teacher ought to be the one to determine both the content and the processes of instruction, *but* in an enlightened and systematic manner. You should always know why you are teaching what is being taught—and should know alternatives to accomplish the same objective! Further, the chapter discusses the role of the microcomputer in lesson planning.

Deciding on Appropriate Interactions

After making the prerequisite decisions, you as teacher must decide how the classroom interaction will take place. The primary verbal interaction is through teacher questioning. But did you know that there are several different styles and techniques of classroom interaction? There are even ways to determine whether the students ought to ask the questions. The process of questioning (Chapter 6) can be fun and worthwhile. Bear in mind that all of this should be accomplished after planned, systematic analysis.

Chapter 7 presents one of the more detailed discussions of its kind about the decisions that must be made for meaningful discussions in the classroom. A thoroughly tested set of discussion strategies is presented so that you can decide which technique will accomplish the process and cognitive goals. By the way, most teachers really do not conduct discussions—they conduct recitations. But that is their decision.

Many teaching techniques are called "expository": the teacher tells or has the students tell. In Chapters 8 and 9 we introduce a realm of decision-making that will cause your students to "think." Several techniques are presented so that you, as teacher, may settle on the appropriate ones to use. Also given are some methods that you can use with inquiry teaching—how to teach inductive-oriented lessons, problem-solving exercises, and even deductive inquiry strategies.

In our opinion the activities given in Chapter 8 are so enjoyable that the students will not notice the work involved. With the teaching methods given here you will need to make fundamental instructional decisions because they demand a different set of teaching behaviors.

How to teach *thinking* is introduced in Chapter 9. In recent years supportive citizen groups and critics have joined in a chorus to emphasize thinking; "thinking" is being marketed. We provide some generic processes that will allow you to make an intelligent decision about teaching thinking.

Deciding About Classroom Procedures

One fact will stand out more clearly than all others: teaching requires the use of trust, power, and responsibility. It would be simple if all you had to do was to plan for instruction and to interact with the students. But real life is tough. The schools draw students who are quiet, shy, and gentle as well as those that are loud, angry, and unruly. What decisions do you, as teacher, make to structure the organization and management of your class? These topics form the framework for Chapter 10.

Teachers do not leave teaching because they are incompetent but mainly because they cannot "handle" the students in the classes. Many teacher dropouts just did not know what kind of decisions had to be made by whom, when, where, and for whom. We want you to be better prepared.

You should also understand that some decisions are made for you, whether you like them or not. Often, you must use the already selected learning materials, because there are no others available. If you do not find the adopted materials to be to your liking, then you must make the effort to begin the change process. Furthermore, you do not decide on what students you will teach; you simply take them all! The latter is one aspect of teaching in the public schools that is not apparent in the private schools. You must realize that you have no command over the students' home lives or value structures—outside the school context. To be sure, you will affect their values and, in some cases, profoundly change both their standards and outlooks in the future. We submit that the moment one is taught to read, one's values are changed.

But we caution you that schools have their constraints as well as their opportunities for experimentation. Schools are institutions and, as such, like it or not, the institutional dimensions usually take precedence over personal ones. If you decide to humanize the institution, then you must decide to commit yourself to a long-term change effort. For example, report cards, attendance reports, athletic teams, and administrative channels are all part of the institutional structure of the school. Although you can change these in any desired direction, you need first to know all about the politics of change.

By now you should begin to appreciate that one just does not "stand up front and teach." What to teach, what the students should learn, how to teach, how to manage the environment, and what and how to evaluate all require professional decisions. This is where you begin.

INTRODUCING FORMATIVE EVALUATION

Before moving to the next chapter, you will be asked to complete a short evaluation. A basic objective of any evaluation system is to determine the extent to which the intended learner objectives are being achieved and the impact that the instruction or assignments are having on the learners. To accomplish this evaluation objective, educators use two well-known evaluation methodologies. These modes, as Michael Scriven (1967) suggests, are formative and summative.

Formative Evaluation

Formative evaluation is designed to provide feedback in a rather immediate sense. Formative instruments are designed specifically to monitor selected aspects of any assignment or to determine where learning problems are emerging. By using formative evaluation, teachers may quickly identify and correct problems. For example, if some methodology is being used that causes the students to do poorly, quick remediation may take place through formative evaluation. Often, the teacher gives assignments but does not check the students' work until the conclusion of the unit, which is usually too late. By continually checking the "small steps," the teacher may identify instructional problems. This means that the teacher observes many different facets of a course while it is being conducted.

A teacher needs to check only a few selected items in any one formative evaluation. These items would all be based on the stated or intended learning objectives. There is no need for a lengthy set of test items. The important point is that the feedback is collected while there is adequate time to make adjustments for the student.

The rationale for formative evaluation is to provide data to the student and teacher so that they may make corrections—immediately, if not sooner! When both students and teacher realize that instructional activities are being monitored constantly, they tend to become more responsible and more productive. The instructional climate and total program environment become positive and supportive. This is precisely the kind of learning climate that the teacher always ought to foster when teaching. Conversely, classes have "gone on the rocks" because the teacher was not evaluating student activities over short periods of time, but waited until the very end of the course or unit to accomplish a one-shot final evaluation.

Using formative evaluation is much more subtle than simply specifying performance objectives. Formative evaluation requires that the teacher carefully observe a selected set of *experiences* for all participants. For example, in most courses, some form of activity is used to build a cluster of skills for future use. A teacher subscribing to formative evaluation monitors the skills and, if a student performs inadequately, provides a new set of experiences that relate to the instructional objectives. To correct any noted learning deficiency, teacher and student cannot wait until the "final exam." Periodic correctives are an integral part of the formative evaluation plan.

One simple method by which to record formative data is to tabulate the absolute numbers or percentages of both individual and group activities. The teacher can compare group data on a graph so that the directions of the students could be displayed for instant visual analysis.

The essential characteristic of formative evaluation is that "hard data" are being collected for decision-making. But, what is more important, corrections are built into the scheme so that feedback is used when it is needed most—not stored for future judgment.

Summative Evaluation

Evaluation that is conducted as the final or concluding task is called summative evaluation. It may be the final formative evaluation of a course or unit. Summative evaluations may take several forms, as long as they are consistent with the prescribed objectives of the unit, course, or module. Again, summative data can be tabulated as absolute responses, with a percentage then calculated for each item. Comparisons between students also can be made from summative data (but not from the formative measures). The final grade is, of course, determined by the summative evaluations. Note the use of the plural: good teachers do not have one summative evaluation. They place evaluations at logical points in the course, such as at the ends of units, chapters, modules, or learning activity packages. The summative sets can then be arranged in a profile to illustrate the sum of evaluation activities. Formative data thus provide feedback, whereas summative scores lead to "grades" or to "judgments" about the quality of the performances.

Of course, it may be argued that formative and summative techniques will cause the teacher to change directions for several students. We agree and submit that if these techniques are properly used, the objectives of the entire class may even be altered. Success is the underlying goal. If a course needs to be modified because of unrealistic expectations (objectives), then why not alter it?

Perhaps the most convincing advantage of the formative and summative model is that there are no surprises at the end of the prescribed work block. With early feedback evaluations built into the system, all elements should stress student success.

The Authors' Technique

At the end of each chapter, or in some cases integrated within it, will be a set of formative evaluation questions. If you score perfectly on the set, you have adequately studied the chapter. If, however, you miss several items, we suggest that you restudy at least that section. Or you may even ask your instructor for another, more detailed book that relates to the topic.

Now let us move on to the formative evaluation—and then to Chapter 2.

FORMATIVE EVALUATION *Decision-Making*

How well did you achieve the basic objectives that we presented? To aid you, we have developed a short formative evaluation (test) by which you may check how well you did. If you miss any questions, review the appropriate section in Chapter 1.

1. The authors strongly support:
   (a) A rationale for teaching acts.
   (b) Using current trends as the basis for instructional decision-making.
   (c) Continuous stability in teacher roles.
   (d) One major method of teaching.

2. Content and process decisions:
   (a) Are mandated by law in forty-three states.
   (b) Tend to be textbook-dominated.
   (c) Will be made for a teacher.
   (d) Are identified in most cases.

3. The authors conclude that innovations:
   (a) Have been a positive force in the schools.
   (b) Have been neglected in the schools.
   (c) Are uniformly implemented.
   (d) Have tended to be failures in the schools.

4. One problem identified in the school culture relates to instruction. The authors:
   (a) Identify ephemeral norms.
   (b) Stress the use of locally prepared instructional materials.
   (c) Conclude that instructional methodologies have had a weak research basis.
   (d) Provide evidence that state legislatures have remedied instructional problems.

5. "Forget that university nonsense. You're in the real world now" implies that:
   (a) You can learn only on the job.
   (b) Teaching is not a rational area.
   (c) A few people really know what is best.
   (d) All of the above.

6. The key incentive for teachers is:
   (a) Salary.
   (b) The uncertainties of teaching.
   (c) Student achievement.
   (d) Working alone in the job without interference from others.

7. Teacher expectations for students:
   (a) Are very mixed.
   (b) Vary by geographic area of the country.
   (c) Show a great deal of warmth and feedback.
   (d) Have been validated as being genuinely compassionate.

8. Which characteristic is essential to be able to do the tough job of teaching?
   (a) Conformity to the school's culture.
   (b) Using a subject-centered approach.
   (c) Having a rationale.
   (d) Being efficacious.

9. From data presented in this chapter, you might conclude that:
   (a) Few techniques are used by most teachers.
   (b) Highly interactive teaching styles are the norms.
   (c) Teachers use virtually all the techniques taught in schools of education.
   (d) Senior high school teachers are the most flexible of all studied.

10. List four or five areas in which process and content seem to be indistinguishable.

11. Select one or two of the studies conducted in the 1980s. Analyze the implied or stated assumptions; also list the conflicting points of view.

12. Why is it essential that teachers understand school cultures?

13. In what way will you influence how you teach?

14. Prepare a checklist of the eleven main points about effective schools. Compare that list with your personal schooling experience.

15. What impact will "high tech" (computers) have on the way you teach?

16. Examine Table 1-2. How would you like to adjust the priorities in the data? Why?

Responses

1. (a)   Having a rationale for decision-makers.
2. (b)   Textbooks are yet a dominant force. Their use tends to restrict content and process.
3. (d)   While some have "made it," the big innovations have had little impact on the classroom teacher.
4. (c)   The conclusion is a weak knowledge base, at this time.
5. (d)   All responses illustrate anti-intellectualism.
6. (c)   Refer to the Mitchell work; student success is the key teacher incentive.
7. (a)   Mixed they are indeed; review that list of 17.
8. (d)   Efficacy is the idea that you can do it!
9. (a)   Teachers use very few techniques; refer to treatment of *A Place Called School*.
10.–16. These questions require some activity from you. We suggest that you work with a peer or a small group of three or four and discuss these questions.

REFERENCES

Ashton, Patricia. "Motivation and Teacher's Sense of Efficacy." In *Research on Motivation in Education, Volume 2: The Classroom Milieu.* Carole Ames and Russell Ames, eds. Orlando: Academic Press, 1985.

Barter, Richard F. "Rejuvenating Teachers." *Independent School* 43:1984, 37–42.

Blum, Robert E., and Jocelyn A. Butler. "Managing by Improvement by Profiling." *Educational Leadership* 42(6):1985, 54–58.

Brophy, Jere. "Successful Teaching Strategies for the Inner City Child." *Phi Delta Kappan* 63:1982, 527, 529.

Burden, Paul. "Teacher Development." In *Handbook for Research on Teacher Education.* W. Robert Houston, Martin Haberman, and John Sikula, eds. New York: Macmillan, 1990.

Chance, William. ". . . *the Best of Educations.*" Chicago: The John D. and Catherine T. MacArthur Foundation, 1986. (Released in 1988 by The Education Commission of States, Denver.)

Coleman, James S., et al. *Equality of Educational Opportunity.* Washington, D.C.: U.S. Government Printing Office, 1966.

Conant, James B. *The American High School Today: A First Report to Interested Citizens.* New York: McGraw-Hill, 1959.

Cruickshank, Donald R. *Reflective Teaching.* Reston, Va.: Association of Teacher Educators, 1987.

Cuban, Larry. "Persistent Instruction: Another Look at Consistency in the Classroom." *Phi Delta Kappan* 68:1986, 7–11.

Darling-Hammond, Linda, and Barnett Berry. *The*

Evolution of Teacher Policy. Santa Monica, Calif.: RAND Corporation, JRE-01, March 1988.

Edmonds, Ronald. "Effective Schools for the Urban Poor." *Educational Leadership* 37:1979, 15–27.

Edson, C. H. "Risking the Nation." *Issues in Education* 1(2 & 3):1983, 171–184.

Engleking, Jere L. "Teacher Job Satisfaction and Dissatisfaction." *ERS Spectrum* 4(1): 1986, 33–38.

Good, Thomas L. "Research on Classroom Teaching." In *Handbook of Teaching and Policy.* Lee S. Shulman and Gary Sykes, eds. New York: Longman, 1983, pp. 42–80.

Good, Thomas L., and Jere E. Brophy. *Looking in Classrooms,* 4th ed. New York: Harper & Row, 1987, pp. 128–130.

Good, Thomas L., and Douglas A. Grouws. "Increasing Teachers' Understanding of Mathematical Ideas Through Inservice Training." *Phi Delta Kappan* 68(10):June 1987, 778–783.

Goodlad, John I. *A Place Called School.* New York: McGraw-Hill, 1984.

Goodlad, John I., ed. *The Ecology of School Renewal.* Part I. Eighty-Sixth Yearbook of National Society for the Study of Education. Chicago: University of Chicago Press, 1987.

Gump, Paul V. "The Classroom Behavior Setting: Its Nature and Relaxation to Student Behavior." Lawrence: University of Kansas, Department of Psychology, 1967.

Guskey, Thomas R. "Staff Development and the Process of Teacher Change." *Educational Researcher* 15:1986, 5–12.

Harnischfeger, Annegret, and David E. Wiley. *Achievement Test Score Decline: Do We Need to Worry?* Chicago ML-Group for Policy Studies in Education, Central Mid-Western Regional Educational Laboratory, 1975.

House, Ernest R. "How We Think About Evaluation." In *Philosophy of Education.* Ernest R. House, ed. San Francisco: Jossey-Bass, New Directions for Program Evaluation, No. 19, 1983.

Jackson, Phillip W. *Life in Classrooms.* New York: Holt, Rinehart and Winston, 1968, p. 11.

Jencks, Christopher, et al. *Inequality: A Reassessment of the Effect of Family and Schooling in America.* New York: Basic Books, 1972.

Kluckhohn, Clyde. *Mirror for Man: The Relation of Anthropology to Modern Life.* New York: Whittlesey House, 1949.

Lieberman, Ann, and Lynne Miller. *Teachers, Their World and Their Work.* Alexandria, Va.: Association for Supervision and Curriculum Development, 1984.

Marshall, Hermine H. "Work on Learning: Implications of Classroom Metaphors." *Educational Researcher* 17(9):1988, 9–16.

Mergendoller, John R., Virginia A. Marchman, Alexis L. Mitman, and Martin J. Packer. "Task Demands and Accountability in Middle-Grade Science Classes." *The Elementary School Journal* 80:1988, 251–265.

Mitchell, Douglas E., Flora Ida Oritz, and Tedi K. Mitchell. *Work Orientations and Job Performance: The Cultural Basis of Teaching Rewards and Incentives.* Albany: State University of New York Press, 1987.

Mitman, Alexis L., Virginia A. Marchman, and John R. Mergendoller. *Teaching for Scientific Literacy. Guide Book II: How Is Science Currently Taught?* San Francisco: Far West Laboratory for Educational Research and Development, November 1985.

A Nation at Risk: The Imperative for Educational Reform. Washington, D.C.: National Commission on Excellence in Education, U.S. Department of Education, 1983.

A Nation Prepared: Teachers for the 21st Century. New York: Carnegie Forum on Education and the Economy, Task Force on Teaching as a Profession, 1986.

NWREL Onward to Excellence Project. Portland, Ore.: Northwest Educational Regional Laboratory, 1988.

Orlich, Donald C. "The Dilemma of Strong Traditions and Weak Empiricism." *Teacher Education Quarterly* 12:1985, 23–32.

Porter, Andrew C., and Jere Brophy. "Synthesis of Research on Good Teaching: Insights from the Work of the Institute for Research on Teaching." *Educational Leadership* 45:1988, 74–85.

Purkey, William Watson, and John M. Novak. *Inviting School Success,* 2nd ed. Belmont, Calif.: Wadsworth, 1984.

Rubin, Louis J. *Artistry in Teaching.* New York: Random House, 1984.

Sarason, Seymour B. *The Culture of the School and the Problem of Change,* 2nd ed. Boston: Allyn and Bacon, 1982.

Scriven, Michael. *The Methodology of Evaluation.* AERA Monograph Series on Curriculum Evaluation, 1967, No. 1, pp. 39–83.

Shulman, Lee S. "Knowledge and Teaching: Foundations of the Reform." *Harvard Educational Review* 57(1):1987, 1–22.

Silberman, Charles E. *Crisis in the Classroom: The Remaking of American Education.* New York: Random House, 1970.

Sizer, Theodore R. *A Celebration of Teaching: High Schools in the 1980s.* Reston, Va.: The National Association of Secondary School Principals and the Commission on the Educational Issues of the National Association of Independent Schools, 1983.

"Standardized Exams Aren't a 'Quick Fix' for Education." *Lewiston Morning Tribune,* October 30, 1983, p. 4. From the Associated Press Wire Service reporting Gregory R. Anrig's comments.

Tomorrow's Teachers: A Report of the Holmes Group. East Lansing, Mich.: Holmes Group, 1986.

Wise, Arthur E. "Legislated Learning Revisited." *Phi Delta Kappan* 69(5):1988, 328–333.

2

Deciding on Objectives

*T*he first step in systematic decision-making is the planning phase. This chapter presents two major concepts to begin that phase: (1) the specifying of student objectives, and (2) the preparing of standards of student performance.

Objectives   After completing this chapter, you should be able to:

- State that there are three levels of objectives generally used in the teaching-learning process
- Identify four domains under which objectives are classified
- Identify and write performance objectives in various styles
- Prepare performance objectives
- Describe why performance objectives are necessary for selected instructional strategies
- Specify elements of curriculum alignment
- Produce objectives that stimulate right hemispheric functions
- Defend or criticize the use of performance objectives

PLANNING FOR SUCCESSFUL INSTRUCTION

One hallmark of schooling as an organized activity is the process called planning. If you as a teacher wish to instruct in a systematic manner, then you will devote a substantial proportion of your time and activity to planning—deciding what and how you want your students to learn. It appears that teachers who are most successful exhibit three common traits: (1) they are well organized in their planning, (2) they communicate effectively with their students, and (3) they have high expectations of their students.

We may generalize that, although learning can take place anywhere and spontaneously, the more systematic the teacher, the greater the probability for success. Instructional planning or lesson planning implies the establishment of priorities. Setting priorities mandates a continuous set of teacher decisions. The objectives that you specify establish learning priorities for the students. This does not mean that the learners may not specify their objectives. But, to be realistic, the teacher, through lectures, discussions, learning modules, assignments, textbooks, and other educational experiences, is responsible for establishing the priorities.

Written lesson plans make known in advance the priorities about time, learning materials, objectives, and type of instruction. They are tools for success for two important groups—the teachers and the students. Chapter 5 is devoted to lesson planning, so we mention that subject only briefly here.

Performance Objectives

A large group of educators stress that objectives ought not emphasize what the teacher will be doing—for example, teach about photosynthesis—but rather should identify the performance or behavior that is to be expected of the students as a result of instructional experiences. For example, if the instructional topic happens to be the introduction to photosynthesis, then one performance objective may be for the student to "illustrate the general reaction of the photosynthetic process, using the components of O_2, H_2O, CO_2, glucose, sunlight, and chlorophyll in the correct sequence of events."

Because the emphasis is on student outcomes, these objectives are called *performance objectives*. Instructional, learner, behavioral, and specific objectives are also used as synonyms, but these terms should not confuse you. The main point is that you should be able to distinguish between objectives that emphasize student behavior and those that state what the teacher is supposed to do.

Another distinction is made between performance and process objectives. *Performance objectives* generally refer to student mastery of the *content* to be taught. Content is the cognitive material (facts, concepts, skills, and generalizations) that makes up the body of information that you want students to learn. *Process objectives* focus on the *mental skills* (observations, evaluations, or inferences) that allow students to interpret the content they master. Performance and process objectives are not exclusive outcomes but are complementary. Whenever you prepare a performance objective that emphasizes content to be learned, some mental skills are always involved in the student's learning. When the student needs to learn mental skills to make use of the content, that is, when learning skills are the principal purpose of instruction, you should prepare process objectives that aid the student's ability to assimilate that content.

One important use of performance objectives is that they give the teacher some clear and precise guidelines to achieving specific student outcomes. That is, the objectives prescribe exactly which behaviors the students must manifest as a result of the instruction. Likewise, performance objectives are given to students prior to instruction to inform them specifically of what they will learn to do. This eliminates much of the guesswork related to teaching ("What should I teach today?") or to the student's learning ("What should I study for the test?").

Note the implicit assumption that, because told in advance what is expected, the student will be self-motivated to do the tasks. This is not always the case, just as it is not always the case if general statements are made to students about what is expected of them. A more detailed critique of the uses and abuses of performance objectives is presented later.

Because performance objectives are widely used, you, as a prospective teacher, need to understand and develop the technical skills that are necessary to prescribe and state these types of objectives. If you ever become involved in any "individualized" program, it is mandatory that you skillfully write and analyze performance objectives; nearly all individualized programs using "mastery" learning techniques refer to performance objectives. Furthermore, by law, some states require that they be specific, as do some school districts.

Public Law 94-142 and Objectives

The year 1975 witnessed a far-reaching federal act, Public Law 94-142, the Education for All Handicapped Children Act. The basis for this act is the assumption that all handicapped children can benefit from public education. *Every* teacher in the United

States must understand its implications, for there is no teacher, school, or class that may be exempt. There are five concepts that you must understand about PL 94-142.

Basically, this law establishes that all handicapped children between the ages of three and twenty-one are entitled to free public education. *Handicapped* is defined by the law as those who are mentally retarded, hard of hearing, deaf, speech-impaired, visually handicapped, seriously emotionally disturbed, orthopedically impaired, multi-handicapped, or those who have other health impairments or have specific learning disabilities and, because of impairments, need special educational services. It is estimated that approximately 12 percent of the children in age group three to twenty-one are included in this broad definition of *handicapped*. Thus the numbers of persons covered under the law ranges in the millions!

The second point that will affect you as a teacher is the need to prepare a written *individual education plan* (IEP) for every handicapped child in your class. This plan must be developed to meet that specific child's needs. The IEP must specify the goals of the educational services, the methods of achieving those goals (objectives), and the exact number and quality of exceptional services to be rendered to the child. The federal laws require that the IEP be formulated by (a) a parent, (b) a child, (c) a teacher, (d) a professional who has evaluated the child within a "recent" time span, and (e) others as designated by the local education agency. The last category usually includes the school principal or a special education resource person.

The IEP must list all special activities and "regular" class activities in which the child will participate. Dates and duration of services must be stated. Objectives and evaluation procedures must also be given. A minimum of one IEP meeting must be held each year. The law is most specific in requiring that parents receive written notice of the IEP meeting.

The third stipulation of PL 94-142 requires that a handicapped child's records be kept secure. The parent has unlimited access to all educational records. Furthermore, a parent may amend (in writing) any statement in that child's file. Finally, the school must keep a record of all persons who have access to the child's record and why.

The fourth element of PL 94-142 requires that when an agency (the school) and the parents fail to agree on an IEP or an evaluation of the child's abilities, then an impartial hearing must be held. The rules for conducting the hearing are very explicit. A hearing can be lengthy and time-consuming for all.

The final component of PL 94-142 prescribes that all handicapped children have the right to be served in the "least restrictive environment." The latter phrase led to a general interpretation of "mainstreaming"—that is, placing handicapped children in "regular" classrooms. A least restrictive environment means that handicapped children must be educated and treated in a manner similar to nonhandicapped peers. There can be no separation of handicapped children in lunchrooms, recess, games (where appropriate to the child's abilities), classes, or any education service or function if the child is able to participate in these activities.

However, a least restrictive environment may simply mean that the child will always be placed in a special room, not in a regular classroom. It may even mean that the child can be institutionalized in a special school or even in a private school. The deciding factor in placement is whether the child can receive profitable services. We discuss this law at some length in part because it is important legislation that illustrates how educational objectives regarding individual uniqueness are implemented through a federal act. But we also stress the second element of the act, which requires that a precise IEP with performance objectives be written for each handicapped student. Since you probably will have handicapped children in your classrooms and will be responsible for helping to prepare an IEP for those students, you must be able to write clear performance objectives. This chapter will give you the skills you need to meet this demand.

Beginning the Process

Identifying and writing performance objectives takes much planning. One way to begin is to identify objectives at a very broad level, then work toward specifics. Developing performance objectives is, therefore, a deductive process: The direction of movement is from a general frame of reference to more specific ones. Most simply, there are three levels of specificity. These levels may be classified as (1) general—very broad objectives, (2) intermediate, and (3) specific performance. This chapter deals only with these behavioral, performance objectives. General goals were discussed briefly in Chapter 1.

Intermediate-range objectives, while useful as guidelines, are still too general for direct implementation in instruction; thus, the classroom teacher states even more specific objectives so that explicit direction is given to learning. These specific objectives usually are called behavioral objectives because learning is defined as an observable change in the behavior of students. That is, learning is assumed to have occurred when the student demonstrates some behavior that could not be shown prior to the learning experience. At the instructional level, therefore, objectives are statements about the *behavior of the student*. Rather than describing what the teacher will do, *specific performance objectives describe what the learner will do*.

If you followed the rationale of some proponents of performance objectives to its ultimate conclusion, you would find yourself creating an individual set of objectives for every student. Although this may be an interesting and worthy "goal," we view it as being fiscally and procedurally not feasible. It is doubtful that any society with limited resources would decide to pay for total individualization of instruction. Fortunately, such individualized instruction is not required to provide effective, appropriate, and meaningful learning opportunities for all students.

We have discussed previously some of the past attempts to identify a consensus on the kinds of goals that could be of value to American schools. The common element in these statements was that the student should be able and willing to demonstrate some acceptable behaviors as a consequence of the educational experiences.

Rationale for Performance Objectives

Whereas many teachers are able to recognize educational goals and to translate them into effective conditions for learning, others have not carried their thinking beyond the stage of selecting the content to be presented. The danger is that the teacher will not recognize effective ways of reaching the necessary objectives if, in fact, the objectives are not individually formulated. Also, unless students know what the objectives are, they are likely to resort to memorization and mechanical completion of exercises rather than to attempt more relevant learning activities. When the teacher tells the student what is expected, a model is provided around which learning activities can be individually organized. When this is done, the teacher and student have established a "perceived purpose" for all that is to follow. Unless you specifically state objectives, you cannot determine the student's achievements at any given moment. Therefore, you must make statements available that define what is expected of the learner. These are the basic assumptions associated with the performance objective movement.

Currently, more than four-fifths of the state legislatures or state education agencies are considering or have already mandated plans that "make the schools accountable." In general, making schools accountable means that teachers will be evaluated in terms of how their students perform. The only way you can "prove" that your students have learned is by providing measurable evidence that they are different at the completion of a sequence of instruction than they were before instruction. The only way you can provide measurable evidence is by stating in advance of instruction the performance you expect of your students—performance objectives. Therefore, in the many states where accountability programs are a part of the teacher's daily life, performance objectives will be a primary part of your planning and implementing of instruction.

It is assumed that teachers who prepare and use performance objectives have a mastery of their academic disciplines. This, however, is not applicable to the majority of preservice individuals (prospective teachers) who have just begun intensive study of their respective disciplines. Therefore, because the preparation of performance objectives demands a critical analysis of the subject matter to be learned, a variety of aids—such as textbooks, curriculum guides, and print and nonprint materials—may be useful to preservice teachers.

Curriculum Alignment

Another rationale for performance objectives centers around the concept called "curriculum alignment" (S. A. Cohen, 1987). In simplest form a curriculum is composed of objectives, instruction, and assessment. When all three elements match— that is, instruction and assessment focus on stated objectives—there is curriculum alignment. While it seems obvious that this should exist in all curricula, curriculum alignment is much more difficult to attain than it seems. Teachers emphasize different learning experiences based upon their skills and interests. Students have differing talents and have mastered different skills at different levels. Teachers have a variety of materials to use for instruction. Performance objectives do, however, provide the key for teachers to align their curriculum in their own room. For that matter, performance objectives are essential for curriculum alignment at the district and building level as well.

The basis for successful curriculum alignment is in the process of carefully analyzing the skills, competencies, and other measures of student learning that you want to result from instruction. Performance objectives focus and define your thinking, and that of your students, about the outcomes of instruction. Without the clarity of performance objectives, instruction may lack a specific focus. With carefully constructed performance objectives, choices about instruction become much easier and more direct. In effect, instructional choices flow from the objectives you write. Finally, your performance objectives act as a powerful check on your assessment of student learning.

As an example of how difficult it can be to focus on careful curriculum alignment, two of the authors of this text once provided students in a teaching methods class with the following objective. "Given class notes and a test booklet, the student will write three performance objectives that have all of the elements of a performance objective correctly written." At the end of the unit on performance objectives, we administered a test that asked our students to underline the conditions, circle the performance statement, and bracket the criterion measure for twenty-five objectives that we provided. At the end of the test period several of the students pointed out that our test did not match the objective we had given them at the start of the unit. Our curriculum was not aligned. Of course, we administered a second test that asked our students to write several performance objectives that we read and graded for the test. This time our curriculum was aligned.

You test what you teach and you teach what is in your objectives—an idea that is simple to state but difficult to do without carefully planned and written performance objectives. Curriculum can be aligned from either end of the process—the objective end or the assessment end. Too often, what teachers teach is influenced by what they know or anticipate will be on the tests. To make instructional decisions based on what is to be tested is to pervert the process. Done correctly, assessment/testing flows from the decisions you will make about what is best for your students to learn. Start from the objectives and make the rest of the process fit. If your objectives are clear and sharp, instruction and assessment will be aligned.

When all parts of the curriculum—performance objectives, instruction, and assessment—are congruent (in alignment), student learning improves dramatically. Curriculum alignment has been identified, after much research, as a principal sign of effective schools. After observing successful schools in all kinds of environments, researchers have noted that without exception, some form of curriculum alignment is present. Curriculum alignment has been demonstrated as a major tool in changing less successful schools into successful centers of student learning. All in all, curriculum alignment is a powerful concept that begins with performance objectives.

Taxonomies of Behaviors

In 1948, a group of evaluation specialists formulated a theoretical framework to facilitate more precise communication about the learning process. The group assumed that educational objectives, stated in behavioral form, are reflected in the behavior of individuals. That is, behavior can be observed and described, and these descriptive statements can be classified.

The plan for classification involved a complete taxonomy in four major parts—the cognitive, the affective, the psychomotor, and the perceptual domains.

The Cognitive Domain includes those objectives that deal with the recall or recognition of knowledge and the development of intellectual abilities and skills. This is the domain in which most of the work in curriculum development has taken place and in which the clearest definitions of objectives phrased as descriptions of student behavior occur (Bloom et al., 1956).

The Affective Domain is the area that concerns attitudes, beliefs, and the entire spectrum of values and value systems. This is an exciting area that curriculum-makers are now exploring (Krathwohl et al, 1964).

The Psychomotor Domain attempts to classify the coordination aspects that are associated with movement and to integrate the cognitive and affective consequences with bodily performances (Harrow, 1972).

The Perceptual Domain, less developed than the others, provides a hierarchical structure for sensory perceptions organized on the principle of integration (Moore, 1967).

These taxonomies or domains were designed as classification systems for student behaviors that represent the intended outcomes of the education process. By combining the principles of any taxonomy with the careful preparation of performance objectives, the teacher can focus instruction on outcomes that vary from the simple to the complex. Chapter 4 is devoted entirely to the topic of learning the taxonomies and to further clarification and amplification of this educational tool.

Hemisphericity

Over the past several decades a major theory about how the brain works, called hemisphericity, has given teachers another tool to use in planning for instructional experiences. Hemisphericity is the study of where in the brain—left hemisphere or right hemisphere—different types of mental functioning occur. Research suggests that the right hemisphere is involved with visual, nonverbal, spatial, divergent, and intuitive thinking. The left side of the brain is involved with verbal, logical, categorical, detail-oriented, and convergent thinking. The right brain works more with approximations and creativity, whereas the left brain works more with specifics and analysis. As an example, it is the right side of the brain that processes the visual information allowing you to recognize a face, but it is the left side that provides the name to go with the face. The facts that allow us to understand the kinds of function occurring on each side of the brain are not important here except as they help educators understand that instruction must be planned to enhance both hemispheres.

Research conducted over many years has demonstrated that teachers persistently emphasize objectives and instruction focusing on the left side of the brain. The vast majority of objectives focus on the cognitive, analytical, and convergent functions dominated by the left side of the brain. To the degree that teachers ignore the more creative right-side functions of the brain, it can be said that they are teaching only half the child. While we certainly want our students to be logical and orderly, it is equally important that our students have the opportunity to develop creatively. This includes objectives that specifically focus on the creative functions characterized by the right side of the brain. They are the key to enhancing the balanced development of the true potential of all children and adolescents.

The research tells us that, although each side of the brain emphasizes a specific kind of function, the most productive intellectual functioning occurs when there is cooperation between both sides of the brain. Learning exercises that are focused on the left side of the brain (the majority of the learning objectives and instructional experiences we plan for students) are improved significantly when the right side of the brain is included in the experience. So, not only have we largely ignored the right-side functions of the brain in devising objectives and instructional experiences, we have also weakened the effectiveness of our instruction to the functions centered in the left side of the brain. To teach most effectively to either side of the brain, we must balance objectives and learning experiences to involve both sides of the brain whenever possible.

Creating objectives and their associated learning experiences that address the intellectual functions of the right side of the brain are important, but you need a brief caution about writing objectives for these creative functions. Because objectives for the right side of the brain emphasize the creative functions, the criterion portion of a performance objective for the right side of the brain can be difficult to write. By their nature, the more creative functions of the brain are less measurable in terms of quantity and quality. If you remember that effective instruction includes a balance between left and right brain emphasis, you will have taken care of most of the problem. Objectives are not written in individual isolation, but rather as sequences of learning expectations that lead to a general outcome. If you write carefully constructed objectives that allow students to master left-brain activities, you will construct a framework for assessment of the right-brain objectives that are part of the whole sequence of learning. With that caution in mind we offer a brief sample of objectives that emphasize right-brain functions. (See Mannies, 1986.)

1. Using only a pencil and blank sheet of paper, draw a caricature of a fellow class member that is recognizable by the majority of the class.
2. Presented with ten objects of different size, shape, and texture, develop a classification scheme that will enable another person to identify accurately all ten objects, using only the senses.

3. Given a story starter, create a short story in which all the physical elements of the story starter are incorporated into the plot.
4. Using only the three primary colors, create a painting that includes all the elements of the modern style.
5. Using the computer simulation "Oregon Trail" as a model, construct a simulation for travel from an earth orbit space station to the moon that adheres to the physical principles regulating movement in an airless and weightless environment.

ELEMENTS OF PERFORMANCE OBJECTIVES

Although performance objectives are written in a wide variety of styles, three elements generally can be included in the specification of a performance objective.

1. The statement of an observable behavior or performance on the part of the learner.
2. An elaboration of the conditions under which learner behavior or performance is to occur.
3. The prescription of a minimally acceptable performance on the part of the learner.

You will observe the first element in almost all performance objectives—that is, the specification of the *intended* behavior or performance. According to purists *only* when all three elements are stated is an objective written appropriately. As learners of the skill, you should always state the three elements for practice. This repetition will then give you insights (nonbehavioral term) into how you will feel (affective term) about their use in your teaching or how to evaluate (cognitive term) curricula that use such objectives. Again, it will be your decision (affective behavior) as to what style *you* choose. It was *our* decision (arbitrary and cognitive behavior) to illustrate a three-element type.

Element One: Performance Statement

The first element of a behavioral objective is the specification of a word, generally a verb, that indicates how the learner is performing, what the learner is doing, or what the learner is producing. Verbs such as *match, name, compute, list, assemble, write, circle,* and *classify* result in observable learner behaviors that will help you to evaluate the achievement of performance objectives.

For example, if you state that the student must name the capitals of ten states listed, the student's behavior is manifested when this performance takes place; everyone will know that the student has attained the stated student objective.

The specifications of the performance, of course, come from the general goals and intermediate objectives. If you teach social studies, one goal always will be to provide instruction about our form of government and the Constitution. An intermediate objective surely will be to study the Bill of Rights. Specific performance objectives may be as follows. The learner will

1. Write verbatim or paraphrase the first ten amendments to the U.S. Constitution.
2. Distinguish between statements from the Bill of Rights and those that are not.
3. Conduct a survey to determine how many students in the high school can identify the Fifth Amendment.
4. Select one of the amendments and prepare a 200-word essay on its meaning to the learner.

All these objectives are written with a prescribed student performance in mind. Table 2-1 contains a handy list of action verbs that will help you in constructing the first element of performance objectives.

When you examine the table, you will notice that it contains mainly *transitive verbs,* the "action verbs." They suggest that the actions are done *to direct objects,*

Table 2-1 *Some Action Verbs That Describe Observable Cognitive Behavior*

A	discriminate among	**I**	**O**	substitute
add	dissect	identify	order	subtract
alphabetize	distinguish between	inscribe	outline	
alter	divide	insert		**T**
amend	draw	integrate	**P**	tabulate
apply a rule	duplicate	interpolate	perform	transcribe
arrange		itemize	place	translate
assign values	**E**		point out	
	enumerate	**J**	predict	**U**
B	extrapolate	join	print	underline
bisect			punctuate	undertake
	F	**K**	put in order	
C	factor	keep		**V**
calculate	figure	knit	**Q**	verbalize
capitalize	fill in		qualify	
chart	find	**L**	quote	**W**
circle	fix	label		write
classify	fold	list	**R**	
combine	formulate	locate	rank	**X**
complete			rate	x-ray
compute	**G**	**M**	recall	
construct	gather	manipulate	reproduce	**Y**
correct	graph	mark off		yell
count	group	match	**S**	
		measure	select	**Z**
D	**H**	memorize	set down	zip
define	hit	mix	specify	
delineate	hold	multiply	state	
describe			state a rule	
diagram		**N**		
		name		

which must also be specified. This is critical, since the intended action is meaningless unless the verb and its direct object are specified. The performance objective thus tells what will be done in observable and measurable terms.

Words such as *know, understand, analyze, evaluate, appreciate, conprehend,* and *realize* are not action verbs. While such terms are important in the processes of learning and behaving, they are not observable actions and thus cannot be used when writing performance objectives. Use terms such as these when you specify goals or intermediate objectives. Remember that you make the decisions about the kind of performance you think is most appropriate or relevant.

Thus, the first and most important element of any performance objective is the selecting of the action verb and its direct object. In certain cases, this is the performance objective. However, according to Robert F. Mager (1962), the exponent of the performance objective movement, there must be two additional elements to make a performance objective truly communicative: the conditions under which the performance is to take place and the criterion statement.

Element Two: Elaboration of the Conditions

The second element in the prescribing of a performance objective is the statement of the *conditions* under which the learner is to perform the behavior. The conditional element prescribes the circumstances under which the learner must perform. Generally, conditional elements refer to

1. What materials may be used to do the tasks
2. How the performance may be accomplished—for example, from memory, from the textbook, or from a handout
3. Time elements (although time may also be used in evaluation)
4. Location of the performance (in the classroom, in a gymnasium, or in the library)

Observe this example: "With the aid of the Periodic Chart, the student will list the atomic weights of the first ten elements . . . ." Note that the conditional statement is "with the aid of the Periodic Chart." This tells a student that there is no need to memorize the atomic weights; the student should simply identify them from the Periodic Chart. We often refer to the conditional component of a performance objective as a "statement of givens": "Given this" or "given that," the learner will accomplish something.

The conditional element of a performance objective is the "fair play" part of the instruction. How many times have you walked into a class to find that when the teacher said to "study" a lesson, the actual or implied meaning, at least according to the teacher, was to "memorize" the lesson? The imprecision of such conditions is confusing, if not demoralizing. We recommend that this element of instruction always be given explicitly to students whether you use performance objectives or not.

The following is a list of a few conditional statements that could be included in the appropriate performance objectives.

1. "From memory . . ."
2. "Using a map of . . ."
3. "On a handout, which describes . . ."
4. "Given six different material samples without labels . . ."
5. "From the notes taken while viewing technicolor 35 mm slides . . ."
6. "Within a ten-minute time span and from memory . . ."
7. "Using the Income Tax Form 1040A . . ."
8. "With a compass, ruler, and protractor . . ."
9. "Using the chemicals and glassware provided in the tray . . ."
10. "Using the film 'The Joel E. Ferris Story' . . ."

These are some examples of the conditions under which a student can achieve a desired performance objective. The conditional statement is set by the teacher and given to the learners in advance. We recommend that the condition be written as the first component of the performance objective, although its placement is not a major issue over which to argue. We simply view it as having significant impact on instructional planning and teacher behavior and so should not be omitted.

Conditions must be realistic. Even though feasible, "reciting the Declaration of Independence from memory in five minutes" would be a very irrelevant condition. One must always ask, "What is my main priority for the objective?" If memorizing is the priority, then that condition will define the attainment of the objective. If identifying the key elements of the Declaration of Independence is the priority, then a condition less rigorous than memorization would be more compatible with the objective.

We highlight this point to warn you of possible pitfalls. We have witnessed performance objectives with outrageous conditions. Conditions must not act as an unreasonable impediment to the student in completing an objective in an effective manner.

Element Three: The Criterion Measure

The third element is perhaps the most difficult decision of all to make in a three-part performance objective—the definition of an acceptable standard of performance. This standard is usually called the "criterion measure," "level of performance," "minimum criterion," or the "minimum acceptable performance." Whatever the term used to define this element, it must be kept in mind that the designated level is the *minimum or lowest level of acceptable performance*. With this truly unique element in instruction, a student knows in advance exactly what the standards are by which the work will be judged.

Examine the following criterion measures, remembering that the condition and the performance verb are missing from the statements.

1. ". . . 70 percent of a given list of problems."
2. ". . . within 2mm. . . ."
3. ". . . nine out of ten of the elements. . . ."
4. ". . . within five minutes, with no more than two errors of any kind."
5. ". . . the project will be compared to the two models completed by the instructor."
6. ". . . without any grammatical or spelling errors."
7. ". . . containing one dependent and one independent clause."

Each of these criterion elements illustrates a well-defined standard toward which the student can strive. These standards are always devised so that the students have a high probability of achieving them and thus will be encouraged to continue to achieve the established criterion. We also caution that many teachers expect far too much from their students and set standards that are too high or impossible to reach. You must know at what level your students are working so that you may establish "reasonable" minimum standards—an accomplishment that is both an art and a science!

Frequently an instructor will require 100 percent of the class to attain 100 percent of the objective—that is, complete mastery. Such criterion measures are called 100/ 100 criterion measures because 100 percent of the class must obtain a 100 percent score. There are many times when an instructor will require mastery, such as when building skills, constructing something, using equipment, learning safety procedures, and other key tasks. In these cases, mastery or the top level is the minimum acceptable level. Again, you, the professional, must make that decision. The mastery criterion is most appropriate when completing prerequisite or entry-level tasks, since later skills are contingent on performing the initial ones.

While carefully defined standards of student performance are essential to a well-written performance objective, we recognize that much of what is taught in the classroom focuses on activities, experiences, and competencies. Providing meaningful criterion measures for instruction of this type can be difficult but can be made easier if you keep two things in mind as you prepare your performance objectives. First, remember that activity, experience, and competency learning experiences are made up of preceding instruction and learning that can be given clear standards of student performance. For example, the activity of playing volleyball is made up of a number of specific behaviors that can be isolated and given clear criterion measures. The experience of visiting an art museum is best preceded by study of the history and principles of art, which can be given clear criterion measures. Competence in building a garage is preceded by many skills that more easily provide clear standards of student performance. Performance objectives that focus on activities, experiences, and competencies are often more global in scope, and criterion measures for them can be difficult to write. However, they are always preceded by smaller increments of learning for which clear standards of performance can be written. In effect, the totality of each of the objectives that precedes an activity, experience, or competency objective make up the criterion measure for that objective.

Second, to write only narrow, skill-based performance objectives would destroy much of the richness that should be part of every classroom. Many times it is the activity or experientially focused instruction that gives a classroom spice and interest. Do not avoid writing objectives in which the criterion measure is not as precise and tight as you might like. Broadly stated objectives in which the criterion measure is less well defined are to be desired as long as they flow from a sequence of clearly articulated objectives forming their base. As you will learn in Chapter 4, much of the most exciting, high-level learning must come from the mastery of lower-level material and skills preceding it. (See Docking, 1986.)

Criterion Grading

A word of caution must be expressed about criterion levels. Far too frequently, a percent number or a time is prescribed by the teacher as establishing the evaluation element of the performance objective. If time is a critical factor in the real world—as in life-saving, in brake-reaction situations, and in manipulating machinery—then a timed criterion is appropriate. But to set the time of early or initial experiences identical to that of practitioners in the field is inappropriate on the teacher's part. Skills can be built or improved by using variable criterion measures just as with any systematic method aimed at improving skills. Thus, a criterion measure of thirty seconds for a skill in the first experience may be reduced systematically as learners improve. Typing teachers have observed this principle in action many times. As time progresses in the course, the students are allowed fewer mistakes per time period. In short, the standards for an A or top grade or even a C or average grade are shifted to higher levels of achievement as the course progresses.

Some educators have criticized performance objectives for seeming to force them into giving A grades for minimum student performance. This need not be the case. As a teacher, you may write performance objectives with clear criterion measures and make the meeting of those objectives worth any letter grade you choose. You may establish the standard that the meeting of criterion measures in your objectives will earn your students a C grade. Not meeting the criterion measures in your objectives will earn students a grade of less than C, and achieving a grade higher than C will require performance beyond those prescribed in your objectives.

Several other alternatives concerning performance objectives and grades are available to the teacher. You may choose to write several performance objectives for a sequence of instruction. Each objective can be progressively more difficult, with each worth a higher letter grade. Thus, performance objective 1 is worth a grade of D, while objective 2 is worth a grade of C, and so on. Rather than pressuring the teacher into giving a high grade for mediocre performance, carefully used performance objectives enable the teacher to prescribe precisely the value and meaning of letter grades in terms of overt learner performance.

We have a wide continuum of assessment techniques by which to judge student performances. Following is a list of techniques that may be easily applied in the classroom:

1. Observation of the student's performance
2. Prepared product
3. Practical application tests
4. Laboratory quizzes
5. Proportion of successful trials
6. Timed tasks
7. Checklists with specific criteria
8. Scales to rate activities or products
9. Objective tests
10. Essay tests
11. Student self-reports

Perhaps the establishment of reasonable levels of excellence is the most difficult task in writing a three-element performance objective. It certainly is the part requiring teacher decisions that reflect discretion and fairness.

Models of Completed Performance Objectives

The following is a series of performance objectives that contain the three elements described in this chapter. As you read each objective, identify each element; then compare your analyses with those in the model set that follows.

1. From those alternatives discussed and listed in this class, from memory, list three of the apparent causes of the American War Between the States.
2. Using the textbook and the supplemental readings listed in the bibliography, compare the events leading to Richard M. Nixon's resignation from the presidency with Lyndon B. Johnson's refusal to run for reelection in 1968. The criteria for evaluation will be the six major points prepared by the instructor and distributed to the class.
3. Using the six descriptions of elements for a good short story, identify in writing the six elements in the short story by O. Henry, with complete accuracy.
4. Given a compass and a straightedge, construct a pentagon, within 5 degrees of accuracy, on any of the inside or outside angles.
5. Following the pattern for a "hot mitt," construct a mitt from the materials in the class bin so that a steam iron set at 400°F may be held for six seconds without burning the mitt and without making your hand feel uncomfortably hot. The project must be completed in two class periods.

The model set of responses that follows is coded to reveal each element. Conditions are identified between the parentheses ( ). Each learner performance is stated between the brackets [ ]. The criterion measure is underscored.

1. (From those alternatives discussed and listed in this class, from memory), [list] three of the apparent causes of the American War Between the States.
2. (Using the textbook and the supplemental readings listed in the bibliography), [compare the events leading to Richard M. Nixon's resignation from the presidency with Lyndon B. Johnson's refusal to run for reelection in 1968.] The criteria for evaluation will be the six major points prepared by the instructor and distributed to the class.
3. (Using the six descriptions of elements for a good short story), [identify in writing the six elements in the short story by O. Henry,] with complete accuracy.
4. (Given a compass and a straightedge), [construct a pentagon,] within 5 degrees of accuracy, on any of the inside or outside angles.
5. (Following the pattern for a "hot mitt,") [construct a mitt from the materials in the class bin] so that a steam iron set at 400°F may be held for six seconds without burning the mitt and without making your hand feel uncomfortably hot. The project must be completed in two class periods.

ARE PERFORMANCE OBJECTIVES NECESSARY?

The establishing of performance objectives is not an educational panacea that will resolve all learning problems. It must be emphasized that there are limited purposes for writing performance objectives. *Performance objectives are only a means to an end, not an end per se.* The purpose of the objective is to communicate the exact intent of the lesson, the behavioral objective being one component of the lesson plan. *The teacher can construct technically correct objectives but can fail completely in the classroom because of a lack of teaching skills and interpersonal competencies or strategies.*

When developing lessons that use behavioral objectives, the teacher must accept the following assumptions:

1. Learning is defined as a change in the learner's observable performance.
2. Behavioral changes are observable in some form and may be measured by *appropriate* measuring devices over a specified period of time.
3. Observed learner outcome is *primary* to the teaching strategies, the content, or the media used.
4. The majority of all children at all ages can master appropriate subjects at some acceptable level if they are given enough time *and* adequate, appropriate learning experiences.

Problems in Writing Appropriate Objectives

We have noticed at least four major problems that teachers encounter when writing performance objectives. Each of these four problems is discussed in the following sections.

Confusing Instruction with the Conditional Statement

One of the common traps into which teachers fall is that of writing a performance objective that is nothing more than the condition under which the instruction is to take place. For example, written objectives that state, "after viewing a film" or "after classroom instruction," are statements referring to teaching behaviors that take place prior to student performance. They are not performance conditions as we have defined the term; teachers have confused their instructional behavior with their students' learning behavior. Condition statements should refer to the circumstances of the student at the moment of performance. More appropriately written conditions may specify "from memory" or "using classroom notes taken while viewing a movie" when the student is to recall a concept or set of concepts.

Incomplete Criterion Statement

In developing the criterion statement for an objective, you need to avoid a statement such as "define eight out of ten terms." This specifies only the quantity of the performance, not the quality. In such a case, you must first have a set of criteria by which to judge the quality of each definition before determining whether the student has given the *minimum* number of eight definitions.

Unspecified Level of Performance in Criterion Statement

For a long time our society has accepted a graded level of performance: 90 percent = A, 80 percent = B, 70 percent = C, and so on. Using the behavioral objective approach to teaching requires a different system of grading because the criterion level is related to the performance. A teacher must ask two questions: (1) "At what level must my students perform in order to be successful in subsequent instructional tasks?" and (2) "What level is considered successful in the world in which the student lives?" In a beginning reading class, the teacher strives for a 95–100 percent mastery of vocabulary and sounds, whereas in a beginning archery course, the instructor considers an acceptable level to be 50 percent of the arrows hitting the target. At best, the teacher establishes a hypothetically acceptable level of performance and keeps collecting data to substantiate, modify, or reject that level. Remember that in nearly all cases standards are subjective, if not arbitrary!

Another problem related to the establishment of minimal levels of performance is the tendency to convert all levels to percentage scores. Asking the student for 80 percent of a definition or for 100 percent of an essay is a misuse of a criterion measure and is inappropriate. A more reasonable approach would be to define clearly the elements necessary for an acceptable essay. Once you state the attributes or elements, you may reasonably request that a certain percentage of these attributes or elements be included. For example, the criterion that "each written sentence must have a subject and predicate" provides a valid standard by which to judge the essay.

Still another problem is the overuse of time statements within the criterion measure. By placing time in the statement, the instructor is suggesting that time is at least as important as quality, and even more important, if the quality criterion is omitted from the objective.

Irrelevant and Misused Objectives

We assume that at this point you have asked yourself, "Couldn't all this performance-objective writing lead to compilations of millions of trite, useless, and seldom-used lesson plans?" Advocates of performance objectives sometimes fail to caution that you can write a series of performance objectives that are totally and irrevocably irrelevant.

There is a general assumption among educators that specifying performance objectives is *the* technology for enhancing accountability. To be sure, the curriculum alignment movement is an excellent example of "tightening" the links of instruction. However, be alert: there is little published evidence showing that alignment alone is powerful enough to improve student achievement in a significant and sustained manner. One may point to "effective schools" research as supporting the curriculum alignment process. Yes, but that process is just *one* of several used in schools that have demonstrated instructional efficacy.

Teachers and curriculum writing teams have tended to produce objectives so trite that they insult a learner's intelligence. We know a school district that proudly announced that it had computerized over 250,000 performance objectives. (Mind you, one-quarter of a million discrete learner statements! That collection illustrates *reductio absurdum.*) And in at least five different inservice projects, one of the authors could not observe *one* teacher who provided those school districts' objectives to the students—in spite of the objectives being typed, categorized, and neatly bound.

Your objectives are statements of teacher intent only. You must provide meaningful activities, drill, practice, reflection, and feedback. You alone can help expand a child's educational horizons by planning for truly important classroom experiences that add meaning to sterile performance objectives.

In most school districts the objectives are already written, published, and distributed for each grade level and subject. Such widespread practice shows a gross misinterpretation of the intent and rationale of specifying learner objectives.

Using performance objectives will probably not help your charges to develop an *understanding* of what they are doing. Yet, understanding *why* some action takes place is far more important than recognizing that the action took place. Performance objectives have notoriously lacked the qualities of enhancing creativity, problem-solving, or applying basic knowledge.

In short, we are cautioning that overuse of performance objectives is just as absurd as not using any at all. Your decision to use this technology must always be predicated on the potential benefit to the learner.

Summary Reasons for Using Performance Objectives

Performance objectives clarify the intent of the lesson for the teacher. With clearly stated outcomes in mind, the teacher is better able to design appropriate learning experiences for the class—and for each child, if the program is individualized.

Performance objectives also clarify the intent of the lesson for the learner. Students are able to use time more efficiently, since they know what is to be performed.

Performance objectives make it easier to measure student achievement. Since the criteria are stated in the objective, both student and teacher know what is expected of the student, and the student gets immediate feedback about the performance. It is simpler—but unfair—to assign students an A, B, C, or F arbitrarily without specifying what is being measured.

A teacher may still assign A's, B's, and F's, but only with a *prior* explanation of the criteria by which such grading standards will be applied. Also, by specifying peformance objectives, a contract grading system may be developed, or a different *qualitative* component may be prescribed, for each different level of performance for each grade.

Performance objectives make it easier to measure effectiveness of instruction. The teacher's job is to aid student learning. Because the level of performance is stated, it is easy to determine if the selected materials, visual aids, and teaching strategies have been helpful to the student in achieving the stated objectives. As a result, effectiveness of instruction is based on student achievement of the instructional objectives.

Performance objectives should help develop a more effective communication system among teachers, students, administrators, and parents. A well-stated performance objective gives them all a common frame of reference for discussion. Because instruction is the primary purpose of education, precisely written instructional objectives are essential to any meaningful interaction.

Charles Clark (1988) and W. James Popham (1987) reviewed the research concerning the effect of performance objectives on student learning. They noted that the findings of reported research are very conflicting. However, there do seem to be several generalizations that are supported by some research evidence.

1. Performance objectives do act as guides to student learning and as advance organizers. (This is discussed in Chapter 3.)

2. Performance objectives tend to depress incidental learning.
3. Providing students with performance objectives after a learning sequence tends to improve incidental learning.
4. Distributing performance objectives throughout the textual material may improve learning—that is, distributing the objectives over an assignment may be more effective than giving all the objectives at once.

If you teach in a school that uses "direct instruction," "teacher-directed instruction," or "mastery learning," then you must master the process of writing three-part performance objectives. If you teach in a school that has adopted Madeline Hunter's "Instructional Theory into Practice" (ITIP) model, then you will also use performance objectives.

A Final Caution

Specifying learning activities in performance terms is just *one* element in the totality of teaching acts. A teacher who uses appropriately designed performance objectives may develop into a better instructor. A disorganized, haphazard, or slovenly teacher with or without performance objectives will still be disorganized, haphazard, or slovenly. But more important, the *quality* of the objectives is of prime concern. A teacher with well-conceived and relevant objectives will help students demonstrate more relevant learning behaviors.

FORMATIVE EVALUATION

Congratulations. You have just completed the text of Chapter 2. Below are two components of a formative evaluation with which to check your knowledge and understanding of the concepts presented in this chapter. Section 1 contains three lists with four items each. The appropriate responses for each list follow. If you score 4 for each list, continue to Section 2 of the formative evaluation. If you score 3 or less, restudy the text on that section so that you may bring yourself up to mastery for each list.

Section 1

A. Read each item below. Place an X next to each item that states an identifiable behavior or an observable performance.

_____ 1. The learner will understand that multiplication requires a place value numbering system.

_____ 2. The student will comprehend the racial subplot in the novel *To Kill a Mocking-bird*.

_____ 3. The student will discern the relationship between interest rates and inflation.

_____ 4. The learner will describe the function of baking powder in the making of bread.

Responses

1. Item 1 should not have an *X*, as the verb *understand* does not offer an observable behavior.
2. Item 2 should not have an *X*, as the verb *comprehend* does not offer an observable behavior.
3. Item 3 should not have an *X*. *Discern* is internal to the learner and there is no observable behavior.
4. Item 4 should have an *X*. The verb *describe* offers an observable behavior.

B. If you had 3 or fewer correct, restudy the text on observable behavior or reexamine the performance words. If you had 4 correct, do the formative evaluation on conditions, which follows. Read each of the following items. Place an *X* next to each item that states a condition under which the learner's behavior is to occur.

_____ 1. Given ten different leaf samples, the student will correctly identify all the plants from which they come.

_____ 2. Identify all the nouns and adjectives.

_____ 3. Given the height, width, and depth, the student will draw an accurate two-point perspective of the Post Office Building.

_____ 4. Within the constraints of the budget and food list provided, the student will create a five-day meal plan that provides minimum nutritional values.

Responses

Items 1, 3, and 4 should be marked with an *X*. The following are the conditions for these items:
Item 1: Given ten different leaf samples
Item 3: Given the height, width, and depth
Item 4: Within the constraints of the budget and food list provided
All these phrases *tell the condition* under which behavior is to occur, what will be provided to the student, or where something is to be done. Item 2 does not present any condition at all.

C. If you had 3 or fewer correct, restudy the text on "Element Two: Elaboration of the Conditions." If you had 4 correct, do the formative evaluation on criterion measures, which follows. Read each of the following items. Place an *X* next to each statement that establishes a minimum level of acceptable learner performance.

_____ 1. The student will reduce 70 percent of a given list of fractions to their lowest terms.

———————— 2. Given a printed copy of a 100-line program, the student will enter the program so that it runs without error.

———————— 3. The student will assemble the DNA model within fifteen minutes.

———————— 4. The student must create a program using Basic or Pascal.

Responses

Items 1, 2, and 3 should have an *X*. The criterion measures are as follows:
Item 1: 70 percent; to their lowest terms
Item 2: Runs without error
Item 3: Within fifteen minutes
Item 4: Does not provide any information on minimal standards

Now proceed to Section 2 of the formative evaluation, in which you are given six objectives to evaluate.

Section 2

D. Examine each of the following six objectives and write whether the statement is *true* or *false* in the space provided.

———————— 1. *To list the criteria for evaluating "user friendly" computer software.* This objective is worded in terms of the learner performing or producing something.

———————— 2. *Use a straightedge and compass to construct a geometric form.* This statement is worded in terms of the learner performing or producing something.

———————— 3. *To identify a parallelogram, given five different geometric shapes.* This objective describes the conditions under which the learner's behavior is to occur.

———————— 4. *Using a copy of "The Student Users Library Handbook," the student will prepare a three-page report on the United States' relations with Central America that contains six references to articles in the periodical literature, none of which are more than three years old.* This statement contains the minimum acceptable criteria.

5. *Given three articles, the textbook, and class lectures, the student will understand the relationship between the "prime rate," changes in the money supply, and consumer interest rates.*

———————— (a) This statement contains all the elements of behavioral objective.

———————— (b) This statement does not contain a minimum acceptable criterion.

———————— (c) This statement does not contain a verb that identifies observable learner behavior.

6. *Given a theorem to prove by coordinate geometry, the student will apply the coordinates that make the least complex algebraic calculation.*

_____ (a) This statement does not contain the conditions under which learner behavior is to occur.

_____ (b) This statement does not contain minimum acceptable criterion.

_____ (c) This statement contains all the elements of a behavioral objective.

Check your answers in the key that follows. If you had all 6 items correct, you are certified as being able to identify and analyze performance objectives. Of course, we don't know if you can write one! If you had 5 or fewer correct, restudy the entire chapter.

Responses

1. true
2. true
3. true
4. true
5. false, false, true
6. false, false, true

REFERENCES

Bloom, Benjamin S., et al. *Handbook on Formative and Summative Evaluation.* New York: McGraw-Hill, 1971.

————. *Taxonomy of Educational Objectives: Handbook I, The Cognitive Domain.* New York: David McKay, 1956.

Carroll, John B. "A Model for School Learning." *Teachers' College Record* 64:1963, 723–733.

Clark, Charles. "The Necessity of Curricular Objectives." *Journal of Curriculum Studies* 20:1988, 339–349.

Cohen, M. "Instructional Management and Social Conditions in Effective Schools." In *School Finance and School Improvement: Linkages in the 1980's.* A. O. Webb and L. D. Webb, eds. Cambridge, Mass.: Ballinger, 1983.

Cohen, S. Alan. "Instructional Alignment: Searching for a Magic Bullet." *Educational Researcher* 16(8):1987, 16–19.

Docking, R. A. "Criterion Referenced Grading Techniques." *Studies in Educational Evaluation* 12:1986, 281–294.

Harrow, Anita. *A Taxonomy of the Psychomotor Domain: A Guide for Developing Behavior Objectives.* New York: David McKay, 1972.

Hunter, Madeline. "Teaching Is Decision Making." *Educational Leadership* 37:1979, 62–64, 67.

Keefe, James W. *Learning Style Theory and Practice.* Reston, Va.: National Association of Secondary School Principals, 1987.

Krathwohl, David R., Benjamin S. Bloom, and Bertram B. Masia. *Taxonomy of Educational Objectives: Handbook II, The Affective Domain.* New York: David McKay, 1964.

Levine, Daniel U. "Successful Approaches for Improving Academic Achievement in Inner-City Elementary Schools." *Phi Delta Kappan* 63: 1982, 523–526.

Mager, Robert F. *Preparing Instructional Objectives,* 2nd ed. Belmont, Calif.: Fearon, 1975.

Mannies, Nancy. "Brain Theory and Learning." *Clearing House* 60:1986, 127–130.

Moore, Maxine Ruth. "A Proposed Taxonomy of the Perceptual Domain and Some Suggested Applications." Princeton, N.J.: Educational Testing Service, 1967.

Popham, W. James. "Two-Plus Decades of Educational Objectives." *International Journal of Educational Research* 11:1987, 31–41.

Slavin, Robert. "The Hunterization of America's Schools." *Instructor* 96:1987, 56–58.

3

Decisions About Sequencing Instruction

*C*hapter 1 discusses teaching as a decisions-making process. You make some of these decisions before you teach the lesson (*planning*), some during the lesson (*instructing*), and some after you have taught the lesson (*evaluating*).

One of the basic components of planning is the writing of educational objectives, a skill amply illustrated in Chapter 2. In this chapter we will describe four models of lesson or unit organizations, which include: (1) the sequencing of instruction; and (2) the use of task analysis to illustrate relationships among bodies of knowledge.

Objectives   After completing this chapter, you should be able to:

- Provide several reasons for using sequencing in the planning process
- Explain how task analysis will provide teacher assistance in the planning process
- Provide some examples from your teaching area for each model

SEQUENCING

By sequencing instructional tasks, one assumes that the student can better master any organized body of knowledge or discipline. One also assumes that the learning of skills or knowledge in a carefully interrelated manner helps the student to develop those skills that ultimately aid with information-processing, that is, thinking.

If we are willing to accept these key assumptions about schooling, then sequencing has two basic purposes. One is to isolate knowledge (a fact, concept, generalization, or principle) so that the student can understand the unique characteristics of the selected information or to isolate a thinking process so that the student can master the process under varying conditions. The second purpose is to relate the knowledge or process being taught to the larger organized body of knowledge. The first function—isolating what is being taught—helps *make learning more manageable,* and the second function—relating the information—*makes learning more meaningful.*

For example, if you want to teach the concept of *metaphor,* you teach the characteristics of metaphor using illustrations of metaphors. This process provides students with a manageable amount of information and with the focus for their study. You proceed to a second figure of speech—*simile*—and use the same process. After the students have mastered both concepts, you then can illustrate how both concepts are figures of speech; that is, they have common characteristics. This process illustrates the relationship of the lesson content to a larger body of knowledge.

This example also shows the relationship between sequencing and hierarchies of knowledge. *A hierarchy is content-related* in that it usually portrays the relationships among items of information, whereas *a sequence is process-related* in that it establishes a schedule for learning the various parts of the related content. In a subject area such as mathematics, in which there is an accepted hierarchy of knowledge, the sequence and hierarchy are very similar because the relationships of the content almost dictate a sequence of learning activities. In a subject such as social studies, in which it is difficult to agree on an established hierarchy of information, the sequencing of learning is usually established by either the interest or the experience of the teacher. The selection sequence of novels or poetry taught in an English literature course or the sequence of regions taught in a geography course is usually determined by teacher experience or background, not by an accepted hierarchy of knowledge within these disciplines. If a learning hierarchy exists, it influences the instructional sequence. If a learning hierarchy does not exist, the sequences of instructional learning establish a loosely knit hierarchy for the student.

At this point, we must once again emphasize how important it is for the teacher to specify objectives to be learned. Chapter 2 recommended the three-part performance objectives made popular by Robert F. Mager (1962). We realize that the linear approach to teaching, that of specifying objectives and sequencing learning activities, is stressed in most teacher education programs (Tursman, 1981). In reality the planned lesson sequence often becomes blurred during the interactive instructional process. Because of students' previous learning, environmental conditions, school schedules, and other conditions affecting instruction, planned instructional objectives, sequences, and activities are continuously altered or adjusted. To be an effective teacher, the student learning objectives must be sequenced to illustrate the relationship between the various components of the curriculum so that prerequisite conditions or entry level competencies can be identified and taught at an appropriate stage.

MODELS OF LESSON ORGANIZATION

This chapter will describe four models of lesson or unit organization. Each model presents a guideline for sequencing objectives and activities and establishes a hierarchy or relationship of knowledge. Yet, each model has unique characteristics that assist the teacher in selecting a planning model. For example, content is the guiding force in the concept analysis model, whereas the student provides the stimulus for planning in the diagnostic-prescriptive model. The models and their primary characteristics are illustrated in Table 3-1. Each model has intrinsic strength: no model is inherently superior. The teacher, as a decision-maker, should choose the one that provides the greatest assistance in lesson planning, organizing, and implementing.

The Task Analysis Model

Suppose you were teaching your class a lesson and you assumed that the students would be able to answer successfully nearly all the questions asked on an examination covering the materials of the lesson. From all indications, the students were enjoying the lesson and no big problems were anticipated. Then, to your dismay, the class performed poorly on the examination. Could the test have been poorly constructed,

Table 3-1   *Models of Lesson or Unit Organization*

Model	Primary Characteristics
Task Analysis	Careful sequencing of intermediate and terminal objectives
Concept Analysis	Sequencing of concept characteristics examples and relating the concept to a concept hierarchy
Advance Organizer	Developing an advance organizer that provides an "ideational scaffold" to teach the interrelationships of an organized body of knowledge
Diagnostic-Prescriptive	A four-step teacher-student interaction model based on student entry-level knowledge and skills

or was the performance the result of poor instruction? An incident similar to this happened to one of America's foremost learning theorists, Robert M. Gagné (1962), several years ago. The lesson was in elementary school mathematics, but the content could have been high school chemistry, college calculus or, for that matter, social studies, English, physical education, or *any* other level study. What is important is that Gagné was not satisfied with the results and wanted to determine why.

Gagné began to study the sequence in which the learning activities (teaching) were planned. He soon concluded that some instructional elements should have preceded others and that some concepts that he had not taught the students should have been introduced prior to attempting the particular learning objective. This initial study led Gagné to rearrange some of the learning sequences and to try the lesson again. The result was a dramatic change in student success as measured by test results. The concomitant learning experiences were arranged in a chartlike format, so that the top of the chart contained the end of the instructional sequence, usually called the *terminal objective.* Those objectives below the terminal objective are called *intermediate* or *entry-level objectives.* The terminal objective is what the students finally should achieve after a series of planned instructional encounters. Note in Figure 3-1 that the terminal objective is to "solve solubility product problems," and it is labeled with a Roman numeral. In Gagné's model, Roman numerals are sequenced by levels, with Roman numeral I being most difficult and the larger Roman numerals being those leading to the terminal objective—that is, the prerequisite behaviors. Figure 3-1 outlines a task analysis chart that James R. Okey and Robert M. Gagné (1970) devised for a chemistry class. Typically, the lowest-level objective is to acquire *prerequisite* or *entry-level skills.* Unless students have already mastered these basic skills, they will probably *not* be able to reach the learning objective in any higher levels.

To study the effects of a hierarchical structure on learning, Gagné employed a methodology that has long proved valuable in the sphere of business and industry. That method is known as "task analysis." Careful sequencing of tasks has been and continues to be a critical element of efficient production in the industrial and technological sectors and even in education. You can imagine how chaotic and costly your

Figure 3-1   *One Task Analysis for a Science Topic*

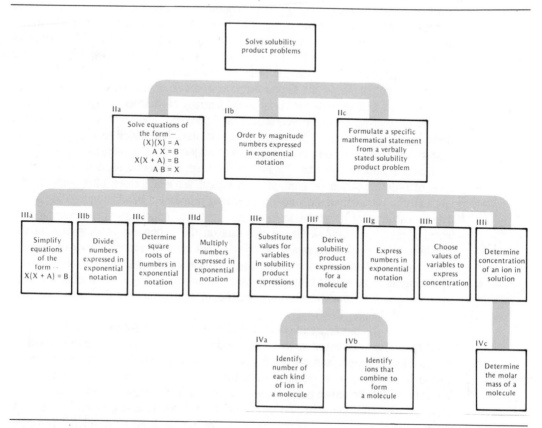

Source: From James R. Okey and Robert M. Gagné, "Revision of a Science Topic Using Evidence of Performance on Subordinate Skills," *Journal of Research in Science Teaching* 7(4):1970, p. 323. Reprinted by permission of the National Association for Research in Science Teaching and John Wiley & Sons, Inc.

education would be if there were no grade levels or if there were no methods of identifying the difficulty level of your university courses. If you think that your program of studies seems disorganized, think of the problems you would have if each piece of information you learned was taught in isolation and not as a part of a course and if the courses had no titles or identifying numbers. Your education would be longer and more expensive.

Industry has not been alone in recognizing the value of carefully analyzing tasks and of identifying the sequential relationships of component activities. In education, the importance of sequencing *subject matter content* for instructional purposes has been acknowledged for a considerable length of time. Ralph W. Tyler (1949) viewed sequencing as one of the three major criteria that must be met in organizing a curriculum; continuity and integration were the other two.

Through the impetus of Gagné's investigations of learning sequences, however, emphasis shifted from the sequencing of content per se to the analyzing and ordering of content *as it relates to the learning process.* The Okey and Gagné (1970) model asserts that before the learner can acquire a complex cognitive skill, such as problem-solving, he or she must first advance through a series of *enabling learning conditions.* Rather than relying on armchair theorizing to determine the nature and order of these enabling skills, Gagné empirically investigated and tested prerequisite performances that were needed prior to the learning of a particular higher-order skill. He used numerous refined psychological methodologies and techniques to construct these learning hierarchies. He amply demonstrated that skilled teachers should no longer rely exclusively on the organization of subject matter to determine sequence.

It seems noteworthy that "logical" is the term frequently used to describe the type of order imposed on content; this logical sequence more often reflects the instructor's, rather than the students', thinking processes. In addition to being sensitive to patterns of organization in subject matters, educators are encouraged by learning theorists such as Gagné to focus on the sequential relationships of the subskills (thinking processes and behaviors) that must be acquired *prior* to learning higher-ordered behaviors and skills (Gagné, 1985 and Gagné and Paradise, 1961). The content to be learned, in other words, is subdivided into descending levels of *cognitive products and processes*—from the most abstract to the most concrete (Gagné and Briggs, 1974).

If you use the hierarchy of content illustrated in Figure 3-2 to plan a lesson, you must take into consideration the relationship of levels 1 and 2 to levels 3 and 4. Principles and generalizations are formed from facts through observational and inferential processes. For example, each time two magnets are manipulated so that like poles repel and unlike poles attract, there is a single event; the action is observable; and the single event itself does not predict values. This single event is a fact. A series of such events (facts) provide data that can be used to develop a principle about magnets, one of many principles that we teach students in our public schools. The teacher has the option either of presenting the principle first and then substantiating it with the facts or of organizing and presenting the facts and then allowing the students to develop the principle. These two options constitute another important teaching decision. Both options demand that the teacher plan for sequencing of lesson activities.

Task Analysis and Sequencing

You can arrange almost any set of learning concepts, generalizations, or principles into the Gagné system. Gagné suggested that all instruction *can* (and indeed *should*) follow the systematic identification of content and process illustrated in the preceding hierarchical analyses.

There are several principles that apply to all kinds of sequencing. The first principle is that you always *begin with a simple step.* This does not mean that you "talk down" to your students. Rather, it means that you structure the teaching elements

Figure 3-2   *Task Analysis of Knowledge and Processes of Thinking*

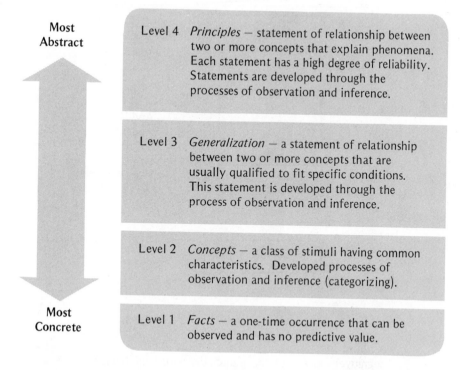

Most
Abstract

Level 4   *Principles* — statement of relationship between two or more concepts that explain phenomena. Each statement has a high degree of reliability. Statements are developed through the processes of observation and inference.

Level 3   *Generalization* — a statement of relationship between two or more concepts that are usually qualified to fit specific conditions. This statement is developed through the process of observation and inference.

Level 2   *Concepts* — a class of stimuli having common characteristics. Developed processes of observation and inference (categorizing).

Most
Concrete

Level 1   *Facts* — a one-time occurrence that can be observed and has no predictive value.

so that learners can understand easily identified characteristics. At this step you should provide numerous examples. Using analogies often helps.

The second principle is to *proceed to the concrete*. This means that you may have to use materials, simulations, models, or artifacts that illustrate the lesson, objective, or concept being taught.

The third principle suggests that, from the concrete, you may plan to *structure a lesson or learning sequence so that it becomes more complex*. Additional variables may be introduced, new sets of criteria may be generated, and relationships may be established between the content of the lesson and other content. It is at this level as well as the next level that you should try to get students to apply the information presented by using the two principles previously described.

Finally, you may introduce abstractions. You may require the students to generalize, predict, or explain the information generated, using principles 1, 2, and 3.

Do not be fooled into thinking that on Monday your lesson should be "simple," on Tuesday it should be "concrete," on Wednesday you should address "complex" issues, on Thursday you should deal with "abstract" issues, and on Friday you should test. The four principles may take years to apply when developing sequenced concepts—for example, grammar and creative writing, mathematical analysis, fine arts, or social studies. What we wish to stress is that understanding the interrelationships

Figure 3-3 *A Hierarchy for Student Success*

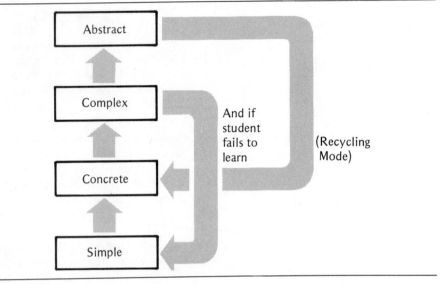

of these four principles helps students learn. If you realize this, then you will be cognitively aware of the sequential nature of thinking skills and will incorporate appropriate learning experiences to complement the levels. Figure 3-3 is a concrete model of this instructional technique.

Let us examine a concrete example. In the first grade, teachers introduce the concept of graphing, a skill that even college freshmen often do not attain. The overall goal is to provide a series of experiences through which the concept of graphing will emerge. Although the concept of graphing is introduced in the first grade, the sequence that includes all types and levels of difficulty of graphs may take as long as ten years or more. The time duration could be reduced but probably not appreciably.

Systematic graphing experiences require all teachers in the school to communicate with one another for a long time concerning what has transpired in their classrooms. In some schools this process would be articulated by means of a curriculum guide.

The lesson begins in a first grade science class. The children plant bean seeds and begin a study of plant growth. The teacher raises the question of measuring the growth on certain days, say, on every Friday afternoon. All plants are watered as uniformly as possible. As the seeds germinate, the teacher gives each child a strip of paper. The paper is placed by the seedling and the strip is torn to equal the length or height of the plant on the prescribed day. This technique is called a scale of 1:1 or, mathematically speaking, one-to-one correspondence.

The teacher then has each child glue the strip to a large piece of paper, with a label made for the strip and bearing that date. This process continues until the teacher and children grow tired of it. Of course, the teacher asks the children to observe other changes, which they discuss. Finally everyone has a concrete histogram—a simple graph. Although there will be some variation, the results will be somewhat uniform. Then comes a discussion about making histograms, and the concept of a one-to-one scale is introduced. The graphs are saved for the next year. Ultimately, similar histograms are constructed, using the concept of scale. The class members can develop a histogram using their own heights, weights, or some other quantifiable, but varying, personal characteristic.

The next year the teacher continues to use the histograms and makes them more complex. Finally, the teacher can show that if a dot is placed at the top of the line and if scales are made in opposite directions (labeling the axes), all the information will be available in a form that is easier to use. This will take us through the second, maybe the third, grade. (We caution that some learning tasks take a long time to develop.)

Ultimately, the teacher provides other data, such as daily maximum temperatures, then maxima and minima simultaneously. The graphing concepts thus become more complex and begin to approach the abstract; yet these activities reflect an experience that the class shares in common. The culmination of the set of experiences would be to have the children obtain data of their choosing and make their own graphs. The initial instructional episode may take three or four years.

Obviously not all concepts take that amount of time. In a high school, it often takes several days to complete a segment (unit) of work. Often the modules are sequenced to progress to more complex aspects of instruction. Each unit should illustrate the use of the principles described previously. Our main point is that you, as teacher, control the learning environment. If you desire to make learning more systematic, then here is one technique that has been tested. You have to *decide* how you will apply task analysis in your teaching so that students learn better—that is the fun of live instruction!

Procedures for Task Analysis

The major purpose of task analysis is to discover the relationships of subskills and to use this information to plan for effective instruction. Although it is unrealistic to assume that you as a classroom teacher will have the time or methodological expertise to identify and validate enabling skills empirically with the precision afforded by Gagné's investigations, you can effectively and efficiently use task analysis in your own teaching. The following procedures (tasks) need to be accomplished to analyze learning tasks successfully.

1. *Select an instructional objective that is at the appropriate level of difficulty.* To make this initial determination of what is to be learned, the teacher obviously must know the structure of the content area (such as physics, health, education, mathematics, or social studies). It is essential that the teacher know what the learner has *already* achieved in the content area.

This first step, which entails the specification of the learning objective, may seem very obvious. (After all, it would be difficult, if not impossible, to analyze an unspecified, ill-defined objective, or to spend laborious hours analyzing the subskills of tasks that are inappropriate for the particular learner.) The importance of this stage of planning is often overlooked. For example, teachers sometimes make such statements as, "When students are in the ninth grade, they should read Chaucer," or "Seventh graders should study world geography." Such curriculum decisions are based on the incremental nature of content, but they neglect to identify where *learners* are located in the curriculum plan. For example, it makes little sense to teach students problems of percentage if they do not first understand decimals—regardless of *grade* level considerations.

Therefore, in selecting appropriate learning objectives, you will need to identify the general area where student knowledge ends. This is the point at which to formulate new learning objectives and to analyze the subskills that lead to the attainment of these new objectives. We will refer later to the importance of using *diagnostic vigilance* when you help learners to achieve an objective through a classroom lesson. The technique of diagnostic vigilance allows the teacher to check on whether or not the original objective is, in fact, at the right level of difficulty.

2. *Identify the independent and dependent sequences of enabling skills that lead to the attainment of the desired objective.* For any given set of subskills, there are two basic types of sequences: independent and dependent. (Sometimes the component behaviors may be *both*.) In an independent sequence, the ordering of a particular set of enabling skills is not incremental. For example, in learning to tie a pair of shoes, it does not matter whether one starts with the right or the left foot. These activities are independent of each other. Similarly, in constructing a house, it does not make any appreciable difference if one starts by laying the foundation for the garage or for the main part of the house.

In the dependent sequence, on the other hand, the accomplishment of one subtask (that is, subskill or behavior) is essential before attainment of the next subtask in the series. In putting on shoes and socks, therefore, the ordering of the tasks does make a difference. The socks need to be on before proceeding to the next behavior: putting on the shoes. In the same way, the construction company would be remiss in attempting to shingle the roof prior to raising the walls of the structure.

3. *Arrange the independent and dependent sequences as they relate to each other and perform the task yourself to identify possible steps that were omitted. Use this sequence to construct a lesson that will systematically facilitate the learning of the terminal objective.* Once you have analyzed the objective and discovered its component parts (independent and dependent sequences), these parts (or enabling skills) will provide an entry point of learning for all students. The enabling skills themselves become objectives as you use them to help students reach the terminal objective.

It is doubtful that you will be able to identify all the prerequisite enabling skills consistently before implementing the lesson. As you teach, your judgment will allow you to adjust, to add other subskills to the list, and to emphasize certain subskills with particular students. Keep notes about such skills in the daily lesson-plan book that is used by most teachers. These notes will be a handy reference for your next class, as you monitor and adjust your teaching activities.

4. *As you plan for the sequencing of specific tasks for the students, you must first plan the sequence in which you will conduct the class.* For example, there are some set tasks that *you* must accomplish every time you attempt to reach your objective of preparing and implementing a lesson. You must (1) identify the instructional objectives; (2) plan the appropriate educational activities or experiences; (3) obtain the materials; (4) read the materials yourself; (5) plan the strategies that you will employ in the teaching act; (6) evaluate the students; and (7) critique the lesson—that is, decide how you would improve it.

The sequence of events and the decisions that you make in planning the lesson will be the easy part of teaching. The "moment of truth" arrives when the lesson is taught. Suddenly, you will observe that there are students who do poorly despite your best efforts to plan systematically. It is at this point in the teaching process that teacher differences occur. Some teachers simply continue with the lesson plan and complete the unit of study. This technique, of course, is the worst—from the learner's perspective. Others will use another technique, that of a concept analysis.

Concept Analysis Model

The teaching of concepts entails a substantial portion of all instruction. For example, science requires students to understand concepts of matter, energy, plant, and animal; language arts applies the concepts of communication, paragraph, parts of speech, and punctuation; mathematics requires students to apply concepts of set, commutative property, and inverse operation. A lengthy list could be compiled for every subject area.

For students truly to understand, a teacher must consider the five following components of teaching concepts.

1. *Name or label of concept.* In Figure 3-4, *verb* is a label referring to a concept in parts of speech.
2. *Definition.* "A verb expresses an act, occurrence, or mode of being" is an example of an abbreviated definition.
3. *Characteristics.* In Figure 3-4, the characteristics of a proper noun are persons, places, or things.
4. *Examples.* In Figure 3-4, Jim and Mary are examples of proper noun person.
5. *Hierarchies.* In Figure 3-4, if the teacher is teaching the concept of noun, then the coordinate concepts are verb, adverb, and adjective. Subordinate concepts are common, proper, and pronoun.

In teaching concepts, the teacher must use both sequencing and task analysis. Sequencing contains two options: (1) the teacher may start the lesson by describing the concept, followed by an analysis of characteristics (facts) and a series of illustrations or examples (facts) so that the students have a thorough knowledge of concept;

Figure 3-4   Concept Analysis

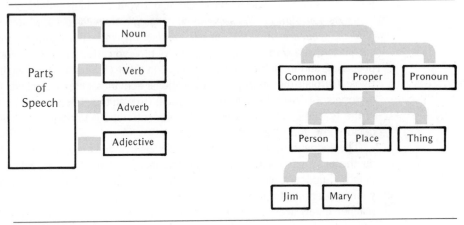

or (2) the teacher may provide examples (facts) of the concept and allow the student to discover the concept. In either instance, a procedure called *concept analysis* is helpful. For example, if you were teaching the concept "proper noun," it would be helpful to develop an outline of the content to illustrate the characteristics of the content (show its uniqueness) and its relationship (make it meaningful) to the larger body of content covered by the course. An example of this kind of outline is shown in Figure 3-4.

The concept analysis procedure provides the teacher with a sequence-planning technique. To teach the concept "proper noun," the teacher must first teach the characteristics of both "noun" and "proper" as they relate to the concept "proper noun." This is followed by an analysis of characteristics, in which the teacher provides examples that illustrate the characteristics of the proper noun—the *names* of *persons, places,* or *things.*

In the second phase of the procedure, the teacher determines whether the lesson should be taught inductively or deductively. Should the student be given the concept and then be provided with examples of its characteristics, or should the student be given examples from which to induce the concept? Whether the lesson is taught inductively or deductively, a thorough analysis of concept characteristics and examples is necessary. The concept analysis hierarchy is an excellent procedure for accomplishing this task. The characteristics of inductive and deductive teaching are presented in this chapter and in Chapter 8.

To apply the four levels of knowledge in a learning hierarchy (see Figure 3-2), instruction at levels 3 (generalization) and 4 (principles) must be preceded by instruction at levels 1 and 2; thus, levels 1 and 2 are prerequisites to levels 3 and 4. You may recall that many of your teachers bypassed one or more levels when developing a lesson, thus leaving many of your classmates—if not yourself—totally "in the dark."

One of the most effective methods in teaching concepts is the use of examples. In planning a lesson, the teacher must have enough examples to illustrate all the dominant characteristics adequately. For concrete concepts such as dog or verb, it is rather easy to find good examples. For concepts such as anger, fear, or worry, the teacher must spend considerable time developing good examples. Using negative examples often helps students to understand the characteristics of the example being taught. For example, when teaching the concept of anger, you may want also to have examples of hostility, indignation, and wrath to help the students understand the concept of anger. Obtaining enough examples that illustrate the characteristics of a concept and having examples from coordinate concepts are an important part of planning when the lesson involves concept.

An Example   The value of sequencing learning activities is that you can quickly learn the technique. You can arrange any number of learning components or tasks into a "map" to be accomplished. In this manner your students will have a better chance at success. Often students do not understand concepts or principles because the teacher made too large an intellectual leap. By developing a task analysis, the teacher is able to identify learning deficiencies before lessons are assigned.

One of the authors, a teacher of science, once observed that teachers often have difficulty teaching the concept of density. Then, by observing student errors, he inferred that if the tasks associated with the learning concept were identified and structured, some of the problems would be reduced. Table 3-2 lists the various tasks or elements that were prerequisites to mastering the concept of density. On examining the table carefully, are you surprised at the number of operations, skills, and prerequisite skills that are needed? Several teachers were, and so were we.

After all the major tasks were listed, as in Table 3-2, they were then sequenced, using Gagné's approach. Figure 3-5 illustrates a simplified task analysis and hierarchy chart for the concept of density. What becomes apparent is that it is useless to even try to teach this concept before the seventh grade. The children simply do not have the necessary intellectual background until that time—and may not until one year later. Nonetheless, we still find teachers and professors who wonder why their students cannot learn certain concepts or principles. Therefore, in many cases you the teacher must revise even the order of the text pages to be read by the students. In short, you may have to sketch "rough" hierarchy charts for every chapter, unit, or module that you assign, so that the benefits to the learner will be maximized. Preparing a rough chart may take just a few minutes as you analyze a unit of work.

When you observe student learning deficits, you can construct your own hierarchy chart to determine if key elements of the instruction are missing. No doubt, other charting modifications can be devised, using these techniques. Try your hand at creating such a chart, say, for a concept in English grammar, biology, mathematics, or social studies. We believe that if more teachers were cognitively aware of this technique, then teaching would be improved immeasurably; both teachers and students would be happier in school—and more successful!

Table 3-2   *Task Analysis for the Concept of Density*

Concept: Density   Tasks associated with concept

1. Weighing in metric system units
2. Using linear measurement in metric system
3. Understanding two-dimensional measurements: compute areas for rectangle and circle
4. Computing volumes
   (a) Rectangular
   (b) Cylindrical
   (c) Irregularly shaped objects
       (1) Those that float in water
       (2) Those that sink in water
5. Defining and using a "Unit Standard"
   (a) Linear
   (b) Volumetric
6. Using mathematics skills
   (a) Division
   (b) Multiplication
   (c) Ability to solve sample linear equations (a = b/c)
7. Knowing that the mass of water in grams approximates the volume of water in cubic centimeters (cc)
8. Deriving that density is mass per unit of volume

Advance Organizer Model

David P. Ausubel, a proponent of deductive learning as an alternative to discovery or inductive strategies, proposes a model that is based on meaningful verbal learning. In *Educational Psychology: A Cognitive View* (1968), Ausubel argues that much of the empirical framework supporting discovery learning strategies is based on conducted research, which compares discovery modes with rote modes. Differentiating between rote learning (memorization), problem-solving, and meaningful verbal learning, Ausubel maintains that, through careful structuring of materials and learning experiences by the teacher, the learner will be able to translate newly learned content into something meaningful.

Ausubel's Deductive Learning

The deductive mode of inquiry, according to Ausubel, includes three basic components: (1) *advance organizers;* (2) *progressive differentiation;* and (3) *integrative reconciliation.* His model also requires a body of knowledge that can be organized hierarchically. The purpose of Ausubel's model is to provide students with a structure so that they understand *each part of the hierarchy of knowledge* in the lesson as well as the relationships among *all parts of the knowledge hierarchy.*

Figure 3-5   *Simplified Task Analysis and Hierarchy Chart for Concept of Density*

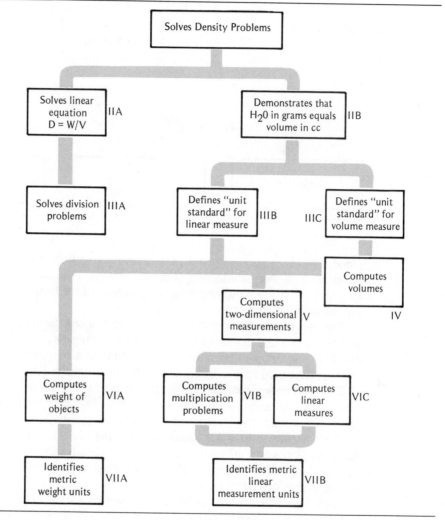

An Ausubel lesson begins with the *advance organizer*. This is a broad term encompassing those elements that the learner will be required to master in the lesson. The English teacher starting a unit that includes metaphor, simile, and personification will want to start the lesson with a definition or generalization about figures of speech. The teacher will follow a simple hierarchy chart like the one shown in Figure 3-6.

If the advance organizer is understood by each student, it will provide a frame of reference for the lesson, so that each part of the lesson can be more easily under-

Figure 3-6   *Hierarchy Chart for Figures of Speech*

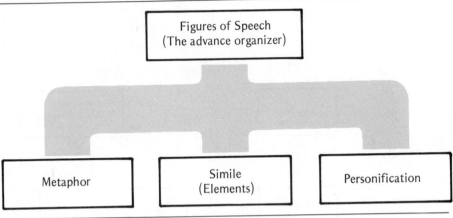

stood. Also, the organizer provides an "ideational scaffold" that enables the learner to relate the lesson material to previous knowledge. The teacher's task is to develop an abstract statement that *encompasses* all aspects of the lesson and that the student can relate to previously learned material.

The advance organizer is usually a *generalization* or a *definition*. For example, the authors have found that using the structure of sentences as a hierarchy chart is an effective way to teach grammar. An illustration of a partially developed hierarchy chart on figures of speech can look like the one shown in Figure 3-6.

The teacher has considerable latitude in organizing and developing the lesson. Therefore, two teachers using the same advance organizer, such as sentence structure, may develop and teach the lesson differently, whereas lessons on figures of speech will tend to be more similar because the subject is based on a conceptual hierarchy. A practical note is helpful here: write the advance organizer on a transparency or large sheet of paper. This allows students to refer to it throughout the lesson; it provides direction and focus.

After the advance organizer has been presented and the teacher is assured that it is understood, the second phase of the model begins. This phase, *progressive differentiation,* is the process by which the content is subdivided into more complex ideas. The English teacher can start a lesson on metaphors with the statement: "A metaphor is *one* kind of figure of speech. The primary characteristics of a metaphor are . . ." The teacher has taken a broad abstract concept (figure of speech) and narrowed it to a smaller, more complex concept (metaphor). Progressive differentiation is the procedure of isolating each idea, concept, generalization, or skill within a hierarchy of knowledge so that it can be learned as an independent piece of knowledge. Highlighting the unique and discrete characteristics of an element makes the information easier to learn.

The third component of the Ausubel model is *integrative reconciliation.* It is in this phase that you make a deliberate attempt to help students to understand similarities and differences among the components of the hierarchy of knowledge and to reconcile real or apparent inconsistencies between the ideas presented. In our English lesson example, the teacher makes certain that the students understand the relationship between figures of speech and metaphor—which is a case of vertical reconciliation—and that they comprehend the differences and similarities between a metaphor and a simile—which is an example of lateral reconciliation. The basic purpose of integrative reconciliation is to ensure that the material is comprehended in a meaningful way. In this phase the teacher makes sure that students grasp the relationships among all parts of the hierarchy.

In summary, the Ausubel model is a deductive model designed to teach organized bodies of content. The advance organizer provides the students with an overview and focus; progressive differentiation provides items of information that can be more easily understood; and integrative reconciliation provides meaningful learning by helping students to understand the relationships among the elements of the content being taught.

Although the three components are presented as sequential, in reality they are interactive, especially progressive differentiation and integrative reconciliation. If the comparison and differentiation discussion develops the students' understanding of a specific concept or generalization, the teacher should not hesitate to use the two steps concurrently. As with any teaching model, the teacher should use the model and its components so that they help the students to learn. The model should be applied with flexibility and not be used as a straitjacket.

Be careful not to confuse deductive thinking with lecturing. Often lectures are neither deductive nor inductive. A deductive lesson can contain as much teacher-student or student-student interaction as an inductive lesson does. According to Ausubel, after presenting the advance organizer, the teacher can hold the students responsible for progressive differentiation and integrative reconciliation. In this instance, the teacher becomes the facilitator of the learning process much in the same manner as in an inductive lesson.

One can argue that Ausubel has developed a model for guided and sequenced deductive inquiry. The degree of guidance provided by the teacher may be the criterion according to which various modes are classified. For example, Table 3-3 presents Lee S. Shulman's (1970) interpretation of four inquiry possibilities.

Ausubel Example Lessons

Assume that the class is studying about government and the concepts associated with the institution of government. The class has already studied about different basic forms of government. The teacher may introduce the lesson with the following advance organizer:

> Government is but one of the institutions serving society. The state or government is essential to civilization and yet it cannot do the whole job by itself. Many human needs can be met by the home, the church, the press, and private business.

Table 3-3   *Classification of Inquiry-Expository Learning Modes*

Rule	Solution	Type of Teacher Guidance
Given	Given	Exposition
Given	Not given	Guided discovery (deductive)
Not given	Given	Guided discovery (inductive)
Not given	Not given	"Pure" discovery

Source: Lee S. Shulman, "Psychology and Mathematics Education," in *Mathematics Education.* The Sixty-Ninth Yearbook of the National Society for the Study of Education, Part I, Edward G. Begle, ed. Chicago: The University of Chicago Press, 1970, p. 66. Used with the written permission of the National Society for the Study of Education.

With the presentation of the advance organizer, the teacher is ready to proceed with the progressive differentiation component of the lesson. Materials are made available to the students so that they may begin their investigations on the human needs that are met by different institutions. Prior to beginning the study, the teacher and the class prepare a list of different problems that can be studied. As an alternative, they list the steps that should be taken to identify the areas in which the various institutions serve the society and in which institutional functions overlap. Functions that are not covered by any institution would also be listed. In the true "Ausubelian" sense, the teacher utilizes some guided discovery techniques in conducting the class. As the material is gathered by students and presented to the class, the teacher leads the students in the progressive differentiation and integrative reconciliation processes. The result is an interactive, deductive lesson.

How successful is this mode of instruction? Jim McBride, sixth grade teacher in Spokane, had his students make advance organizers of the three branches of the federal government (1988). But each branch was attached to a coat-hanger mobile to add a visual and third dimension effect. Students could then see "the balance of power."

Parmalee P. Hawk (1985), using graphic organizers to increase achievement at sixth and seventh grades, found that the organizers enhanced student learning. Dale Dinnel and John A. Glover (1985) found that college students dealing with the semantic of "base organizers" had significantly greater memory for the organizers and subsequent essay content. In a study of the effect of graphic organizers on fourth graders' comprehension of study, Donna E. Alvermann et al. (1984) found that graphic organizers improved students' ability to read and to retain social studies information. Ian Tudor (1986) wrote that advance organizers helped low-ability students on comprehending the study of French. Several others have discussed the efficacy of advance organizers; thus, the concept is important in lesson design. (See Clark and Peterson, 1986; Doyle, 1986; Kallison, 1986; Levine and Loerine, 1985; and Tudor, 1986.)

Another example is the lesson plan in Table 3-4 prepared by Cathy Valencsin

Table 3-4   *An Ausubel Lesson Plan About Verbs*

Advance Organizer	1. Review sentence elements to conclude that the subject is one of the two basic elements of a sentence. 2. What is the function of the subject in a sentence? 3. After we have a subject, what is the second basic element of a sentence? 4. Usually, there are more than only two words in a sentence. But we will concentrate on these two most basic sentence elements because they are necessary in writing a sentence.
Progressive Differentiation	5. Today, we will talk specifically about verbs. 6. What is the primary function of a verb? 7. There are many types of verbs, but today we will want to focus specifically on action verbs. 8. Why is it important that we use action verbs in our writing? 9. Administer list of verbs to determine how much the students might already know about verbs. Tell them to circle action verbs. 10. Ask students to read those verbs that they did not circle. 11. Tell students that these verbs are called "forms of the verb *to be*" and are used to show being or existence. 12. If teachers have ever told the students that their writing was lifeless or dry, it could be that they were not using enough action verbs.
Integrative Reconciliation	13. A verb is one of the two basic what? 14. How is a verb related to a subject? 15. When can one of these basic sentence elements be left out of a sentence but the sentence still be considered correct? (Awareness of inconsistencies.) 16. Put a box on the table. Ask the students to list at least three actions that can be done to the box, or that the box performs. 17. Review importance of action verbs in writing. 18. Give the next day's assignment—to write a paper that describes the student's favorite sport and that uses ten action verbs.

Duffy and used with her permission. It illustrates the three elements of an Ausubelian lesson.

In summary, for the advance organizer model to work effectively, the teacher must have an advance organizer that provides students with an understandable focus for the lesson and a visual representation that illustrates the relationships of the lesson information.

A Diagnostic-Prescriptive Model

Because of its interactive and cyclic nature, the diagnostic-prescriptive instructional model aids in planning for anticipated learning problems. Diagnosing teaching-

Figure 3-7   *Simplified Diagnostic Model*

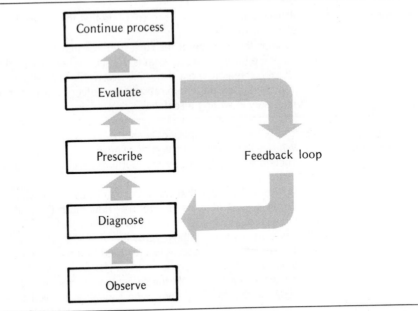

learning effectiveness is very complex; but, if some students do not experience success the first time they are exposed to a topic, it behooves the teacher to prepare some type of educational diagnosis. The diagnosis is then followed by a prescription. This teaching model may be viewed as having a cycle with at least four elements: (1) observation; (2) diagnosis; (3) prescription; and (4) evaluation. Figure 3-7 shows this cyclic process.

As you examine Figure 3-7, you will note that we urge that the evaluation phase of teaching be used for decision-making. This may seem to be a novel method of using tests, as most teachers use them only for grading. We want you to use tests as one method of making learning more efficient; that is, use them to help the students to master the materials in the lesson. This also means that evaluation is used in considering future educational material, in substituting lessons, or in identifying other class members who can help as tutors. Let us expand the concept of a diagnostic-prescriptive decision-making tool.

Observation   The observation phase begins either before an assignment is made or while some specific tasks are being completed by the learners. What does the teacher observe? There are at least three types of clues: activity, verbal, and nonverbal student clues. Most learning takes place through the building or transmitting of concepts or skills. This generalization will hold true for most disciplines and at most grade levels of instruction. As a teacher, you will observe the three types of clues in every class. Do students tend to master selected concepts? Do students prefer to do certain tasks? Do students look amazed when selected tasks are assigned? Do students tend to discuss or evaluate verbally the type of work assigned? The communication network is already established in the classroom. Your job is to monitor it continually.

On a more individual basis, you may observe that only one or two students have trouble with selected, or perhaps most, assignments. The general tendency is to ignore these learners and to allow them to "drift." We suggest that you structure your class period so that if you do identify students who need specific aid, you can establish the mechanism by which they may obtain it. In some cases, you the teacher, will do the aiding; in other cases, peers, tutors, programmed instruction, or other assignments will be put into action. But, before taking action, you must first observe. We have known teachers who were simply not aware that students were expressing clues indicating that they needed help in completing the lesson.

Other activity clues are incomplete assignments, inaccurate work, plagiarized work, or work showing that the student has not completed the assignment in the manner the teacher expected. Sometimes your observations will be made during oral recitations or discussions. You may sense that a student does not respond to the work or to an oral question in exactly the appropriate manner, that the logic used in responding is a bit faulty, or that a student seems to be making the same type of error repeatedly. Also, when grading papers, you may note that the same kind of mistake prevails throughout a set of examples, or, at worst, throughout the entire assignment. It is at this point that you should begin to implement the elements of the diagnostic-prescriptive model.

Diagnosis   The diagnostic phase of the model begins when you, as teacher, realize that a student or a group of students seems to need additional work in specific skills, processes, or content. At this point, you have made an initial diagnosis, which focuses on small or discrete units of learning (for example, the subskills of the task analysis). Each unit of study is related to the student's learning need. In other words, the teacher who uses this system will never be heard to say to a student, "You've got to try harder." Nobody likes to or tries to fail. Yet teachers mistakenly assign more drill or other such tasks to the student who has been unsuccessful. Such decisions only lead to futility. If a student does not meet the expected standard of performance on the first lesson or set of problems, then more of the same will probably yield the same result—student failure.

It is the purpose of the diagnostic phase of instruction to determine which prerequisite lessons a student needs in order for success to follow. Also, as you plan the prescription that follows the diagnosis, you need to make decisions that allow the student—not you or the tutor—to do the work. Such a strategy helps the student to work more independently and to gain greater self-confidence and self-esteem. You maintain the student's self-confidence by adjusting the difficulty level or by substituting different learning materials.

Diagnosis is an analytic task for the teacher. It is an inductive process in which, after observing specific errors in the student's work or other clues indicating that the student needs help, you begin to frame a general plan attempting to remedy the problem. You may even think of yourself as the world's greatest detective, with your goal being the eradication of unachieved objectives!

The diagnostic phase of the model is concerned with pinpointing exact problems—for example, the student cannot conjugate a set of verbs; the student does not know the primary colors; or the student cannot compute ratios. Each of these diagnoses identifies a specific learning deficit or behavior.

During the diagnostic phase you personally communicate your desire to help the student master the lesson at a higher level. You can test your diagnoses with a few carefully chosen problems or tasks. If the learner exhibits the same learning deficit, then you probably made an incorrect diagnosis and should try again. Now, play the part of the kindly medical doctor who writes the necessary prescription after the disorder is identified.

Prescription   In this model your prescription is an explicit set of instructional objectives for the student who has *not* achieved at a standard that *you* feel is adequate. The prescription usually contains the following elements:

1. Identification of the prerequisite skills, if any, that the student needs to be able to accomplish the desired objectives.
2. Selection of necessary materials, equipment, and activities that will be made available to the student.
3. Selection of the instructional strategies that are appropriate to the learning episode.

The prescription may be written or stated orally. As you begin this teaching technique, it may be better to write the prescription. This way the learner may check off those objectives that are completed, and you can quickly conduct an evaluation to determine whether the student learned the assignment. Most of the time you would construct a chart that would sequence the prescribed tasks for the learner. The chart need not be elaborate—the simpler the better. The main point is that you should analyze the instruction in a very logical and efficient manner.

Evaluation   The final phase of the model, evaluation, may be conducted separately, or it may be combined as an active part of the prescription. After the students complete the prescribed activities, they are evaluated immediately. If they have corrected the errors they made previously, then you have improved their learning. If the prescription was not successful, then—as was illustrated in Figure 3-7—you begin the entire cycle again.

The evaluation may be conducted by several means. You may simply inspect the newly completed work and observe whether or not the work meets your criteria. Or you may conduct an oral evaluation by asking the student a few key questions. How you conduct the evaluation is unimportant. Striving to improve instruction and learning is important! The evaluation is needed to provide feedback to you, the teacher, for instructional decision-making. Our chief concern is that you know there is a way of systematically making decisions to aid those who are not successful on the initial instructional assignment.

Conducting Tutorial Sessions   The process of task analysis may frighten you into thinking that you must write all kinds of prescriptive learning activities every day for many students. That is the exception, not the rule. Generally, you will find that, after you have observed and diagnosed, the prescription element may be very informal and may be needed for only a small number of pupils. As one alternative, you may sit and chat with a student or perhaps a small group and may decide to use an oral approach to help each student correct his or her work. In such cases you may employ a set of questions that are diagnostic—at least from the student's point of view. These may be "How did you arrive at this response?" "Are there any words that you do not understand?" "Tell me in your own words what . . . means." "Why . . . ?" "How . . . ?" "What . . . ?" We expand the tutorial concept in Chapter 7.

You must conduct all sessions in a supportive mode. The teacher *must not* be angry, disrespectful, or intolerant toward the students. We mention this because many teachers do exhibit such behaviors, just when they think that they are being helpful to students; in fact, they are perceived by the students as being critical or spiteful: unintentionally uninviting!

CONCLUSION

Every discipline has different types of learning problems. Mathematics is very different from social studies or English. Thus, the instructional planning models presented in this chapter must be adapted for specific situations. Perhaps the one valid generalization is that, more often than not, the teacher assumes that the students have the prerequisite knowledge when, in fact, they do not.

The following quote from one of America's foremost psychologists, Sidney L. Pressey (1959), summarizes our position on the topic.

> One of the most pernicious problems in teaching is the teacher's desire to "cover ground." Many teachers feel that they do not have time to discover and remedy their pupil's lack of information and skill because they would never be able to "cover" the material called for in the course; so they plunge ahead from a starting point that many of their students have never reached, and they proceed to teach the unknown by the incomprehensible. The result is that the student cannot learn effectively and ends the course about where he started.*

---

*From Sidney Pressey, F. P. Robinson, and J. E. Horrocks, *Psychology in Education* (New York: Harper & Row, 1959), p. 201. Quoted with written permission of the publisher.

A Postscript

In most cases, you will be teaching from a textbook or some type of printed material. Only through a detailed analysis of the content will you be able to determine which planning model should be used for any specific unit of instruction. The textbook sets the pace for most teachers and learners; however, you may have to supplement the text with short presentations or demonstrations that provide the students with the necessary prerequisite skills or background. Once you have mastered the idea of sequencing major blocks of information, you will be able to implement any model in a short period of time.

As was mentioned in Chapter 2, the advent of PL 94-142 brought about some mainstreaming of special-education children. Every classroom teacher, from kindergarten to grade 12, must be able to provide the most meaningful and effective educational environment for these students. You will be responsible, as a member of the school's instructional team, for helping to prepare an Individual Educational Plan (IEP). The techniques described in this chapter will be the ones that you will probably use most frequently.

In addition, and of greater importance, these same techniques are easily used in teaching children from lower socioeconomic classes who need positive experiences. The diagnostic-prescriptive model discussed here will be of critical importance in this context. It has been verified that many, if not most, of these children have not had the appropriate prerequisite learning experiences to be successful. By spending a little more time with these students and by using the techniques described in Chapter 2, you will be able to effect substantial improvement in students who have shown gross educational deficits.

Even the most difficult and challenging instructional concepts may be made more teachable—and, most important, more learnable. In short, you structure lessons to become intentionally inviting to learners.

FORMATIVE EVALUATION   *Sequencing and Task Analysis*

1. State two basic purposes of sequencing.

   (a) _____

   _____

   (b) _____

   _____

2. Describe three ways in which task analysis provides assistance in the planning process.

   (a) _____

(b) _____

(c) _____

3. Arrange the following task analysis characteristics in an appropriate sequence, and explain the reason for each item in the sequence.
   (a) Arrange the independent and dependent sequences.
   (b) Identify the independent and dependent sequences of enabling skills.
   (c) Select an instructional objective.

4. Explain how a hierarchy is helpful in each of the following components of the diagnostic model.
   (a) Observation.
   (b) Diagnosis.
   (c) Prescription.
   (d) Evaluation.

5. Develop a figure using advanced organizers to represent the levels of hierarchy of the branches of the federal government.

6. What is the relationship between sequencing and hierarchies for the discipline or subject for which you are prepared to teach? How much is primarily determined by the content, and how much is determined by your interest and education?

7. Reflect on planning for your own area. Which of the four models of lesson and unit organization provides the best framework for planning within your subject matter? Which one fits your planning style the most accurately?

8. Using Figure 3-1 as a model, select a topic from your subject and develop a task analysis.

9. Using the concept analysis model in Figure 3-4, develop a similar structure for several major concepts from your teaching major.

10. Explain why it is important to use examples in teaching concepts.

11. How is the Ausubel deductive learning model different from, or similar to, other expository approaches? What unique feature(s) characterizes the model?

12. How can the diagnostic-prescriptive model be used for group instruction?

Responses

1. (a) Isolates the properties and unique characteristics of the desired learning.
   (b) Relates the desired learning to the larger organized unit of learning so that the acquisition of skill or knowledge becomes meaningful.
2. (a) Provides a map for sequencing learning activities.
   (b) Provides a conceptual framework for diagnosing student progress.
   (c) The relational aspect of a hierarchy provides information that can be helpful in selecting the appropriate thinking mode (deductive or inductive) and in choosing the most efficient teaching materials and techniques.

3. (c) *Select an instructional objective.* You must be able to specify first what the student should be able to do at the end of the learning sequence.

(b) *Identify the independent and dependent sequences.* You must identify the activities necessary to achieve the desired learning and must determine whether the nature of these activities necessitates a specific sequence.

(a) *Arrange the independent and dependent sequences.* You must arrange the activities so that, if dependent, the sequence is followed and, if independent, the activities are done at the appropriate time.

4. (a) *Observation.* This allows the teacher to look for problems with specifics—that is, the unique characteristics or properties of each component in the hierarchy—or to pinpoint difficulty in relationships between components in the chart.

(b) *Diagnosis.* This careful observation allows for a detailed probing of the problem situation. A student may not understand a concept characteristic and, therefore, not the concept. Hierarchy provides a map of the possible difficulties.

(c) *Prescription.* Once a problem is pinpointed, the teacher can select material or procedures to resolve the difficulty. Pinpointing the difficulty helps identify the many solutions available.

(d) *Evaluation.* This makes the development of measurement items easier. It takes the guesswork out of evaluation.

5. Compare your chart to Figure 3-8 that follows. It should be similar but may differ in the details of the subcategories.

6.–12. These questions are developed for discussion, and answers should be substantiated by information in the chapter. There is no single correct response.

Figure 3-8   *A Hierarchy on Branches of the Federal Government*

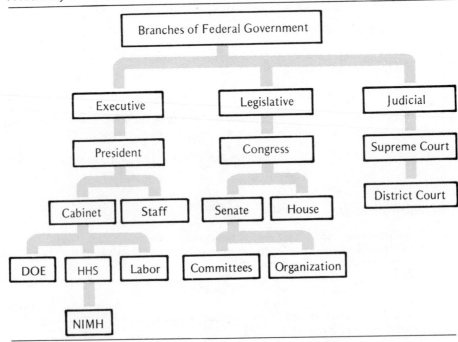

REFERENCES

Alvermann, Donna E., et al. "The Effect of Graphic Organizer Instruction on Fourth Graders' Comprehension of Social Studies Text." *Journal of Social Studies Research* 14(1):1984, 13–21.

Ausubel, David P. *Educational Psychology: A Cognitive View.* New York: Holt, Rinehart & Winston, 1968.

Brophy, Jere. "Research on Teacher Effects: Uses and Abuses." *The Elementary School Journal* 89:1988, 3–21.

Clark, Christopher M., and Penelope L. Peterson. "Teachers' Thought Processes." In *Handbook on Research on Teaching,* 3rd ed. Merlin C. Wittrock, ed. New York: Macmillan, 1986, 255–296.

Dinnel, Dale, and John A. Glover. "Advance Organizers: Encoding Manipulations." *Journal of Educational Psychology* 77(5):1985, 514–521.

Doyle, WIlliam H. "Using an Advance Organizer to Establish a Subsuming Function Concept for Facilitating Achievement in Remedial College Mathematics." *American Educational Research Journal* 23(13):1986, 507–516.

Gagné, Robert M. *The Conditions of Learning and Theory of Instruction,* 4th ed. New York: Holt, Rinehart & Winston, 1985.

Gagné, Robert M., and Leslie J. Briggs. *Principles of Instructional Design.* New York: Holt, Rinehart & Winston, 1974.

Gagné, Robert M., and N. E. Paradise. "Abilities and Learning Sets in Knowledge Acquisition." *Psychological Monographs* 76:No. 14, Whole No. 518, 1961, p. 23.

Gagné, Robert M., et al. "Factors on Acquiring Knowledge of a Mathematical Task." *Psychological Monographs* 76:No. 7, Whole No. 526, 1962, p. 20.

Hawk, Parmalee P. "Using Graphic Organizers to Increase Achievement in Middle School Life Science." *Science Education* 70(1):1986, 81–87.

Kallison, James M. "Effects of Lesson Organization on Achievement." *American Educational Research Journal* 23(2):1986, 337–347.

Levine, Lawrence H., and Beatrice M. Loerine. "Investigating the Scope of an Advance Organizer for Compiler Concepts." *Journal of Educational Technology Systems* 13(3):1985, 175–183.

Mager, Robert F. *Preparing Instructional Objectives.* Belmont, Calif.: Fearon, 1962.

McBride, Jim. Personal observations, November 1988.

Okey, James R., and Robert M. Gagné. "Revision of a Science Topic Using Evidence of Performance on Subordinate Skills." *Journal of Research in Science Teaching* 7:1970, 321–325.

Pressey, Sidney L., Francis P. Robinson, and John E. Horrocks. *Psychology in Education.* New York: Harper & Row, 1959, p. 201.

Shulman, Lee S. "Psychology and Mathematics Education." In *Mathematics Education.* Edward G. Begle, ed. The Sixty-Ninth Yearbook of the National Society for the Study of Education, Part I. Chicago: University of Chicago Press, 1970.

Tursman, Cindy. "Good Teachers: What to Look For." *Education USA Special Report.* Virginia National Schools Public Relations Association, 1981.

Tudor, Ian. "Advance Organisers as Adjuncts to L2 Reading Comprehension." *Journal of Research in Reading* 9:1986, 103–105.

Tyler, Ralph W. *Basic Principles of Curriculum and Instruction.* Chicago: University of Chicago Press, 1949, p. 85.

4

Deciding on Levels of Instruction: Introducing the Taxonomies

*T*he previous chapter discussed the concept of learning hierarchies and task analysis and showed how these could be used to sequence instruction and to facilitate learning. The present chapter builds on these ideas by describing three hierarchical classification systems that can be used to sequence instruction in the areas of cognitive, affective, and psychomotor learning.

Educational objectives can be divided into three main areas on the basis of their primary focus. Cognitive objectives deal primarily with the development of intellectual skills and abilities. The majority of educational activities is involved with the attainment of cognitive objectives (Goodlad, 1984). For the most part, society as a whole, as well as parents, students, and teachers, views the cognitive growth and development of students as being the primary function of the schools. For that reason, the principal focus of this chapter will be on developing your understanding of the *cognitive domain.* In the cognitive domain, we have seen an increased emphasis on the development of students' thinking skills. This has come out of a realization that our modern technological society needs people who can understand changes, apply information, analyze problems, and create and evaluate solutions. These are the micro-skills (Beyer, 1984) contained within Bloom's Taxonomy, the major topic of this chapter. (See Chapter 9 for a detailed treatment relating to teaching "thinking skills.")

The second major area emphasized in our schools today is the development of students' attitudes and values. We call this part of the school curriculum the *affective domain,* and later in the chapter we discuss a system that educators use to describe and sequence instruction in this area.

The third major focus of learning in the schools today is the *psychomotor domain,* which involves the development of muscular skills and abilities. We also include the *perceptual domain* as a special application of the psychomotor domain. The area of the curriculum that places the greatest emphasis on the psychomotor domain is physical education, but a later part of this chapter will show how all areas of the curriculum are either directly or indirectly concerned with psychomotor skills.

Central to our discussion of each of these three areas is the concept of a taxonomy. A *taxonomy* is a hierarchical classification system for describing and sequencing learning activities. Before describing each of the three major areas of learning (the cognitive, affective, and psychomotor domains), we will discuss the idea of taxonomies and their value to prospective teachers.

Objectives   After completing this chapter, you should be able to:

- Describe what a taxonomy is and how it can be used in teaching
- Describe in your own words the differences between the three domains
- Classify objectives in the three domains as cognitive, affective, or psychomotor
- List the six major levels of the cognitive taxonomy
- Classify objectives at appropriate levels of the cognitive taxonomy
- Apply the levels of cognitive taxonomy when constructing classroom questions or test items

- Identify the major elements of the affective taxonomy
- Identify the major elements of the three psychomotor taxonomies
- Construct a rationale for the use of the three taxonomies in your major area of interest
- Apply a novel analogue to the cognitive taxonomy

TAXONOMIES: AN INTRODUCTION

The concept that underlies all taxonomies as decision-making tools is simply this: not all teacher behaviors are the same. And these different behaviors, accordingly, elicit different responses from the student. That is, as the teacher acts in various ways, the student will respond in various ways. From this we may infer that the student is thus learning different behaviors. Taxonomies are classification tools that teachers use to describe these different learning outcomes. For example, consider students who read a story in their basal text. Afterward, do they answer low-level, recall questions, or are they asked to make inferences not explicitly stated in the story? This may seem like a slight difference, only reflected in the questions, but in fact the difference is major. First, the products are different. Recall questions require only knowledge of the story information, while inferential questions require the ability to sort the knowledge and construct a set of conclusions. Second, the teaching procedures, as well as the mental operations of students, will be very different. In teaching inferential skills, the teacher first directs the students to read for understanding and then asks students to make inferences and to defend their basis for making them.

Because producing their own inferences is initially difficult for learners, the teacher has to model the skill and demonstrate patience, tolerance for uncertainty, and zest for inquiry. Besides the story, the teacher may need supplementary materials that give students practice in making inferences in different contexts. Also, to reflect the different products, operations, and student processes, test items must be written to be consistent with the emphasis. Writing test items to measure students' ability to form conclusions is much harder than selecting simple fact-level items.

The cognitive processes induced in students as they learn to make inferences are much different than those leading to recall facts. In one case they are given opportunities to learn cognitively complex skills; in the other, they can form stimulus-response associations only. This consistency between teacher objectives, instructional strategies, student learning activities, and evaluation items is another example of curricular alignment discussed in Chapter 2.

Jean Chall (1983) has made an important note that textbook materials change dramatically at grade 4. Before that year, children are taught to read for the sake of learning to read, and stories for them are written in a narrative style. Abruptly, at grade 4 the textbooks shift to an expository style. Children must now read to learn new content. The cognitive level of that content becomes an important decision-making point for all teachers.

In planning for learning at these different levels, teachers perform various actions in the course of a school day. These actions include the formulation of performance objectives, of questions to be asked, or of tests to be administered. Within these clusters of teacher behaviors (performance objectives, questions, or tests), teacher actions can vary widely. One way of examining and comparing the differences in teacher emphasis is to analyze these teacher behaviors in terms of a *taxonomy*. This is a classification system that educators use to observe, compare, and evaluate performance objectives, questions, written materials, and evaluation methodologies (tests).

Although a taxonomy is basically a classification system—a way of grouping selected objects together, such as plants, animals, performance objectives, or questions—it is more than just that. What differentiates a taxonomy from a classification system is that a taxonomy is *hierarchical;* that is, a taxonomy is a classification system with a hierarchy of *classes* or groupings by level or rank. Not all the classes are at the same level. The method by which the classes are arranged in a hierarchy depends on the organizing principle and the type of taxonomy.

In the taxonomy of the animal kingdom, the phyla are arranged according to evolutionary complexity. Thus the phylum Chordata (animals with backbones) is higher than Porifera (sponges), which is higher than Protozoa (one-celled animals). In most educational taxonomies the organizing principle is that of complexity. The higher levels in taxonomies involve more complex student behaviors than the lower levels do. In addition, the higher levels in taxonomies build on the lower levels. If a student can perform at a third level, then we also assume that the student can perform at the two lower levels. This idea is discussed further later in the text.

How Can Taxonomies Be Used?

Teaching can be envisioned as a triad of acts, as illustrated in Figure 4-1. In this model the formulated objectives determine the teaching procedures and the evaluation procedures, but with all elements affecting each other. A taxonomy can be used in each of these processes: in writing objectives at an appropriate level, in developing classroom questions and learning exercises, and in constructing evaluation instruments that are congruent with the objectives and strategies previously employed. In other words, you can use taxonomies to decide what to teach, how to teach, and how to evaluate the effectiveness of your teaching.

Taxonomies: Tools for Planning

As you have seen, not all objectives are the same, nor do different questions or test items evoke the same thinking processes in students (Smith, 1985). Effective teaching requires that teachers think strategically about the level of objectives, questions, and test items when they plan. Some different ways that a taxonomy can help in the

Figure 4-1   *A Model of Teaching*

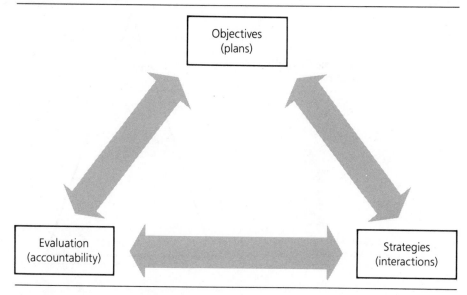

planning process are listed below. (You may want to add your own after reading ours.)

1. Provide a Range of Objectives

A taxonomy provides a list of possible ranges of objectives available in any subject. Closely examining the categories may prevent you from overemphasizing one dimension of learning, such as the memorization of facts, in your teaching. In this respect, a taxonomy not only adds variety to your repertoire but also gives greater breadth to your objectives.

2. Sequence Objectives

An analysis of learning tasks indicates to the teacher the learning experiences necessary for the student to obtain the intended outcomes. A taxonomy provides one means of sequencing learning, from simple to complex outcomes. Other means were discussed in Chapter 3.

3. Reinforce Learning

Because each lower category of the taxonomy is subsumed by the next higher category, reinforcement of previous learning occurs if learning experiences are se-

Figure 4-2   *Time, Complexity, and Taxonomies*

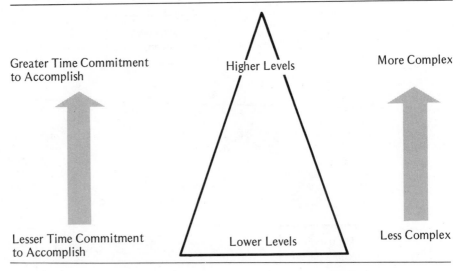

Greater Time Commitment
to Accomplish

Higher Levels

More Complex

Lesser Time Commitment
to Accomplish

Lower Levels

Less Complex

quenced in terms of a taxonomy. Further, activities can be focused on a specific level.

4. Provide a Cognitive Structure

Research has shown that students learn and retain information better if it is organized into some type of cognitive structure rather than presented as isolated items (Shuell, 1986; Woolfolk, 1987). Taxonomies can provide cognitive structure to students by showing them how facts can be used in the application, analysis, synthesis, and evaluation of other ideas.

5. Provide a Learning Model

By experiencing a series of learning activities sequenced in terms of a taxonomy, students are able to perceive that learning is logical and sequential, thus obtaining a model of learning that they, too, can use when they leave the classroom.

These first purposes of taxonomies can be illustrated by Figure 4-2, which shows the relationship of the sequencing of instruction to the complexity of the levels. In this figure note that the broader categories are the first to occur in terms of time. In sequencing objectives, teachers typically begin a unit by laying a foundation of lower-level knowledge. Since the taxonomy is hierarchical, each higher objective builds on a sequence of lower ones. In addition, as students progress through each level of the taxonomy, they experience a learning sequence that builds on successive levels. Further, it takes greater instructional intensity to achieve higher-level learning goals and objectives.

6. Ensure Instructional Congruency

Once an objective (or question) is written and classified at a particular level, it helps the teacher in selecting more appropriate teaching strategies and evaluation techniques that coincide with the level of the objective. If you write an objective at the application level, you must provide learning experiences for students at the application level. In addition, you should test or evaluate the student at that level. If the goal of a particular physical education course is to teach a person how to swim certain strokes, then the teaching activities should be geared toward this goal and the evaluation should match. In this situation, a paper-and-pencil test would be incongruent with the learned behavior. As teacher you can prevent such mismatches by analyzing your objectives, learning activities, and evaluation procedures, making sure that they are compatible. This is the instructional component of curriculum alignment.

7. Design Appropriate Test Items

Teachers who understand the principle of fairness will be quick to use the taxonomy as a self-evaluation device to check the appropriateness of test items. Evidence shows that most teachers at most levels of instruction teach at rather low levels; yet, tests are often constructed to measure higher levels of thinking. This is not fair to the students. The teacher can match learning objectives and teaching activities with the test items to determine whether or not the test approximates the level described in the objective and at which the lesson was taught. This is an application of the concept of congruency. Standardized tests can also be analyzed to determine levels at which they test. These activities form the measurement component of curriculum alignment (see Gronlund, 1985; Tanner, 1988).

8. Diagnose Learning Problems

Should a student fail to perform at one of the higher levels of the taxonomy, you can check to see if prerequisite knowledge or skills at the lower levels is a problem. (Recall the prescriptive-diagnostic model in Chapter 3.) This use of taxonomies may become increasingly important in view of the growing acceptance and retention in our schools of students with diverse cultural backgrounds, as well as the mainstreaming of special education students into the regular classroom.

9. Individualize Instruction

Related to the idea of sequencing instruction is the use of taxonomies as tools for individualizing instruction. Several recent developments in education make this an especially persuasive argument for using taxonomies. One such development is the growing realization on the part of educators that there is a great deal of heterogeneity in most classrooms. Students not only enter classrooms with different experiential and knowledge backgrounds, but they also learn at different rates and in different optimal situations. This problem of heterogeneity is further complicated by the mainstreaming of some special education students into the regular classroom. By identifying and sequencing a number of learning objectives and activities in terms of a taxonomy, the teacher allows the students with differing capabilities to start at different points in a taxonomy and to proceed through the sequenced activities at different rates.

Keep these different uses in mind as we progress to the section that describes the taxonomy and explains how it can be used to teach thinking skills.

BLOOM'S TAXONOMY: A VEHICLE TO TEACH THINKING SKILLS

Renewed emphasis is being placed on the development of students' ability to think (Costa, 1985). The argument for this trend is that our modern technological society requires citizens who can process and use information rather than store it. After all, we have computers to perform the storage function.

Thinking skills allow people to use information to solve problems. Experts in the area divide thinking skills into micro-skills such as applying and analyzing, and larger, more inclusive macro-skills that include problem-solving and decision-making (Beyer, 1984).

Our focus in this section of the chapter is on the foundational thinking skills found in Bloom's Taxonomy (1956). These are foundational because they form the basis for later, more complex processes. Bloom's Taxonomy, a classic work in the area of thinking skills instruction, was named after Benjamin Bloom, coauthor of the taxonomy and a seminal thinker in education. The fact that this taxonomy has entered its fourth decade guiding research in such diverse areas as instructional research (Woolfolk, 1987), curriculum design (Posner and Rudnitsky, 1986), and research on classroom interaction (Cazden, 1986) is testimony to its value as a tool for analyzing teaching and learning in the classroom.

Bloom's Taxonomy classifies cognitive behaviors into six categories ranging from fairly simple to more complex behaviors. These categories are briefly described in Table 4-1. Like other taxonomies, Bloom's Taxonomy is hierarchical, with learnings at higher levels being dependent on attaining prerequisite knowledge and skills at lower levels. These features of the taxonomy will be discussed and illustrated in the text that follows. We begin our discussion of the taxonomy with a description of the first level—knowledge.

Knowledge

Knowledge is the category that emphasizes remembering—either by recall or recognition. An example of a recall operation is a fill-in-the-blank exercise, and an example of a recognition operation is a multiple-choice exercise requiring the recognition of

Table 4-1   *Six Major Levels of Bloom's Taxonomy*

Level	Characteristic Student Behaviors
Knowledge	Remembering; memorizing; recognizing, recalling
Comprehension	Interpreting; translating from one medium to another; describing in one's own words
Application	Problem-solving; applying information to produce some result
Analysis	Subdividing something to show how it is put together; finding the underlying structure of a communication; identifying motives
Synthesis	Creating a unique, original product that may be in verbal form or may be a physical object
Evaluation	Making value decisions about issues; resolving controversies or differences of opinion

Source: From *Taxonomy of Educational Objectives: The Classification of Educational Goals. Handbook I: The Cognitive Domain,* edited by Benjamin S. Bloom et al. Copyright © 1956 by Longman, Inc. Reprinted with permission of Longman.

information previously encountered. Both processes involve the retrieving of information or facts that are stored in the mind. For the most part, the information retrieved is basically in the same form as it was stored. For example, if an elementary social studies teacher teaches the students on one day that Washington, D.C., is the capital of the United States, then an appropriate Knowledge-level question to ask on the next day would be "Name the capital of the United States." In answering this question, the student would be trying to remember the knowledge in basically the same form as it was learned. Other situations involving Knowledge-level activities include memorizing a poem, remembering the steps to follow in making a dress, learning the lyrics to a song, and answering true-false and matching questions on a test.

Knowledge-level objectives have as their primary focus the storage and retrieval of information. In answering a Knowledge-level question, the student must find the appropriate signals in the problem that will most effectively recall the relevant knowledge stored. In the Knowledge category the student is not expected to transform or manipulate knowledge, but merely to remember it in the same form as it was presented.

Knowledge-level activities may consist of:

1. Recalling specific *facts* or *bits of information* (for example, Who was the first President of the United States?)
2. Recalling *terminology* or *definitions* (for example, What is a noun?)
3. Recalling *conventions* or *rules of usage* (for example, What goes at the end of an interrogatory sentence?)

Teachers generally recognize that the Knowledge category forms the basis for the other categories. In fact, teachers overuse this category. Studies indicate that the majority of teachers (and textbooks) formulate most of their questions (both in class and on tests) at the Knowledge level. The thought processes of the students (and the teachers) are consequently kept at very low levels. Perhaps this is why so many young people find school boring and unchallenging.

This is not to say that the Knowledge category serves no purpose. Because of the hierarchical design of the taxonomy, Knowledge serves as the foundation for the other categories. It provides the subject matter on which the higher categories are based. Thus, Knowledge-level questions can be very useful at the beginning of a lesson or unit by providing necessary background information.

Although the Knowledge level forms the factual foundation for the rest of the categories, there are certain problems with its overuse in the classroom. Some of these problems are as follows:

1. Basically a passive operation, the recall of information does not actively involve the learner. Students are often poorly motivated when the major part of the curriculum consists of the memorization of facts.
2. Because each Knowledge question usually has one right answer, such questions do not lend themselves to classroom sessions in which the students work together in solving or discussing a problem. Consequently, the students' interpersonal and problem-solving skills are not adequately developed.
3. Related to this second problem is the lack of development of communication skills in students. Because, typically, Knowledge-level questions each have one right answer, classroom dialogue tends to occur between teacher and student rather than between student and student.

Barak Rosenshine and Robert Stevens (1986) provide evidence from effective-schooling studies that drill and practice on the lower-level skills do help students learn higher-order skills more effectively. A general rule of thumb to use in judging whether certain Knowledge-level objectives should be included in the curriculum is to ask yourself: "Will this knowledge be useful to the student at a later time in one of the higher categories?" If the answer is no, you should reevaluate the reason for focusing on isolated bits of information and possibly redesign the lesson.

Comprehension

The *Comprehension* category embraces the transforming of information into more understandable forms. Like all categories above the Knowledge level, the Comprehension category is used to emphasize ways of handling information that has already been stored. Comprehension activities require students to demonstrate an understanding of the material through some type of processing or altering of the material before answering a question. The distinction between this processing and recall is important because, through the act of processing, students transform information into a form that makes sense to them.

The basic idea behind the Comprehension category is to get students to understand the material, not just to memorize it. (An example of the difference between the two would be the difference between second graders reciting the Pledge of Allegiance and understanding what the words mean.) However, unlike some of the higher categories, the Comprehension level does not ask students to extend information, merely to integrate it into their own frame of reference.

A Comprehension-level question requires a greater degree of active participation by the student. In responding to a Comprehension-level question, the student must somehow process or manipulate the response so as to make it more than simple recall. This distinction is important from a learning-theory point of view. That is, if students rephrase material into their own words or if they organize it to "make sense" personally, they will probably learn the material more quickly and retain it longer.

The Comprehension category is an essential gateway to higher levels; if students don't understand something, they can't use it to solve or analyze problems, which are higher-level processes (Good and Grouws, 1987). It is worth your time and effort to ensure that all students understand an idea before you ask them to use it in more complex activities. One effective way to assess student comprehension is through classroom questioning (see Gall, 1984).

Types of Comprehension Questions

The Comprehension category is divided into four groups: interpretation, translation, examples, and definition. Examples from each category follow so that you can become familiar with the variety of questions available to you.

Interpretation   This concept involves the student's ability to identify and comprehend the major ideas in a communication and to understand the relationship between these ideas. For example, a student asked to relate one point in an essay to another must go through the process of interpretation: giving meaning to a response by showing its relationship to other facts. This relationship may be shown by comparing or contrasting or by demonstrating similarity. "How" and "why" questions often call for some type of interpretation. In answering these questions, the student relates major points and, by so doing, shows an understanding of them. Some interpretation questions may include the following:

a. *How* do professional and collegiate basketball rules differ?
b. *What* are some *similarities* between French and German sentence structure?
c. *Compare* sociology and psychology with respect to their early histories.
d. *What differences* exist between the high school curricula of today and those of the 1920s?

Note that the italicized key words may be used in a variety of disciplines.

Translation   Translation involves changing ideas from one form of communication into a parallel form, with the meaning retained. Reading a graph or describing the main point of a pictorial cartoon are examples of translation. Another type of translation exercise is summarization. In summarization the student translates a large passage into a shorter, more personal, form. Translation exercises would be like these:

a. Describe in your own words the first paragraph of the Declaration of Independence.
b. Record the results of your laboratory findings in tabular form and summarize your findings.
c. Reconstruct the main story plot of *Moby-Dick*.

These types of exercises require the student primarily to translate or change the material into a different form.

Examples   One of the best ways a person can demonstrate comprehension of an idea is to give an example of it. Some exercises requiring examples are as follows:

- Give an example of a quadratic equation.
- Bring to class tomorrow a poem that uses iambic pentameter.
- Name two countries that are constitutional monarchies.

In asking students to provide examples of an abstraction, the teacher should require that these examples be new or previously undiscussed. Otherwise, the student would be operating at the Knowledge level, remembering examples from previous classes.

Definition   A definition requires students to construct in their own words a description or idea of a term or concept. This involves more than just repeating verbatim a textbook or dictionary definition. The teacher expects students to formulate the definition with words that are familiar and meaningful to them. Some definition exercises follow:

- Define, in your own words, the Knowledge category.
- Give a definition of your particular discipline (for example, home economics, mathematics, or physics) that a fifteen-year-old student can understand.
- Explain in your own words the meaning of the term *pornographic*.

Note that these examples call on the student to do more than just open the dictionary and copy meaningless words or synonyms. We have more to discuss about comprehension in this chapter.

Application

The *Application* category, as the name implies, involves applying or using information to arrive at a solution to a problem. In operating at the Application level, the student typically is given an unfamiliar problem and must apply the appropriate principle (method of solving the problem) without having to be prompted regarding how to resolve it. Also, the student must know how to *use* the proper method after having chosen it. When evaluating an Application problem, you should check both

Figure 4-3 Application Problems As Two-Step Processes

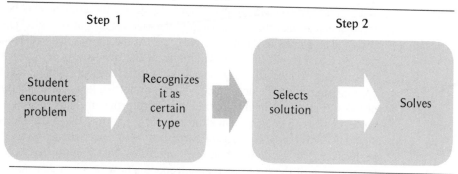

the solution and the process. Both of these are important subcomponents in the Application-level problem because how a student solves a problem may be more important than the answer obtained. To be sure that a question reaches the Application level, you must make the problem *unique* or *novel*. If the problem has been *gone over* the day *before* in class, the *task* for the *student* would involve mere *recall*, thus making it a Knowledge-level activity.

The two-step application process can be visualized as shown in Figure 4-3. In the first step of the process, the student encounters a problem not seen before and recognizes it as a subset or type of problem solved before. Note that we have used the words *subset* and *type* rather than *same* with the problem encountered before. The novelty or originality of the problem is an essential characteristic of an Application-level problem.

During the second step of solving an Application-level problem, the student selects an appropriate solution and applies it to the data at hand. This solution can consist of an algorithm, a formula, an equation, a recipe, or a standardized set of procedures for handling a specific type of problem.

If you view Application problems as a two-step process, you can analyze students' responses and diagnose problems on the basis of the error patterns. If students are having difficulty in recognizing certain equations, then you need to give them a wide variety of these types of problems to recognize and to prescribe the correct solutions. However, if students are able to perform this function but are unable to plug the values in the problem into the correct formula or equation, give them practice in the computational aspects of the problem. Here you can see another use of the taxonomy in individualizing instruction for diverse student needs.

Examples of Application

A few examples will help differentiate the Application category from other categories. Typically, an Application problem has one solution, but there may be other correct ways to solve the problem. This usually involves the use of some formula or principle that has been learned previously.

For example, the formula $a^2 + b^2 = c^2$ describes the relationship between the sides of a right triangle. At the Knowledge level, the student may be asked for the formula concerning the relationship of the sides of a right triangle. The student may reply, "The square of the hypotenuse . . ." At the Comprehension level, the student may be asked to put the formula into his or her own words or, given a triangle with some sides delineated, may be asked to plug the appropriate numbers into the appropriate places. To determine whether or not students can apply their knowledge of the formula, you might give them a word problem that requires computing distances across an imaginary field or lake. In computing these distances, the student would need to recognize that the formula $a^2 + b^2 = c^2$ should be used. To evaluate performance at the Application level optimally, wait a few weeks after the original presentation of the content; then introduce a new problem dealing with right triangles. This ensures that students can demonstrate the knowledge in a unique and novel situation. They are doing more than using the formula on the math test just because it was the only topic taken up for the previous three weeks.

An example involving home and family living may differentiate between understanding the processes of frying and sautéing and knowing when and why to use each process. The student may know the definition of both sauté and fry (Knowledge level) but, when given foods that have been cooked differently, may not be able to identify which foods have been sautéed and which fried (Comprehension level). An Application-level operation may involve a situation in which the student is given a selected food to cook and told what the food should taste like when cooked. The student should not only choose the correct method but also apply it correctly to produce the desired product.

An example involving physical education further illustrates the relationship between the three levels. At the Knowledge level, a basketball coach can give a definition of a certain defensive alignment or formation. At the Comprehension level, the coach can explain how the defense strategy works or can identify an example of it in use. At the Application level, the coach can recognize, in a game situation, where the strategy would be appropriate and can successfully implement it.

In all these examples, note that the student must know *when* and *how* to use a particular method of solving a problem. Now take the formative evaluation on the three previously described levels.

FORMATIVE EVALUATION *Knowledge, Comprehension, Application*

Place a **K** next to each Knowledge question or objective. Place a **C** next to each Comprehension question or objective. Place an **AP** next to each Application question or objective.

_____ 1. Approximately what proportion of the population of the United States works in a service industry?
(a) 10 percent (b) 20 percent (c) 35 percent (d) 50 percent (e) 60 percent

_____ 2. According to the statistics, which team was more accurate at the free-throw line?

HARVARD (51)	B	F	P
Sanders	2	1–2	5
Lewis	9	2–4	20
Mustoe	1	3–10	5
Brown	3	0–6	6
Dover	7	1–2	15
	22	7–24	51

MICHIGAN (84)	B	F	P
Wilmore	10	7–11	27
Johnson	6	3–5	15
Brady	7	2–3	16
Fife	7	0–1	14
Grahiec	5	2–4	12
	35	14–24	84

_____ 3. A person who lays brick is called
(a) A carpenter (c) An architect (e) A mechanical engineer
(b) A mason   (d) A draftsman

_____ 4. Ontogeny recapitulates phylogeny means that
(a) Man is descended from apes.
(b) All life has evolved from ancestors in the sea.
(c) The embryonic development of an animal retraces evolution.
(d) Amphibians developed into reptiles when they finally became independent of the water.

_____ 5. Using paper, pencil, and dictionary, compose an essay of approximately two pages on "The Scariest Dream I Ever Had." Incorporate the principles of proper usage of grammar, logical sentence structure, logical development of ideas, and clarity of expression.

_____ 6. How would you explain performance objectives to someone who is unfamiliar with the term?

_____ 7. Given the materials and the stated problem for an experiment, the student, without being told to do so, will perform each phase of the experiment, following the steps of scientific method.

_____ 8. Using James Joyce's *Ulysses* as the reference, summarize the plot. The summary must relate to the three criteria in class, and these must be illustrated with examples from the novel.

_____ 9. Given the power factor and the reactive power of a generator, the student will determine the power of the generator to the closest watt.

_____ 10. Given a schematic of a diesel engine, the student will be able to read the schematic, identifying ten of the twelve major parts.

Responses

1. K. This question requires the student to recall a statistic.
2. C. The behavior required here is a type of table-reading. The student must understand what the different columns mean to answer the question.

3. K. This question requires knowledge of terms.
4. C. This question would be translation but could be a Knowledge question if the student had seen this particular phrase before.
5. AP. Note how the criteria for evaluation were made specific. This component of higher-level objectives is often ignored.
6. C. The key phrase here is "How would *you* . . . ?"
7. AP. Again note how criteria can be applied to Application-level objectives.
8. C. The student is being asked for a summary.
9. AP. In this situation the student must recognize the problem type, select an appropriate solution, and determine the answer—a sequence that is typical of Application-level objectives.
10. C. This objective requires students to read a schematic and translate it into words.

Analysis

Application involved the bringing together of separate components to arrive at a solution. *Analysis* involves the converse of this process, in that complex items—such as speeches, written communications, organizations, or machines—are taken apart and the underlying organization behind them explained. The emphasis in Analysis-level operations is on explicating how the various parts of a complex process or object are arranged and work together to achieve a certain effect. Another common kind of Analysis question offers an example of reasoning and asks the student to judge whether it is logical. Yet another type of Analysis question asks the student to discover the personal motives behind a communication.

Analysis can be differentiated from Comprehension in terms of the depth of processing. Comprehension involves finding similarities and differences and making comparisons. Basically, the task at that level is to show relationships that can be discovered by understanding the communication itself. Analysis, however, goes beyond just understanding a communication and involves being able to look beneath the surface and discovering how different parts interact. In this sense Analysis builds on Comprehension but goes beyond it. Analysis involves working backwards, taking a situation or event and explaining how all the parts fit together to give a total effect; Comprehension, on the other hand, primarily involves describing what that effect is.

Types of Analysis Questions

As in the Comprehension category, we can subdivide the Analysis category into groups. This is done to offer you the opportunity to see the Analysis category in various forms.

Identification of Issues   In this type of Analysis operation, students subdivide a broad communication into its constituent parts. This may be like discovering the "skeleton" of a communication, as the issues involved are sometimes not explicitly stated in the communication. In this sense you are asking the student to go beyond the information in the message and to show the relationship between assumptions and key points, stated or otherwise. Examples of this type of Analysis objective are as follows:

- Using the six campaign speeches of the presidential candidates, point out the major differences between the candidates, relating the differences to specific sections of the speeches.
- Given the Bill of Rights, the student will be able to explain its main points in terms of the injustices suffered under British rule.

Implications   This type of Analysis question requires that students point out relationships between two propositions. The relationships may be expressed by inference, association, or necessary consequences and may not be stated directly. Some examples are these:

- What does the slogan "America: Love It or Leave It" imply about the people to whom it is addressed?
- What are the educational implications of a voucher system that would allow all parents to purchase an education for their children at a school of their choice?

Note that in both the identification of issues and implications subcategories, the main task is to acquire some meaning beyond the denotation level. This is what distinguishes Analysis from Comprehension; the connotation of the message is important.

Motives   Questions or objectives that ask students to identify reasons for behavior are examples of the motive subcategory. The student must again be able to use connotative meanings and to discover two bases of behavior—one overt, the other covert. A caution is in order here. Because these tasks can lead students to speculate, insist that they provide evidence to support the probable motive given. Examples of such questions are these:

- What were some of the motives behind President Bush's historic visit to Poland and Hungary?
- Why do many organizations keep lobbyists in Washington, D.C.?

The Analysis category has many uses besides those just illustrated. Examples of Analysis objectives from the various disciplines may include:

Physical Education   When given a game film, list the main turning points of the game and explain why or how they contributed to the final outcome of the game.

Physical Education   Given a video tape of golf swings to analyze, identify the actions that result in a hook or a slice. The analyses must include body movements as well as the position of the club face.

Home Economics   Given some dish (or meal) that did not turn out right, pinpoint the error and correct it.

Literature   Given a poem or other piece of literature, try to explain how the different elements interweave to achieve an effect.

Art   Given a painting, show how form, color, and texture all blend together to give a certain impression.

All these examples involve the analysis of a complex phenomenon so that its constituent parts are discovered. Now complete the next formative evaluation.

FORMATIVE EVALUATION   *Analysis*

Place a **K** next to each Knowledge question or objective. Place a **C** next to each Comprehension question or objective. Place an **AP** next to each application question or objective. Place an **AN** next to each Analysis question or objective.

_____ 1. What logical fallacies can you list relating to the supply side of economics?

_____ 2. What are the different parts of the human eye?

_____ 3. Why have labor unions and the Democratic party been closely connected in the history of our country?

_____ 4. What does the word *taxonomy* mean?

_____ 5. What were the author's motives in writing *Uncle Tom's Cabin*?

_____ 6. Formulate a definition for the term *urban crisis.*

_____ 7. What implications does the advance in medicine, namely, organ transplantation, have for the legal profession?

_____ 8. Given a set of data, compute the arithmetic mean to the nearest whole number.

_____ 9. Given a description of an experiment that has been conducted, the student will describe how the six steps of scientific method worked together to make a valid experiment.

_____ 10. Given $10, plan a dinner for four that will have at least one of each of the basic food types (protein, carbohydrates, etc.) and that will not have more than 1,000 calories per meal.

_____ 11. Given four major components of a computer, define in your own words the function of each. Definitions must correspond in meaning to those discussed in class.

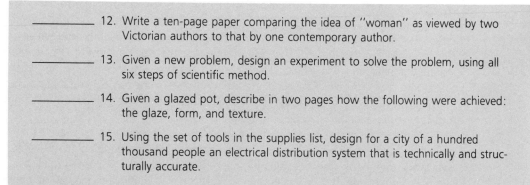

12. Write a ten-page paper comparing the idea of "woman" as viewed by two Victorian authors to that by one contemporary author.

13. Given a new problem, design an experiment to solve the problem, using all six steps of scientific method.

14. Given a glazed pot, describe in two pages how the following were achieved: the glaze, form, and texture.

15. Using the set of tools in the supplies list, design for a city of a hundred thousand people an electrical distribution system that is technically and structurally accurate.

Responses

1. AN. "Logical fallacies" should have been the clue here.
2. K. The student is asked to recall information.
3. AN. The student is asked to search below the surface and discover implications and motives.
4. K. It is a hierarchical classification system.
5. AN. The student is being asked to supply motives.
6. C. The student is being asked to formulate his or her own definition.
7. AN. The student is being asked for implications.
8. AP. This classification assumes that the formula for finding the mean is not given to the student.
9. AN. In this problem, students are asked to describe the interrelationship of the component parts of an experiment.
10. AP. The student is asked to use principles of nutrition to solve an everyday homemaking problem.
11. C. "In your own words" is the key characteristic here.
12. AN. The student is being asked to show how different novel components (plot, characterization) interact to depict women.
13. AP. The student is applying a solution to a specific problem.
14. AN. Given the final product, the student must work backwards to determine how different procedures affected the finished pot.
15. AP. In this Application exercise, the student is using electrical laws and principles to solve a practical problem.

Synthesis

Synthesis entails the creative meshing of elements so as to *form* a new and unique entity. Because its key is creativity, the Synthesis category may be the most distinctive and one of the easiest to recognize. Synthesis is the process of combining parts in such a way as to constitute a pattern or structure that did not exist before. A research paper can belong to either the Application or Synthesis category, depending on the level of originality. If the paper is comprehensive and thorough but does not add anything to the topic that is not already known, we consider the writer to be operating at the Application level. If, however, the writer puts ideas together in new or unique patterns or creates new idea configurations, then we consider this to be a Synthesis-level activity.

This category probably stimulates the most creative behavior. In fact, by definition, the Synthesis category requires the creation of something unique, a product of the individual and his or her unique experiences. Consequently, the whole of the creation is more than just the sum of its parts; the parts are held together in a unique combination—the whole. This is not to say that every Synthesis operation must be a work of art. A second grader writing a poem can be working at the Synthesis level. What is important in this case is that the second grader is translating a unique experience into poetic expression.

Because of the stress on creativity, operations at the Synthesis level are usually difficult to grade objectively. You need to use more subjective judgment in evaluating Synthesis operations than in evaluating operations at other levels. Be careful, too, about stifling creativity. To encourage it, give your students full leeway in their creative expression.

As with the other levels, Synthesis can be subdivided in terms of the type of processing involved and the products of those operations. In one subcategory the product or performance is a unique type of communication, such as a poem, essay, speech, or original art form. (Though language is the most common medium, other media, such as music or painting, are also part of the arts.) In operating at the Synthesis level, students attempt to use the medium to achieve one of these functions—to inform, to describe, to persuade, to impress, or to entertain. Students' originality and creativeness in attempting these are among the criteria used in evaluating these products. (See also McAlpine et al., 1987; Ennis, 1985b; and Paul, 1985.)

The second subcategory of the Synthesis level involves the developing of a plan or proposed set of operations to be performed. Bloom illustrates this subcategory in Table 4-2. Note that all these operations result in the creation of a tangible product. This tangible product and the quality of creativity are the two distinguishing characteristics of the Synthesis level. Often, because of resource limitations in our schools, the final product cannot be constructed, so we often judge the quality of the Synthesis operation on the basis of the plans themselves. As opposed to creative art

Table 4-2   *Synthesis Operations Involving the Development of a Plan*

Proposed Set of Operations	Process (i.e., carrying out the set of operations)	Expected Outcome
Plan for an experiment	Carrying out the experiment	Experimental findings; probability statement
A teaching unit	Teaching	Changes in behavior
Specifications for a new house	Building the house	The house

Source: From *Taxonomy of Educational Objectives: The Classification of Educational Goals: Handbook I: Cognitive Domain,* edited by Benjamin S. Bloom et al. Copyright © 1956 by Longman, Inc. Reprinted with permission of Longman.

projects, teachers generally feel more comfortable evaluating a project or project plan than an "original" art form.

The third subcategory involves the creation of a set of abstract relations as a product of Synthesis. This set of relations typically is derived from working with observed phenomena or data and forming patterns that did not exist before. These may include formulating hypotheses, which are guesses about potentially fruitful directions for research, and formulating principles, an example of which is the Peter Principle. This principle states that in an organization people advance or are promoted until they unknowingly (at least before the principle was formulated) reach their level of incompetence. Another example is the Premack Principle, which states that, in psychology, more frequently occurring behaviors can serve as reinforcers for less frequently occurring behaviors. In addition, the taxonomy that we are presently discussing can surely be considered a creative set of abstract relations.

Some examples of Synthesis operations in various disciplines follow.

- *Home economics.* Creating a new dish or designing a new clothing pattern.
- *Social studies.* Developing a new constitution for school or designing a survey to measure people's attitudes on a topic.
- *Language arts.* Writing a play or a short story.
- *Music.* Putting words to a melody or composing a tune in a certain rhythmic time.
- *Science.* Designing an experiment or a new computer program.

Now proceed to the formative evaluation on the Synthesis category.

FORMATIVE EVALUATION *Comprehension, Application, Analysis, Synthesis*

Based on the information in Figure 4-4 on page 112, try to construct higher-level questions or objectives of your own: one Comprehension, one Application, one Analysis, and one Synthesis. You may wish to consult the text to refresh your memory and to reexamine the examples given.

Comprehension

_____

_____

Application

_____

_____

Analysis

_____

_____

Synthesis

_____

_____

Some possible questions and objectives are shown on page 113. Try to write some of your own before consulting them.

Figure 4-4   *Worldwide Military Expenditures in Current Dollars: 1978–83*

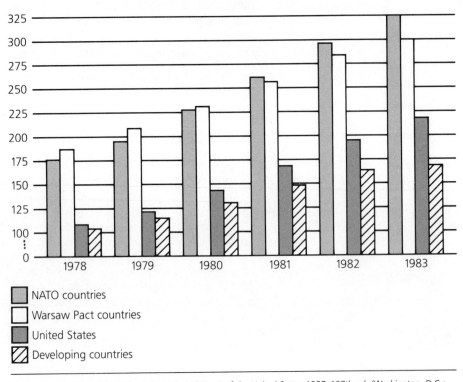

NATO countries
Warsaw Pact countries
United States
Developing countries

Source: U.S. Bureau of the Census, *Statistical Abstract of the United States 1987,* 107th ed. (Washington, D.C.: U.S. Government Printing Office, 1987), p. 321, Figure 530.

Responses

Comprehension
1. Which of these powers has increased its expenditures the most from 1978 to 1983?
2. Which of these powers shows the most fluctuations in its military spending?

Application
1. What effect would border conflicts in the following areas have on military expenditures?
   (a) The Middle East
   (b) Central America
   (c) Eastern Europe
2. What effects would a worldwide recession have on military expenditures?

Analysis
1. Why did the military expenditures for the United States increase so dramatically during these five years? In answering the question, relate your response to the political and economic conditions in both the United States and abroad.
2. What do the increases in military spending over this five-year period tell us about defense priorities for the different groups of countries?

Synthesis
1. Given appropriate data and a model treaty to follow, devise a treaty that reduces military spending by 10 percent for all four countries or groups of countries listed in Figure 4-4. The treaty will be evaluated on internal logic as well as by accurate use of data.
2. Given a map of the world and current military expenditures, develop a proposal for the United Nations to reduce current military expenditures. The proposal will be evaluated on the direct link between geographical and monetary considerations.

Evaluation

The *Evaluation* category involves making decisions on controversial topics and substantiating these decisions with sound reasons. Creativity is to Synthesis what judgment is to Evaluation. Evaluation questions ask the students to state their thoughts, opinions, and judgments and to give the criteria on which these are based. Evaluation uses standards for appraising the extent to which particulars are accurate, effective, economical, or satisfying. To qualify for this category, the student must (1) set up appropriate standards or values, and (2) determine how closely the idea or object meets these standards or values.

The Evaluation category projects the Analysis category into another dimension. An Evaluation question requires the student, besides analyzing, to make some type of value judgment. The criteria for judgment must be clearly identified, and the quality of the Evaluation response should be graded according to how well the student has met the criteria. The Evaluation category requires the student to make reasonable judgments, to have rational opinions or personal reactions to a stimulus, and to defend them in a logical and coherent fashion.

Although the Evaluation process is subjective to the extent that the student chooses the criteria, emphasis should still be placed on rational, well-developed, rather than emotional, responses. This prepares the student for situations in later life in which critical thinking will be needed (see Kunen et al., 1981).

An Evaluation response should consist of two parts:

1. The student should establish criteria on which to base judgment.
2. Using the prescribed criteria, the student should make his or her judgment accordingly.

For example, with the question "Would Lee Iacocca make a good President?" you are first asking the student to decide which qualities are necessary for a good President. Then the student should compare these presidential qualities with those possessed by Lee Iacocca. It is obvious that there will be some difference of opinion about the qualities necessary for a good President. This brings out the subjective or even creative component of Evaluation. The student must be analytical in matching these criteria with the subject being evaluated.

Criteria are formed usually from one of three sources:

1. Cultural or social values
2. Religious or historical absolutes
3. Individual justifications

Examples of each follow:

1. "Is it proper for a woman to ask a man for a date?" This question could be answered in several ways, depending on which social or cultural values the person believes are important.
2. "Should abortion be legalized?" To some people this is a religious question, to others it is a personal moral decision, and to still others it is a medical decision.
3. "Should the Equal Rights Amendment be passed?" Different people would probably arrive at different answers based on different value systems.

Because students have varying value orientations, you will receive different responses to the same Evaluation question. You can use Evaluation questions to help students learn to live with, and accept, the different views of others, thus preparing them for life in a pluralistic society.

You also prepare the students for taking a stand on some issue with an Evaluation question such as "What do you think is best/worst or more/most important?"

FORMATIVE EVALUATION   *Evaluation*

Write two Evaluation questions for the following passage.

THE ENERGY CRISIS

As the existing stock of crude oil diminishes, energy experts debate what measures should be taken to remedy possible shortages of oil products and continually rising prices. The United

States is affected more by these growing shortages and subsequent rises in prices because its technologically oriented economy is heavily dependent upon energy from other countries. With only 6 percent of the world's population, the United States is using one-third of the world's energy. As often happens when the government is asked to take action, the question is not whether it should take action, but what that action should be and which segments of the economy will be affected.

A major energy question involves the kinds of energy sources in which the United States should be investing in the following years. Conservative experts on energy claim that the United States, for the next fifty years, will still be heavily dependent on oil and, consequently, should be investing its energy research money in ways to find more oil and not use it more efficiently. More radical critics advocate loosening our grip on oil dependence and exploring alternate sources of energy such as nuclear and solar energy. The latter position is more speculative, but advocates of this position claim that the time is right for bold experimentation.

Even on the topic of oil, experts disagree on how to save the oil that we do have. One controversial method of oil conservation that is being discussed is the limiting of car use either directly or indirectly. Direct means would include enforced car pooling and limiting the number of driving days for each vehicle. Indirect means would include closing gas stations on weekends and gas rationing. Public debate on these issues has centered on their feasibility and their fairness. For example, opponents of gas rationing contend that extensive bureaucratic controls needed to enforce the gas rationing laws would cost more than they would save. Critics of indirect means of saving gas claim that these methods have not worked in the past and have the potential of being unfair to states with tourist economies.

The energy problem has also spilled over into another area of government control—the air. In an era of plentiful fuels, the environmentalists' demands for clean air seem reasonable and feasible. However, with cleaner fuels becoming increasingly expensive, more and more manufacturing and utility companies are turning to cheaper, dirtier sources of fuel such as coal. Environmentalists contend that now is the time to test the Americans' commitment to a cleaner, healthier environment, and they are advocating the maintenance of present Environmental Protection Agency clean-air standards. Opponents say that these standards are unrealistic and should not be enforced in times of energy shortage.

Evaluation Questions

1. _____
   _____
   _____

2. _____
   _____
   _____

Responses

1. Do you think that the United States should spend most of its energy research dollars on oil or on alternate sources of energy? Explain why.
2. If gasoline consumption needs to be curtailed, do you favor direct or indirect means of doing so? In your answer, include at least three historical precedents.
3. Should the United States relax its clean-air standards during an energy shortage or maintain them as they are? Discuss the economic and political implications of one particular position.

Bloom's Taxonomy: A Critical Analysis

In the more than thirty years that Bloom's Taxonomy has existed, it has been widely used and accepted by educators at all levels. Research on the taxonomy, as well as research in cognitive psychology, has generally supported the ideas behind the taxonomy but has also raised some questions about its internal structure. This section of the chapter focuses on that research.

Uses of the Taxonomy

The taxonomy has been much used in curriculum and test construction. John Feldhusen et al. (1974) successfully used it to focus on higher levels of learning in curriculum design. Donald Bailey and Judith Leonard (1977) demonstrated the taxonomy's usefulness in early childhood education, using it to plan learning experiences for preschoolers. Test specialists have also applied the taxonomy to test construction (McDaniel, 1979; Wolfe and Heikkinen, 1979; Nelson, 1978), translating goals at different levels into tangible evaluation procedures. Dale Halpain and colleagues (1985) demonstrated that using curriculum and instruction at higher levels of the taxonomy induced greater levels of student attention. And Doris Redfield and Elaine Rousseau (1981) concluded that an increased emphasis at higher levels of the taxonomy enhances higher level student performance.

Researchers have found Bloom's Taxonomy to be a serviceable analytical tool as well. Donald Freeman and collaborators (1983) used the taxonomy to analyze questions in elementary mathematics texts. They found an overemphasis of lower level questions and exercises with corresponding little emphasis on the development of students' thinking skills. Richard Clevenstine (1987), focusing on the ISIS science program, found a similar imbalance, with the activities of the curriculum relating to lower levels of the taxonomy. Other researchers (Cazden, 1986; Gall, 1984) have made use of the taxonomy for analyzing verbal interactions in a classroom.

Perhaps Bloom's Taxonomy's greatest contribution has been in the development of a professional language. Teachers and administrators describing and analyzing their efforts know that terms such as "knowledge level" and "higher levels of learning" will be understood by educators everywhere. This universal vocabulary, reflecting a specialized body of knowledge, was an essential step in the professionalization of teaching (Metzger, 1987).

Some Lingering Questions

Despite its widespread acceptance and use, Bloom's Taxonomy has raised some persistent questions. One question is about the comprehensiveness of the taxonomy. Some critics are concerned that the taxonomy is too narrow and may not include all the important outcomes taught in our schools (Furst, 1981). When you think about the broad range of goals existing in such diverse areas as home economics, art, music, and physical education, you can see that this concern is probably valid. As this chapter points out, teachers in these diverse areas can still use the taxonomy but will have to adapt its use in their classrooms. (In fact, all teachers seem to do this—personalizing any educational idea to make it their own.)

A second concern centers on whether the levels are discrete or highly sequenced. You may have encountered this problem yourself as you tried to keep the levels separate. (Your authors have encountered similar problems and may have a novel solution in the next section.) Though a problem for researchers, this concern is not as great for individual teachers using the taxonomy to guide their teaching.

Researchers raised some questions about the sequence of the levels (Kunen et al., 1981; Madaus et al., 1973). Though supporting the general idea of increasing cognitive complexity, researchers question whether progress through the taxonomy is in six uniform steps. Again, this is more of a research problem than a pedagogical one. As you will see in the next section, evidence from diverse areas of psychology supports the idea of a learning hierarchy embodied in Bloom's Taxonomy.

The Taxonomy: Psychological Evidence

Does Bloom's Taxonomy make sense psychologically? Evidence from a number of sources supports the idea that increased processing means better student learning. Perhaps the most fundamental of these is evidence that teacher actions influence student academic tasks, which ultimately influence learning. Research from both public school classrooms (Doyle, 1983; Nickerson, 1985) and experiments of cognitive psychologists (Schuell, 1986) support this conclusion. Teacher efforts to have students process information in different ways results in different kinds of learning. This is the essence of the idea of curriculum alignment discussed earlier. Further, the more thoroughly and thoughtfully students think about an idea, the better they learn it and the longer they retain it.

Support for these latter ideas comes from a broad spectrum of research areas. In the area of verbal learning, research has shown that the depth with which students process information significantly affects retention (Craik, 1979; Haller et al., 1988). Work in the area of concept learning (Tennyson and Cocchiarella, 1986) has documented the importance of students' internalizing concept definitions through analyzing examples and attributes and putting these in their own words. Research in the area of generative learning (Wittrock, 1986) has demonstrated the importance of having students summarize, apply, and analyze ideas; and research in junior high classrooms (Pratton and Hales, 1986) has illustrated the importance of students' active participation in the learning process.

The importance of the Comprehension category as a gateway to the other levels is also becoming clear. In a perspective review of this area of cognitive psychology, Raymond Nickerson (1985), in his article "Understanding Understanding," argues convincingly that comprehending an idea or concept is an essential prerequisite to applying it, analyzing it, or using it creatively or evaluatively. (We will expand that concept shortly.) Teachers need to make a special effort to determine that students understand an idea before asking them to use it.

Even the importance of the often overused and much-maligned knowledge category has been documented by researchers (Shuell, 1986). Research in such diverse areas as chess expertise and mathematical problem-solving has demonstrated the importance of a knowledge base in higher level process. Students cannot problem-solve in a knowledge vacuum.

The overriding message is clear. If your students are to learn effectively, you need to plan and implement strategies that require internal processing of information. Establish goals, lay a knowledge base, and actively teach for higher cognitive levels.

A NEW ANALOGUE
FOR THE COGNITIVE TAXONOMY

In over three decades of use, Bloom's Taxonomy has provided a number of useful insights about teaching and learning in the classroom. Then came Raymond Nickerson's monumental "Understanding Understanding" (1985). That paper triggered serious reexamination of the nature of understanding and its role in Bloom's Taxonomy. When Arnold B. Arons (1988) examined concepts similar to Nickerson's, his studies created more speculation about the role that comprehension plays in "learning." Merlin C. Wittrock (1986); Beau Fly Jones (1986); Robert H. Ennis (1985a); Barry K. Beyer (1984); Arthur Whimbey (1984); Eileen P. Haller, David A. Child, and Herbert J. Walberg (1988); and John E. McPeck (1981) all contributed pieces to our dilemma and puzzle. Based on these works, we constructed a novel interpretation of how the cognitive taxonomy may operate. It goes beyond the traditional display of the six major categories of the taxonomy (Figure 4-5), which assumed that the steps must be climbed one at a time. That analogue has generally persisted since 1956.

We now offer Figure 4-6 to illustrate the interactive nature of the cognitive taxonomy's categories. This analogue (model) is actually to be perceived as being three-dimensional, similar to a solar system analogue. Our model shows that knowledge and all other categories are continuously expanding. The breaks in the "boundary lines" attempt to show that. Further, after analyzing the several writers above, and based on our own experiences in teaching, especially with hands-on science programs, we concluded that knowledge is simply a precursor to the other categories.

Comprehension, that is, *understanding,* is the real key to unlocking entry into the other levels. Once you comprehend or truly understand a concept, principle, law, set of conditions, or skills, then you can branch into any of the remaining four categories—application, analysis, synthesis, or evaluation. We submit that the categories are not discrete entities; they are interactive. *Critical to the interaction is under-*

Figure 4-5   *Traditional Analogues (Models) of Cognitive Taxonomy*

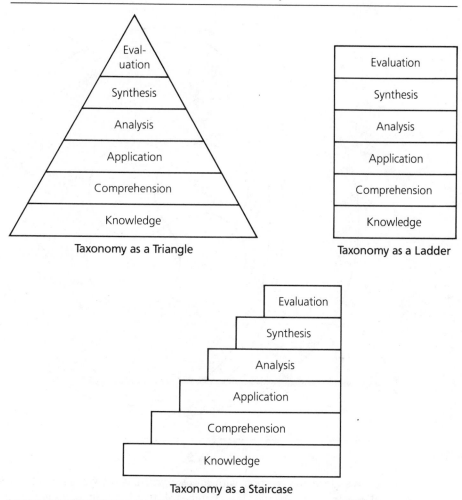

Taxonomy as a Triangle

Taxonomy as a Ladder

Taxonomy as a Staircase

standing. Teach to understanding, and the other categories are easily attainable. We assert that teachers do *not* teach to understanding but to a superficial knowledge level. Thus, students in the United States do rather poorly on achievement tests, especially on the thinking skills areas. The Japanese have long been held in high esteem for their educational achievements. The instructional element to which Japanese teachers strive is for their students to achieve understanding! (We will not enter into a discussion about the cultural differences—and there are many—that also account for their student overachievements.) UNDERSTANDING is the key to instructional success. (For an extended treatment, see Crooks, 1988.)

Figure 4-6   *Interactive Model of Cognitive Taxonomy*

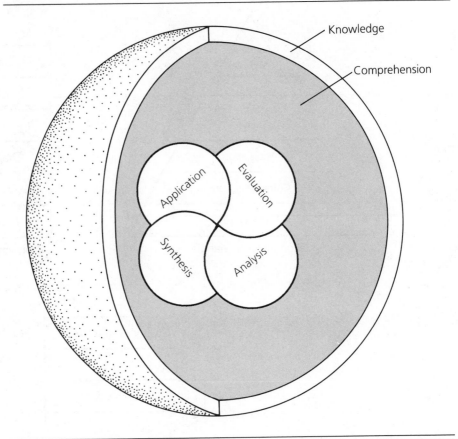

We close this section with an *emergent theory*. We want you to send us your thoughts on this model. We hypothesize that the higher categories of the cognitive taxonomy act similarly to the interactions of an atomic nucleus. There is a "force" that binds the nucleus, just as there is a "quality" that holds the cognitive processes as a unity. One moves rapidly from understanding to creativity, analytic thinking, evaluation, or application without having to proceed one step at a time. We offer the profession a novel analogue to explain the interactions of all elements of the cognitive domain.

Lest you infer that we have made too much out of this topic, we close with a quote from John I. Goodlad's *A Place Called School.*

> Only *rarely* did we find evidence to suggest instruction (in reading and math)
> likely to go much beyond merely possession of information to a level of under-
> standing its implications and either applying it or exploring its possible applica-

tions. Nor did we see activities likely to arouse students' curiosity or to involve them in seeking a solution to some problem not already laid bare by teacher or textbook.

And it appears that this preoccupation with the lower intellectual processes pervades social studies and science as well. An analysis of topics studied and materials used gives not an impression of students studying human adaptations and exploration, but of facts to be learned (p. 236).*

THE AFFECTIVE DOMAIN †

Whereas the cognitive domain concerns those intellectually related goals of the schools, there is another domain that involves the development of students' feelings, attitudes, values, and emotions—the affective domain. Lorin and Jo Anderson (1982) describe affective measurement techniques in the classroom and point out that some affective goals, such as honesty and truthfulness, are ends in themselves, whereas other goals, such as positive attitudes toward mathematics or science instruction, may be viewed as means toward an end. Most parents, as well as most professionals in the field, tend to view the development of students' thinking skills, rather than their attitudes, as the most important job of the schools. Our discussion of the affective domain will not be as detailed as that of the cognitive domain because of the cognitive focus of most schools.

The developers of the taxonomy of the affective domain (Krathwohl et al., 1964) had goals similar to workers in the cognitive area. They wanted to develop a classification system that would help to design and analyze instruction in the affective area. As they developed their taxonomy, they arrived at the following five levels.

1. Receiving (attending)
2. Responding
3. Valuing
4. Organization
5. Characterization by a Value or Value Complex

These five categories are then subdivided, as are the categories in the cognitive domain. Like those in the cognitive domain, the categories in the affective domain are hierarchically arranged along a continuum, in this case one of internalization rather than of complexity. Internalization refers to the extent to which an idea has been integrated into a person's belief structure. If taken through each category of the taxonomy, the learner would begin by being willing to receive a particular attitudinal or value position and would conclude by incorporating or internalizing this position

---

*From: John I. Goodlad (1984). *A Place Called School*. New York: McGraw-Hill. Used with permission.
†From *Taxonomy of Educational Objectives: Handbook II: Affective Domain* by David R. Krathwohl et al. Copyright © 1964 by Longman, Inc. Reprinted by permission of Longman, Inc., New York.

into his or her lifestyle. Following is a very brief outline of the entire affective domain.

Receiving (Attending)

The overall focus of the affective taxonomy is on the development of attitudes and values. The first step in this process and the initial level in the affective domain relate to the willingness of learners to be open to stimuli and messages in the environment. At this level, students are willing to receive some message or to acknowledge that some phenomenon is taking place. To receive an affective message, one must demonstrate *Awareness,* which is the first subdivision of Receiving. Awareness implies that one is conscious of some stimulus occurring. Awareness is similar to the cognitive behavior of observing, which we presented previously as being one of the major scientific processes.

Being aware is only the entry step. This is followed by the subcategory of *Willingness to Receive.* Someone may be aware that a message has been sent, but does that same individual willingly attend? The attitude of simply being willing to listen to others is a demonstration of Willingness to Receive.

The final subdivision of Receiving is *Controlled or Selected Attention.* Receiving is also contingent on one's ability to focus attention further on a selected set of stimuli. You demonstrated selected attention when you decided to focus on this page rather than on the newspaper, which may be on the same desk as this text. Students are operating at this level when they make a conscious effort to attend to a classroom presentation rather than to daydream or to look out the window.

Some examples of this level of the taxonomy include the following performance objectives:

1. Students will listen to other students who disagree with their point of view and use their ideas in response.
2. Students will develop an openness toward other cultures so that, when other cultures are encountered in and out of the classroom, students will be willing to hear or read about them.

Responding

The second level in the affective domain is called *Responding.* Although one may be willing to receive, this is not enough for internalization, which needs an action component. The second level places the students in a position to make choices about an issue.

Acquiescence in Responding is the first subdivision of Responding and is demonstrated when one complies with regulations or conventions. *Willingness to Respond,* the second subdivision, takes responding one step further. Acquiescence in Responding suggests that one complies without knowing the reasons, but Willingness to Respond indicates that one complies and knows the reasons why.

The third subdivision in the major category of Responding is *Satisfaction in Response.* This subcategory implies that, after making a decision within the Responding realm, a person is emotionally satisfied. For example, you may have a difficult work assignment that ought to be done. After completing it, you feel good about having done it.

Following are some objectives that teachers have written for this level of the taxonomy:

1. Students will develop an appreciation for poetry, so that during a free reading period they will select a book of poetry as one of their choices.
2. Students will develop an appreciation of good hygiene habits, so that they will wash their hands with soap and water without being reminded after going to the lavatory.
3. Lower elementary students will learn to understand and appreciate the value of sharing, so that in a free play situation, the student will share toys with other children at least once.

Valuing

The third major category in the affective domain is called *Valuing.* Valuing means that one internalizes the concept of "worth." What differentiates this category from earlier ones is that Valuing is exhibited by the individual as a motivated, deliberate behavior, not simply as a willingness to acquiesce.

There are three subdivisions in the Valuing category: (1) *Acceptance of a Value,* (2) *Preference for a Value,* and (3) *Commitment.* Acceptance of a Value means that an individual believes that a certain value is preferable to others, but that this belief is flexible. If one accepts a value and is willing to be identified with it, one demonstrates a Preference for a Value. If one becomes involved and acts in accordance with the value, then one displays behaviors that are classified as Commitment. An important element of behavior is characterized by this level; behavior is motivated not by the desire to comply but by the individual's commitment to the underlying value guiding the behavior.

The following three objectives with a respective goal are examples of this level:

1. *Goal:* Appreciate democratic processes.
   Objective: In a mock election, students will vote and will urge at least three others to do the same.
2. *Goal:* Develop commitment for clean air and water.
   Objective: In voluntary, nonschool settings, students will demonstrate that commitment by becoming active in organizations set up for this purpose and by encouraging others to do so.

3. *Goal:* Appreciate safe shop practices.
   Objective: In unsupervised shop settings, students will police their own work areas for unsafe practices.

Organization

As a learner's experiences broaden, there comes a point at which values begin to be ordered or classified. When such behaviors occur, then that individual is operating according to the fourth major category of the affective domain—*Organization.*

Within Organization there are two subcategories. The first is *Conceptualization of a Value,* which is demonstrated when one determines how values relate to each other in an abstract framework. We interpret Conceptualization of a Value as being very similar to the final category of the cognitive taxonomy, Evaluation, in that the individual takes a value position and can defend it if necessary.

The second subcategory of Organization is *Organization of a Value System.* This is the level for ordering one's commitments. In a broad sense, Organization of a Value System is similar to stating one's "philosophy of life."

Some objectives and their goals at this level are as follows:

1. *Goal:* Learn importance of good study habits.
   Objective: Demonstrate study habits by voluntarily organizing free time, both in school and out, by preparing a schedule of assignments to be done.
2. *Goal:* Importance of neat work areas.
   Objective: Without being reminded by the teacher, students will put away their materials, clean up the area, and be ready for dismissal by the time the bell rings.
3. *Goal:* Prepare career choices.
   Objective: Students will attend a career fair and will voluntarily seek and organize information relating to their career goals.

Characterization by a Value
or Value Complex

The highest category of the affective domain is the demonstration of behaviors showing that an individual acts in a manner consistent with those internalized values in which he or she believes. In the terms of the affective domain, this category is known as *Characterization by a Value or Value Complex.*

Generalized Set is the first of two subdivisions within this category. Generalized Set refers to one's commitment to certain attitudes, beliefs, or values, as reflected in one's consistent behavior. By knowing one's Generalized Set, one's behavior may be predicted for specific situations, which either conflict or converge with those values.

The highest level of the affective domain is described in the final subdivision, *Characterization.* Values so influence an individual's thinking as to be completely controlled by them. In other words, at this stage in the taxonomy, words and actions are entirely consistent with value orientation.

Sample objectives and goals for this level of the taxonomy follow:

1. *Goal:* Value honesty.
   Objective: In actual classroom situations, students will monitor their own behavior on tests and assignments and will discourage others from cheating.
2. *Goal:* Value free speech in a society.
   Objective: In classroom discussions, students will acknowledge the rights of others—including those with whom they disagree—to express their views and opinions. These will be expressed without any personal attacks or slurs.
3. *Goal:* Value human rights.
   Objective: In an unsupervised school setting, students will treat other members of the school community in a way in which they, too, would want to be treated.

A Very Brief Analysis

Although our introduction has been brief, we will attempt, nevertheless, to analyze the affective domain as it relates to instruction. We feel that this domain is a complex one, and it is sometimes hard to differentiate objectives at the various levels (a criticism that could also be leveled at the taxonomy of the cognitive domain). The affective domain also poses difficult evaluation problems because of the need for noncoercive and unobtrusive measures. On the positive side, however, the affective taxonomy provides a conceptual framework within which to view the entire instructional process. In other words, if teachers understand the major ideas in the affective taxonomy, they have tools for improving their educational endeavors.

We also believe that the variations between subdivisions are too artificial and hard to differentiate. Again, if this taxonomy is used as a conceptual framework rather than as a planning tool for instruction, this problem is not too important.

Finally, the time that is needed in the schools to provide all the necessary experiences for both the cognitive and affective dimensions of learning is overwhelming. This problem is becoming increasingly important as teachers and schools are being held more accountable for students' cognitive performance.

Yet, we can counter with the question "What are schools for?" The kinds of attitudes we develop as children and the values we espouse as adults are certainly influenced by the schools. Our attitudes toward learning are school-related, our approaches to personal interaction are shaped largely in school, and our belief in ourselves is school-connected. All of these affective behaviors are more important than learning and promptly forgetting the difference between transitive and intransitive verbs (see Hellison, 1987).

Abby L. Hughes and Karen Frommer (1982) devised a system by which to state, identify, and monitor affective objectives: a checklist called "Rating the Affective Domain" (RAD). This seventy-item RAD checklist uses a five-point rating scale.

Their system has four major behavioral skill areas: (1) individual tasks, (2) social interaction, (3) relationship to teacher, and (4) emotional responses. A teacher using their RAD system may monitor on a yearly basis the affective objectives selected for each student.

The very best of our teachers subtly interweave both the cognitive and affective consequences into their instruction. Bear in mind that very probably the teachers you liked best just happened to teach the most effectively and to teach the subjects that you liked most. Perhaps this was no accident. Good teachers have been incorporating affective goals into their curricula for years. It is our hope that knowledge of the ideas in the affective taxonomy will help make these teachers more effective and encourage others to be sensitive to the attitudes and values they are developing in students.

We close this section with an observation by Robert F. Mager (1968), the person responsible for popularizing behavioral objectives. He wrote: "If I do little else, I want to send my students away with at least as much interest in the subjects I teach as they had when they arrived." This perceptive statement is the essence of incorporating the affective domain into your *value complex* of instruction.

FORMATIVE EVALUATION   *Affective Domain*

Write the answer to each item below in the space provided.

_____ 1. Cognitive domain is to complexity as affective domain is to _____?

_____ 2. Cognitive domain is to the head as affective domain is to the _____? (What metaphorical place in the body would form the locus for the affective domain?)

_____ 3. True/False. Cognitive and affective behaviors are distinct and separate entities.

_____ 4. True/False. Getting someone to listen to an idea is the first step to getting her or him to act on that idea.

_____ 5. Is there more of a cognitive emphasis at the lower or higher levels of the affective domain? Explain your answer.

Categorize the following statements as cognitive or affective by inserting *C* or *A* as appropriate in the space provided.

_____ 6. Given a list of ten words, the student will identify all of the five that are nouns.

_____ 7. The student will follow classroom rules as prescribed by the teacher.

_____ 8. The student will recite the Bill of Rights.

_____ 9. In an unsupervised classroom setting, the student will use objectives to plan for instruction at least three times per week.

_____ 10. During a discussion, the student will listen at least twice to others, demonstrating this by using others' ideas in his or her comments.

Responses

1. Internalization. The affective domain is hierarchically organized on the basis of internalization. Objectives at the higher levels of this taxonomy require a greater degree of internalization than those at lower levels.
2. The heart. We commonly describe feelings as being from the "heart."
3. False. Though these taxonomies have been presented as separate systems for the purpose of clarity, there are a number of interrelations between the two areas.
4. True. The taxonomy of the affective domain is organized in such a way that a person must first be willing to receive an idea before any other type of internalization can occur.
5. There is more of a cognitive emphasis in the higher levels of the affective domain than at the lower levels because at the higher levels an individual must logically organize feelings into a coherent system.
6. Cognitive (Comprehension level)
7. Affective
8. Cognitive (Knowledge level)
9. Affective (the clue here is the phrase, "in an unsupervised classroom setting")
10. Affective

THE PSYCHOMOTOR DOMAINS

The psychomotor domain, that area of the curriculum dealing with the development of muscular skills and abilities, is the latest to be analyzed by educational taxonomies. Unlike the other areas, the psychomotor domain has several taxonomies that the following sections will take up briefly.

Each taxonomy treats skill learning as a series of inputs and outputs. The inputs involve perception of information from the outside environment, and the outputs are the actual motions or movements the students perform. Consideration of both inputs and outputs is important in complex motor activities because movements must be coordinated in terms of the outer environment. Think of a gymnast on a balance beam or a basketball player in a game: both must take in information from the environment (input) and synchronize their movements to this information (output).

Figure 4-7   Moore's Taxonomy of the Perceptual Domain

Level	Example of Behavior
1. Sensation	Ability to discriminate rough detail
2. Figure perception	Resolution of part/whole relationship
3. Symbol perception	Ability to perceive the overall picture and complex relationships within a stimulus
4. Perception of meaning	Ability to reproduce a complex movement
5. Perceptive performance	Ability to reproduce, interpret, and adapt a complex phenomenon

Moore's Taxonomy

A logical starting point for our discussion of the psychomotor domain is the *perceptual taxonomy* developed by Maxine Moore (1967, 1970, 1972). Hers was the first developed and places most emphasis on the initial stages of psychomotor development, the perceptual aspect of information.

As shown in Figure 4-7, the lowest levels of Moore's taxonomy deal with discrimination of sensation, starting with simple discriminations and progressing to more complex. At level 4, *perception of meaning,* students not only can perceive complex relationships in a movement but also can copy or reproduce those movements. A swimmer, for example, faithfully replicates a dive, and a musician plays a concerto as other musicians have played it previously. In the final level, *perceptive performance,* students are expected to improvise original variations of the movements replicated in level 4. In keeping with this taxonomy's focus on perception, the emphasis at this level is on the extraction of subtle information from the stimulus, not on the motor skill involved in the behavior. Here we can see a parallel with the emphasis on creativity in the last two levels of Bloom's Taxonomy.

Harrow's Taxonomy

Anita Harrow's taxonomy, published in 1972, incorporates perceptual elements but places more emphasis on output or performance variables. As shown in Figure 4-8, the two lowest levels deal with basic fundamental movements, the building blocks of higher levels.

The third level, *perceptual abilities,* is involved with stimulus interpretation and is very similar in focus to Moore's *symbol perception.* Physical abilities, which are at Harrow's level 4, include components such as endurance, strength, flexibility, and agility—considered part of the foundation for higher levels. The last two levels, *skilled movement* and *nondiscursive communication,* stress performance, or output. At the *skilled movement* level, emphasis is on performance of a skill in a complex environment, such as in a game or in a performance with other musicians. The

Figure 4-8   *Harrow's Taxonomy of the Psychomotor Domain*

Level	Example
1. Reflex movement	Knee-jerk and other reflex movements innate at birth
2. Basic fundamental movements	Visual tracking of an object, crawling, walking, grasping an object
3. Perceptual abilities	Body awareness, figure-ground differentiation, auditory awareness, memory
4. Physical abilities	Muscular endurance, agility, strength
5. Skilled movement	Simple behaviors such as sawing wood and complex behaviors such as playing tennis
6. Nondiscursive communication	Moving interpretatively and using the body creatively to express ideas or emotions

From *Taxonomy of the Psychomotor Domain: A Guide for Developing Behavior Objectives* by Anita J. Harrow. New York: David McKay, 1972. Reprinted with permission of Longman Inc., New York.

highest level, *nondiscursive communication,* stresses expressive and creative movement. Here again we can see parallels with the cognitive taxonomy.

Jewett and Mullan Psychomotor Domain

The final taxonomy to be discussed is not only the most recent but also the most comprehensive. Its major concepts, endorsed by the American Alliance for Health, Physical Education and Recreation (AAHPER), were synthesized by Ann E. Jewett and Marie R. Mullan (1977). Combining elements of the two previous taxonomies, the Jewett and Mullan psychomotor domain begins with generic movement and concludes with creative movement. As you read through the levels, notice the similarities with the taxonomies discussed earlier. Note also how many of these processes can be applied to vocational, music, and art education.

    A. *Generic Movement:* Those movement operations or processes that facilitate the development of characteristic and effective motor patterns. They are typically exploratory operations in which the learner receives or "takes in" data as he or she moves.

        1. *Perceiving:* Awareness of total body relationships and of self in motion. These awarenesses may be evidenced by body positions or motoric acts; they may be sensory in that the mover feels the equilibrium of body weight and the movement of limbs; or they may be evidenced cognitively through identification, recognition, or differentiation.

        2. *Patterning:* Arrangement and use of body parts in successive and harmonious ways to achieve a movement pattern or skill. This process is dependent on recall and performance of a movement previously demonstrated or experienced.

   B. *Ordinative Movement:* The processes of organizing, refining, and performing skillful movement. The processes involved are directed toward the organization of perceptual-motor abilities with a view to solving particular movement tasks or requirements.

     1. *Adapting:* Modification of a patterned movement to meet externally imposed task demands. This would include modification of a particular movement to perform it under different conditions.

     2. *Refining:* Acquisition of smooth, efficient control in performing a movement pattern or skill by mastery of spatial and temporal relations. This process deals with the achievement of precision in motor performance and habituation of performance under more complex conditions.

   C. *Creative Movement:* Those motor performances that include the processes of inventing or creating movement that will serve the personal (individual) purposes of the learner. The processes employed are directed toward discovery, integration, abstraction, idealization, emotional objectification and composition.

     1. *Varying:* Invention or construction of personally unique options in motor performance. These options are limited to different ways of performing specific movement; they are of an immediate situational nature and lack any predetermined movement behavior that has been externally imposed on the mover.

     2. *Improvising:* Extemporaneous originations or initiation of personally novel movement or combination of movement. The processes involved may be stimulated by a situation externally structured, although conscious planning on the part of the performer is not usually required.

     3. *Composing:* Combination of learned movements in personally unique motor designs or the invention of movement patterns new to the performer. The performer creates a motor response in terms of a personal interpretation of the movement situation.*

This taxonomy is structured in terms of purposes and processes. The *purpose concepts* describe the functions of movement in achieving human goals and thus define the scope of the physical education curriculum. The *processes* by which one learns to move must also be an integral part of curricular planning. The purpose-process conceptual framework promotes an action-oriented system focusing on the individual learning to move. Movement processes represent one large category of human behavior. Process learnings are, therefore, essential curricular outcomes. Sequence in physical education can best be facilitated if a teacher organizes curricular content in terms of a hierarchy of movement-learning process outcomes. This classification scheme conceptualizes a hierarchy of movement-learning processes and offers a taxonomy for the selection and statement of educational objectives in the motor

---

*Ann E. Jewett and Marie R. Mullan, *Curriculum Design: Purposes and Processes in Physical Education Teaching-Learning* (Washington, D.C.: American Alliance for Health, Physical Education and Recreation, 1977), pp. 9–10. Reprinted by permission of AAHPER, Washington, D.C.

domain, which is applicable to any curricular area dealing with physical movement. But a serious question must be raised: "Does the psychomotor domain operate in a linear manner as the sequencing of skills implies?" The solutions to that question we leave to you.

Summary

The functions of the psychomotor domain relate to human movement, and the classification outlines just given analyze instructional objectives through a hierarchy of tasks. Also, learning objectives can be applied in those areas of instruction that make use of the domain. Those areas include mathematics (spatial analysis), home and family living, fine arts, vocational-technical education, science, business, and occupations. Think of how you could use this taxonomy in your own discipline.

FORMATIVE EVALUATION *Psychomotor Domain*

_____ 1. True/False. The psychomotor domain is only for physical education majors.

_____ 2. In which of the following areas would the psychomotor domain *not* be used?
(a) Music
(b) Art
(c) Home economics
(d) All of the above involve psychomotor learning

_____ 3. Categorize the following performance objectives as cognitive (C), affective (A), or psychomotor (PS).

_____ (a) In an unsupervised setting, third grade students will obey traffic rules on foot, on bicycle, or on another conveyance at intersections and elsewhere.

_____ (b) Given a caliper graduated to millimeters, the student will measure objects to within one millimeter of a standard set by the instructor.

_____ (c) On a timed five-minute test, type at least thirty-five words per minute with a maximum of five errors of any kind.

_____ (d) In a game of Pickleball, players will abide by the decisions of the official. Disputing any call is unacceptable behavior.

_____ (e) Given the text and class notes, construct a proof for the commutative property of real numbers. The proof must be mathematically testable.

_____ 4. Which psychomotor taxonomy is most concerned with the input aspects of movement?

_____ 5. Where is creativity provided for in each of the taxonomies?

RESPONSES

1. False. Psychomotor components exist in virtually all subject matter areas.
2. (d). There are psychomotor components in all these areas. For example, music students use psychomotor skills in learning how to play an instrument; art and home economics students also use psychomotor skills in manipulative aspects of their subjects.
3. (a) (A) Affective (the key here is the phrase, "in an unsupervised setting").
   (b) (PS) Psychomotor
   (c) (PS) Psychomotor
   (d) (A) Affective
   (e) (C) Cognitive
4. Moore's taxonomy of the *perceptual domain* places the most emphasis on incoming stimuli.
5. All three of the taxonomies place creative behavior at the highest level. In Moore's taxonomy, the final level, *perceptive performance*, stresses interpreting and adapting a complex phenomenon, such as a musical piece. Harrow's taxonomy stresses creativity in the sixth level, *nondiscursive communication*, and Jewett and Mullan's taxonomy does this at the third level, *creative movement*.

CONCLUSIONS

This chapter presented three discrete taxonomies that describe cognitive, affective, and psychomotor goals in the schools. We describe these taxonomies as analytical tools that teachers can use purposefully to help them understand more clearly what their objectives are and to help them make their teaching more effective. These taxonomies are treated as separate entities, but interconnections among the three domains are numerous; very seldom do we think without feeling, and action on the part of the learner is a major component of all learning.

Most of the chapter was consciously devoted to the cognitive domain because the major thrust of our schools is in the development of cognitive skills and abilities. We describe this taxonomy as a hierarchical classification system in which students first know about a topic and then become increasingly familiar with the topic through a series of progressively complex mental operations. These operations, or levels of the taxonomy, require the learner to understand the topic, then to use it in solving problems, in analyzing ideas, in creating new ideas, and in evaluating other ideas. Each of these steps is sequential, with subsequent steps building on previous ones. Because of this, the taxonomy has proved to be a valuable tool for sequencing instruction and for determining the base of difficulty.

The second area of the curriculum discussed is the affective domain, which deals with feelings, emotions, attitudes, and values. Like the cognitive domain, the affective domain also contains a series of sequential levels in which objectives or student behavior can be categorized. The organizing principle for this domain, however, is one of internalization, or the degree to which feelings and attitudes are integrated into the individual's personality and lifestyle. At the lowest level of this taxonomy, the individual is merely open to messages from other people. Then the person willingly responds to those messages, values them, integrates them into his or her own value structure, and finally leads life according to these ideas. Like that of the cognitive domain, the taxonomy of the affective domain can be used to analyze educational objectives and to order these objectives in a learning sequence.

The final taxonomies discussed concern the psychomotor domain. We described this area of the curriculum as being broader in scope than just physical education skills and as including coordinated manipulative movements in a number of disciplines. Like the other two, the psychomotor domain is organized along a sequential continuum—in this case, organizational complexity—with lower behaviors involving simpler movements and higher behaviors requiring more complex and integrated movements.

Although our presentation is admittedly limited, you have at least been introduced to the three interrelated taxonomies; in the case of the cognitive domain, you will have acquired more than a superficial understanding of the topic. While not perfect, each taxonomy can contribute to your understanding of what you teach, the possible components that can be included, and the more creative means by which to structure both learning activities and evaluative tasks. We urge you to use these three taxonomies as you analyze the work that you receive in higher education. Finally, ask yourself this question: "How could my classes be made better through the application of the principles and concepts presented in the taxonomies?" If you can become more systematic, analytical, and evaluative, then we have attained one of our goals.

We assume that if taxonomies were applied to their optimal use, there would be far more cognitive success in the schools of the world, students would be more serious about their studies and would enjoy them more, and physical education would be supported for its own sake rather than be considered merely an adjunct of athletics. As we state in Chapter 1, our aim is to provide you with a better understanding of the decisions that are made by great teachers. By understanding the potentials of the taxonomies, you will be adding one more tool to your "bag of professional skills."

REFERENCES

Anderson, Lorin, and Jo Anderson. "Affective Assessment Is Necessary and Possible." *Educational Leadership* 39:1982, 524–525.

Arons, Arnold B. "What Current Research in Teaching and Learning Says to the Practicing Teacher." Robert Karplus Lecture. National Science Teacher Association, National Convention, St. Louis, April 9, 1988.

Bailey, Donald, and Judith Leonard. "A Model for Adapting Bloom's Taxonomy to a Pre-School

Curriculum for the Gifted." *Gifted Child Quarterly* 21:1977, 97–103.

Beyer, Barry K. "Improving Thinking Skills: Practical Approaches." *Phi Delta Kappan* 65:1984, 556–560.

Bloom, Benjamin S., Max D. Engelhart, Edward J. Furst, Walker H. Hill, and David R. Krathwohl. *Taxonomy of Educational Objectives. The Classification of Educational Goals. Handbook I: Cognitive Domain.* New York: David McKay, 1956.

Cazden, Courtney B. "Classroom Discourse." In *Handbook of Research on Teaching,* 3rd ed. Merlin Wittrock, ed. New York: Macmillan, 1986, pp. 432–463.

Chall, Jean. *Stages of Reading Development.* New York: McGraw-Hill, 1983.

Clevenstine, Richard. "A Classification of the ISIS Program Using Bloom's Cognitive Taxonomy." *Journal of Research in Science Teaching* 24:1987, 699–712.

Costa, Arthur, ed. *Developing Minds.* Alexandria, Va.: ASCD, 1985.

Craik, Fergus I. M. "Human Memory." *Annual Review of Psychology* 30:1979, 63–102.

Crooks, Terence J. "The Impact of Classroom Evaluation Practices on Students." *Review of Educational Research* 58(4): Winter, 1988, 438–481.

Davis, O. L., Jr., and Francis P. Hunkins. "Textbook Questions: What Thinking Processes Do They Foster?" *Peabody Journal of Education* 43:1966, 285–292.

Doyle, Walter. "Academic Work." *Review of Educational Research* 53:1983, 159–199.

Ennis, Robert H. "Critical Thinking and the Curriculum." *National Forum* 45:1985, 28–31. (a)

———. "A Logical Basis for Measuring Critical Thinking Skills." *Educational Leadership* 43: 1985, 44–48. (b)

Feldhusen, John, Russel Ames, and Katheryn Linden. "Designing Instruction to Achieve Higher Level Goals and Objectives." *Educational Technology* 14:1974, 21–23.

Freeman, Donald, Theresa Kuhs, Andrew Porter, Robert Floden, William Schmidt, and John Schwille. "Do Textbooks and Tests Define a National Curriculum in Elementary School Mathematics?" *Elementary School Journal* 83:1983, 501–513.

Furst, Edward. "Bloom's Taxonomy of Educational Objectives for the Cognitive Domain: Philosophical and Educational Issues." *Review of Educational Research* 51:1981, 441–443.

Gall, Meredith. "Synthesis of Research on Teachers' Questioning." *Educational Leadership* 42: November 1984, 40–47.

Good, Thomas J., and Douglas A. Grouws. "Increasing Teachers' Understanding of Mathematical Ideas Through Inservice Training." *Phi Delta Kappan* 68:1987, 778–783.

Goodlad, John I. *A Place Called School.* New York: McGraw-Hill, 1984.

Gronlund, Norman. *Measurement and Evaluation in Teaching,* 5th ed. New York: Macmillan, 1985.

Haller, Eileen P., David A. Child, and Herbert J. Walberg. "Can Comprehension Be Taught? A Quantitative Synthesis of 'Metacognitive' Studies." *Educational Researcher* 17(9):1988, 5–8.

Halpain, Dale, John Glover, and Anne Harvey. "Differential Effects of Higher and Lower Order Questions: Attention Hypotheses." *Journal of Educational Psychology* 54:1985, 702–715.

Harrow, Anita J. *A Taxonomy of the Psychomotor Domain: A Guide for Developing Behavior Objectives.* New York: David McKay, 1972.

Hellison, Diane. "The Affective Domain in Physical Education: Let's Do Some House Cleaning." *Journal of Physical Education, Recreation and Dance* 58:1987, 41–43.

Hughes, Abby L., and Karen Frommer. "A System for Monitoring Affective Objectives." *Educational Leadership* 39:1982, 521–523.

Jewett, Ann E., and Marie R. Mullan. "Movement Process Categories in Physical Education in Teaching-Learning." In *Curriculum Design: Purposes and Processes in Physical Education Teaching-Learning.* Washington, D.C.: American Alliance for Health, Physical Education and Recreation, 1977.

Jones, Beau Fly. "Quality and Equality Through Cognitive Instruction." *Educational Leadership* 43:1986, 4–11.

Krathwohl, David R., Benjamin S. Bloom, and Bertran B. Masia. *Taxonomy of Educational Objectives. The Classification of Educational Goals. Handbook II: Affective Domain.* New York: David McKay, 1964.

Kunen, Seth, Ronald Cohen, and Robert Solman. "A Levels-of-Processing Analysis of Bloom's Taxonomy." *Journal of Educational Psychology* 73:1981, 202–211.

McAlpine, Jim, Sue Jeweler, Betty Weincek, and Marion Findbinder. "Creative Problem Solving and Bloom: The Thinking Connection." *Gifted Child Today* 10:1987, 11–14.

McDaniel, Thomas. "Designing Essay Questions for Different Levels of Learning." *Improving College and University Teaching* 27:1979, 120–123.

McPeck, John E. *Critical Thinking and Education.* New York: St. Martin's Press, 1981.

Madaus, George F., Elinor M. Woods, and R. Nuttal. "A Causal Model Analysis of Bloom's Taxonomy." *American Educational Research Journal* 10:1973, 253–262.

Mager, Robert F. *Developing Attitude Toward Learning.* Palo Alto, Calif.: Fearon, 1968.

Metzger, W. "A Spectre Haunts American Scholars: The Spectre of Professionalism." *Educational Researcher* 16:1987, 10–18.

Moore, Maxine R. "Consideration of the Perceptual Process in the Evaluation of Musical Performance." *Journal of Research in Music Education* 20:1972, 273–279.

———. "The Perceptual Motor Domain and a Proposed Taxonomy of Perception." *A.V. Communication Review* 18:1970, 379–413.

———. "A Proposed Taxonomy of the Perceptual Domain and Some Suggested Applications" (Test Development Report 67-3). Princeton, N.J.: Educational Testing Service, 1967.

Nelson, Gerald. "A Proposed Taxonomy of Student Assessment Techniques in the Cognitive Domain." *Educational Technology* 18:1978, 24–26.

Nickerson, Raymond. "Understanding Understanding." *American Journal of Education* 93:1985, 201–239.

Paul, Richard. "Bloom's Taxonomy and Critical Thinking Instruction." *Educational Leadership* 42(8):1985, 36–39.

Posner, George, and Alan N. Rudnitsky. *Course Design,* 3rd ed. New York: Longman, 1986.

Pratton, Jerry, and Loyde W. Hales. "The Effects of Active Participation on Student Learning." *Journal of Educational Research* 79:1986, 210–215.

Redfield, Doris, and Elaine Rousseau. "Meta-Analysis of Experimental Research on Teachers' Questioning Behavior." *Review of Educational Research* 51:1981, 237–245.

Rosenshine, Barak, and Robert Stevens. "Teaching Functions." In *Handbook of Research on Teaching,* 3rd ed. Merlin Wittrock, ed. New York: Macmillan, 1986, 376–391.

Seddon, G. Malcolm. "The Properties of Bloom's Taxonomy of Educational Objectives for the Cognitive Domain." *Review of Educational Research* 48:1978, 303–323.

Shuell, Thomas J. "Cognitive Conceptions of Learning." *Review of Educational Research* 56:1986, 411–436.

Smith, Lyle. "The Effect of Lesson Structure and Cognitive Level of Questions on Student Achievement." *Journal of Experimental Education* 54:1985, 44–49.

Tanner, David. "Achievement As a Function of Abstractness and Cognitive Level." *Journal of Research and Development in Education* 21:1988, 16–21.

Tennyson, Robert O., and Martin J. Cocchiarella. "An Empirically Based Instructional Design Theory for Teaching Concepts." *Review of Educational Research* 56:1986, 40–71.

Trachtenberg, David. "Student Tasks in Text Materials: What Cognitive Skills Do They Tap?" *Peabody Journal of Education* 52:1974, 54–57.

Whimbey, Arthur. "The Key to Higher Order Thinking Is Precise Processing." *Educational Leadership* 42:1984, 66–70.

Wittrock, Merlin. "Students' Thought Processes." In *Handbook of Research on Teaching,* 3rd ed. Merlin Wittrock, Ed. New York: Macmillan, 1986, pp. 297–314.

Wolfe, Drew, and Henry Heikkinen. "An Analysis of the Construct Validity of a Test of Higher Cognitive Learning in Introductory Chemistry." *Journal of Research in Science Teaching* 16:1979, 25–31.

Woolfolk, Anita E. *Educational Psychology,* 3rd ed. Englewood Cliffs, N.J.: Prentice-Hall, 1987.

5

Decisions About Lesson Planning

*T*ime—we have only so much of it. Master teachers cannot create a single extra second in the day—any more than their less effective counterparts can. But master teachers do *control* time by systematically and carefully planning its productive use for instruction.

One of your primary roles as a teacher is that of designer and implementor of instruction. Teachers at every level prepare plans that aid in the organization and delivery of their daily lessons. These plans vary widely in their style and degree of specificity. Some instructors prefer to construct elaborately detailed and impeccably typed outlines; others rely on the briefest of notes handwritten on scratchpads or on the backs of discarded envelopes. Regardless of the format, all teachers need to make wise decisions about the strategies and methods they will employ to help students move systematically toward learner goals.

Teachers need more than a vague, or even a precise, notion of educational goals and objectives to be able to sequence these objectives or to be proficient in the skills and knowledge of a particular discipline. As an effective teacher you will also need to develop a plan to provide *direction* toward attaining the selected objectives. Numerous studies on the characteristics of competent teachers show that being well organized correlates highly with instructor effectiveness.

To aid you in deciding how to organize your lessons, we now introduce the topic of planning for your consideration. The principal goal of this chapter is to enable you to be effective and systematic in planning. To do so, you must become aware of the decision areas and techniques of lesson preparation.*

Objectives   After completing this chapter, you should be able to:

- Identify the major elements of lesson planning, including prelesson, lesson implementation, and postlesson activities
- Provide formats for designing lesson plans
- Illustrate the Madeline Hunter model of lesson design
- Illustrate how to plan for direct instruction
- Give examples of planning with the Kaplan Matrix
- Introduce the concept of micro-teaching as a means of applying lesson-planning concepts
- Consider the many ways that the microcomputer can be used as a tool for lesson preparation and lesson delivery

LESSON-PLANNING PROCEDURES

First, we would like to introduce you to the concept of lesson planning and to present a format that many successful practitioners have used. We will discuss a general model of lesson planning in much the same way that an architect might present the

---

*We thank Connie Kravas for her contributions to this chapter.

basic design and functions for a new building. When architects first enter their profession, they tend to follow closely the recommendations of authorities. But, once they experience success in the process, they make personal adaptations to suit their talents.

Similarly, as a classroom teacher, you will probably begin by imitating a favorite teacher; later, after study and experience, you will expand the acquired "basics" for lesson preparation and delivery. Classroom innovations usually come once you are in the classroom with your own set of learners, have developed your own instructional resources, and have experimented with various strategies. Although fundamental lesson-planning elements tend to remain stable, their basic formula is always modified to suit the individual teacher's lesson preparations or style of presentation.

Figure 5-1 graphically illustrates a general planning cycle. The model contains three primary stages, each with several interrelated steps. These stages refer to your major prelesson, lesson, and postlesson activities in designing, implementing, and evaluating your daily plan.

Note that the main object of lesson planning is that all activities and processes provide an educative environment for the learner. Teachers sometimes forget about the learner and become more interested in their respective disciplines. If lesson planning is to be a useful task, it must always focus on the *interaction* between what is to be learned and the learner.

As shown in Figure 5-1, lesson planning involves much more than making arbitrary decisions about "what I'm going to teach today." Many activities precede the process of designing and implementing a lesson plan. Similarly, the job of systematic lesson planning is not complete until after the instructor has assessed both the learner's attainment of the anticipated outcomes and the effectiveness of the lesson in leading learners to these outcomes.

Before discussing each element of lesson planning, we must add one more caveat. Although there is a logical distinction between various lesson-planning stages, in reality these different activities are *not linear*. Even teachers who develop highly structured and detailed plans rarely adhere to them in lock-step fashion. Indeed, such rigidity would probably hinder, rather than help, the teaching-learning process. The lesson-planning elements described in this chapter should be thought of as *guiding principles* to be applied as aids, but not blueprints, to systematic instruction. Your precise preparation must allow for flexible delivery. During the actual classroom interaction, you need to make adaptations and to add artistry to each day's plan. For these reasons, Figure 5-1 depicts the process of lesson planning as being cyclical.

PRELESSON PREPARATION

Before you can construct a lesson plan, there are at least four major considerations to take into account. These include (1) information about the major *goals* that are to be pursued through the programs of the school, (2) the *content* to be included in your course, (3) the *entry level* of your students, and (4) *activities* to be used in attaining

Figure 5-1   *The Lesson-Planning Cycle*

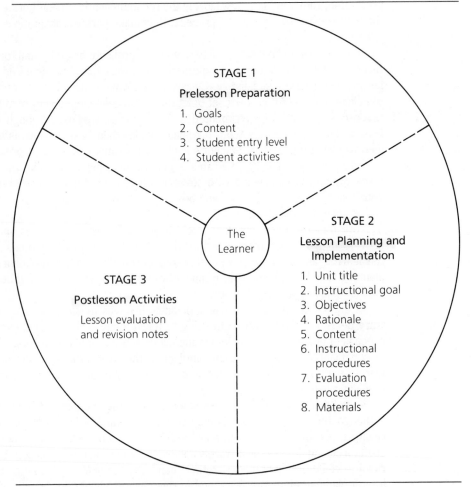

STAGE 1

Prelesson Preparation

1. Goals
2. Content
3. Student entry level
4. Student activities

The Learner

STAGE 2

Lesson Planning and Implementation

1. Unit title
2. Instructional goal
3. Objectives
4. Rationale
5. Content
6. Instructional procedures
7. Evaluation procedures
8. Materials

STAGE 3

Postlesson Activities

Lesson evaluation and revision notes

the goals. Although in actuality these considerations are interdependent, we separate them for the purpose of illustration.

Goals

Within the pages of *Alice's Adventures in Wonderland* by Lewis Carroll, there is a memorable exchange in which Alice, not knowing which road to take, asks the Cheshire Cat for directions. Their subsequent conversation goes like this:

"Would you tell me, please, which way I ought to go from here?"
"That depends a good deal on where you want to get to," said the Cat.
"I don't much care where—" said Alice.
"Then it doesn't matter which way you go."

In contrast to Alice's situation, decisions about destinations and about how to reach them are critical to educators as they plan their courses and lessons. For the teacher or school administrator, the starting point of curriculum planning is usually to identify broad educational goals.

A *goal* describes the major, culminating outcome that results from the educational process. It is more abstract, more visionary, than an objective. A goal is something toward which to work—a guiding star, so to speak. It gives us that affective quality of commitment.

Whereas goal statements are effective in suggesting certain types of content and actions for the school to include in the curriculum, they are too general for organizing the daily activities of teachers and students. General goals must be translated into progressively specific outcomes as you plan for daily lessons. The sources of educational goals are many. As a new teacher, you may find some, perhaps all, of the following resources helpful.

State, District, and School Goals

Most states, districts, and schools have developed written statements of general educational goals—outcomes that are to be sought for *all* learners. The *process* of developing goal statements is often as critical as the *content* of the goals. Selected goals are accepted widely only if they are formulated by representatives of the many different groups who have a vested interest in them—teachers, administrators, students, parents, and other citizens of the community.

Whether formulated by a national curriculum commission, a state board of education, or a group of local citizens and teachers, goals are usually long-range and inclusive. Note, for example, the comprehensive nature of the following goal statement written in 1983 in the form of a recommendation developed by the Committee on Educational Policies Structure and Management of the State of Washington (1983).

> It is recommended that the core curriculum ensure that *all* high school students pursue a common core curriculum designed to assure graduation with effective communication (written and oral) and thinking and reasoning skills; study in the arts (appreciation or performance); knowledge of American civilization and government; comprehension in at least one language other than English; computation skills and the ability to use computers; understanding of geography, economics, and history; job acquisition and retention skills; and the capability to assume future roles as parents, consumers and home managers. Students with special educational needs should share in this core to the extent of their abilities.

Curriculum Guides and Courses of Study

District and school-level goals are often converted into more concrete goals at the program and course level—social studies, physical education, language arts—and presented in documents known as curriculum guides. As the term *guide* implies, these manuals provide the framework within which you, as a teacher, can organize your course outlines, units, and lessons.

Guides spell out, in greater detail than goals do, the types of competencies students are expected to attain in a course of study. They may or may not include specific student objectives and learning activities. The content of curriculum guides is usually developed by a group of local teachers after careful consideration of the various subject-matter elements and their relation to the abilities and needs of those who will receive the instruction. Most districts have guides available for each main component of the school's curriculum. The guides that have been developed for the subject you teach will help you, as a new teacher, in identifying the major content and learning experiences to which students have been exposed in previous years. They will also suggest topics that are recommended for learners at your particular grade level.

Needs-Assessment Information

Increasingly, school districts are developing new programs and revising current ones based on needs-assessment information. The purposes of such data collections are twofold: (1) to identify the goals of the district; and (2) to determine how well these goals are being met. A discrepancy between what is viewed as ideal (a goal) and what is seen as the present status (the actual condition) is defined as a *need* that should be addressed through curricular or instructional changes.

Clearly, identifying goals is a critical part of all curriculum planning. One of your tasks as a teacher will be to select from various sources those goals that will provide focus for your course-planning endeavors. Because of the ages and abilities of your particular students, you will want to design lessons that, in an incremental way, assist the students in approaching the selected goals.

At this point you may begin to realize that there is definitely more to planning a lesson than just assigning the odd-numbered problems for the next day and the even-numbered ones for the day after. This is why teaching is such a demanding profession. Once the goal question is resolved, you must determine what it is that will be taught.

Course Content

Decisions about course content—that is, what subject matter to include and how much material to cover in a course, a unit, or a lesson—are, initially, among the most difficult facing the beginning teacher. They demand that the teacher have a strong command of the discipline and the ability to analyze it carefully to isolate those concepts, principles, rules, and facts that are most significant.

A lesson plan will help a teacher articulate clearly stated ideas, activities, and assignments. Jere Brophy and Thomas L. Good (1986) reported that *clarity* was a critical element for effective instruction. Ellen Gagné (1985) observed that teacher vagueness and lack of clarity had a negative effect on student achievement. Thus, for many of you, the lesson plan will be your guide to clear verbal or written communication in the classroom.

Several sources of information may be helpful in making these significant choices about content. Two of these sources are experts in the field and local curriculum developers.

Expert Opinion

For each content area taught in our schools, subject-matter specialists have suggested key questions that should be raised and critical concepts that should be learned. Publishers frequently rely on the opinions of content experts to develop textbooks, which in turn establish a "tradition of content" that is typically included in a particular field of study. Although the exclusive use of textbooks for selecting subject matter has certain limitations, it is presently one of the more influential determiners of content.

Curriculum Study Teams

Many schools have content-based curriculum study teams composed of teachers who work together to develop general outlines and materials for one or several areas of study. In a more informal way, your colleagues—particularly those who majored in a particular content area at the college level—may prove to be invaluable resources as you begin the process of developng your courses.

Student Entry Level

At the same time that you are selecting major course goals and choosing content in relation to these goals, you must accomplish another prelesson planning task: identifying student entry levels. This activity requires you to find out what students already know about the content, to determine whether there is a need for instruction in the particular area, and to assess whether students are at a state of readiness to receive the instruction. It is not an overstatement to say that at *every* step of the planning process, it is imperative to consider your audience, the students. What they already have learned, the degree to which they have retained the learning, their motivations, their abilities, their social and cultural backgrounds, and their academic achievements are all crucial data. Such information takes on special significance as teachers prepare to mainstream handicapped children into their classrooms. Often, the teacher who is aware of special student disabilities can adapt the physical environment and the instructional strategies employed for daily lessons in ways to accommodate unique learner needs. (Review PL 94-142 in Chapter 2.)

The function of the student entry level as a prerequisite for planning is demonstrated in Figure 5-2, which shows the major components of the instructional process

Figure 5-2   *Major Components of the Instructional Process Cycle*

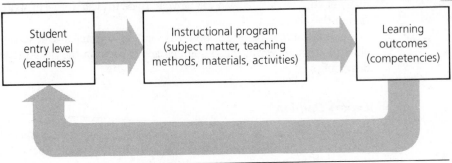

cycle. Note the direct relationship between the entry level and the subsequent learning experiences provided and the learning outcomes attained. You should also recognize that this process, like that of lesson planning, is a never-ending cyclical one.

How do you obtain all this information about the students, especially when you may not meet them until the day after school begins in the fall? One technique is to set up a series of conferences with the principal, school counselor, and vice-principal (if the school has one). Inquire about the general kinds of problems that the students have had in your particular grade level or specialization. Ask to examine any class composites on either school-district-sponsored or nationally administered achievement tests.

One critical fact to know is the students' reading achievement levels. If your potential students are two or three years below their grade level in reading, you will have to secure materials that they can comprehend. You may even have to prepare taped cassettes so that students with special reading problems can listen to, and follow, the written assignments.

In short, when you are assigned five or six different classes or preparations per day, you will not have much time to determine student entry levels. (At the start, you may even rely on intuition until you can make more accurate observations.) Perhaps one final method is to ask your colleagues for appropriate advice.

In a very general way, identifying student entry level is done by assigning groups of students to specific instructional units and courses and then monitoring their progress closely as they complete the material in a particular sequence. On a more specific level, it is much more difficult to determine the entering level of students because the entry level is influenced by numerous interacting factors. However the assessment is accomplished, it is important for you to determine that students have the requisite knowledge, skills, and attitudes necessary to address the lesson's goals. In determining the entry level, ask yourself, "For which concepts and generalizations do my students have the requisite knowledge, skills, and attitudes?"

Student Activities

Deborah Sardo Brown (1988) reported that middle school teachers tended to make lesson decisions that focused on student activities. Obviously, activities must relate to the unit's goals or performance objectives (if specified). (We have implied the need for student activities throughout.) The activity is the *hands-on* or *experiential* component of a lesson. Activities can be—to list but a few—worksheets to complete, assignments to finish, projects to create, or student-led discussions. Not only is the activity the usual way for students to attain comprehension or application, it also provides the teacher with a means to monitor student achievement and to make any necessary changes to accommodate individual differences.

In summary, the preliminary preparation stage plays a vital role in teacher decision-making. The choice of a particular lesson, the content selected, and the methodologies used are determined by the knowledge of broader *goals,* by the *subject matter,* by the entry level of the *learners,* and by *activities* to be done. The lesson, in essence, represents the daily implementation of the teacher's interpretation of these important interacting elements.

LESSON PLANNING AND IMPLEMENTATION

Although there is no one best way to develop and present a lesson plan, the format presented here should help you meet the requirements for nearly all instructional activities. You may follow the format or amend it to suit your individual needs as you become proficient in lesson planning. A sketch of the recommended format is provided in Figure 5-3. An explanation of the various components of the format and an example of a completed plan are also provided in the following sections.

Lesson-Planning Elements

Section 1. Unit

As we discussed in the preceding text, daily lesson plans do not spring out of thin air. Rather, they relate to, and originate from, the broader goals and culminating experiences that are planned for the students. These major synthesizing goals are achieved by learners as a result of completing various *units* of study. Thus, the purpose of the first section of the lesson plan is to identify, in a sentence or two, the larger unit of instruction of which the particular lesson will be a part and in the context of which the lesson will be taught.

Figure 5-3   *A Model Lesson Plan Format*

Teacher _____

Course Title _____

1. Unit _____

2. Instructional goal _____

3. Performance objectives _____

4. Rationale _____

5. Content	6. Instructional procedures
	(a) Focusing event (b) Teaching procedures (c) Formative check (d) Student participation (e) Closure

7. Evaluation procedures _____

8. Materials and aids _____

9. Notes/File comments _____

Section 2. Instructional Goal or Unit Objective

An instructional goal is an outcome that students should achieve on completing the total unit of instruction. For example:

1. The goal of this unit is to present a variety of musical rhythmic features.
2. The goal of this unit is to write short themes in the past tense.

An *instructional goal* gives focus and direction to the lesson. The *performance objectives* that you write represent the more specific subskills or behaviors that students require to demonstrate attainment of the broader instructional goal. Whereas behavioral objectives specify measurable student outcomes, *an instructional goal usually is general and is stated in nonperformance terms.* Thus, although it is inappropriate to use verbs such as *know, value,* and *understand* in stating performance objectives, these words are not only acceptable *but even preferable* at the instructional goal level of planning, where they provide overall guidance and organization to the instructional process.

The instructional goal or unit objective will *not* be reached at the end of a single lesson. It represents an organizing element from which to develop as few as one, or as many as a dozen or more, specific performance objectives. Thus, attaining the instructional goal may take from a few minutes to several days—even weeks—

depending on the complexity of the topic and the type of learner change that is sought.

Section 3. Performance Objectives

Once you have selected your instructional goal, the next step is to identify the subordinate skills that your students must learn in order to achieve the goal. This process results in the identifying concepts, rules, and information that each student will need, along with the sequence of behavioral objectives that must be attained before mastering the overall goal.

Each lesson that you prepare should include one or more performance objectives, each consisting of one element of knowledge or skill that forms part of the broader instructional goal or unit objective. Performance objectives describe specifically what the student will be able to *do* as a consequence of the lesson. (Chapter 2 discusses performance objectives in detail.)

Beginning teachers frequently ask, "How many objectives should be included in a single plan?" Because there are so many variables in the instructional process— different outcomes, learners, teachers, and conditions—it is impossible to respond to this question by specifying any set number. In general, the average secondary student can grasp only two or three major ideas (and often only one) within a class period of forty-five to fifty minutes. On the average, therefore, the daily lesson plan for secondary classes should contain no more than two or three performance objectives. Lessons prepared for younger students should be even shorter, ranging from fifteen to twenty minutes, and should focus on attaining perhaps a single performance objective.

To assist students in achieving maximum performance, you need to have specific objectives, to present a challenge, and to be "close at hand." Objectives that are perceived by the students as somewhat difficult do result in higher task achievement than those that are viewed as too easy, provided that the challenge is within reach and objectives that are close at hand can be attained within a reasonable time period. Merlin C. Wittrock (1986) reported that motivation is appreciably strengthened when the student perceives that the objective is within reach rather than distant. Finally, the inclusion of explicit performance objectives in a lesson plan should never inhibit you from capitalizing on these unexpected, serendipitous learning opportunities during lesson implementation.

During the instructional implementation stage itself, you will need to monitor student understanding and progress continuously, so that you do not forge ahead to the next objective before the student has mastered related subordinate skills. Such diagnostic activities serve the added purpose of preventing unnecessary duplication of instruction, which should be avoided because it fosters student boredom (unless, of course, the repetition is being used intentionally and sparingly to reinforce earlier learning).

Not all objectives need to be organized and presented in hierarchical fashion. In addition to *dependent* sequences, some learning outcomes can be arranged in *inde-*

pendent patterns. To use the analogy of the construction of a building, although it is imperative to lay the floor of a house before raising its walls, it is not necessary to wait until the entire house has been completed before constructing the garage. In fact, it makes little difference whether the garage is built before, during, or after the construction of the main house, so long as the overall blueprint is kept in mind. Similarly, departures from the objectives are acceptable, so long as the instructional goals and course outlines are considered.

Section 4. Rationale

A statement of rationale or purpose provides a brief justification of why you feel your students should learn what you are teaching. In preparing this section of your lesson plan, imagine a visitor to your classroom asking, "Why are you teaching this at this time?" The rationale would be your response.

One of the best reasons for including a rationale in your formal planning activities is that it helps clarify the intent of the lesson for *you,* the teacher. The rationale will prompt you to think about both content and goals, separating the most significant aspects of subject matter from the ephemeral, and the most important learner objectives from the trivial. In turn, you will be more likely to communicate this sense of purpose to your students. When instructors know not only *what* they are trying to accomplish, but also *why* they are attempting to accomplish it, they are more likely to teach with enthusiasm and purpose, to stay on task, and to avoid tangents that confuse their learners.

Section 5. Content

The content section of the lesson plan provides an outline or a description of *what* is to be taught. At the minimum, it should include a "key word" checklist of the material to be presented, arranged in the order that you intend to teach it.

An important question at this juncture of the planning process is, "What is the most appropriate sequence to use in presenting the subject-matter content to my students?" Fortunately, you will have conducted a task analysis to determine the subskills and knowledge that your students must learn prior to reaching a particular unit objective or instructional goal. You will be able to answer this question without too much additional effort. The hierarchical analysis will tell you what entry behaviors are required before students can progress toward the intended outcomes. The analysis will also tell you which lower-level skills must precede higher-level ones and the order in which these subskills should be learned. (You may want to review Chapters 3 and 4 concerning this section.)

Section 6. Instructional Procedures

Whereas in the content section of the lesson plan the teacher lists *what* is to be taught, in the instructional procedures column the teacher states *how* it will be taught. Based on information provided in the five previous sections of the plan, the teacher identifies the strategies that will be most effective in leading students toward attaining each of the performance objectives.

Although for any one objective there are probably numerous procedures that teachers could employ, current research and knowledge about learning suggest that five major components should be included in a lesson to maximize student opportunity for learning. The five major elements of an effective instructional procedure on which we will elaborate are as follows:

1. Focusing event
2. Teaching procedures
3. Formative check
4. Student participation
5. Closure

Focusing Event

A memorable lesson usually starts with a memorable beginning. All teachers have just a bit of Shakespeare in their blood. Every one of us has a touch of the dramatic, a flair for the unusual, a mad dream to "put on one they won't forget." It is with these theatrical notions that the stage for learning experiences is set. If you fail to capture the interests and imaginations of the students, you have wasted the remainder of the lesson. Irrespective of how significant the subject matter may seem to the instructor or of how capable the students are, if their interests are not stimulated early during the instructional sequence, they will not be motivated to develop an understanding of the content.

The main purposes of the focusing event are to provide *lesson orientation* and *learner motivation*. When presented effectively and creatively, the focusing event makes subsequent learning more efficient because students are prepared to engage actively in the lesson. A motivated learner acquires new knowledge and skills more readily than one who is not motivated. A student's desire to learn can be a mighty force in the instructional process. You need to capitalize on this powerful learning variable as you commence each day's activities.

A focusing event can take many forms: a clever story common to the students' experience, a humorous anecdote, an analogy that relates to the main concept of the lesson, a puzzling experiment or confusing situation, and even a "touch of magic" that encourages students to ask questions. It is important to remember, however, that the focusing event is not an end in itself. Use it as a building block to influence positively the way your students approach the lesson. If you choose a joke for the focusing event, make sure it relates clearly to the content of the lesson; do not introduce it at the start of the class period simply to relax or to entertain the students. Although a joke can serve effectively as a rapport builder (and rapport is certainly a very important element of teacher-learner interaction), when used as a focusing event, it should serve the additional function of readying the students for the lesson ahead. The two examples following illustrate the use of the focusing event as a lesson "booster."

Imagine you are a student in a sixth grade class; your teacher enters and says:

"Let me read you a story from today's sports page. 'Darryl Strawberry went to bat eight times in yesterday's double-header. He was walked twice, struck out once, flied out in deep center field once, doubled twice, tripled once, and hit a ninth inning grand slam home run in the second game.'"

At this point, a little boy in the back of the room raises his hand and says, "All right!"

The teacher responds, "All right!" Then the teacher states, "Class, we are going to work on fractions today. But first let's figure out what kind of fractions we can find from Darryl Strawberry's games for yesterday."

In the preceding example, the mood or climate was established quickly by a focusing event that was relevant to the purpose of the lesson—learning about fractions. Let us look at one more example.* This time you are a student in a tenth grade class; your teacher begins the lesson by saying:

"This week we have been studying Southwest history and I have been thinking that there is one area that it would be fun to know a great deal more about. I would like to find out the origin of the names of the towns in our own state of Texas. For example, how many of you know where the name Austin came from?

"Can you tell me why they named Austin Austin? . . . John.

"Can you add anything? . . . Sue.

"It's intriguing to know why towns were given their names, and today we are going to learn a great deal more about the names of towns. At the end of class today, each of you will demonstrate the ability to do research on the names of towns by sharing the origin of the names of two towns with the rest of the class and telling us where you found this information."

The way you present the focusing event is equally as important as its content. To stimulate student interest and motivation, the teacher must present it with a great deal of gusto. Being enthusiastic does not require that you lead your students in a rousing cheer at the start of each period or that you perform a humorous monologue in the tradition of a stand-up comic. It does require, however, that you *believe* in what you are teaching and, even more important, that you *think positively about your learners* as individuals capable of significant growth in all dimensions—cognitive, affective, and psychomotor.

To conclude your focusing event, you may want to *verbalize* the performance objective(s) that your lesson plan specifies. Many teachers find that this technique provides a smooth transition to the next stage of the instructional sequence—the presentation of the day's lesson. The teacher, in other words, may use the focusing event first to "grab the learner's attention" and then to announce briefly what the student is expected to be able to do at the end of the instructional activities.

---

*This example was provided by Dr. David Lundsgaard and is reprinted with his permission.

It is crucial that, in stating the performance objectives, you translate what you have written on your plan into a form that is both understandable and interesting to your students. Indeed, the language used to specify a performance objective on paper is seldom identical to the language needed to express the objective orally in class. The way you communicate the objectives must correlate with the level of sophistication of your audience. For example, notice the difference between the way the following performance objective is written for a third grade lesson plan (developed for the *teacher's* use) and the way the teacher actually presents it to the third grade students:

> *Lesson plan objective:* Given ten problems, the student will demonstrate the ability to add two-digit numbers and will get nine out of ten correct.

> *Oral statement of objective:* Today we're going to learn to add two-digit numbers. Last week we worked on adding one-digit numbers. Adding two-digit numbers is a lot like what we did then.

Teaching Procedures

At this point in the instructional procedures section, you have set the stage for the lesson. Now it is time to present content—the "input" that you will provide to foster student learning. But *how* will you give students the intended information? This decision requires you to choose from a wide variety of teaching methods and possible learning experiences those that are most appropriate for the particular lesson.

Because there are so many variables that characterize any given classroom situation, decisions regarding teaching procedures are very complex. Figure 5-4 identifies some of the important components of such decision-making and their apparent interactions with the learning environment that must be considered.

As noted, there are at least four elements associated with selecting a teaching procedure. Every teacher has a unique set of personal strengths, abilities, previous learnings, and experiences to rely on when selecting teaching methods. The strategies you choose should be ones that bring student success. This does not mean that you should hesitate to try new methods and techniques. Even though your own preferences influence your methodology choices, you should continually seek opportunities to develop your teaching skills in additional directions. With practice, you will feel confident about your ability to handle an extensive selection of teaching methods. We are very familiar with a traditional teacher excuse, "That teaching method doesn't match my personality." This often-heard statement means simply that the teacher has decided to quit learning. The emphasis of modern curricula is on highly interactive instructional methodologies, not on static principles.

The methodology used to impart content also must match the students' experiences. Just as every teacher brings unique skills and preferences to the learning situation, so too every learner enters the classroom with a special combination of likes, dislikes, interests, values, abilities, and needs. It is doubtful that any two students will respond identically to you or to the lesson; thus, give careful considera-

Figure 5-4   *Variables Affecting the Choice of Instructional Procedures*

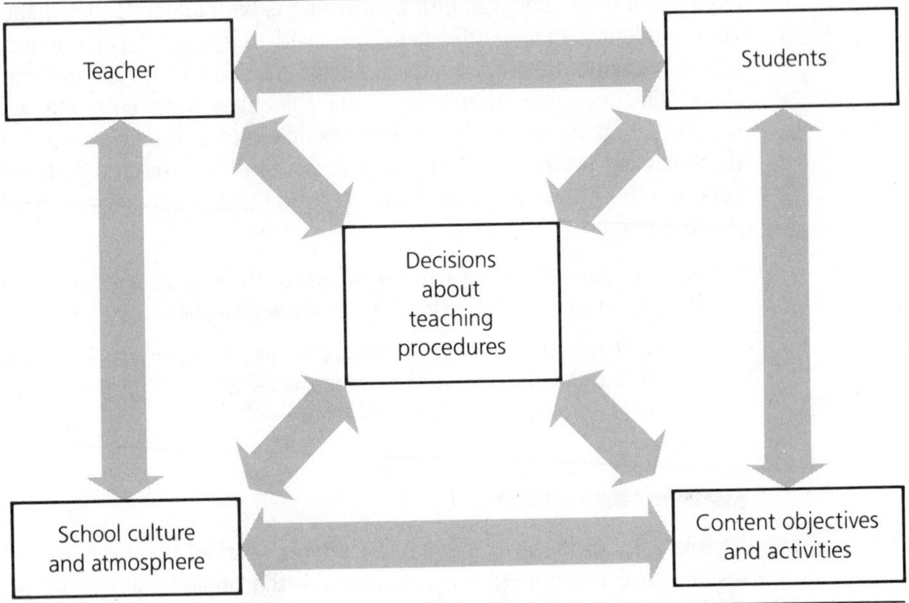

tion to these student variables when making decisions about teaching methods. If a student interacts comfortably with peers in a small-group setting but stutters uncontrollably when asked to stand up in front of the entire class, the sensitive instructor will select teaching methods and learning experiences that help the student attain the intended outcomes without experiencing personal frustration or embarrassment.

As we have discussed previously, all lesson planning activities have purposes. The purposes—the desired ends of the learning experiences—involve the goals, the related performance objectives, and the subject matter of the lesson. Obviously, your decisions about appropriate methodology must correspond to these other planning elements. If the desired learning is in the affective domain, you will need different methods than if a psychomotor skill is being sought. Although small-group discussions may be appropriate in helping students to clarify their personal values and to be tolerant of the feelings and attitudes of others, such discussions are not very effective in teaching students a new gymnastics event.

Still another consideration influencing the choice of teaching procedures is that of the physical environment, including such related elements as time, place, and context of the learning situation. To use a rather extreme example, a ninth grade biology teacher in Jacksonville, Florida—where abundant marine life can be observed and numerous natural museums visited—will want to plan different types of field trips than does a ninth grade biology teacher in Terre Haute, Indiana. Because instructional procedures are often dependent on *where* the learning is to take place, you always need to ask the question, "Is this environment the best one for the method planned?"

Formative Check

One of the most vital elements of *any* lesson is the formative check, an activity that allows the teacher to assess student understanding up to the point of the check and to make adjustments to the lesson in accordance with this information.

Actually, it is slightly erroneous to imply that the teacher should check for student understanding *after* the content of the lesson has been presented. In reality, formative checking is a continuous process that needs to be done throughout the instructional process from the moment you first introduce a topic for the day (for example, the focusing event) to the time you bring the lesson to closure. Just as the skillful weather forecaster constantly monitors the movement of fronts, so too the effective teacher conscientiously monitors student understanding and progress by means of the formative check. The resulting data permit the teacher to adjust the lesson to compensate for any confusion, gaps, or advances in learning not anticipated during the planning phase.

Formative checks vary widely in their specificity and level of formality. Sometimes it is most appropriate to conduct the formative check on a one-to-one basis, and at other times it is best done in small-group settings; some lessons require written tests, and others call for verbal question-and-answer periods. Curriculum designers, especially developers of programmed instructional materials, frequently rely on formative quiz items to direct the learning sequence. The student, in such cases, cannot progress to the next learning activity until the preceding step has been successfully completed; this is usually demonstrated by answering correctly a true-or-false, multiple-choice, or fill-in-the-blanks test item.

Other formative checks are markedly less structured. For example, on some days you may want to initiate a class session by finding out in an informal way the degree to which students remember the content and outcomes of the previous lesson. You may, for instance, begin by saying: "Please summarize what we learned about the incident at Harpers Ferry yesterday. . . . Pablo?"

The use of formative checks helps ensure that students are not pushed to new topics and objectives before they achieve success in the subskills that make attainment of the later task possible. Whatever their format, formative checks help the teacher avoid situations in which learning problems are not identified until the *end* of an entire unit or sequence. Sadly, situations in which students feel hopelessly lost and hence consider themselves learning failures occur too frequently in education. You can prevent many of these problems if you conduct frequent and relevant formative checks and then *use* this information to make appropriate changes in your teaching procedures. Sometimes a formative check will alert you to the need for remediation or for enrichment, and sometimes the information will suggest that students need more practice to internalize the concepts they are studying. Formative checks may be difficult to practice in some situations, but these will be the exceptions, not the rule.

Student Participation

Another powerful element in the teaching process is that of student practice accompanied by feedback of success. The purposes of such practice are many. First, a practice session can serve as a *formative check of student understanding*. Second, the *degree that learning is retained* is highly related to the degree to which the student was given an opportunity to practice that learning. Third, student *learning can be enhanced* greatly with practical activities that relate directly to the objectives of the lesson. The activities give relevance and practicality to what may otherwise seem (to the students) to be a series of meaningless words. Finally, student practice, when followed by feedback of progress, can be very informative and *intrinsically rewarding for the student*. It allows learners to say to themselves, "I'm able to *do* this!" The latter provides for student efficacy.

Plan student practice carefully. Requiring students to "fill out a worksheet" or to "do a homework assignment" does not guarantee that the activity will be meaningful or constructive. Practice, unfortunately, is one of the elements of instruction that frequently is abused, particularly in those situations in which the teacher employs it simply as a method of "killing time" by keeping students occupied with "busy work." Even worse, some teachers use student practice as a tool for punishment—for example, they may threaten: "If you don't quiet down, I'm going to assign you extra homework tonight."

In contrast to these forms of abuse and misuse, student practice should be thought of as an integral component of the lesson. Students need to know that you view it as an important, rather than peripheral, part of the learning process. One of the best ways to communicate this belief is by giving students feedback, or knowledge of results, regarding their practice activities. In other words, you conduct a formative check on the practice and report the results to the students so that they realize what they do during the practice is of high priority.

One additional note should be made about student practice. Before being asked to perform a particular task or to demonstrate their understanding of a concept via a practice activity, students need to know precisely what it is that the teacher expects them to do. This requires that you *describe the assignment clearly* and *model the correct procedures* as a means of providing students with a good example to follow. For example, after *explaining* "how to multiply fractions," you need to *demonstrate* "how to multiply fractions" by using the chalkboard, the microcomputer, overhead projector, or bundles of sticks. The old adage "a picture is worth a thousand words" has never been more apt. Once you have completed modeling and have conducted a short formative check to assess student understanding, *then* the learners are ready to practice the assigned task.

Closure

Public speakers are often advised that their delivery should adhere to the following formula:

1. Tell them (the audience) what you're going to tell them.
2. Tell them.
3. Tell them what you've told them.

This advice has some merit for teachers as well. The focusing event, including the statement of the objective(s), serves as a way of telling students what you are going to help them to learn. The content and methodology components of the lesson serve as a means of helping them to attain the intended outcomes. Lesson *closure* serves to synthesize and summarize all the elements of the lesson at the end.

An effective closing puts the "icing on the cake." As the finale of the learning experience, it not only provides a vehicle for *summarizing* the day's lesson but also, more significantly, allows you to *single out those aspects that are of greatest importance.* Closure solidifies the whole lesson by reinforcing what has just been learned, while simultaneously telling students that "now we're ready to move on. You've got it!"

The techniques that you use in bringing a lesson to closure often are as critical as the content of the closure itself. We recommend that, whenever possible, you design closing sequences that actively engage your learners. Ask *them* to identify the main points of the lesson—for example, "What have we been trying to learn today?" Request *them* to suggest meaningful relationships between what the class has learned previously and what it has learned today.

Sometimes, of course, you may not want to bring a lesson to closure, such as when you wish to challenge students to pursue a special research project. On the other hand, some lessons may require three or more separate closures. Lesson closure, like all other aspects of the teaching process, needs to be adapted skillfully to the particular learning situation. Although at the outset it may seem comforting to follow "the perfect prescription for lesson excellence," no one will ever be able to identify such an all-encompassing system. With teaching, nothing is cast in cement—nor would any good teacher want it to be.

Section 7. Evaluation Procedures

Student evaluation, as we are defining it here, entails postinstruction assessment of student performance. At this stage in the instructional sequence you determine to what degree the learner has attained the anticipated outcomes of the lesson. These measurement activities frequently are referred to as student *summative evaluation.*

At the end of the lesson, a clear picture of how well students have mastered the stated objectives should emerge. If you find a discrepancy between what was intended and what has been achieved, then you must decide where additional instruction is needed.

The evaluation procedures should describe in detail the testing technique to be followed in evaluating student summative behavior. These procedures must relate directly to the behavioral objectives stipulated at the beginning of the lesson, including the conditions, content, and criteria being employed to assess student mastery.

A word of caution is in order about evaluation procedures. *Be sure you measure the behavior you have taught students to perform.* Congruence among stated objectives, instruction, and evaluation procedures is very important. It is only fair to expect students to behave in ways that closely duplicate how they have been taught to behave. Some teachers are notorious for writing clear statements of desired terminal performance, but for testing students on other, sometimes even unrelated, behaviors. When this happens, instead of channeling their energies to learn the most important material and skills, students are left confused and anxious about course requirements and testing procedures.

The "condition" element of the performance objective is commonly misconstrued by teachers in planning for evaluation. The *examination* situation needs to parallel closely the *practice situations* in which the learning has taken place. For example, if a student is expected to learn how to swing a golf club, the appropriate testing situation will involve the actual swinging of a club, rather than exclusive reliance on a paper-and-pencil test!

Not all lessons require students to demonstrate attainment of the behavioral objective—that is, to perform on the test—on the exact day that they receive instruction. It is hard to imagine a classroom situation in which the teacher would not collect *formative* evaluation data on a daily basis, but *summative* evaluation may be postponed to a more appropriate time. You may want, for example, to combine several objectives to show their cumulative relationship before you test student terminal behavior.

Irrespective of when you implement the evaluation procedures, try to include some assessment procedure within each day's plan. This strategy will help to remind you of the one-to-one correspondence that should exist between the lesson intentions and the measurement of the intended outcomes.

One final point should be mentioned before we discuss materials and aids. Although the examples given in this chapter tend to be consistent with a performance objective–based curriculum, we recognize that some, if not all, of the important learning may take weeks, months, or even years. Thus, all learning is not neatly divided into daily lesson plans. As you know from the presentation on taxonomies, the higher cognitive levels and most affective levels take a long time to assimilate.

Section 8. Materials and Aids

The materials and aids section of your plan should provide a checklist of everything you expect to use to teach the lesson. The list should include audiovisual equipment, handouts, books, microcomputer and software, and lab facilities—in short, anything that the student does not have that you must supply. The principles in *The Medium Is the Massage* (McLuhan and Fiore, 1967) are certainly relevant here. The *way* that ideas and skills are presented may have more impact on the learning process than their content does.

Although much could be mentioned about the importance of selecting materials and aids that will foster learning, we do not go into detail on this point here. Suffice it to say that you need not only to identify the types of audiovisual and print media that will enhance the learning environment but also to *prepare for the use of the selected aids.* You will want to take all the preliminary steps necessary to ensure that the materials are ordered in ample time and that the equipment required is available for your use (and in good operating condition) before you begin the lesson.

A Rationale for Postlesson Evaluation

Evaluation occurs on a number of levels in the development and implementation of instructional plans. We already have discussed some of these evaluative activities— namely, the formative and summative assessment of student achievement.

Evaluation occurs on another level—that of the lesson itself. At the conclusion of every class session, ask yourself a series of questions about the effectiveness of the plan—for example, Were the objectives realistic and appropriate? Did the instructional methods work? For which learners and to what degree? What components of the lesson succeeded? What aspects could be improved? Your answers to these and other inquiries help you to identify difficulties experienced by learners and to relate these problems to specific elements of the lesson.

Jot down any notes or comments about the lesson that can assist you the next time you teach the lesson. Brown (1988) stated that this feature is a very important aspect for efficiency. The teachers with whom she interacted always referred to the previous year's notes and resource files as they planned their lessons.

A lesson plan should be an *emerging document;* thus, the initial creation of a plan is only the *first* stage of its development. After initial use, the *actual* classroom conditions that account for learner entry level, teaching procedures, and learner outcomes need to be compared to the *planned* situation. The resulting data allow for refinement and recycling to make the lesson plan more effective as an instructional tool. In summary, you *continually evaluate* the lesson each time you implement it and always attempt to improve its techniques and approaches.

A General Note

In closing, we must introduce the six basic teaching functions described by a long-time contributor to the field, Barak Rosenshine. After synthesizing several research reports and conducting his own studies, Rosenshine (1983) concluded that truly effective teachers (1) have a general pattern of well-organized procedures, (2) stress comprehension, and (3) tend to be more direct than implicit. The six functions that he includes follow.

1. The teacher conducts a daily review of the previous day's work.
2. The new content or skills are introduced and are directly related to the previous lesson.
3. Students practice the new learning. At this stage the activities are provided, and the teacher gives prompts to all students who need them.
4. The teacher provides feedback to students, makes corrections as needed, and reteaches some component of the lesson. When reteaching, the teacher sequences the learning in even smaller bits than originally taught.
5. Students are given practice work in which they independently show that they comprehend the material. (Refer to our treatment in Chapter 4.)
6. The teacher periodically reviews the material on a weekly or monthly basis. In Chapter 6 we discuss one technique—*concept review*—that can be easily integrated into the recitation periods.

You cannot cover every possible lesson, objective, question, activity, or project that might be suggested in the school district curriculum guides, the adopted textbooks, or other print materials. Effective teachers build a "topic" calendar of essential learnings.

Brown (1988) observed teachers just *sketching* yearly and monthly plans. In unit plans, themes, concepts, and principles are identified and emphasized. Finally, a key idea for each day is determined as lesson plans are constructed. Lesson plans need not be elaborate or detailed. To be systematic in providing learning experiences, some form of written plan must be prepared, used, critiqued, and filed for "next year." As Mitchell, Ortiz, and Mitchell (1987) stressed, it is the lesson, the actual stuff of instruction, that transforms youngsters into students. Learning is the primary goal of the schools. Your job is to make planning decisions for ensuring that learning is always *intentionally inviting.*

No plan is a magical elixir that will guarantee intended learning; it can be only as effective as the instructor using it. The critical activity for you as a planner is to identify the type of format that will help you most in facilitating the learning process. The format you choose should be easy for you to use—a tool to lend direction to the lesson, but not a manuscript from which to read verbatim statements.

OTHER LESSON FORMATS

To complement the lesson-planning format introduced earlier in this chapter, Figures 5-5 through 5-8 illustrate some of the many other options that are available. Some of these styles will be more applicable to your teaching situation than others are.

In selecting a format, you need to consider (1) the subject or content that is taught, (2) the types of instructional methods you are able to use, and (3) the interests and learning styles of the students. Also, you may use several different forms of lesson plans in any one unit or module of instruction.

As you examine the following lesson plan formats, you will quickly observe that

Figure 5-5   *Weekly Lesson Plan Format 2*

Identify goals _____

Specify objectives _____

Taxonomic levels _____

Sequence objectives (process) _____

     Independent _____

     Dependent _____

Select materials (content) _____

     Textbooks assignments _____

     Laboratory or computer activity _____

     Supplemental materials _____

Prepare hierarchy (content) _____

     Arrange logically _____

     Rearrange for learning _____
       Preentry skills
       Entry skills
       New skills
       Apply new skills
       Relate skills
       Review

Formative test _____

Review as needed _____

Report _____

This format encourages the instructor to plan for the inclusion of an array of objectives in a sequential order. Further, it allows a teacher to build a larger unit of material to be planned, studied, and completed.

each contains a set of common elements: topic, goal or rationale, objectives, and procedures. Furthermore, you will note that each format is logically structured and developed, qualities that are highly critical, as you usually will be introducing or expanding concepts as you teach. It is imperative that you build a lesson systematically and logically so that the learners likewise build systematic and logical study skills.

Figure 5-6   *Lesson Plan Format 3*

INQUIRY/PROBLEM SOLVING

Subject _____

Teacher _____

Goal _____

Topic for this lesson _____

Objectives _____

_____

_____

Procedures or Steps

1. Problem identification _____

_____

_____

2. Data collection _____

_____

3. Formulation of hypothesis or assumption(s) _____

_____

4. Analysis of data or materials _____

_____

5. Testing hypotheses or assumptions _____

_____

6. Conclusion or judgment _____

_____

_____

_____

_____

_____

This format is easily adapted to any inquiry-oriented lesson.

Figure 5-7   *Lesson Plan Format 4: Outline of Key Questions or Key Statements*

Unit topic _____

Instructional goal _____

Objectives _____

_____

_____

Procedures for recitation or discussion _____

_____

_____

Key questions

1. _____

2. _____

3. _____

4. _____

Summary _____

_____

Key statements

1. _____

2. _____

3. _____

4. _____

Summary _____

_____

Conclusion _____

_____

_____

This format may be particularly suitable when questioning and/or teacher-led discussion will be the primary learner activities. Further, the addition of "Key statements" reflects the research evidence provided by J. T. Dillon ("Cognitive Correspondence Between Question/Statement and Response," *American Educational Research Journal* 19:1982, 540–551; and "Do Your Questions Promote or Prevent Thinking?" *Learning* 11:1982, 56–57, 59). Dillon suggests that teachers' statements rather than questions will promote more higher-level student responses. (See Chapter 6 for the discussion.)

THE HUNTER MODEL

Instructional Theory into Practice (ITIP) is a method for planning and implementing instruction developed by Madeline Hunter (1984) and promoted through her own instructional materials. Hunter's ITIP has been widely adopted (and adapted) by many school districts, often as *the* instructional "formula" composed of several "locked steps," for assuring accountability of instruction. Some school districts expect teacher-applicants to be familiar with ITIP and offer inservice training in the method for their teachers and administrators.

Hunter provides neither a "formula" nor a series of "steps" to guarantee teacher effectiveness. Instead, ITIP is a lesson design process—very similar to the processes described in this text—that considers relevant factors in making instructional decisions. The following three categories are considered basic to lesson design.

1. *Content.* Within the context of grade level, student ability, lesson rationale, the teacher decides what content to teach.
2. *Learner behaviors.* Teachers must decide what students will do (a) to learn, and (b) to demonstrate that they have learned.
3. *Teacher behaviors.* Teachers must decide which "research-based" teaching principles will most effectively promote learning.

To plan and implement instruction based upon the above categories, Madeline Hunter asserts that the following factors must be considered. It is these factors that her advocates identify as *the* "steps" of the model and *mistakenly insist* must be part of each lesson. As you read the list, notice how closely it parallels what you have already learned.

1. *Select an objective* at an appropriate level of difficulty and complexity, as determined through task analysis, diagnostic testing, and congruence with Bloom's cognitive taxonomy.
2. *Motivate instruction* by emphasizing the learning task, its importance, and the learning that led to this objective (*anticipatory set*).
3. *State the objectives* to the students.
4. *Identify and teach* main concepts and skills, emphasizing clear explanations, frequent use of examples and diagrams, and active student participation.
5. *Check for understanding* by observing and interpreting student reactions (active interest, boredom) and by frequent formative evaluations with immediate feedback. Adjust instruction as needed and reteach if necessary.
6. *Provide guided practice* following instruction by having students answer questions, demonstrate skills, or solve problems. Give immediate feedback and reteach if necessary.
7. *Assign independent practice* to solidify skills and knowledge when students have demonstrated understanding.

When used as intended—to select objectives and to plan instruction—ITIP is a useful tool. (It should be! It contains the elements that educators have long associated with effective teaching and learning—careful goal identification, task analysis, appropriate levels of complexity, clear instruction, and frequent feedback to students. These elements, and many, many more are precisely the concerns of this text.) At least two problems, though, have arisen with ITIP's adoption and adaptation in practice. Both relate to extending the model beyond its intended use.

The first problem is that many school district administrators, by insisting upon the near-universal application of the model, imply that ITIP *is a panacea* for instructional ills if teachers will only follow the steps. Indeed, some districts evaluate teachers on how well they demonstrate ITIP principles (Slavin, 1989; Garman and Hazi, 1988; Gibboney, 1987). The fallacy, of course, lies in using ITIP as a teaching checklist rather than as a planning tool. Few educators, of course, would argue seriously that *any* teaching model is equally effective for all subjects, students, and contexts. (Hunter herself is shocked at the model's misuse.)

Second, it is easier to follow ITIP principles (or any other teaching model) if the objectives are *easily measured,* as is the case with basic reading and computing skills. Although higher-level thinking skills and affective goals might be attempted from the ITIP rationale, they rarely seem to be in practice. Thus, an insistence upon following this method to the exclusion of others forces us, as Elliot Eisner (1983) noted in regard to a "back to basics" emphasis, to expect too little of our students.

Virtually all students can develop their thinking skills into the application and higher cognitive levels, but few will do so if teachers do not deliberately plan relevant instruction. Such development is best done through a variety of teaching methods—discussion, small-group learning, learning projects, problem-solving—rather than a single method that is best adapted for large-group, basic skill instruction and that is closely related to direct instruction. Figure 5-8 provides elements of Hunter's lesson design format as a framework for your lesson plan.

DIRECT INSTRUCTION

Let us address a technique that emphasizes competency, particularly regarding basics, and a shift away from the individual to the group. However superficial these shifts may seem, we need to study them critically, as the technique of direct instruction shows promise for specific educational needs.

The emphasis on "basic education" is a natural link to direct instruction. While reviewing nearly two hundred studies that compared educational outcomes of indirect, student-centered teaching with direct instruction, Penelope Peterson (1979) concluded that with direct instruction, students tended to do better on achievement tests and slightly worse on tests of abstract thinking than students did in open classrooms. Her findings demonstrate a commonly held belief that direct instruction is useful for teaching basics and the learning disabled, but inappropriate for higher cognitive learning.

Direct instruction foments heated debate among proponents and opponents. It has been readily adapted by those teaching *the basics* and for *special education*

Figure 5-8   *Lesson Plan Format 5*

Goal _____

Objectives _____

Purpose _____

Cognitive levels _____

Materials and activities _____

Set (initiating or motivating experience)   Techniques of presentation

_____   _____

_____   _____

Information to be learned   Formative check

_____   _____

_____   _____

Modeling   Guided practice

_____   _____

_____   _____

Evaluation   Independent practice

_____   _____

_____   _____

Advocates of Madeline Hunter's ITIP often illustrate this lesson plan as useful.

(Cotton, 1982; Unks, 1986; Ross and Kyle, 1987). Already used in reading, mathematics, and instruction of the learning disabled, direct instruction has received a boost from researchers and school districts looking for ways to increase student on-task learning time or the amount of time a student is actively engaged in achieving the learning objective (Lysiak, 1985; Doyle, 1984). A review of the research indicates that direct instruction consistently extended skills across a broad range of learners and subject areas. There is demonstrated effectiveness of the direct instruction model (Barr and Dreeben, 1977; Moore, 1986; Ornstein, 1987; Condon and Maggs, 1986; Gersten and Guskey, 1985).

Principals, teachers, and entire school districts have turned to direct instruction for help in increasing on-task learning time (Gettinger, 1986), thinking skills (Gersten, 1986), problem-solving (Schaaf, 1984), language training (Cornick and Thomas, 1984), social studies (Beyer, 1985; and Rooze, 1986), computer literacy (Gelder and Maggs, 1983), writing (Hornick, 1986; and Balajthy, 1986), and science (Yore, 1987). As you can see, direct instruction has widespread applicability.

Direct Instruction—A Definition and Discussion

Many different definitions for direct instruction have been published. Eclectically, the technique involves an *academic focus,* presents *little choice of activity* by the students, favors *large-group* over small-group instruction, and focuses on *factual questions* and *controlled classroom practice.* Before deciding to use direct instruction, study the list below; ask yourself if your instructional outcomes are best suited to the strengths of direct instruction, which are as follows:

- Provides for delivery to the entire class
- Controls focus of attention
- Makes the most of the time available
- Assesses feedback quickly from the class to ensure understanding
- Allows the teacher to answer student questions which may be of interest to the class as a whole only once
- Provides the teacher with the option of using student reactions to modify a lesson or an activity
- Allows the teacher to use a student to explain directions or provide insight into the lesson or activity
- Requires less preparation time than many alternative instructional strategies
- Stresses the teacher's ability to motivate
- Allows all students the same amount of time on task

The weaknesses of direct instruction are these:

- Allows for very little individualization of the activity or lesson
- Requires the teacher to direct instruction at the median ability level
- Relies on the delivery capabilities of the teacher
- Requires using audiovisual materials for maximum effectiveness
- Allows teachers to use direct instruction as an excuse for lack of preparation

Using Direct Instruction

In direct instruction you as teacher are in control in a reasonably formal manner as you tell, show, model, demonstrate, and teach the skill or concept to be learned. It is this teacher behavior in the classroom that guides the instructional strategy. In brief, direct instruction tends to be a five-step approach consisting of (1) an introduction,

(2) a demonstration, (3) a presentation, (4) guided practice, and (5) independent practice. Following is an elaboration on these steps.

Step 1. *Introduce.* Gathering the attention of the entire class, you tell the students what the lesson will be about. At this time you may detail your expectations for learning outcomes.

Step 2. *Demonstrate.* You provide an example and clarify the value and purpose of the concept of the lesson.

Step 3. *Present.* You present the instructional scenario in a sequential manner, moving from the simple to the complex. Frequently, you will build upon previous lessons or student-known concepts and experiences.

Step 4. *Practice—Guided.* You have the class practice the concept through questioning techniques, boardwork, and teaming methods. Often, the entire class will shout out the answers to a teacher command. Everyone answers every question.

Step 5. *Practice—Independent.* You turn the class to individual or group seatwork while carefully monitoring class progress.

You have to approach long-range goals in a step-by-step manner to teach successfully. After identifying what the students already know and what they must learn, you then divide it into "segments" that are learnable in single lessons. These segments must be properly sequenced when you teach a concept to students: you provide concrete examples, have them practice the skill, and arrange for evaluation and feedback. At all times you watch for examples and point them out. If a student makes a mistake, you correct it and have the student practice the correct process and outcome. These steps are necessary to teach the students how to learn and the process you will follow in *directing the instruction.*

Keep the following in mind while leading your students through the five steps.

Explanation   Good explanation usually includes definitions in concrete terms, reasons for rules or procedures, and demonstration of correct outcomes. If a concept is a complex one for the age/grade level, then you should present the task in a step-by-step fashion (task analysis). Make sure after each step that the students have understood the concept correctly. Never accept students "nodding heads" as evidence of understanding. Ask two or three students to reexplain the concept, or ask the class as a whole to demonstrate the process.

Rehearsal   Students need time for practicing the process or demonstrating understanding of a concept. This serves two purposes: it helps students to learn the desired concept, and it allows you to determine whether students have truly learned or require further instruction. It is a good idea to rehearse all activities and procedures that are complex or that are to be performed by the whole class (for example, test taking, oral reading, team assignments, homework). Be certain to rehearse the desired or correct procedure or strategies.

Feedback   It is desirable to get feedback from students who have participated in a demonstration or an exercise. Feedback from the teacher provides the individual and the class an assessment of how well or how poorly they have understood the concept you presented (Meyer, 1985). Remember, this assessment is also a gauge of how well you presented your instruction.

Jane Stallings (1976) found that teachers who stayed at their desks without interacting with students during seatwork had more student absences and lower student reading gains. This finding indicates that when students are doing seatwork, the teacher should actively monitor their independent work by moving among them, giving assistance and getting feedback. Teachers who closely monitor students' learning throughout the entire instructional period have fewer behavioral problems, greater student involvement and success, and higher student achievement.

Practice—Follow-Up   If the first run-through is unacceptable, then you want to review the concept, demonstrate the correct process, and state what you think went wrong. The review may include reexplanation. If the students perform well, *praise* them. You might also consider another quick practice session to reinforce their learning and to assure yourself that luck did not play an unusual part in their success.

No matter what your instructional strategy, you will find that the attention span of your students varies dramatically. Time of day, interest level, capabilities, and dozens of other variables affect how long an individual student can focus on any given activity. You should consider twenty-minute instructional scenarios. Less than that creates havoc with your planning cycle; more than twenty minutes puts undue demands on your creative efforts. Stay short and keep them involved.

Implementing the Technique

Get Attention   All students must be listening; you should use a signal such as a raised hand to indicate desired silence. Don't pass out papers before directions, as this easily distracts students; you don't need competition while giving directions.

Give Directions   Give them clearly. Repeat any new or unusual aspect of the directions and demonstrate these portions before proceeding to the next step.

Check for Understanding   Giving clear directions does not guarantee comprehension. Students need to repeat the directions. Be certain to call on students who, you feel, will repeat the directions correctly. This is not the time to catch the student who isn't listening. For example: Who can repeat the directions? How will you begin? What next? And then?

Transfer to Action   You've given directions, checked for understanding, and modeled the behavior you want. What do you do next? Provide the class with the specifics that guide the activity.

Motivate the Students   Circulate around the room, encouraging those that got a quick start and prodding those that are letting the minutes pass unproductively.

Remediate if Necessary   Even after listening to the best of directions, some students may not be following them. Remember to scan the room quickly for visual cues. When you spot someone who seems to be having difficulty, move to clarify the directions and push in the right direction.

Direct instruction requires planning and practice. Direct instruction is NOT lecturing! To make the most of direct instruction, you must be thorough and follow a logical sequence of activities. Feedback and careful monitoring of student work is essential to guarantee reaching the desired learning outcomes. As we noted, direct instruction is exactly that: You are in charge and you pace the class. It is not for every class, every hour; use it with discretion when you decide that it is most effective.

THE KAPLAN MATRIX

One of the special challenges facing the teacher is the need to develop lessons that adapt to the specific skills and abilities of students. Nowhere is the challenge more pronounced than in situations involving the gifted student or the student with specific learning disabilities. To assist educators in this critical area, Sandra Kaplan (1979) has created a matrix that *extends* the basic curriculum, thus allowing the instructor to plan appropriate activities for the student's individual level of learning.

The format in Table 5-3 (p. 171) is an extended sample of the Kaplan matrix. The content (unit objectives) is listed down the left side. The differentiated processes are identified across the top. In each box the teacher develops an activity or assignment *and* specifies the outcome that aligns the thinking process and objective or content. Through this extended format, the teacher develops a wide array of alternatives to the regular curriculum that can be matched to each student's readiness level.

The Kaplan matrix looks complex but is not. The performance objectives describe student activities that must be performed. We suggest preparing a Kaplan matrix for any activity-oriented topic or laboratory.

In the first stage of this model, the teacher lists all the major concepts or ideas to be taught. For example, a social studies unit on immigrants might have the topics listed, as in Table 5-1.

The next step is to take these content areas and translate them into objectives at the various levels, as in Table 5-2.

Table 5-3 illustrates how the teacher expands the concepts of cognitive objectives into a working plan that is used both by the teacher and the class. This model, adapted from Sandra Kaplan, shows the relative ease with which detailed planning can be accomplished to provide a broad spectrum of learner experiences.

This approach to planning takes time, but the time spent prior to instruction will pay off in the classroom itself. The teacher will have a clear idea of where each lesson is going, how it relates to other lessons, and the various kinds of learning students will encounter. Further, Kaplan's matrix can help a teacher individualize selected

Table 5-1   *An Initial Expansion of Performances*

Content, Concepts	Places of Origin	Hardships Encountered	Contributions of Immigrants
Knowledge	Students will know the dates and the countries of origin of the major immigrant groups to the U.S.		
Comprehension	Students will construct a graph showing the national origin of various immigrant groups to the U.S.		
Application	Students will predict from where future immigrant groups to the U.S. will come		
Analysis	Students will explain the motives of different immigrant groups in coming to the U.S.		
Synthesis	Students will design an immigration policy that is fair to future various immigrant groups		
Evaluation	Students will decide whether the current U.S. immigration policy is fair to various immigrant groups and tell why		

aspects of the curriculum by prescribing a set number of evaluation points to each objective.

MICRO-TEACHING

We now turn our attention to the topic of micro-teaching, a technique that affords both beginning and advanced teachers excellent opportunities to *plan* and *practice* a wide array of new instructional strategies. Our goal is not only to introduce you to micro-teaching but also to provide instructions to guide you in applying this very widespread teacher-education method. By the end of this part of the chapter, you will be able to plan and present a micro-teaching lesson for school-age children or for peers in your education classes. Subsequent chapters describing numerous teaching methods will encourage you to develop and implement additional micro-teaching

Table 5-2   *Teacher–Student Work Plan*

Content	Level of Objective	Teaching Activity	Learning Experiences	Student Product
Places of origin	K	Lecture/Recitation Reading assignment Worksheet	Note taking Reading	Worksheet completed
Places of origin	C	Demonstration of how to construct graphs	Note taking Constructing a graph	Graph
Places of origin	AP	Small-group pre-sentations	Each group makes a prediction and presents to class	Presentation by small groups to whole class
Places of origin	AN	Presentation of assignment Discussion of resources Description of final product Break class into groups	Each group focuses on one immigrant group and is re-sponsible for ex-plaining their mo-tives for coming, using references, film strips, and other resources	Report to class

Used with permission of Sandra Kaplan.

lessons so as to experience, and experiment with, various instructional techniques or methods.

What Is Micro-Teaching?

Micro-teaching is a scaled-down sample of teaching. It is essentially an opportunity for preservice teachers and experienced professionals to develop and/or improve specific teaching skills with a small group of students (four to six peers or "real" students) by means of brief (four–fifteen minutes) single-concept lessons. These lessons are recorded on videotape for reviewing, refining, and analyzing very specific teaching processes. Micro-teaching is a technique that allows the teacher to place small aspects of teaching under the microscope. More specifically, micro-teaching is an empirically tested procedure that allows you to do the following:

1. Practice a new technique, strategy, or procedure in a supportive environment
2. Prepare and deliver a lesson with reduced anxiety
3. Test new ways to approach a topic or lesson

Table 5-3   The Kaplan Matrix for Extending the Curriculum

Content or Concepts	Performance Objectives and Related Student Activities					
	Knowledge	Comprehension	Application	Analysis	Synthesis	Evaluation
Volcanoes	List facts about Mount Saint Helens' devastation	Compare Mount Saint Helens to the volcanoes of Hawaii	How could we use the piles of volcanic ash?	What do the people near Mount Saint Helens feel?	Make a volcano model for our class	Are all things about Mount Saint Helens bad? Why?
Minerals and gems	List the important gems found in the Northeast	Contrast the hardness of the minerals found in the Northeast	Field test the hardness of ten minerals	What would happen if the government imposed tougher mining regulations?	Grow crystals of various shapes and colors	What do you think of people who hoard gems? Why?
Space travel	Name all the people who have gone to the moon	Compare the Russian space program to the U.S. program	If you were an astronaut, what would you study about space?	What do you think would happen if we found life elsewhere?	Make a rocket and fly it	What are some of the negative things about being an astronaut? Why?
Weather and climate	Name the different types of clouds	Contrast the climates of the Southwest and the Southeast	Chart the amount of rainfall for the next week	What effect did El Chiconal have on the world's weather?	Create a wind generator	Which climate best suits your lifestyle? Why?

Adapted with the permission of Sandra Kaplan.

4. Develop very specific delivery techniques such as introducing a topic, giving an assignment, or explaining an evaluation procedure
5. Be evaluated both by *others* and by *yourself*
6. Gain immediate feedback of your performance by viewing the video playback
7. Risk little but gain much in valuable experience
8. Subdivide complex teaching interactions into related elements
9. Manage your own behavior in a systematic manner

The micro-teaching approach to developing teacher competencies is not without its drawbacks, and two questions have been raised about its effectiveness. (1) How do you apply the effects to real classes? and (2) Does it matter significantly that college peers are not really authentic students? But micro-teaching has considerable merit in its own right because, outside of the actual classroom setting, micro-teaching provides the closest simulation of teaching yet devised. As a future educator you will want to strive for excellent, not merely satisfactory, performance, so we encourage you to practice your skills—with the constant goal of self-improvement. The Far West Educational Laboratory report shows that micro-teaching is a powerful way to change teaching behaviors (Borg et al., 1970). Janice Bertram Vaughn (1983) provided evidence that it did not matter whether college peers or students from the appropriate grade level made up the "micro-class." The results are equally positive and beneficial.

Micro-teaching has the basic objective of subdividing multifaceted teaching acts into simpler components, so that the task of learning new instructional skills will be more manageable. When prospective or inservice teachers engage in a micro-teaching lesson, they focus on a specific aspect of teaching until they develop a satisfactory minimum competency of that skill. If they see that a specific skill is not mastered, they schedule a reteach session to perfect it. The teacher proceeds to new skills only after having achieved success with each preceding one.

Before developing any micro-teaching lesson plans, however, you need to consider the circumstances. First, *not every topic, concept, or process automatically lends itself to every teaching method.* Each concept needs to be analyzed carefully to determine whether or not it is appropriate for the assigned skill or for the specified time allotted to conduct the micro-class.

Second, *in situations where it is not possible to obtain school-age students for the teaching sessions, a modified form of micro-teaching may be used.* For example, students enrolled in your education classes may be recruited to play the role of the school students. Also, because of a limited amount of class time, your reteach sessions may need to be kept to a minimum.

Cognitive *skills* (in the form of single-concept lessons) as well as *processes* may be perfected through micro-teaching. The notion of single-concept lessons will be addressed later in this chapter. But first we need to define what we mean by *processes* of instruction.

Instructional processes concern how you do a specific teaching act. Some illustrations of processes that you may want to learn through the micro-teaching technique include these:

1. Introducing a new topic or concept
2. Giving an assignment to a class
3. Specifying how the students will be evaluated in the course
4. Asking questions
5. Conducting recitation sessions
6. Tutoring an individual or small group
7. Leading a discussion
8. Practicing inquiry and problem-solving skills
9. Providing summaries of student statements
10. Closing a discussion or a class period

The list is far from complete. You may think of many others. What is comforting to the learner (or prospective teacher) is that micro-teaching allows one to practice a skill in "safety." It is a simulated form of teaching; the reality is there, but not with *all* the realism of a classroom. With the micro-teaching approach, you can isolate one tiny segment of the totality of teaching and practice it until the process is mastered. With this approach you have the opportunity to practice and master a skill before using it in a classroom.

Preparing for Micro-Teaching

Micro-teaching is not just "getting up front and teaching." The technique requires that you first prescribe carefully selected behaviors that you want to practice. As in "regular" daily lessons, the objective(s) must be carefully specified. Furthermore, you must establish a set of criteria by which to judge how effectively you were able to accomplish the desired skills, processes, or behaviors. The whole idea of micro-teaching is to *help you improve* your teaching techniques through practice, feedback, and evaluation.

Usually, micro-teaching sessions last only five to ten minutes. To conduct your lesson, you will need a portable videotape recorder, one TV camera, and one microphone for a videotape recorder (VTR) setup. This requires that you plan for at least one or two technicians to help you operate the needed equipment. These may be students or your peers in class. If a VTR setup is not available, use a cassette audiotape recorder, which will be nearly as effective.

At this point, you should be able to combine all of the competencies learned in the preparation of a micro-teaching lesson plan based on content from your major discipline. Here is an instructional objective for you to use in designing and demonstrating your lesson.

> Within the prescribed time limitation and focusing on a prescribed process or
> teaching technique, teach a preselected concept to either a peer group of ap-

proximately five students or to five "real" students. The members of your miniclass must achieve the performance objective as it is stated in the lesson plan, or you must accomplish the teaching process that you have specified in the plan.

To accomplish this objective, you should perform the following tasks for each micro-teaching session. You should

1. Prepare a lesson plan, using the suggested format. We recommend an abbreviated version of the lesson-plan format found in the early part of this chapter.
2. Make two copies of your lesson plan, one for your group leader and one for your own use while micro-teaching.
3. Teach the lesson to the student group within the time limitation stipulated for the particular micro-teaching session.
4. Evaluate student achievement or your correct use of the process you tested by using a stated performance objective and a specific evaluation device.
5. Play the role of a micro-session student when not teaching; operate the recording equipment or evaluate other micro-teaching performances.
6. Critique in writing, by using an evaluation instrument, the teaching of the other students in the group. Each group should provide an immediate oral critique following each micro-lesson.
7. Critique your own lesson after viewing and listening to the recording of the teaching. You may want to use a critique checklist or other evaluation criteria to aid you in your self-evaluation (see Figure 5-10).
8. Reteach the lesson, time permitting, to master the new technique.

Deciding on Micro-Lesson Content and Lesson-Plan Format

A critical decision you will need to make in preparing for your lesson is how to *narrow your topic*. The purpose of micro-teaching is not to demonstrate everything there is to know about effective instruction; rather, it is to focus on one aspect of the teaching process at a time. To accomplish this, you will need to select a *single subconcept* from the discipline of your choice and to develop a lesson aimed at helping your micro-session students learn this concept in the short span of five to ten minutes.

Initially, making decisions about the content to be covered in a single-concept lesson is often difficult for the beginning teacher. It demands that you have a strong command of your discipline, along with the ability to analyze it carefully and to isolate those concepts, principles, rules, and facts that are *most significant*. The work of experts in the various disciplines can greatly assist you with this task. Of course, textbooks, curriculum guides, course outlines, and models or collections of sequenced performance objectives also may be useful tools to employ in this context.

Once you have selected a single concept as the basis for your micro-lesson, your next step is to develop a *limited number* (perhaps only one) of performance objectives. That is, you need to determine what behavior the micro-student is to manifest in relation to the concept and to what extent he or she is expected to recall, recognize, or apply the concept.

To aid you in developing your single-concept lesson for micro-teaching, we suggest that you follow the organizational format for lesson planning described previously in this chapter. Instead of using the format in toto, however, make careful "editing" decisions so that the resulting plan will be manageable within the limits of the micro-setting. For example, you may not have enough time to allow for extensive "student practice." Although the planning procedures recommended previously will be generally applicable, they may need to be abbreviated to fit your particular objective(s) and circumstances. The ultimate criterion of your plan's effectiveness is: *Does it work for you during the actual implementation of the lesson?*

Micro-Teaching Planning Checklist

Since micro-teaching entails much preparation (just as does systematic teaching), the checklist in Figure 5-9 is provided to assist you in this important planning process.

Micro-Teaching Feedback

Once you have completed your lesson and have received immediate verbal and written feedback from your micro-students, you will be ready for what may be the

Figure 5-9   *Micro-Teaching Planning Checklist*

Activities	Check When Completed
1. Student entry level known	_____
2. Unit title, instructional goal/unit objective and performance objective(s) properly written	_____
3. Focus on a *single* concept	_____
4. Rationale clearly stated	_____
5. Content determined	_____
6. Instructional procedures specified	_____
7. Micro-session evaluation or critique form developed	_____
8. Audiovisual materials and special instructional items prepared	_____
9. Two copies (original for instructor, copy for self) of lesson plan completed	_____
10. Lesson delivered and peer evaluations given	_____
11. Tape replayed	_____
12. Self-critique conducted	_____
13. Decision made about whether to reteach	_____

most significant aspect of the technique—your self-evaluation. The replay of your micro-teaching session has great potential value in helping you to identify strengths and weaknesses in your use of particular teaching approaches and strategies. The playback (learner feedback) is aimed toward helping you become the best possible teacher. The replay of your micro-teaching gives you an approximation of how you appear, sound, and interact with your students.

In the interest of effectiveness and efficiency, you should view the video recording as soon as possible after the actual micro-teaching session, preferably immediately, but certainly no later than twenty-four hours after you have taught your lesson.

While observing the replay of your micro-session, you will find it helpful to use an evaluation form with appropriate criteria for judging the effectiveness of your teaching skills. The micro-teaching evaluation form in Figure 5-10 may help you design similar evaluative instruments to assess your own lessons.

PLANNING WITH MICROCOMPUTERS

It is fitting to close Chapter 5 with a short discussion of that apparent wizard of modern technology, the microcomputer, for it has emerged as a powerful teaching aid. Without question, microcomputers have had a significant impact on the classroom; it is mandatory to discuss their potential.

Technology never has been and never will be the panacea for our educational needs; the microcomputer will not replace the teacher as the basic instructional planner or provider. But insightful educators find that the computer can improve lesson planning and the management of instruction and thereby enhance the teaching

Figure 5-10 *A Sample Micro-Teaching Evaluation Form*

Name of Micro-Teacher _____

Class Hour _____

Tape No. _____

	SCALE					
	Needs improvement	1	2	3	4	5	Very effective

I. Lesson Plan

Unit and instructional goal _____

Objective _____

Rationale _____

Figure 5-10 (Continued)

	Needs improvement	1	2	3	4	5	Very effective
			SCALE				

Focus on single key concept _____

Distinction between content
  and procedures _____

Sequencing of lesson _____

Evaluation procedures specified _____

II. Management and Delivery

Focusing event _____

Teacher-student eye contact _____

Pacing of lesson _____

Monitoring and adjusting _____

Teacher verbal behaviors _____

Teacher nonverbal behaviors _____

Lesson closure _____

Use of materials _____

III. Evaluation (knowing that the
objective was reached)

Evaluation plan followed
  as specified _____

Students performed tasks
  or met stated objective _____

Teacher and students know whether
  objectives were reached _____

General comments _____

_____

_____

_____

and learning process. We will review how the microcomputer can be used (1) as an instructional tool, (2) with teacher- or student-made software, and (3) as an aid for implementing lesson design.

The Microcomputer As an Instructional Tool

Computer-assisted instruction (CAI) enables a lesson to be delivered through a computer program without constant teacher interaction. Jack A. Culbertson and LuVern L. Cunningham (1986) noted that CAI takes one or more of the following forms:

1. *Tutorial programs* present the student with material, followed by a set of questions concerning that information. It is assumed that the pupil has not had prior knowledge of the subject matter. Tutorial programs may be used in conjunction with, or independent of, the classroom teacher.
2. *Drill and practice* help ensure that the learner attains complete understanding of concepts that have been taught.
3. *Simulations* provide for the study of events beyond the normal capability of our senses, such as events that occur too quickly or too slowly for us to perceive. For example, the internal operation of an automobile engine, which normally operates at very high speeds, may be studied through a simulation of its operation.
4. *Interactive* systems enable students to input their own data. These data are integrated with other data sets. Displays such as graphs or charts present the original data in new formats. Such systems may link the microcomputer with a videodisc or overhead projector.

Higher-level thinking skills are also promoted through technological advances such as *display devices* in which the computer is used to organize raw data and present information in the form of graphs and charts. *Calculations* can be made that offer relief from the drudgery associated with repetitive mathematical exercises (which sometimes precludes the learning of more important conceptual objectives). *Information retrieval* is made accessible from large library data bases, which provide vast amounts of material not otherwise available to the student. *Word and music processing,* which promotes writing and musical composition, are easily programmed.

Teachers of the handicapped have discovered another major advantage of the microcomputer as an instructional tool: computer technology can enable students with speaking, writing, or visual disabilities to communicate at levels that would have been impossible only a few years ago.

Teacher- and Student-Made Software

As school personnel prepare to purchase computer hardware, they must ask the corollary question: "How will we acquire the necessary software?" Adequate planning for computer technology demands that educators conduct a careful needs assessment and plan for the provision of software *prior* to allocating resources for the acquisition of hardware. In 1988 a Northwest Regional Educational Laboratory report cautioned that lack of planning for software integration with curriculum activities is *the* major problem confronting educators.

Although it may be argued that local production of programs is often inefficient (a similar product already may have been developed elsewhere), locally developed programs do create interested and enthusiastic teachers and students. Another advantage of teacher-made software is that a product developed by a classroom teacher is more likely to relate directly to instructional objectives, course content, and student reading and language skill levels. External products, however sophisticated, may miss the mark in each of these important areas, causing frustration and feelings of failure.

When students are involved in computer course development, they too learn quickly that it is not really difficult to program. What is more significant, they are given an ideal opportunity to exercise effective interpersonal abilities (they need to communicate closely with the teacher about the lesson's objectives and intended audience) and to practice organizational skills. We think of this phase as a new "art form" for students.

Just as the organized teacher carefully maintains files of each previous year's curriculum goals, lesson plans, and examinations, the teacher who collects or produces programs needs to catalogue them. Such systematic efforts help ensure their later accessibility and enable good programs to be distributed to other educational settings. The computer itself, of course, provides an excellent vehicle for this cataloguing process.

Implementing Lesson Design with Microcomputers

As computer-assisted instruction must be carefully planned, it is essential that the students be given lists of both performance and process objectives. These will help them know what is required of them as they work at the microcomputers. As an instructional tool, the microcomputer can also be programmed to process individual and class learning outcomes. This processing capacity saves valuable teacher record-keeping time.

Microcomputers also provide a means by which drill and practice—as well as individualized instruction—may be made part of the classroom routine. Performance objectives must be built into such programs so that students understand what degree of accuracy is required in an individualized system.

Microcomputers easily allow for student self-pacing. Self-pacing requires each user to know expected outcomes and standards. If you use student performance contracts with the microcomputer, then outcomes and standards of achievement are critical. Finally, interactive computer programs allow the student to achieve both performance and process objectives with a speed and efficiency that no other system can attain.

Potentials for Computers

Leslie Eiser and Judy Salpeter (1987) described the use of computer-based interactive geography instruction. The systems interface with computers, video displays, maps, stickers, and worksheets. Students are tested via multiple-choice items that are accumulated by the programs. Some programs have simulation qualities, while others are able to receive student data and process it into the general program.

Video discs allow interactive software with a wide range of programs. "Videodiscovery," one of the many new companies in the field, has already produced interactive programs for art, music, history, science, biotechnology, and biology topics. Predator-prey relations in the food chain provide for a dynamic approach to working with a computer.

Word processing is taught beginning in middle grades and has become standard fare in high schools. English teachers now ask their students to draft, compose, and edit their papers on computers. And virtually every high school now offers training on computers to business students. Recall, it was the business sector that put the pressure on schools to introduce computers. (That pressure was about five years premature. Hundreds of school systems now have obsolete electronic junk because they purchased hardware without knowing much about software needs. And the arena has evolved so fast that no school system can keep current.)

Henry J. Becker (1986) and Robert F. Tinker (1984) noted that only a few schools can allow at least thirty minutes a day on a computer. Usually one microcomputer is found in a classroom, and the available software tends to be trivial and unimaginative.

James D. Ellis (1987) suggested three stages for microcomputer use: (1) exploration where students can gain familiarity, (2) accommodation where a variety of tasks are initiated, and (3) integration where the computer becomes an integral element of the instructional process.

William C. Norris (1988), founder of Control Data Corporation, stressed the need for computer-based education so that ultimately the nation's workforce could be more economically competitive. His analysis is perhaps the most compelling reason for using computers in the schools.

It is clear that the computer acts as a motivating mechanism. Students want to "beat the beast"; thus they apparently spend more time on computer tasks than they normally do on traditional work, or "homework."

Anticipated Problems with Microcomputers

We have already amassed observations about the microcomputer. Rather than providing a lengthy discussion of the problems, we simply provide a list of problems (instructional planning and decision-making) that must be solved *before* the microcomputer is integrated into the total instructional system.

- Exactly how will the computer be used?
- How many stations are available each class period?
- Will an adult be available to supervise?
- Will all microcomputers be stored centrally?
- How will computer usage be assigned?
- Will the computer be an integral part of the class or an enrichment component?
- Will peripheral equipment be required?
- How will the microcomputers be safeguarded against theft?
- How many microcomputers will each teacher have?
- Will the teacher's class have access to computers simultaneously?
- How will independent student study or practice be scheduled?
- Will computers be available before and after school hours?
- How long will any one student have access to the computer?
- Will your school stock entertainment games for students to use?
- Will there be a computer course to teach students how to use the hardware and software?
- How will the computer usage affect the traditional student-teacher roles?

The problems are not insurmountable, but the questions must be raised and answered before the equipment is purchased. Problems notwithstanding, we urge you to be a user of the microcomputer, as it is a powerful force in assisting you as a planner of instruction. Our "real world" already is computerized. As a tool for lesson planning and instruction, the computer can be a great asset. It contributes yet another instructional technology to the teacher's already diverse repertoire of planning and teaching methods—and decision-making skills.

CONCLUSION

Our major intent in this chapter has been to illustrate several guiding principles that can assist you in organizing lessons. We have by no means described all the available options. Furthermore, each instructor or school district may have its own required lesson format. If that is the case, you will at least have had some experiences that should allow you to adapt easily. We also recognize that micro-teaching may or may not be used in your situation; thus, some form of peer coaching may be required.

Let us now address a very important technique that will probably involve the largest proportion of your decision-making time—the art of questioning, which is the subject of Chapter 6. But first complete the formative evaluation that follows.

FORMATIVE EVALUATION   *Lesson Planning*

1. What are the three components of prelesson preparation that should precede the process of designing and using a lesson plan?

2. Match the following elements of lesson planning with their definitions by inserting the correct letter in the spaces provided.

_____ Unit

_____ Instructional goal

_____ Performance objective

_____ Rationale

_____ Content

_____ Instructional procedures

_____ Evaluation procedures

_____ Materials

(a) An outline of how the lesson will be taught.

(b) A description of what the students will be able to do as a consequence of the lesson.

(c) Name of the larger element of instruction of which the particular lesson is a part.

(d) Checklist of everything (for example, handouts) the teacher will need to supply to students during the lesson.

(e) An outcome students are to achieve on completion of the total unit of instruction.

(f) Postinstruction assessment of student performance.

(g) A brief justification of why students should learn what is being taught.

(h) An outline or description of what is to be taught.

3. Identify three sources of educational goal statements that you may find useful in the planning process.

4. Which of the following are goal statements (match with a *G*) and which are objectives (match with an *O*)?

_____ (a) Citizenship training will be learned in this unit.

_____ (b) Each student will list the names of the state's governor and attorney general.

_____ (c) The proper safety habits will be taught in this chemistry class.

_____ (d) Please determine the mass of each of the five samples to the nearest gram.

_____ (e) We will learn Picasso's secrets to success in this art class.

_____ (f) Beside each color on the wheel, you will print in the space the complementary color.

5. What is the main purpose of the Hunter model?

6. Direct instruction is the best instructional strategy under all circumstances.
   (a) Very true.
   (b) Only for teaching the basics and for learning disabled students.
   (c) False; it stresses thinking skills.
   (d) No one strategy is the best under all circumstances.

7. Research about direct instruction shows:
   (a) A very consistent trend.
   (b) A change in recent years.
   (c) No trend in findings.
   (d) Very little interest.

8. Teachers, schools, and entire school districts have focused on direct instruction because:
   (a) It offers an opportunity for reducing costs.
   (b) There has been an increased interest in basic education.
   (c) It offers the opportunity to increase academic engaged time.
   (d) Schools of education require it.

9. Direct instruction does not include a focus on:
   (a) Large groups over small groups.
   (b) Academics.
   (c) Controlled classroom practice.
   (d) Student selected activities.

10. Devise a complex lesson that uses the Kaplan matrix. What benefits are there to the teacher and students when using this model?

11. How does a teacher ever get the time to prepare lesson plans?

12. What essentials are needed in making unit plans for elementary, middle, or high school instruction?

13. Review the Brown (1988) and Rosenshine (1983) papers. What similarities and differences do you observe?

14. What contributions do media and audiovisual materials make in lesson implementation?

Responses

1. Goals; content; student entry level.
2. (c) Unit   (h) Content
   (e) Instructional goal   (a) Instructional procedures
   (b) Performance objective   (f) Evaluation procedures
   (g) Rationale   (d) Materials
3. State, district, and school goals; curriculum guides; needs assessments.
4 (a) G   (d) O
   (b) O   (e) G
   (c) G   (f) O

5. Lesson design.
6. (d).
7. (a).
8. (b).
9. (d).
10.–14. These questions require some activity from you. We suggest that you work with a peer or a small group of three or four and discuss these questions.

REFERENCES

Balajthy, Ernest. "Do Writers Really Revise? Encouraging Unnatural Acts in Your Classroom." Paper presented at the Conference on Language and Literacy, 1986.

Barr, Richard, and Robert Dreeben. "Instruction in Classrooms." In *Review of Research in Education*. Lee Shulman, ed. Itasca, Ill.: Peacock, 1977.

Becker, Henry J. "Instructional Uses of School Computers." Baltimore: Johns Hopkins University, 1986.

Beyer, Barry K. "Critical Thinking Revisited." *Social Education* 49:1985, 268–69.

Borg, Walter R., Marjorie L. Kelley, Phillip Langer, and Meredith Gall. *The Mini-Course: A Microteaching Approach to Teacher's Education.* Beverly Hills, Calif.: Macmillan Educational Services, 1970.

Brophy, Jere. "Teacher Behavior and Student Learning." *Educational Leadership* 37:1979, 33–38.

Brophy, Jere, and Thomas L. Good. "Teacher Behavior and Student Achievement." In *Handbook of Research on Teaching,* 3rd ed. Merlin C. Wittrock, ed. New York: Macmillan, 1986.

Brown, Deborah Sardo. "Twelve Middle-School Teachers' Planning." *The Elementary School Journal* 89(1):1988, 69–87.

Condon, Dennis, and Alex Maggs. "Direct Instruction Research: An International Focus." *International Journal of Special Education* 1:1986, 35–47.

Cornick, Craig, and Timothy Thomas. *Beyond Tradition: Innovative Enhancement of Oral Language in the Classroom.* Des Moines: Iowa State Department of Public Education, 1984.

Cotton, Kathleen. *Direct Instruction. Topic Summary Report. Research on School Effectiveness Project.* Portland, Ore.: Northwest Regional Educational Laboratory, 1982.

Culbertson, Jack A., and LuVern L. Cunningham, eds. *Microcomputers and Education.* Eighty-Fifth Yearbook of the National Society for the Study of Education, Part I. Chicago: University of Chicago Press, 1986.

Doyle, Walter. *Effective Classroom Practices for Secondary Schools. R&D Report No. 6191.* Austin: Texas University, Research and Development Center for Teacher Education, 1984.

Eiser, Leslie, and Judy Salpeter. "Where on Earth Is Washington, DC?" *Classroom Computer Learning* 8(3):1987, 28–32.

Eisner, Elliot W. "The Kind of Schools We Need." *Educational Leadership* 41(2):1983, 43–55.

Ellis, James D. "Improving Science Instruction with Microcomputers." *NARST News* 29(4):1987.

Gagné, Ellen D. "Strategies for Effective Teaching and Learning." In *The Cognitive Psychology of School Learning.* Boston: Little, Brown, 1985.

Garman, Noreen B., and Helen M. Hazi. "Teachers Ask: Is There Life After Madeline Hunter?" *Phi Delta Kappan* 69:1988, 669–672.

Gelder, Amanda, and Alex Maggs. "Direct Instruction Microcomputing in Primary Schools: Manipulation of Critical Instructional Variables." *Research in Science and Technology Education* 1:1983, 221–238.

Gersten, Russell. "Direct Instruction: A Research-

Based Approach to Curriculum Design and Teaching." *Exceptional Children* 53:1986, 17–31.

Gersten, Russell, and Thomas R. Guskey. "Transforming Teacher Reluctance to Teacher Commitment." Paper presented at the Annual Meeting of the American Educational Research Association, 1985.

Gettinger, Maribeth. "Issues and Trends in Academic Engaged Time of Students." *Special Services in the School* 2:1986, 1–17.

Gibboney, Richard A. "A Critique of Madeline Hunter's Teaching Model from Dewey's Perspective. *Educational Leadership* 44(5):1987, 46–50.

Hornick, Karen. *Teaching Writing to Linguistically Diverse Students. ERIC Digest. Number 32.* New York: ERIC Clearinghouse on Urban Education, 1986.

Hunter, Madeline. "Knowing, Teaching, and Supervision." In *Using What We Know About Teaching.* P. L. Hosford, ed. Alexandria, Va.: Association for Supervision and Curriculum Development, 1984, pp. 169–192.

Kaplan, Sandra N. *Inservice Training Manual: Activities for Development Curriculum for the Gifted/Talented.* Ventura, Calif.: Ventura County Schools, 1979.

Lysiak, Fae. *Time on Task: Time Utilization 1984–85.* Fort Worth, Tex.: Forth Worth Independent School District, Texas Department of Research and Evaluation, 1985.

McLuhan, Marshall, and Quentin Fiore. *The Medium Is the Massage.* New York: Bantam Books, 1967.

Meyer, Linda. *Strategies for Correcting Students' Wrong Responses. Technical Report No. 354.* Cambridge, Mass.: Bolt, Beranek and Newman, 1985.

Mitchell, Douglas E., Flora Ida Ortiz, and Tedi K. Mitchell. *Work Orientations and Job Performance: The Cultural Basis of Teaching Rewards and Incentives.* Albany: State University of New York Press, 1987.

Moore, Joseph. "Direct Instruction: A Model of Instructional Design." *Educational Psychology* 6:1986, 201–29.

Norris, William C. "Computer-Based Education: A 'Key' to Reform." Speech, Ninth Conference on Interactive Videodisc in Education and Training, 1988.

The Northwest Report. Portland, Ore.: Northwest Regional Educational Laboratory, September 1988.

Ornstein, Allen. "Emphasis on Student Outcomes Focuses Attention on Quality of Instruction." *NASSP Bulletin* 71:1987, 88–95.

"The Paramount Duty: The Interim Report of the Temporary Committee on Educational Policies, Structure and Management." Olympia: State of Washington, Superintendent of Public Instruction, November 1983.

Peterson, Penelope. "Direct Instruction: Effective for What and for Whom?" *Educational Leadership* 37:1979, 46–48.

Rooze, Gene. "Strategies for Teaching Students to Process Information Using Databases." Paper presented at the Annual Meeting of the National Council for Social Studies, 1966.

Rosenshine, Barak. "Content, Time, and Direct Instruction." In *Research on Teaching: Concepts, Findings, and Implications.* Penelope Peterson and Herbert Walberg, eds. Berkeley, Calif.: McCutchan, 1979.

———. "Teaching Functions Instructional Programs." *The Elementary School Journal* 83(4): 1983, 335–351.

Ross, Dorene, and Diane Kyle. "Helping Preservice Teachers Learn to Use Teacher Effectiveness Research." *Journal of Teacher Education* 38:1987, 40–44.

Schaaf, Oscar. "Activities: Teaching Problem-Solving Skills." *Mathematics Teacher* 77:1984, 694–699.

Slavin, Robert E. "PET and the Pendulum: Faddism in Education and How to Stop It." *Phi Delta Kappan* 70(10):1989, 752–758.

Stallings, Jane. "How Instructional Processes Relate to Child Outcomes in a National Study of Follow Through." *Journal of Teacher Education* 26:1976, 43–47.

Tinker, Robert F. *Science and Mathematics Software Opportunities and Needs (SAMSON) Project, Final Report.* Cambridge, Mass.: Technical Education Research Center, 1984.

Unks, Gerald. "Product-Oriented Teaching: A Reappraisal." *Education and Urban Society* 18: 1986, 242–254.

Vaughn, Janice Bertram. "A Comparison of Peer Teaching and Child Teaching in Preservice Teacher Acquisition of Enthusiasm, Praise, Probing and Questioning Behaviors." Ph.D. diss., University of Cincinnati, 1983.

Wittrock, Merlin C. "Students' Thought Processes." In *Handbook on Research on Teaching,* 3rd ed. Merlin C. Wittrock, ed. New York: Macmillan, 1986.

Yore, Larry. "A Preliminary Exploration of Grade Five Students' Science Achievement and Ability to Read Science Textbooks As a Function of Gender, Reading Vocabulary, and Reading Comprehension." Paper presented at the Annual Meeting of the National Association for Research in Science Teaching, 1987.

6

Deciding How to Ask Questions

*N*ext to lecturing, the single most common teaching method employed in the schools of America and, for that matter, in the world may well be the asking of questions. As an art, it may have started with Socrates and remains the most often used of all teaching strategies. Therefore, if you are to become a highly competent educator, you must master the development and application of questioning.

Objectives   After completing this chapter, you should be able to:

- State the general conclusions from a given review of literature on classroom questions
- Distinguish between convergent, divergent, or evaluative questioning operations
- Distinguish between sequential hierarchies and nonsequential hierarchies as they relate to the classification of questions
- Apply the concept of "mapping"
- Use the following techniques:
  (a) Prompting
  (b) Handling incorrect responses
  (c) Promoting multiple responses
  (d) Framing review questions
  (e) Encouraging nonvolunteers
  (f) Encouraging students to ask questions
  (g) Using "wait time"
- List techniques that interfere with student responses
- List areas relating to questioning where there is some empirical disagreement

In addition, you should demonstrate the following affective behaviors:

- Be considerate and courteous to students during a recitation period
- Be open-minded as students respond
- Appreciate the feelings of students who may be too shy or too reticent to participate in class recitation
- Be positive in outlook, not sarcastic or cynical

OVERVIEW

Having gained familiarity with performance objectives, task analysis, lesson planning, and the taxonomies, you may be wondering how to implement these concepts to aid in your teaching decisions. Your next step will be to master one of the most effective and underestimated teaching strategies: classroom questioning. There is little doubt

The authors wish to thank Carol Mandt Doughty for her efforts in preparing the prototype materials originally used for this chapter.

that questioning plays a critical role in teaching. If teachers are to "teach logically," they must be knowledgeable in the process of framing questions so that they can guide student thought processes in the most skillful and meaningful manner. This implies that teachers must design questions that will help students attain the specific goals (that is, performance objectives) of a particular lesson. Although textbook and examination questions contribute to the learning process, most classroom questions are verbal and teacher-formulated. As Todd D. Kelley (1987) pointed out, questions are critical elements with which teachers stimulate student thinking. By studying question patterns, one may even determine the types of verbal interactions that take place in the classroom.

The Status of Classroom Questioning

The purpose of this chapter is to examine the functions of questions, their use as a teaching strategy, and the effects they have on learning. Our brief review of classroom questioning will provide you with an indication of the apparent effects that questioning techniques have on learning processes.

It appears that teachers may have mistakenly equated quantity of questions with quality. One of the earliest studies of questions in the classroom was done in 1912 by Romiett Stevens. She estimated that 80 percent of school time was used for question-and-answer recitation. Eight decades later that ratio would range between 33 percent (Fisher et al., 1984) and 50 percent (Watson and Young, 1986). In 1970 Ned Flanders reported that teachers talked about 75 percent of the time. The study made by J. Nathan Swift, C. Thomas Gooding, and Patricia R. Swift (1988) found that one science teacher spoke "in excess" of 85 percent of the entire class period. These authors further reported that one teacher they studied asked fifty-three questions in a recitation period, while students asked only three.

Meredith D. Gall (1970) cited several studies in which large numbers of questions were used by elementary teachers—ranging from 64 to 180 questions in one class period to an average of 348 questions during the school day! He cited eight studies showing that questioning practices changed little over time. J. T. Dillon (1987) reported that observations of twenty-seven senior high school social studies teachers showed an average of eighty questions per class hour per teacher. Only two questions per hour were asked by students. What makes these data tragicomic was the topics being discussed: racism, revolution, abortion, pollution, and marriage. These are topics that should raise dozens of student questions. Perhaps the teachers were unintentionally disinviting.

Several reasons have been proposed for why teachers use so many fact (low-level) questions. One rationale supported by many teachers is that students need facts for high-order thinking. This is a cogent point, but there are ways to teach facts, such as direct instruction.

Another apparent reason why teachers overuse fact questions is the lack of systematic teacher training in the use of questioning strategies. The Far West

Laboratory for Educational Research and Development developed a self-contained, inservice minicourse to improve teachers' questioning skills. The laboratory program uses 16-mm films to explain the concepts and also includes modeling, self-feedback, and micro-teaching. After the program was used with forty-eight elementary teachers in the Far West Laboratory field tests, the results showed an increase in redirection questions (those requiring responses from more than one student) from 26.7 percent to 40.9 percent; in thought-provoking questions, from 37.3 percent to 52.0 percent; and in probing (that is, prompting) questions, from 8.5 percent to 13.9 percent. There was also a concomitant decrease in the repetition of students' answers from 30.7 percent to 4.4 percent. The repetition of the teacher's own questions decreased from 13.7 percent to 4.7 percent, and the answering of the teacher's own questions by the teacher decreased from 4.6 percent to 0.7 percent (Borg et al., 1970).

We must note here that it is the micro-teaching component of the Far West Laboratory's minicourse that allows the teacher to practice and perfect questioning skills. Studies by Donald C. Orlich et al. (1972, 1973, 1989) revealed that when teachers were trained in questioning, the frequency of higher-level questions used in the classroom increased significantly.

Still another reason why there have been so many low-level questions is that teachers do not use a system to organize and classify questions. This is where Bloom's and other taxonomies can be of use. A majority of the researchers use Bloom's Taxonomy to evaluate the potential for critical thinking in the classroom. Jere Brophy (1986) suggests that the use of a taxonomy per se will not improve the quality of questions but does make the teacher more aware of the process. He implied that students also should understand the various levels of questions. In this chapter we present a total of seven different taxonomies or hierarchies by which to categorize questions.

Questions and Cognitive Effects

Before attempting to demonstrate the ways a teacher may use a classification system such as Bloom's to improve questioning, let us examine a few of the hundreds of published studies to determine how varying the levels of questioning affects student thinking.

Lucille Falkof and Janet Moss (1984) reported that up to 85 percent of all teacher-asked questions are factual. Swift, Gooding, and Swift (1988) found that their sample of middle school science teachers asked 85.9 percent of their questions at the memory or lowest cognitive level. Mary C. Shake (1988) observed six second grade teachers ask low-level questions at least 52 percent of the time. There was also a correlation between questioning levels and the reading group. Highest readers were asked higher-level questions, while the poorest readers were asked lower-level questions.

Teaching by twenty-two high school student teachers of English, social studies, and science was observed by Marylou Dantonio and Louis V. Paradise (1988), who found that 63 percent of the cohort collectively asked questions that were at the lowest cognitive level. These questions had a 100 percent correspondence rate; that is, when the teachers asked low-level questions, students responded 100 percent of the time with a low-level response. When the group asked higher-level questions, there was 76 percent correspondence. Around one-fourth of the students responded at levels lower than the intended context of the question.

All the blame for low-level questions does not rest with the teacher. In a study that still has validity, O. L. Davis, Jr., and Francis P. Hunkins (1966) investigated textbook questions and the thinking processes they apparently foster. They randomly chose a third of the chapters from three recently published fifth grade social studies textbooks. They used the *Taxonomy of Educational Objectives, Handbook I: Cognitive Domain* by Bloom (1956) to categorize the questions. All three books consistently emphasized Knowledge questions and uniformly avoided higher-order questions. A summary of their data indicated that the averages for all three were as follows: Knowledge—87 percent; Comprehension—9 percent; and Application—4 percent. Of the 732 questions analyzed, Davis and Hunkins found that none required analysis, one required synthesis, and two required evaluation! However, Hans Gerhard Klinzing and Gisela Klinzing-Eurich (1988), in summarizing several studies, have concluded that (1) teachers can learn how to increase the cognitive level of classroom questions, (2) higher-level questions predominantly have a positive effect on student achievement, and (3) internationally, the correspondence between cognitive levels of teacher questions and student responses tends to be low.

The above substantiate analyses published by J. T. Dillon that there are wide discrepancies between the teachers' cognitive level of questions and the students' responses. Dillon (1982a) observed that there was a 50 percent chance that a student would respond with a lower-level response when asked a higher-level question, and *vice versa*. Dillon (1982b) further wrote that teachers may have become doctrinaire in their almost exclusive use of teacher questioning at the expense of greater student participation. He very accurately observed that teacher-question student-recitation periods seldom lead to meaningful classroom discussion. (We very much concur with Dillon; see Chapter 7, "Decisions About Discussions.")

Dillon (1981a) also cautioned teacher educators that if teachers dominate classroom verbal interactions, then class members ultimately become dependent on the teacher and illustrate passive behaviors. Indeed, the latter traits would hardly foster ingenuity, creativity, or thinking—traits we all consider desirable.

Dillon (1981b) offers an alternative to the use of teacher questions. He provides some persuasive evidence that teachers should stimulate student responses and thinking by using *declarative statements* rather than questions. This elicits longer and more complex student responses. Writing in 1987, Dillon expanded on the technique, suggesting that teachers explicitly state their thoughts in relation to the student's response. He asserts that students will respond to a teacher's statement because students are conditioned to respond to authority figures. Teachers should keep the statements short—about one sentence—and, when appropriate, seek further comments from the student. Using Dillon's technique requires some practice. This is an ideal situation for perfecting a new teaching behavior via microteaching or peer coaching (Joyce and Showers, 1988).

Using Student Questions

Another source of questions is often overlooked—the students. David and Heather Wood (1988) stated that classes should be oriented toward student communication, giving students a chance to express opinions and ideas; but evidence shows that teachers do most of the talking and questioning.

In 1975 Catherine Cornbleth presented some relevant studies and evidence to support teacher encouragement of student questioning behavior. In general she found that (1) students can be encouraged to ask productive or higher-level questions, (2) the more questions a student asks per period the more probable the questions will be higher level, (3) praise will encourage and stimulate more productive thinking processes with children of lower socioeconomic status, and (4) students become more involved in the classes when they are encouraged to ask questions.

In yet another study, Meredith D. Gall and associates (1978) reported that their experiments on questioning, recitation, and learning seemed to support the idea that recitation teaching was more effective in promoting student learning than was a nonrecitation instructional experience lasting the same time. They also noted that students learned equally well when the teacher gave the answer to a question a student did not know or when information was provided by their peers. This study provides evidence that fact questions were not harmful to the learning of higher cognitive skills.

Gall's studies draw two conclusions: (1) well-designed questions and strategies may be more important than the level of questions, and (2) when you work with very small groups, there is a tendency for greater efficiency in learning. The latter is discussed in Chapter 7.

Although the evidence is somewhat inconclusive, there does appear to be a direct relationship between the level of questions asked by the teacher and the level of student responses. Furthermore, it appears that if teachers decide to raise their expectations for the class and *systematically* raise the level of their questioning, then the students accordingly raise the level of their responses. Of course, this implies a carefully planned questioning sequence that would probably span several weeks of instruction. The major caution is not to jump haphazardly into high-level questions without making the necessary teacher-student attitude adjustments. This means that teachers must plan how to ask appropriate questions just as they plan for the next week's reading assignments. J. T. Dillon adds a caution: There is no guarantee that a higher-level question will elicit a higher-level student response. (Student questioning as a teaching technique is discussed later in this chapter.)

Tips for the Teacher

The implications of these studies for your decision-making are many. First, if you want your students to develop higher levels of thinking, to evaluate information, to achieve more, and to be more interested, then you must learn to ask higher-level questions. Second, encourage your students to ask more questions—and more thought-provoking ones—if you want greater student involvement in the process of learning. We should add that the type of questions to be used is your decision.

Another important consideration if you desire to stimulate critical thinking is how you use textbooks. Be aware of the advantages and disadvantages of your textbook materials. To attain the objective desired, you may have to supplement the materials provided. For example, Cheryl G. Fedje and Ann Irvine (1982) prepare lesson plans with key questions that require students to observe, compare, contrast, group, order, or determine cause and effect. These processes are ones used in developing "thinking."

Finally, you can use questions to (1) diagnose student progress, (2) determine entry-level competence, (3) prescribe additional study, and (4) enrich an area.

Lelia Christenbury and Patricia P. Kelly (1983) collected at least seven different questioning taxonomies or hierarchies. They divided the questioning hierarchies into two general sets: sequential hierarchies and nonsequential hierarchies. These two sets are illustrated in Table 6-1. Observe how there are similarities and also great differences between the sets. Further, one or more of the categories can be used to "analyze" questions or statements and the concomitant student responses. You can

Table 6-1   *Seven Questioning Hierarchies and Classification Methods*

	Benjamin Bloom et al. (1956)	Norris M. Sanders (1966)	Hilda Taba (1967)	Harold L. Herber (1978)
Sequential Hierarchies	To know To comprehend To apply To analyze To synthesize To evaluate	Memory Translation Interpretation Application Analysis Synthesis Evaluation	Form concept Interpret concept Apply concept	Literal comprehension Interpretative comprehension Applied comprehension
	Arthur Kaiser (1979)	Richard Smith (1969)	Ronald T. Hyman (1979)	
Nonsequential Hierarchies	Open Closed Suggestive Rhetorical	Convergent Divergent	Definitional Empirical Evaluative Metaphysical	

Source: Lelia Christenbury and Patricia P. Kelly, *Questioning: A Critical Path to Critical Thinking.* Urbana, Ill.: ERIC Clearinghouse on Reading and Communication Skills and the National Council of Teachers of English, 1983, p. 4. Public Domain Document, NIE 400-78-0026.

select the hierarchy that best fits your instructional objectives. We present this series in keeping with our concept of teacher decision-making.

Summary

Following is a brief list of findings that summarizes the results of a century of research on questioning.

1. Questioning tends to be a universal teaching strategy.
2. Being systematic in the use and development of questioning tends to improve student learning.
3. By classifying questions according to a particular system, the teacher may determine the cognitive or affective level at which the class is working and make adjustments as professionally indicated.
4. Through systematic questioning, the teacher may determine the entry levels of students for specific content areas.
5. Questions should be developed logically and sequentially.
6. Students should be encouraged to ask questions.
7. A written plan with key questions will provide lesson structure and direction.
8. Questions should be adapted to the students' level of ability.
9. Use questioning techniques that encourage the widest student participation.
10. Use statements rather than questions to promote student reactions.
11. A wide variety of questioning options is open to teachers.
12. No one questioning strategy is applicable to all teaching situations.

In addition to these assertions, which are substantiated by research, we also have assumed that higher-level questions demand greater intellectual activity. The research available to date seems to confirm that assumption. Rather than emphasizing a "right" answer, teachers should use questions to stimulate higher cognitive achievements and to make information more meaningful. In the long run, the quality of the questions being asked should be most important. Finally, Walter Borg, one of the creators of the Far West Lab minicourse, concluded that questioning is one of the most essential functions of teaching (Borg et al., 1970). *If* this generally accepted assertion is valid, *then* teachers must achieve a high degree of sensitivity and awareness to use questions in the most efficacious and appropriate manner.

APPLYING QUESTIONING TECHNIQUES

We suggest that all teachers must become aware of the kinds of questions they ask and the kinds of responses that these questions elicit. Our theory states: If *the teacher desires a response at a selected level of thinking,* then *an appropriate question must be framed that will elicit the proper response level from the student.* The simple adoption of the "if-then" strategy gives the teacher the needed awareness of the intellectual level at which the class is being conducted. This strategy also requires concomitant and continued decision-making and evaluation by the teacher and can be applied at *all* levels of instruction and with *all* types of students.

Applying the Taxonomies to Questioning

As shown in Table 6-1, there are several hierarchies or taxonomies from which to select a framework for questioning. The context of the questioning must be taken into account. Dennis Palmer Wolf (1987) notes that a teacher who desires to instruct at higher cognitive levels must develop a questioning hierarchy. The hierarchical list then becomes a plan through which the recitations and discussion are implemented. In short, the hierarchy allows the students to perceive an idea, concept, or issue as being structured into a framework for thinking; thus, the hierarchy becomes a visible blueprint for action. Further, in light of J. T. Dillon's work, a series of declarative statements—rather than questions—could be structured in some hierarchical manner to elicit improved student responses.

Basic Questioning Categories

For convenience you may classify all questioning strategies into three categories: (1) convergent, (2) divergent, and (3) evaluative. This classification is a very slightly modified version of that proposed by James Gallagher and his associates (Verduin, 1967). If the teacher assigns value (affective dimension) to the types of questions being asked of the students, then it becomes necessary to have a method for verifying that the teacher is using specified questioning patterns. Some type of classification scheme is needed. The studies previously cited indicated that the three categories would be an efficient method by which to tabulate the kinds of classroom questions.

Convergent Questions

As the term denotes, the focus of a convergent questioning pattern is on a narrow objective. You would use questions that encourage student responses to converge or focus on a central theme. Convergent questions, for the most part, elicit short responses from students. That is, *if* you have a learning objective that involves manifesting a student behavior consisting of short responses such as "yes" or "no" or very short statements, *then* you should plan to use a convergent questioning pattern. Furthermore, if you are using a convergent questioning pattern, you must be aware that you are focusing on the lower levels of thinking—that is, the Knowledge or Comprehension levels. It should be noted that using a convergent technique per se is not to be construed as "bad." In many situations you will decide that the students need to demonstrate a knowledge of specifics; in such cases, lower-level questioning strategies are appropriate.

What this means, then, is that the *appropriateness* of any set of questioning strategies must be judged solely on the objectives that you have specified. Of course, any teacher who justifies the continual use of low-level questions with the commonly heard comment that "I don't think my students can do any better" may be replaced with a set of programmed instruction materials supplemented by an audio or video cassette learning system.

Why do you want to prepare learning objectives that utilize a convergent type of questioning pattern? There are several possibilities for consideration. For example, *if* you use an inductive teaching style (proceeding from a set of specific data to a student-derived conclusion), *then* you will use a large proportion of convergent type questions. Also, you may wish to use short-response questions as "warm-up" exercises for breaking the monotony of the traditional classroom. These warm-up exercises may follow a "rapid-fire" method, which would be most appropriate when you are building vocabulary skills. Teachers in foreign-language classes may use a convergent, rapid-fire pattern to help develop oral, vocabulary, and spelling skills among students. This technique also allows all students to participate. The same method may be used by a science teacher. For example, a typical high school sophomore biology course has more "foreign" terms and concepts than all the new vocabulary words learned by the average sophomore in any foreign language class! Thus, a biology teacher may wish to use a convergent technique for the first few minutes of the class to maximize participation and to generate constructive verbal motivation among the students.

A convergent, rapid-fire technique focuses on specific learning objectives, skills, terminologies, or short responses. The use of this technique with short answers may be demonstrated in a mathematics class when the teacher wishes the students to practice verbalized rapid calculation. A social studies teacher may want to use a pinpoint technique in identifying specific bits of information or facts.

The basic convergent pattern allows you to "dominate" the thinking of the students by asking for short-length, low-level intellectual responses that involve a single answer or a limited number of logical answers. You should understand that a convergent questioning pattern is *not* an appropriate means of stimulating thought-provoking responses or classroom discussions; rather, it stresses Knowledge or Comprehension levels. The convergent technique is an ideal application of "teacher-directed instruction" or *direct instruction,* where all students in class respond *in unison* to teacher-asked questions. Everyone participates.

A list of convergent questions follows. Note that these questions all meet the criterion of limiting student responses to a narrow spectrum of possible options and are more recall-oriented than analytical.

1. In what works did Robert Browning use the dramatic monologue as a form for his poems?

2. Under what conditions will water boil at less than 100°C?
3. What helps bread dough rise?
4. Where did "Pickleball" originate?
5. Why do relatively few people live in the deserts of any country?
6. Explain the attitudes that the Romantic poets had toward nature.
7. Where and when did Champlain build the first French trading post?
8. Explain the "Big Bang" theory.
9. Describe how parliamentary governmental systems differ from the type described in the American Constitution.

Divergent Questions

Divergent questions are the opposite of convergent questions—the focus of divergent questions is broad. Rather than seeking a single focus, you are, with a divergent questioning strategy, evoking student responses that vary greatly. Divergent questions also elicit longer student responses. Thus, *if* you wish to evoke several different responses from the class, *then* you ask a question that is divergent. The anticipated student reply will be typically longer than a response to a convergent question. In summary, when ideas are being discussed and you want to elicit a variety of responses from the students, you will recognize divergent types of questions as appropriate. This technique is ideal for building the self-concepts of children of minority groups or of lower socioeconomic status because divergent questions often have few "right" or "wrong" responses.

Eliciting Multiple Responses   If you wish to elicit multiple responses, *then* you will use a multiple-response technique. Basically, such a technique is as follows: After you decide that more than one student should respond to a particular divergent question, you then ask a question that can be answered with multiple responses. After stating the question, call on three or four students and then assume a passive role in this minidiscussion. Such a technique teaches the students to conduct a classroom discussion—a rather sophisticated teaching strategy when used properly. This technique also sharpens their listening skills.

Accepting Diversity   Besides eliciting longer and multiple responses, you must also be prepared to accept diverse responses. When you ask a divergent question, then you must expect a multiplicity of responses as well as some creative ones. *If* allowing or encouraging novel solutions and creative responses is your goal, *then* the divergent method is appropriate. Remember, too, that if you elicit diverse responses from the students, then *you have the professional obligation to accept* those students' responses. This is a very important concept in the art of asking questions. To reinforce appropriate response behavior, you must demonstrate a high degree of acceptance for the response of each student. This means that you may not use subtle "put down" tactics, regardless of how seemingly outlandish a student's point of view may be or how opposite from what you expected. The rule of thumb is that when you ask divergent questions, you must allow free responses by the students. Again, this is a great technique for disadvantaged students, as they get to become "stars" in the classroom.

Beginning the Sequence   A helpful technique as you initially frame divergent questions is to write out the questions prior to asking them. Then examine them to ensure that they are clearly stated and convey the precise meanings intended. In using divergent questions for the first time, you will probably find the initial class experience rather difficult or even disappointing, usually because students are not oriented toward giving longer or higher-level thinking responses.

It takes a good deal of reshaping of student behavior patterns to elicit the proper level and type of student responses with the use of divergent questioning techniques. For thousands of classroom hours, students from grade school to high school have been conditioned to respond with short, low-level thinking responses. The teacher who begins to schedule divergent questions in the classroom questioning periods must also have the patience to inform the students that the level of questions is changing and that the level of their responses will also change quite drastically; it will differ from the level of responses given with the convergent or pinpointing technique commonly used by other teachers.

In using a divergent technique of questioning, you will soon discover that the students will respond in the higher-level thinking categories of the cognitive taxonomy—that is, Application, Analysis, and Synthesis. Also, you should develop questions that, over an extended time, will gradually progress to other divergent questions for stimulating analytical and synthetic thinking. This point has been amply demonstrated in classes with large proportions of disadvantaged students. Thus *if* you want your students to be prepared to conduct discussions and to give longer and more diverse oral or written responses, *then* the divergent technique is the appropriate one to use.

The divergent method is appropriate for eliciting multiple responses from students. If this is your intent, then it will be important for you to inform the class that you desire a set of multiple responses, with each student taking cues from the other students' responses. This means that you do *not* repeat student responses for the other class members. (Obviously, there are exceptions to this rule. For instance, if a student speaks in such a low voice that it is impossible for some class members to hear, then the teacher may repeat the student response.) The rationale underlying the technique of not repeating is that if a student knows that the previous student's response will be repeated by the teacher, then most students become conditioned to listening only for the teacher's repetition of the response (which is similar to instant replay on television).

Our prescription for avoiding inappropriate teacher behaviors is to allow all students to present their responses without teacher interference. This has a positive effect on the class. There may be times, however, if using debate techniques, when the teacher may interrupt a student. This is a more advanced technique that is used after mutual trust has been established in the classroom. In general, we find that teachers tend to interrupt their students before students have fully explained their positions. If the teacher is sensitive to this behavior, the students will realize that their responses *are* important and that they must take their cues from one another rather than from the teacher. This technique of not interrupting students reduces the time of teacher's talk in a classroom and increases the "responsibility quotient" of students. In short, students realize that they must now be responsive to each other, and the "attending behavior" of the class will improve. It does little good for the teacher continually to remind the students that they are not paying attention. Such negative reinforcement only makes a class less attentive. By encouraging students to listen to one another, you let them participate in a dynamic fashion and, thus, receive peer reinforcement for positive and constructive classroom behavior.

In summary, *if* you wish to elicit a set of student behaviors that involve higher-level thinking skills, *then* you will plan for a systematic development of divergent questions. Remember that the emphasis is on systematic development of questions over an extended time, with well-conceived and appropriate learning objectives. We cannot overemphasize the amount of time involved; it takes weeks, even months, to incorporate these behaviors into the usual repertoire of school behaviors.

Longer and more diverse responses are the criteria that characterize the divergent questioning framework. Your decision to use divergent questions requires that you help the students locate different sources of information so that they can share a variety of viewpoints in the class. The following list includes questions that may be classified as divergent. Note that we have adapted a few of these from the previously presented list of convergent questions.

1. What type of social and cultural development might have taken place if Christopher Columbus had landed on Manhattan Island on October 12, 1492?
2. What would happen in a school if it had no rules?
3. What do you think are other effective methods of organic gardening that are not listed in the textbook?
4. How does the environment affect human behavior?
5. Why would one select arc welding over gas welding in the fabrication of art objects?
6. How has the popularity of tennis had both a social and an economic impact on our society?
7. What kinds of evidence would you seek if you were an opponent of the "Big Bang" theory?
8. How would a government organized according to a parliamentary system have reacted to our "Iran-contra" incident?
9. What impact will be made on our standard of living if we exhaust our nation's petroleum resources within ten to twenty years?
10. List as many alternatives as you can to an interstate highway system being constructed in a city.

Evaluative Questions

The third pattern of questioning uses divergent questions, but with one added component—evaluation. The basic difference between a divergent question and an evaluative question is that the evaluative question has a built-in evaluative or judgmental set of criteria. In asking *why* something is good or bad, you are raising an evaluation question. It is possible, however, that an evaluative question may elicit nothing more than a poor collection of uninformed student opinions. Therefore, with evaluative questions, emphasize the specificity of the criteria by which a student judges the value or appropriateness of an object or an idea. As with divergent questions, you must accept student responses to encourage students to provide evaluative responses to your questions.

A major component in the evaluative questioning framework is that the teacher systematically helps students develop a logical basis for establishing evaluative criteria. For example, if you ask a question and a student presents a response that is followed by your asking, "Why?", to which the student replies only, "Because," then you should recognize immediately that the student is lacking in logical perception, may be dogmatic or arbitrary, or simply does not understand how to frame a logical, consistent set of evaluative criteria. Once again, we caution that you must *never* use sarcasm or any other disparaging technique; instead, take a positive approach and reinforce the student in an environment conducive to a logical development of evaluative criteria. The typical teacher comment, "You're not being logical," gives the student no basis for improvement. Provide a specific set of criteria from which students may develop their own criteria. In this manner, they will understand why they hold value judgments or opinions. As an introduction to this technique we recommend a joint writing session, with the teacher and small groups of students collaboratively listing criteria.

Observation will verify that as evaluative questions are presented and student responses elicited, you and the students will want to classify the evaluative responses along some type of continuum ranging from "bad" or "illogical" to "good" or "logically developed."

Note that we have been using the term *responses,* not *answers. Answers* carry the connotation of being final, complete, or the last word. To be sure, convergent questioning patterns may elicit student answers; but when divergent and evaluative questions are framed, the students will not be responding with definitive or absolute answers. They will be providing responses that tend to be relative, less than certain, or tentative.

Note also that the term *continuum* can describe a classification scheme. Both questions and responses are not conveniently categorized within the dualistic concept of "good or bad" or "appropriate or inappropriate." Most student responses in the evaluative mode will demonstrate a broad range of thought when based on a set of evaluative criteria. This is precisely your aim in using evaluation questions. You then classify the evaluative responses according to their logical development, internal consistency, validity, and perhaps responsibility. In short, we are suggesting that again you accept all student responses and, as apparent logical inconsistencies develop, discuss them after the student has had an opportunity for classroom discourse. Thus *if* you wish to allow students to make evaluations and judgments about what they have learned, *then* your appropriate behavior is to use the evaluative questioning technique.

The following list provides examples of evaluative questions. Remember that most, if not all, evaluative questions will also be divergent. The one characteristic that separates divergent questions from evaluative ones is that the latter rely on established judgmental criteria. Observe that some examples previously designated as divergent have been converted now into evaluative questions.

1. Why is the parliamentary system of government more responsive to the citizens than our legislative system is?
2. Why is the world a better place because of computers?
3. Why should good teachers strive to be aware of the types of questions they ask?
4. Why will the Court's stand on abortion reform affect social and moral attitudes and behaviors?
5. Why is it better to switch to either "gasohol" or "hydrogen" as fuel for our automobiles?
6. Why has the federal system of interstate highways harmed our city environments?
7. Defend the strip mining of coal in eastern Montana.
8. To what extent is the "Big Bang" theory a more viable one than the "Cold Start"?
9. Why have professional sports grown to be so popular in the United States?

You may disagree that there are three major types of questioning strategies and may want to establish other categories of your own. If so, you may produce a series of classification schemes for your own use. Our objective is to provide an efficient and convenient system for categorizing questions quickly so that you are always aware of the specific questioning strategy you are using and may anticipate an appropriate set of responses from the students. The decision to use such a system for self-improvement or professional development is, of course, yours.

MAPPING AS A QUESTIONING TECHNIQUE

Just when it appears that the concept of questioning is clear, we will add another contemporary technique. You will find this technique labeled mapping, webbing, highlighting, story mapping, netting, or drafting—we will call it *mapping*. It stems from the innovative and creative work of the Bay Area Writing Project (Gray and Meyers, 1978) and the various projects that evolved from it (Barton and Zehm, 1983).

Isabel Beck and Margaret McKeown (1981) adapted the concept of mapping to a "story map," which guides question development so that deeper meaning is constructed from a text. The map is simply a visual plan of the major events and ideas ultimately placed in their logical order. The map begins as a "hub," which is the starting point of the story. Then a list of central events and ideas is made in summary form. These elements, which are student statements or questions, are added as spokes on the hub. A progression of the listed ideas and events becomes the foundation for extending comprehension into higher levels, and a "map" emerges. Additional questions or statements can be used to develop interpretations, themes, use of literary conventions, or relevancy to current issues. (Mapping may also be used to teach basic organizational skills in grades 1 through 9. The technique is also useful in helping high school students improve selected analytical skills.)

Gabriele Lusser Rico (1983) provides examples of mapping under her concept of *clustering;* her work is an excellent resource for the topic. We observed a splendid model in the fourth grade class of Mrs. Meta Gibbs. Figure 6-1 illustrates the actual concept map that she and her students created in 1988 when they were studying volcanoes. This map guided classroom discussions and integrated writing assignments.

THE TEACHER'S APPROPRIATE QUESTIONING BEHAVIORS

To develop a repertoire of questioning skills, you must be aware of a wide spectrum of questioning techniques that may elicit appropriate responses from students. The

Figure 6-1   *Concept Map of Student Ideas*

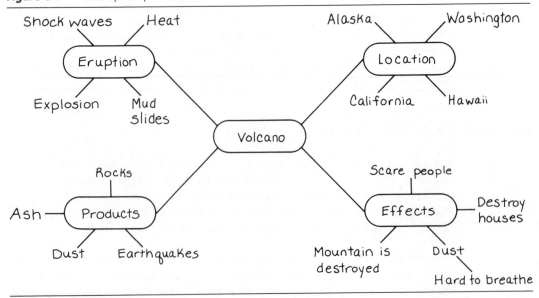

Used with permission of Meta Gibbs, Browne School, Spokane, Washington.

teacher-behavior questioning skills that follow address specific kinds of problems arising in any class using questioning strategies. Each skill is discussed so that you may identify and practice that particular skill. Thus, when you decide to use the strategy, you will know how to use it and why.

Technical and Humane Considerations

The questioning in a recitation period, a tutorial period, or an inductive session is always predicated on the assumption that some meaningful or purposeful learning activity will take place, allowing the student to gain another learning experience. For this to happen, questions must be asked in a positive reinforcing manner—that is, so that the student will enjoy learning and responding. All students should receive positive reinforcement by virtue of the questions being asked and the types of responses elicited. Our basic premise is that questions should *never* be used for punitive means. The teacher who asks a question to punish the student is turning a learning situation into a negatively reinforcing one. The result is that, rather than creating a friendly atmosphere conducive to learning, the teacher "turns off" not only the learner but the learning process as well. This is extremely critical, especially when working with disadvantaged or young students. In short, our philosophy is that questioning must be used only in ways that are meaningful, purposeful, and positively reinforcing.

Framing Questions

How does one frame a question? The logical method is to think through your question plan, just as a quarterback or a coach plans the game strategy *prior* to the playing of the game. As a teacher, you establish goals with objectives to be met *and* the appropriate questioning strategy to reach those goals. Once the initial preparation has been accomplished, then it becomes a matter of implementation: Ask the question and elicit an appropriate response.

The basic rule for framing a question is as follows: *Ask the question; pause, then call on a student.* This rule is grounded in the psychological principle that when a question is asked and then followed by a short pause, all students will "attend" to the communication. The nonverbal message (pause) communicates that any student in the class may be selected for a response. Thus, the attention level of the class remains high. If you reverse this pattern by calling on a particular student before you ask the question, then all those students who are not involved have the opportunity "not to attend" to the communication between teacher and student.

The technique of framing thus entails (1) asking the question, (2) pausing, and (3) calling on the student. You can use this same question-framing technique even with a multiple-response method in which you specify that several students will be selected to respond. Furthermore, once you and the students have mastered this technique, you can modify the third element to a nonverbal action simply by pointing or nodding to a student for response. This technique becomes easy with a little practice.

We mentioned that the teacher ought to pause after asking a question. There are several justifications for this teacher behavior. The first is that the pause, or *wait time,* gives students a chance to think about their responses to the question. This is especially essential when you ask higher-level thinking questions.

A pause after the question also provides you with a little time to "read" the nonverbal cues from the class. With some practice you can readily observe such nonverbal signals as pleasure, apprehension, fright, excitement, joy, or shame. As teachers become more affectively sensitive to humanistic considerations in the classroom, this dimension of teaching becomes very important.

Finally, the teacher who acquires the habit of pausing after asking a question will not dread the wait time. Mary Budd Rowe (1969, 1974, and 1980) discovered that teachers are most impatient with youngsters when asking questions. Measuring the wait time of many metropolitan elementary school teachers, she found that the wait time between asking a question and answering it before the student does or calling on another student had to be measured in *fractions of seconds!* Is it any wonder, then, that some students dread to be called on? They know that it will elicit impatient behaviors from the teacher and that they will simply be "in Dutch" again.

In subsequent studies, Rowe (1978) described the results of "wait-time 2." In the first set of studies, the teachers paused (wait-time 1) prior to calling on a student to respond. Rowe then discovered that if a teacher waits to respond to the student after the student responds initially, then students will continue to respond—without teacher prompting.

By using the wait-time 2 technique Rowe found that (1) lengths of student responses increased, (2) the number of questions asked by students increased, (3) there was a decrease in failure to respond, (4) student involvement in the lessons increased, (5) student reasoning improved, (6) slower students responded more, and (7) student disciplinary actions decreased.

The effectiveness of wait time has been well documented. The most significant review of wait time emerging from the 1980s was by Kenneth Tobin (1987), who analyzed fifty published studies regarding wait time reflecting over a twenty-year period. He summarized changes that took place in *teacher questioning behaviors* when they used the wait time technique. In general, the teachers using this strategy

1. Had less teacher talk
2. Repeated themselves less
3. Asked fewer questions per period
4. Asked more questions that had multiple responses
5. Asked fewer lower-level questions
6. Did more probing
7. Repeated students' responses less
8. Asked more application questions
9. Had some increased anxiety as they implemented the technique

Reflect on the above findings. They support the total method presented in this chapter.

What impact does wait time have on student behavior? In general, students

1. Made longer responses
2. Had more student discourse
3. Had fewer nonrespondents
4. Increased complexity of answers
5. Had more student-initiated questions
6. Had more student-to-student interactions
7. Had less confusion
8. Had more confidence
9. Had fewer peer interruptions
10. Had higher achievement (Tobin, 1987)

Again, these findings illustrate the efficacy of the total questioning method endorsed herein. The results reported by Tobin and others demand that *any responsible teacher* must master the total method of questioning.

We do add one cautionary footnote. Joseph P. Riley, II (1986) reported that wait time had no effect on student responses to lower-level questions. But when a teacher asks a higher-level question, it is essential to "wait." Riley found that lack of wait time with higher-level questions led to lower level student responses—the correspondence problem we mentioned earlier. That is, if you ask a low-level question, then there is a probability you will receive a low-level student response.

We want you to know that classroom silence is not all bad—even when asking questions. So make the decision to wait—not only once, but twice, even three times if students are interacting.

Prompting Techniques

Once you have asked the question and have called on a student to respond, there is the possibility that the student will either not answer the question *completely* or not answer it at all. When this happens, you should promptly conduct strategies to clarify the question so that the student can understand it better, should try to have the student amplify the response, or should elicit additional responses from the student so that you may verify whether the student comprehends the material. As you develop prompting skills, there are many rules that you can follow; however, to simplify matters, keep one rule foremost in mind: *prompt in a positive manner*. This means that if a student has not answered the question or has not amplified a response to your satisfaction, then you should decide to prompt. To do this, acknowledge the attempted response but then encourage the student to clarify or amplify it.

You may have to prompt a student many times during a questioning session so as to derive a more complete or logical response from an inadequate response. Basically, always aid the student with positive reinforcement so that the student is encouraged to complete an incomplete response or to revise an incorrect one. In most cases, the student will answer with a partially correct response or, to put it negatively, with a partially incorrect response in addition to a partially correct response. Immediately on hearing a response that fits this category, begin to prompt the student so that the response can be completed, be made more logical, be re-examined, or be stated more adequately or more appropriately.

The next two examples illustrate prompting or probing techniques.

Example 1

Teacher: What did the English citizens and American colonists think a constitution should be like? (Pause.) Hector?

Student: Well . . . um . . . they figured it was a bunch of laws all written down in one place.

Teacher: That's a good description of the American point of view. Now . . . what did Englishmen think?

Student: They thought the laws should be written down in different places . . . sort of.

Teacher: O.K. . . . that's part of the answer. Now, did *all* of the laws for the English constitution have to be written down?

Student: Some stuff was just rules that had been set up and everybody knew what they were and followed them. But others were written down in many different . . . ah . . . documents.

Teacher: Fine! Now how about going back and summing up what you've worked out so far?

Example 2

Teacher: American colonists and English citizens both had the highest respect for their constitutions. However, they differed in how they should be interpreted. What is an example of this difference? (Pause.) Angela?

Student: The English thought it should be used to exploit the colonists by taxing really hard.

Teacher: Taxation *was* one of the biggest problems. Good! Now, what made the English think they had the right to tax?

Student: Their constitution said so.

Teacher: That's the basic idea. Can you expand that idea a little?

Student: Their constitution said it was O.K. to tax Americans, so their Parliament made a bunch of tax laws.

Teacher: O.K. Now you've worked out the fundamentals, let's see if someone else can supply additional ideas. (Pause). Zak?

Handling Incorrect Responses

No matter how skillful a teacher is in motivating students, providing adequate and relevant instructional materials, and asking high-quality questions, there will be one continual problem that detracts from the intellectual and interpersonal activities of a classroom questioning session—incorrect student responses.

As was discussed previously, you may use prompting techniques when student responses are partially correct or are stated incompletely. Basically, prompting is an easy technique because you can reinforce the positive aspect of a student's response while ignoring the negative or incomplete component. However, when a student verbalizes a totally incorrect response, a more complex interpersonal situation arises. First, you have little to reinforce positively in such a case. But teacher comments such as "No," "You are way off," or "That is incorrect" should be avoided, as they all act as negative reinforcers and, depending on the personality of the child who responds, may reduce that student's desire to participate in a verbal classroom interaction. This is critical, especially with non-English-speaking youngsters.

Second, if you respond negatively to an incorrect student response, there is a high probability that the "ripple effect" will occur. This effect, which has been described by Jacob S. Kounin (1970), demonstrated that students who are not themselves the target of the teacher's negative strategy are, in fact, negatively affected by what the teacher does to other class members. There is, of course, a difference between a positive or supportive strategy and a negative or threatening strategy. When a student gives an incorrect response, try to move to a *neutral* prompting technique rather than respond with the usual "No, that is not at all correct."

What, then, should you do? Because the entire approach to this method is to stress the positive, the first decision you might make is to analyze the student's verbal response to determine whether or not any portion of the response can be classified as valid, appropriate, or correct. Following this split-second decision-making, you must then provide positive reinforcement or praise for that portion interpreted as valid, appropriate, or correct. For example, if you ask a general mathematics question and the student gives a totally incorrect answer, then you might state, "Your response is in the magnitude of the answer," or "Could you tell us how you arrived at your answer?" "Could you rethink your solution and take another try at it?" These responses are neither entirely negative nor wholly positive; rather, they can be considered *neutral*.

If there is one teacher behavior that is crucial in handling incorrect student responses, it is to avoid being sarcastic or punishing. If you use a punishing verbal response, then you are in fact using a "put down" strategy. Such a strategy tends to produce negative reinforcers and ultimately provides residual effects causing students to ignore opportunities to respond verbally. Verbal teacher abuse is *never* an appropriate *professional* response.

How can a teacher provide either positive or neutral stimuli and yet elicit an appropriate response from the student? One strategy is to rephrase the question in a different manner so that the onus is at least shifted away from the student. As mentioned previously, *if* any portion of the response is correct or appropriate, *then* you can begin a spontaneous prompting session with that student. You carefully lead the student with a set of convergent questions.

Accompanying this strategy is a point that must be kept in mind: You must be careful that nonverbal cues—such as frowning—do not show that you are upset or angry at the incorrect response. Thus, you maintain congruency between verbal and nonverbal behavior when handling incorrect responses. (Chapter 10 has a list of both verbal and nonverbal positive responses.)

Another strategy for helping a student correct an incorrect response is to diagnose immediately the type and level of question that you asked; then ask the student a similar question, but one that is less difficult, without making other verbal comments to the student. This is similar to performing a task analysis on a concept in which simpler ideas must precede the more difficult ones. The latter strategy will be most important where concept learning is being stressed—for example, in social studies, science, grammar, and the humanities. What we are recommending is that you react like a computer programmed with many possible options. This system always allows the students to get another set of opportunities to show that they know some answer.

The human or interpersonal relationships that you experience with the members of the class are subtle and take time to build. After you have the opportunity to analyze the personality types of each individual in the class, you can use some negative as well as positive reinforcers. It is not uncommon for better students to clown or joke with the teacher or to kid the teacher. When you diagnose such situations, you can predict fairly accurately how a specific student will react, and you can, in turn, humor the student.

As a general rule, it is much better to be very *cautious and positive* in handling incorrect responses. For example, it was one of the authors' unfortunate experiences as a junior in high school to be told to "read between the lines" when analyzing poetry. Such deceitful advice is blatantly bad—no wonder some students approach English courses with "avoidance tendencies." If a student makes an error in a written response, unless it concerns spelling or mechanics, provide a set of minimum specifications to guide the student in correcting the error.

The following examples are suggestions for handling incorrect responses.

Example 1

Teacher: Could you suggest some reasons why Secretary of War Root advocated the establishment of a General Staff? (Pause.) Peggy?

Student: Well . . . generals are pretty important and they really needed somebody to keep house, wash, cut grass, shine things, and stuff.

Teacher: Can you think about what you just said? I stated "General Staff" not "Cleaning Staff." Would you try again, please?

Example 2

Teacher: What was one of the military reforms instituted by Secretary Root? (Pause.) Manuel?

Student: He increased the size of the army to a million men.

Teacher: Well, you got the increase part right. He did increase the size of the army. You got the number a little too high, though. Why don't you lower your estimate and try again?

Example 3

Teacher: In this house plan, the living room windows face west. Is that a good idea? (Pause.) Isadore?
Student: I think it's great. You can see the sunset straight on.
Teacher: Izzy's answer is a good example of individual priorities in house design. To some people, the advantage of being able to view sunsets is very important. What kinds of weather-related problems might be created, though, Izzy, if the large windows face west?

Example 4

Teacher: Who do you think will be the next President, and what views can you offer in support of your judgment? (Pause.) Inez?
Student: I don't know. I really don't care either because they are all a bunch of liars anyway.
Teacher: That's a pretty strong opinion. Could you tell us why you think all the presidential candidates are liars?
Student: Well, to begin with. . . .

In these examples, you are responding in a manner that does not criticize the student. We all know of teachers who insult, ridicule, and degrade students who make incorrect responses; such teachers are incompetent professionals. One primary goal of schooling is to provide a positive and stimulating environment in which learning can take place. Learning is blocked by insults or negative teacher responses. The student learns nothing by humiliation—except to despise the teacher and to hate the school. We want you to create an atmosphere in your classes that is supportive—one in which students can react freely without the fear of being attacked for being wrong. Again, you must decide how you will behave.

Interactive Questioning Mechanisms

Promoting Multiple Responses

Teachers typically conduct recitation periods through questioning: they ask one student to respond, then another student to respond, and so on. For the most part, the teacher does the talking. Few students, if any, are listening carefully to their peer responses because there is a closed communications circuit between the two individuals interacting. We recommend using *multiple-response questions,* to each of which at least three or four students may each provide a response. The key to increasing the number of students who respond to a question is to ask either a *divergent* or an *evaluative* question. In this manner you can predict that there will be more than one response or that there ought to be a set of responses not duplicating one another. Thus, you frame a divergent question, ask the question, pause, and then identify three or four individuals to offer responses.

Of course, before you use the multiple-response technique, you must carefully explain the new method to the class. Also caution the students that you will not repeat *any student response*. Thus, students must listen to their peers' responses so that they will not repeat any that have been previously stated.

The use of multiple-response techniques is a logical precursor to student-conducted discussions. Student discussions are extremely difficult to use effectively because students do not demonstrate the needed discussion behaviors or skills. By using multiple-response questions, you subtly condition the students to accept more responsibility to listen to one another and to modify anticipated responses based on previously elicited responses.

The multiple-response strategy also affects your behavior in that it allows you to speak fewer times during the class. This in itself may be cause for celebration among students. But our concern is that the teacher's verbal interaction with the class be kept to an absolute minimum. It is difficult for you to be an empirical observer of student behaviors, be directing a question-and-answer period, be managing the classroom, and be planning for appropriate questions—all at the same time. By using divergent or evaluative questions coupled with the multiple-response strategy, you have the opportunity to analyze the types of responses that are being given. In short, you have the chance to make a qualitative evaluation of each student's response without doing any other work.

By using these strategies, you can expect longer student responses, student statements delivered in greater depth, and the establishment of greater challenges to all students. A slight modification of this technique can be made, in which you subdivide a class into teams of three, four, or five students to add the motivating factors of small-group solidarity and identification. By varying the seating patterns of the desks, you can facilitate more interaction. Also, any competition that develops within the class will be peer-oriented rather than between teacher and student. Friendly intraclassroom competition is established by adapting some type of "game" situation. This is one means of rewarding a whole spectrum of appropriate responses.

Teachers tend to have one major fault: they are very parsimonious with rewards. But by using some adaptations of the multiple-response strategy, you may reward one group for providing the most novel responses, another for the best responses obtained from an encyclopedia, another for the best nonverbal responses (pictures, cartoons, and the like), and another for the best multimedia presentation. All these are motivational strategies that help make the classroom an enjoyable, creative, and interesting place rather than a prison to which the student is sentenced for one hour each day for one year.

Examples of Multiple Response

You can make a mundane or pedantic recitation period more dynamic. Rather than asking the usual questions about where or when a big event happened, you may conduct the recitation as follows:

Teacher: Today I'm going to use a new technique that we'll continue from here on. I'll ask a question, pause for a few seconds, and then call on three or four of you for responses. Listen carefully because I'll not repeat the question. Furthermore, listen to your classmates as they respond because I will not repeat any of their responses either. . . . Any questions? O.K.?

Teacher: Where might Christopher Columbus have landed if he had set sail from London and headed due west?

Teacher: (Pause.)

Teacher: Trudy, Raphael, Billy, Tommie.

Trudy: He'd have landed in Canada.

Teacher: (Smiles and merely points without comment to Raphael.)

Raphael: I think he would miss Canada and land near Boston because the Pilgrims landed in that area.

Teacher: (Nods head and points to Billy, but without verbal comment.)

Billy: You're both off. He'd have been blown right back to England or maybe Ireland.

Tommie: That would not happen, either. Christopher Columbus would have been blown by the Gulf Stream winds right down to the West Indies.

Teacher: Those are all interesting ideas. Class, let's check the direction of the Gulf Stream and the air currents. Hermie, will you please get the big map of ocean and air currents from the closet and give us a reading?

Hermie: O.K.

Trudy: Will you . . . ?

Evidence from the Far West Laboratory for Educational Research and Development would substantiate the previous hypothetical case. Students do learn to take cues from one another and to carry on a "minidiscussion" without much verbal guidance—or interference—from the teacher.

When you use the multiple-response technique, you also aid in building other communication skills. For example, when you start using this technique, you can ask students to write one-sentence summaries of each response given by their peers. Think of the implications that this simple teaching act can have on (1) improving listening skills, (2) structuring logical discussions, (3) identifying main points in an oral discourse, (4) enabling students to classify arguments, positions, or statements systematically, and (5) learning to outline. Thus, teachers of all classes or grades must realize that they are responsible for helping improve student communication skills. Since questioning is such a widely used communication technique in the classroom, it follows that teachers should maximize the usefulness of this technique so that it improves other cognitive skills and processes as well.

Again, the use of the multiple-response technique is an excellent way to introduce the class to a discussion period. We recommend that discussions and discussion techniques be postponed until the multiple-response technique is mastered by teachers and students alike.

Concept Review Questions

As you begin to develop confidence in both yourself and your students, review, in the most efficient manner, previously learned concepts and relate them to knowledge that you will be introducing later. Most teachers tend to schedule a review prior to a summative evaluation. Thus "Review Thursday" tends to be boring for most students—even good ones. It is an ineffective use of student time in that the vast majority of students do not need the review; and, for those who do, such an oral exercise is usually fruitless in expanding their intellectual understanding of the concepts that the teacher is trying to teach.

How can you review previously taught concepts while conducting questioning strategies? One successful method is to reintroduce previously discussed concepts in the context of newly presented material. For example, if you are progressing through a unit on transportation—in which modern transportation systems such as air travel and freeways are being discussed—and you wish to review the topic of the railroads that has already been covered, then you should review the placement of transport terminals in both old and new contexts. That is, most railroad terminals as well as airports were initially built at the edge of a city. Through questioning that uses concept review techniques, you provide opportunities for the students to demonstrate comprehension concerning city growth while noting that transportation terminals become engulfed as a city expands; this, in turn, causes a set of problems that is unique to cities and to the transportation industry.

What we are suggesting, as a viable alternative to review sessions, is constant review. Such a review may be conducted at any level in Bloom's Taxonomy. As students begin to relate previously learned skills or concepts to new ones, they may begin to perceive the interesting relationships between old and new materials. If you truly wish to use the so-called basic liberal arts approach, then you should attempt to relate the ideas of one discipline to those of other disciplines. Rather than telling the students about such subtle interdisciplinary relationships, you can direct the students to the library so that they may discover them on their own and report them to the class. The latter technique is a meaningful one for those students who are always finished with their work and "have nothing to do"—except disrupt the class.

The concept review technique, therefore, requires that you always be on the alert for instances that allow some meaningful relationships to be established, a previous concept to be reinforced, or a synthesis of knowledge to take place, thereby creating added motivation for the class.

Concept Review Examples

(The class is studying the affective domain.)

Teacher: How does the taxonomy of the cognitive domain, which we studied last month, differ from the taxonomy of the affective domain? (Pause.) Bill?

Bill: The cognitive domain is concerned with the intellectual aspects of learning, while the affective domain is more concerned with emotional outcomes.

Teacher: Good. Could someone give us some examples of these "emotional outcomes"? (Pause.) Mary?

Mary: Attitudes and values?

Teacher: Fine. Now, going back to my original question, how are the two taxonomies similar? (Pause.) Sally?

Sally: Well, because they both are called taxonomies, they both are classification systems, and both are hierarchical in nature.

Teacher: Excellent. What do we mean by "hierarchical" in nature, Bill?

Bill: I think it means that each category builds on the ones below it.

Teacher: Okay, could you give us an example of another kind of taxonomy that would illustrate your point?

Bill: Sure, the taxonomy of the animal kingdom. Each phylum supposedly is related in some evolutionary fashion to the one below it.

Teacher: Good. Does everyone see how that example applies to Bloom's Taxonomy? Okay, let's take a second now and try to relate the module on the taxonomy to previous modules. In other words, how could we use the taxonomy with some of the other ideas we've talked about? (Pregnant silence, which does not last for long.)

Teacher: Let me try to be more specific. How could the taxonomy be used in constructing better lesson plans? (Pause.) Jim? Mary?

Jim: You can use the taxonomy to look at your performance objective and see if your procedure correlates with the terminal behavior.

Mary: (With emotion.) You could also use the taxonomy to kind of judge whether the lesson is worthwhile doing at all.

Teacher: How do you mean, Mary?

Mary: Well, if the lesson consists of nothing more than transmitting a lot of facts, maybe the teacher should ask if these facts are ever going to be used again in one of the higher categories. And if the facts are important, there are more effective ways of having the students master them than by a recitation.

Teacher: Good. Anything else? (Pause.) How about the discussion module? Can you make any connections with the taxonomy? (Pause.) Al?

Al: Kind of going along with what we said about lesson plans, the taxonomy might give teachers some new ideas about discussion topics.

Teacher: Could you elaborate?

Al: Well, sometimes it's easy to get in a rut. Though teachers aren't likely to use discussions with performance objectives at the Knowledge level, they may not be aware of the full range or spectrum of possibilities open for discussion topics.

Teacher: Excellent. Anyone else?

Tina: Also, the taxonomy might be useful in analyzing why discussions bog down.

Teacher: In what respect?

Tina: If the students are attempting thought processes at the higher levels and don't have the background at the lower levels, there's likely to be a lot of confusion because the students don't "know" or "comprehend" what they're talking about.

(NOTE: In this interaction, the following topics were reviewed: (1) affective domain, (2) lesson planning, (3) objectives, and (4) discussions.)

Encouraging Nonvolunteers

In most situations you will not have much of a problem encouraging students to respond to questions. To be sure, if you carefully tabulate the students who respond to the questions, you will find that a few students dominate the verbal questioning sessions. Further observation of any class tends to illustrate that there are several students who do not volunteer their responses. *If* your goal is to encourage verbal responses, *then* you must take the appropriate initiative to encourage nonvolunteers to respond. Such encouragement is most difficult at the beginning of a new term when you are relatively new to the students. As you become more knowledgeable about a student's interest, it is easier to prompt a nonvolunteer because you can use a question in that particular student's realm of interest. What, then, are some helpful strategies to motivate nonvolunteers to respond verbally during a questioning session?

The first technique is to *maintain a highly positive approach toward the student.* That is, follow the philosophy that we have been espousing. The emphasis must be on allowing nonvolunteer students to respond appropriately or correctly each time they are called on. This means that you must use questions that foster successful answering by the nonvolunteer. Once the nonvolunteer has responded appropriately, there should be generous positive feedback to encourage the student to continue such behavior. Furthermore, you should inaugurate a systematic plan for devising those questions that require short responses and that lead to those questions that require longer responses. In summary, you progress from a convergent frame of reference to a more divergent one. Also, the opposite approach will ensure at least some response from nonvolunteers, thus allowing for positive reinforcement. You may even begin by using easy evaluative questions because most students respond to questions that concern judgment, standards, or opinion.

Whatever the reason for a student's not volunteering, you must constantly strive to diagnose the verbal deficiencies and assets of each nonvolunteer. This does not mean that you should play the role of an amateur psychiatrist but that you should determine whether or not there is an apparent pattern of verbal deficiencies for specific students.

Another method for increasing nonvolunteer participation is periodically to make a game out of questioning. One way is to place each student's name on a card so that you may draw the cards at random, thus creating a condition in which every student potentially can be called on to recite. Also, in situations where numerous hands are raised each time the teacher asks a question, you can politely ask those students who are raising their hands to "hold all hands for the next three minutes" so that other students may have an opportunity to respond. In this fashion you tend to shape the behavior of those students who are adequately reinforced through verbal participation.

In addition, there is nothing wrong with giving each "nonresponding" student a card with a question on it the day before the intended oral recitation period. Very quietly, hand these students a card and tell them they may review the assignment so that they can summarize their responses for the next class period. At least this method begins to build a trusting relationship between teacher and student.

Implicit in this technique is the fact that you observe and systematically note *who* is volunteering responses in class recitations, and in what class situations. If time permits, it would be even more desirable to make a daily listing of such verbal activities. You can appoint one member of the class to keep a tally each day. At the end of a week, patterns will emerge for each student.

Again, we condemn the use of calling on nonvolunteers as a punishment tactic. Schooling ought to be a positive, enjoyable experience, the affective consequence of which will encourage students to want to learn. As a general rule, your most effective means for encouraging a nonvolunteer to participate is to be sincere in treating each student as a human being. Nonvolunteers have learned—sometimes painfully— that it does not pay to say anything in class because the teacher will "put you down." Teachers may not be the nicest people on earth and students in the junior and senior high schools, especially, have learned to recognize this and to play the game accordingly. No one likes to put a hand in a hot fire. No student will volunteer to answer a question if the response is going to be met with sarcasm, witty innuendoes, snide remarks, or hostility. Be highly considerate and approving at all times.

Developing the Student's Skill in Framing Questions

The previous techniques are all oriented toward improving your questioning skills. The following technique attempts a reciprocal arrangement—that is, to teach students how to frame their own questions.

For the most part, teachers neither encourage nor teach their students to ask questions. As a matter of record, some teachers are upset when students do ask questions. The typical classroom discussion—or, more correctly, recitation period—is conducted by the teacher, who asks the students questions, not vice versa. However, if we desire to encourage critical or reflective thinking, or thinking of any sort, then it behooves all teachers to develop the student's skill in framing questions. To aid in such a strategy, we refer to the game that was made famous many years ago on radio and is currently on many television stations—"Twenty Questions."

The game of "Twenty Questions" is one in which participants ask questions to identify something. The same mode may be applied in the classroom. You may present a problem or identify some concept that needs to be discovered and allow the discovery to take place only through student questioning. Initially you will conduct the session; but, as the students master the technique and become more proficient in the skills, then they may conduct the entire session, and you will merely analyze the various interpersonal reactions.

J. Richard Suchman (1966) prepared the "Inquiry Development Program," which emphasized the development of student questioning skills. The rule of his game is that, after a problem has been presented to the students, the teacher plays a passive role in the learning and responds only with a "yes" or "no" to a student's question. This means that the students must learn how to ask questions on which they may build a pyramid of knowledge, ultimately leading to a convergent response rather than a series of unorganized questions. When this technique is first used, the students have almost no opportunity to ask the teacher questions, thus causing initial results to be discouraging. However, the teacher should review each lesson and give precise and detailed directions on how the questioning can be improved. As one alternative, if it will not be too slow, the teacher may write each student's question on a chalkboard or on an overhead projector transparency, so that those questions being asked by their peers will have been presented visually to all students. In this manner, the gradual accumulation of information and skills can be accomplished in a systematic manner.

Of course, when developing student skills in framing questions, it becomes imperative for the students to understand that each question must encompass numerous specifics. In short, the teacher must give practical application to student skills in deductive logic.

Another method of developing students' skills in framing questions is to have students prepare study or recitation questions based on the subject being discussed. In this manner you select a few students each day to prepare a series of questions for their peers. You may even share with the students a few secrets on questioning techniques, such as following the rationale of Bloom's Taxonomy for cognitive skills. To be sure, most students will be oriented only toward fact because that is what is mostly reinforced in their learning. But a skillful teacher will continually reinforce those questions that are aimed at higher-level thinking skills and ultimately help each student to prepare appropriate higher-level thinking questions.

You will note that as the teacher begins to encourage the class members to ask questions of one another, there is a subtle shift of responsibility to the students. Teachers usually encourage their charges to accept more responsibility. We believe that, by participating in learning situations, students acquire greater responsibility.

This statement implies that responsibility is a "learned behavior" just as so many other behaviors are. As a teacher, you owe it to your students to help them become articulate and thinking individuals. You have a splendid opportunity to do so when you transfer more responsibility for classroom questioning techniques to the students.

As we stated previously, this method must be explained carefully to the students and then practiced for a few class periods so that the students know how to "play the game." Then, perhaps once a week or more often, the students can conduct the questioning sessions. This method is a prerequisite experience to student-led discussions.

You and the class may generate a set of criteria on which to base the various student-framed questions. The criteria also may be applied to a broader context. Students can be requested to evaluate the kinds of questions that are asked on various television quiz shows as a means of improving their own skills in data collection and interpretation.

All the teachers with whom we have worked have been pleased with the results of such techniques. More importantly, these same teachers were amazed at how much they *underestimated* the potentials that existed in their classes. We are not implying that these techniques are simple to implement; they take much work and planning. But the attendant rewards make both teaching and learning more worthwhile.

Teacher Idiosyncrasies: A Caution

One can speculate that all teacher behaviors associated with questioning are positive and encouraging. After all, the teacher is assumed to need only a few tricks and a smile to achieve instant success. Unfortunately, there are inappropriate teacher behaviors that interfere with a smooth verbal interaction pattern in the classroom. Briefly, these idiosyncrasies are (1) repeating the question, (2) repeating all student responses, (3) answering the question, (4) not allowing a student to complete a long response, (5) not attending to the responding student, and (6) always selecting the same student respondents. Each of these behaviors is analyzed in the following sections.

Repeating the Question

A common error often made by teachers is the regular repetition of each question. This habit conditions the students to catch the "replay" of the question instead of "attending" to it—either cognitively or intuitively. Moreover, this habit causes a loss of valuable time, is redundant, and does not help the teacher to maintain efficient classroom management. To be sure, there are appropriate times to repeat questions: in a very large room with poor acoustics; when the question is multifaceted; when the question is not adequately framed; or when you are dictating a question to the class. We do caution that beginning teachers often have difficulty in framing verbal questions that are understood explicitly by the students. In such cases, rephrase the question for added clarity. Repeating a question may be appropriate when you use divergent questions. In most cases, though, avoid repeating a question.

Read the following two sets of repeated questions aloud to friends or colleagues and obtain their reactions.

Teacher: What is the main set of criteria by which to frame questions? In other words, what is the main set of criteria by which to frame questions?

Teacher: What is the population of Boston? What is Boston's population? How many people live in Boston?

How did they respond to the repetitious questions? Listen to teachers or professors in oral discourses to determine whether they repeat their questions. If you have not observed this idiosyncratic pattern, then obtain a tape recorder, tape a simulated version of this pattern, and play it back to a small group of peers. We will wager that after listening to a few of these simulated episodes, your audience will be highly amused. This may make a creative term project for your methods class.

Repeating All Student Responses

An equally distracting and time-wasting technique is to repeat all or nearly all of the student verbal responses. Not only is this a waste of time, but also it causes class members to ignore their peers as sources of information and subtly conditions them to wait until the word comes from the "fount of all wisdom." In short, students either do not attend to the initial student response or wait for the "instant replay" from the teacher. If you are the least bit sensitive to the building of positive student self-images, then you will not want to be the center of verbal interaction and will keep the focus on the responding student. After all, if it is important to call on a student and require a response, then it ought to be equally important that student input be given the same priority as teacher-made statements.

This general rule does not hold for large-group sessions. Because most large-group rooms or halls have poor seating arrangements, you must almost always repeat student responses so that all can hear. The same is true for students with very soft voices. But in the vast majority of cases, there is no need to repeat student responses. Finally, *if* you wish to condition the students to prediscussion behaviors, *then* all must comprehend this technique. To put it positively, by allowing students to take cues from one another, you establish the desired attitude. The introduction of true discussions will be a logical sequence.

Answering the Question

Have you ever observed or participated in a class in which the teacher carefully frames a question, pauses, calls on a student, then quite insensitively answers the question? First of all, this idiosyncrasy is a morale defeater. How can students be encouraged to think when they know that the teacher will hardly allow them to voice their opinions? This behavior also tends to discourage volunteers and causes students to be negatively reinforced. If a question is so complex that no student can answer it, rephrase it, begin prompting, or assign it as a research project. As we mentioned previously, Mary Budd Rowe (1974) found that teachers usually do not wait for student responses or, worse yet, had wait times that measured in fractions of seconds! These findings are a heavy indictment, to say the least.

Not Allowing a Student to Complete a Long Response

One very distracting, inappropriate, and rude teacher idiosyncrasy is to ask a question and then interrupt the student by completing the response or by adding personal teacher comments without attempting to elicit other student responses. An example follows:

Teacher: What impact did the Vietnam War have on our young people? (Pause.) Arnie?
Arnie: Well, I sure don't trust . . .
Teacher: Right, you kids really don't have the confidence in our government. Why, I can remember when I was in high school . . .

Teachers who suffer from excessive talkativeness frustrate students and, worse, neglect to allow them to develop logical response systems. This interruptive technique discourages most students from even participating in the recitation period.

Not Attending to the Responding Student

When you call on a student, show a courtesy to that student by attending to (that is, listening to, or at least appearing to listen to) him or her. After all, you expect to instill attending habits in the students. This habit should be reciprocated during verbal interactions. How would you feel if you were responding and observed that the teacher was gazing out the window or counting some loose change. We *are* suggesting that teachers often fail to reinforce appropriate student behaviors in the class simply by being insensitive to the feelings of others.

Always Selecting the Same Student Respondents

One frequently heard student complaint is that "my teacher never calls on me" or that "the teacher has a few pets that are always being called on." These statements typify the frustrations of students who recognize partiality when they see it. The biased teacher who calls on only a few (usually highly verbal and successful) students is providing a negative reinforcer to the majority of the class members, is making them uninterested in the subject, and is causing serious erosion of the group morale.

If you are skeptical, let us remind you of Ray C. Rist's classic study, which was conducted in a Chicago elementary school. Rist (1970) observed that a teacher in a primary grade was exhibiting great bias in the manner of selecting students for class recitations. Fewer and fewer individuals were being called on by the teacher until only a select few were identified. To make matters worse, the teacher began to move the responding pupils up to the front seats and the others, the nonrespondents, to the rear of the room. Needless to say, there were tremendous disparities between the educational achievements of the students in the front rows and those of all the other students. The teacher and pupils were all of the same ethnic group, so racism can be eliminated as the basis for bias. This may be an extreme case, but in general such situations exist to varying degrees.

A quick way to determine whether you show bias is to ask a different student each day to list the number of times that you call on each student. A quick tally at the end of the week will provide the data.

It is tempting to call on students who often volunteer and who will give you the "right" answer, so that you will appear to be an effective teacher. But *if* you wish to encourage all your students to be winners, *then* you ought to accord them equal opportunity to do so. One motto is fairly accurate in this case: "Nothing breeds success like success." If students are hesitant about responding verbally, then you as the teacher (who is presumably the most secure individual in the class) must gear the questions to suit the individual students, so that all students can enjoy the feeling of success and positive reinforcement.

This is a good point for you to review those seventeen major findings related to student expectations summarized in Chapter 1 by Good and Brophy (1987). The list shows that many teachers exhibit some strong biases against "academically poorer students." For example, the responses of teachers to poor academic achievers and high academic achievers show that teachers (1) wait less time for low achievers to respond, (2) fail to provide low achievers with feedback, (3) generally pay less attention to low achievers, (4) seat the low achievers toward the back of the room, (5) criticize the low achievers more, and (6) demand less from low achievers.

Throughout this chapter we have implicitly suggested that questions must be clear and understandable. Let us now become explicit. To be an effective questioner, teachers must be able to frame clear, concise, and succinct questions. In this respect, M. L. Land (1980) cautioned against teachers using "uhs," false starts, uncertain pauses, and ineffective transitions between topics. All such verbal behaviors by teachers ultimately cause student uncertainty. (See Brophy and Good, 1986; Cruickshank, 1985.) Of all the virtues, clarity remains high on the list of criteria for good questioners.

Conclusion

If you perceive that we are attempting to make a "game" of schooling, then you may be absolutely correct. School ought to be a place in which one may have fun or at least have a positive experience while learning. The "Puritan ethic"—that if something is fun it must be bad—is totally inappropriate now, as it was when first conceived. If learning can be made meaningful and relevant, then students will enjoy working at it. There is a great deal of research demonstrating that students have a strong interest in, and like, those areas in which they are successful. If mathematics is distasteful to students, it is because for the most part students have been unsuccessful in this subject. Such an attitude can be rectified easily by making mathematics or, for that matter, all subjects success-oriented. The essence of mastery learning is that interest is a function of success.

All these questioning strategies provide the teacher with important "tools of the trade." But they are just that—tools. Each technique must be used appropriately and must be congruent with your objective for a specified student, group of students, or class.

Because questions play such an important part in the learning process, we have attempted to provide you with a cognitively ordered set of questioning alternatives based on "if-then" logic. Our goal is to increase the number of techniques available to the teacher so that whenever a question is asked, you cognitively and automatically know what you are attempting to do with the students. We also believe that the questioning sessions in school classrooms ought to be constructive and cheerful experiences, in which the students' opinions are respected, their interests stimulated, and their minds challenged.

FORMATIVE EVALUATION *Questioning Skills*

A. How well did you master the materials on questioning? Here is a quick "knowledge check" to determine your ability to recall the points presented. If you have any problems, you should reread the chapter.

1. Several studies cited by the critics would indicate which trend?
   (a) Teachers tend to use questions that elicit student responses that can be classified in the Knowledge category.
   (b) Most teachers carefully plan their teaching and questioning.
   (c) Teachers stress critical thinking skills when using classroom questions.
   (d) A combination of items (b) and (c) is the best response.

2. The limited evidence on the improvement of cognitive levels of instruction and high-level questions may be interpreted to
   (a) Show that a positive relationship exists.
   (b) Indicate that there is a negative relationship—that is, high-level questions cause low-level responses.
   (c) Substantiate the idea that there is no need whatsoever for teacher training in questioning, since such training is not very helpful.
   (d) Indicate that teachers will ask what they please and that any technique produces high-level thinking.

3. There is evidence to indicate that a vast majority of questions in textbooks are at this level (based on Bloom's Taxonomy).
   (a) Knowledge
   (b) Comprehension
   (c) Application
   (d) Evaluation

B. Here is a list of questions and objectives. Classify each according to whether it is convergent, divergent, or evaluative. (For extra practice, also classify each according to the six major categories of the cognitive taxonomy.)

_____ 1. List as many major problems as you can that relate to urban education.

_____ 2. Given a model of the human eye, correctly label its parts.

_____ 3. From the data presented in Table 1, form generalizations that are supported by the data.

_____ 4. Zero population growth should become a governmental priority of the United States. Defend or refute this position.

_____ 5. What effect did the withdrawal from Vietnam have on our nation's international prestige?

_____ 6. Discuss the differences between evolution and creationism. Which of the two concepts is the better, as supported by the best empirical evidence? List the evidence.

C. Place an X next to each question that has been properly framed by the teacher. If you do not check a question, briefly explain why.

_____ 1. "On what date did Christopher Columbus discover the Americas?" (Pause.) "Christine?"

_____ 2. "Charlie." (Pause.) "Name the ships that Columbus commanded."

_____ 3. "Nancy, I see you horsing around. Please go to the board and write out problem 6."

_____ 4. "Why would an Italian sail for the Spanish Crown?" (Pause.) "Albert?"

_____ 5. "Who knows the port from which Columbus departed?" (Pause.)

_____ 6. "How did the Spanish Crown raise the money for the expedition?" (Pause.) "Alfonso?"

D. Circle the most appropriate response.

1. Read the following teacher-student interaction.
   Teacher: Where does the Ohio River flow into the Mississippi?
   Student: I don't know.

Which questioning technique should be used?
(a) Multiple response   (c) Concept review
(b) Clarification   (d) Prompting

2. You cannot prepare a sequence of questions for prompting before class begins because:
   (a) Generally, the right answer is given.
   (b) It takes too long for a teacher to prepare the list of questions.
   (c) It is nearly impossible to determine the necessity of prompting prior to the lesson.
   (d) Prompting questions are based on specific student responses.

3. A student in your class cries when informed that the response is wrong. Which of the following procedures would you use to help overcome this problem?
   (a) Never call on the student in the future.
   (b) Admonish the student for crying.
   (c) Ignore the crying and proceed.
   (d) None of these is appropriate.

4. One of your better students has given an incorrect response in class. Which of the following techniques should be used?
   (a) Tell the student he or she is right, but correct him or her privately after class.
   (b) Reply with a neutral statement such as "Would you think that through again?"
   (c) Wait for other students to correct the student.
   (d) Ignore the response and proceed.

5. An implied consequence of the multiple-response questioning technique is that
   (a) There will be less student participation.
   (b) The teacher becomes more actively involved.
   (c) It will provide a framework for shaping student interactions.
   (d) None of the above is apparent.

6. Select the multiple-response question from the following list:
   (a) What is the single mineral resource of Georgia?
   (b) List one criterion for good classroom discipline.
   (c) Who was the last Whig President?
   (d) Give sound reasons for the collapse of Chile's economy.

7. A student who is a nonvolunteer is asked to provide a solution to a problem that is being discussed by the class. The response is appropriate but of minimal quality. The teacher should
   (a) Ignore the student because he or she is obviously incapable of contributing to the class.
   (b) Encourage or praise the student for the response and then continue to react with the student.
   (c) Tell the student, "I guess that is about all we can expect from you, anyhow."
   (d) A combination of items (a) and (c) is the best technique.

E. The following statements should be identified as either True or False.

_____ 1. Maintenance of higher-level student thinking is best accomplished by the use of divergent or evaluative rather than convergent, types of questions.

_____ 2. When the teacher asks a divergent question, the teacher reserves the right to accept the responses given by the students.

_____ 3. Under normal conditions the repetition of student responses by the teacher tends to act as a positive reinforcer to the student.

_____ 4. Calling on the student prior to asking the question is the best method by which to gain and keep the attention of all students, not just the student being called on.

_____ 5. Multiple-response techniques tend to place greater student dependence on the teacher for answers and lessen student interactions.

_____ 6. When the teacher repeats the question prior to selecting a student, it means that the question is really important and alerts the students to think this one out carefully.

F. When would you use a sequential hierarchy and when would you use a nonsequential one?

G. How does the logic of a question affect the responses?

H. How do lawyers, medical doctors, and teachers differ in the use of questions?

I. How could you use ''mapping'' to stimulate your students to generate questions?

J. Wait-time 1 and wait-time 2 differ in what respects?

K. Prepare a chart illustrating different questioning uses.

Responses

A. 1. (a)
    2. (a)
    3. (a)
B. 1. Divergent
    2. Convergent
    3. Divergent
    4. Evaluative
    5. Evaluative
    6. Divergent-Evaluative
C. 1. X
    2. The student should be identified after the question is asked.
    3. The teacher is using questioning as a punishment.
    4. X
    5. It is better to call on one or a few students rather than hoping for a response.
    6. X

D. 1. (d)
    2. (d)
    3. (d)
    4. (b)
    5. (c)
    6. (b) or (d)
    7. (b)
E. 1. True
    2. False
    3. False
    4. False
    5. False
    6. False
F. through K.
    Discuss with class members in small groups

REFERENCES

Barton, Thomas L., and Stanley J. Zehm. "Beyond Bay Area: A Description of the Washington State University Writing Project." *English Education* 15:1983, 36–44.

Beck, Isabel, and Margaret G. McKeown. "Developing Questions That Promote Comprehension: The Story Map." *Language Arts* 58:1981, 913–917.

Bloom, Benjamin S., ed. *Taxonomy of Educational Objectives, Handbook I: Cognitive Domain.* New York: David McKay, 1956.

Borg, Walter R., et al. *The Mini Course: A Microteaching Approach to Teacher Education.* Beverly Hills, Calif., Collier-Macmillan, 1970.

Brophy, Jere. *Synthesizing the Results of Research Linking Teaching Behavior to Student Achievement.* Paper presented at the annual meeting of the American Educational Research Association, San Francisco, April 1986. EDRS/ERIC ED.

Brophy, Jere, and Thomas L. Good. "Teacher Behavior and Student Achievement." In *Handbook of Research on Teaching,* 3rd ed. Merlin C. Wittrock, ed. New York: Macmillan, 1986.

Christenbury, Lelia, and Patricia P. Kelly. *Questioning: A Critical Path to Critical Thinking.* Urbana, Ill.: ERIC Clearinghouse on Reading and Communications Skills and the National Council of Teachers of English, 1983, p. 4.

Cornbleth, Catherine. "Student Questioning as a Learning Strategy." *Educational Leadership* 33: 1975, 219–222.

Cruickshank, Donald. "Applying Research on Teacher Clarity." *Journal of Teacher Education* 36:1985, 44–48.

Dantonio, Marylou, and Louis V. Paradise. "Teaching Question-Answer Strategy and the Cognitive Correspondence Between Teacher Questions and Learner Responses." *Journal of Research and Development in Education* 21:Spring 1988, 71–75.

Davis, O. L., Jr., and Francis P. Hunkins. "Textbook Questions: What Thinking Processes Do They Foster?" *Peabody Journal of Education* 43:1966, 285–292.

Dillon, J. T. "Alternatives to Questioning." *High School Journal* 62:1979, 217–222.

———. "Cognitive Correspondence Between Question/Statement and Response." *American Educational Research Journal* 19:1982, 540–551. (a)

———. "Do Your Questions Promote or Prevent Thinking?" *Learning* 11:1982, 56–57, 59. (b)

———. "The Multidisciplinary Study of Questioning." *Journal of Educational Psychology* 74:1982, 147–165. (c)

———. "A Norm Against Student Questions." *The Clearing House* 55:1981, 136–139. (b)

———. *Questioning and Teaching: A Manual of Practice.* London: Croom Helm., 1987.

———. *Questioning and Discussion: A Multidisciplinary Study.* Norwood, N.J.: Ablex Publishing, 1988.

———. "To Question and Not to Question During Discussion." *Journal of Teacher Education* 32: 1981, 51–55. (a)

Falkof, Lucille, and Janet Moss. "When Teachers Tackle Thinking Skills." *Educational Leadership* 42:November 1984, 4–9.

Fedje, Cheryl G., and Ann Irvine. "Questions to Promote Thinking." *Vocational Education* 57: 1982, 27–28.

Fisher, Charles W., et al. "Teaching Behaviors, Academic Learning Time, and Student Achievement: An Overview." In *Time and Learning.* Deborah Strother, ed. Bloomington, Ind.: Phi Delta Kappa, Hot Topics, 1984, pp. 97–122.

Flanders, Ned A. *Analyzing Teaching Behavior.* Reading, Mass.: Addison-Wesley, 1970.

Gagné, Ellen D. "Strategies for Effective Teaching and Learning." In *The Cognitive Psychology of School Learning.* Boston: Little, Brown, 1985.

Gall, Meredith D. "The Use of Questions in Teaching." *Review of Educational Research* 40:1970, 707–721.

Gall, Meredith D., et al. "Effects of Questioning Techniques and Recitation on Student Learning." *American Educational Research Journal* 15:1978, 175–199.

Gray, James, and Miles Meyers. "The Bay Area Writing Project." *Phi Delta Kappa* 59:1978, 410–413.

Herber, Harold L. *Teaching Reading in the Content Areas,* 2nd ed. Englewood Cliffs, N.J.: Prentice-Hall, 1978.

Huenecke, Dorothy. "Cognitive Levels of Teacher Objectives and Oral Classroom Questions for Curriculum Guide Users and Non-Users." *Educational Leadership* 27:1970, 379–383.

Hyman, Ronald T. *Strategic Questioning.* Englewood Cliffs, N.J.: Prentice-Hall, 1979.

Joyce, Bruce, and Beverly Showers. *Student Achievement Through Staff Development.* New York: Longman, 1988.

Kaiser, Arthur. *Questioning Techniques.* LaVerne, Calif.: El Camino Press, 1979.

Kelley, Todd D. "A Teacher's Use of Question." *Questioning Exchange* 1:May 1987, 119–123.

Klinzing, Hans Gerhard, and Gisela Klinzing-Eurich. "Questions, Responses, & Reactions." In *Questioning and Discussion: A Multidisciplinary Study.* J. T. Dillon, ed. Norwood, N.J.: Ablex Publishing, 1988, pp. 212–239.

Kounin, Jacob S. *Discipline and Group Management in Classrooms.* New York: Holt, Rinehart & Winston, 1970.

Land, M. L. "Teacher Clarity and Cognitive Level of Questions: Effects on Learning." *Journal of Experimental Education* 49:1980, 48–51.

Orlich, Donald C. *A Study of Elementary School Science Teaching.* Unpublished field study, Washington State University, Pullman, 1989.

Orlich, Donald C., Frank B. May, and Robert J. Harder. "Change Agents and Instructional Innovations: Report 2." *The Elementary School Journal* 73:1973, 390–398.

Orlich, Donald C., et al. "A Change Agent Strategy: Preliminary Report." *The Elementary School Journal* 72:1972, 281–293.

Raphael, Taffy E., and David Pearson. "Increasing Students' Awareness of Sources of Information for Answering Questions." *American Educational Research Journal* 22:Summer 1985, 237–243.

Rico, Gabriele Lusser. *Writing the Natural Way.* Los Angeles: J. P. Tarcher, 1983.

Riley, Joseph P., II. "The Effects of Teachers' Wait-Time and Knowledge Comprehension Questioning on Science Achievement." *Journal of Research in Science Teaching* 23:April 1986, 335–342.

Rist, Ray C. "Student Social Class and Teacher Expectations: The Self-Fulfilling Prophecy in Ghetto Education." *Harvard Educational Review* 40:1970, 411–451.

Rowe, Mary Budd. "Pausing Principles and Their Effects on Reasoning in Science." *New Directions for Community Colleges* 31:1980, 27–34.

———. "Science, Silence, and Sanctions." *Science and Children* 6:March 1969, 11–13.

———. "Wait, Wait, Wait." *School Science and Mathematics* 78:1978, 207–216.

———. "Wait-Time and Rewards as Instructional Variables, Their Influence on Language, Logic and Fate Control: Part I, Fate Control." *Journal of Research in Science Teaching* 11:1974, 81–94.

Sanders, Norris M. *Classroom Questions: What Kinds?* New York: Harper & Row, 1966.

Shake, Mary C. "Teaching Questioning: Is There An Answer?" *Reading Research and Instruction* 27:1988, 29–39.

Smith, Richard. "Questions for the Teacher—Creative Reading." *The Reading Teacher* 22:1969, 431.

Stevens, Romiett. *The Question as a Measure of Efficiency in Instruction: A Critical Study of Classroom Practice.* New York: Teachers College Contributions to Education, 1912.

Suchman, J. Richard. *Inquiry Development Program in Physical Science.* Chicago: Science Research Associates, 1966.

Swift, J. Nathan, C. Thomas Gooding, and Patricia R. Swift. "Questions and Wait Time." In *Questioning and Discussion: A Multidisciplinary Study.* J. T. Dillon, ed. Norwood, N.J.: Ablex Publishing, 1988, pp. 192–211.

Taba, Hilda. *Teachers' Handbook for Elementary Social Studies.* Reading, Mass.: Addison-Wesley, 1967, pp. 87–117.

Tobin, Kenneth. "The Role of Wait Time in Higher Cognitive Level Learning." *Review of Educational Research* 57:Spring 1987, 69–95.

Verduin, John R., Jr., ed. "Structure of the Intellect." In *Conceptual Models in Teacher Education.* Washington, D.C.: American Association of Colleges of Teacher Education, 1967, p. 93.

Watson, Ken, and Bob Young. "Discourse for Learning in The Classroom." *Language Arts* 63:February 1986, pp. 126–133.

Wolf, Dennis Palmer. "The Art of Questioning." *Academic Connections* Winter 1987, 1–7. (The College Board, New York.)

Wood, David, and Heather Wood. "Questioning vs Student Initiative." In *Questioning and Discussion: A Multidisciplinary Study.* J. T. Dillon, ed. Norwood, N.J.: Ablex Publishing, 1988, pp. 280–305.

7

Decisions About Discussions

*O*ne decision that will have a critical impact on how you interact with your students and how they interact with one another is how you will use small-group strategies as a regular instructional method. Small-group strategies and discussions require much teacher preparation and preplanning, which will be discussed later. Let us now identify what kinds of *process* objectives are described in this learning episode.

Objectives   After completing this chapter, you should be able to:

- Distinguish process objectives from performance objectives
- Understand the rationale for establishing small learning groups as an organizational pattern
- Differentiate between a discussion and other classroom techniques
- Select an appropriate discussion technique from those given for classroom use and defend its application
- Identify communication patterns that both facilitate and impede discussions
- Plan for the organization, orientation, and initiation of small-group learning experiences, including cooperative learning
- Determine the appropriate type of evaluation for judging the efficacy of small-group discussion strategies
- Identify ways that simulations may be used in your classes
- Conduct a small-group discussion.
- In addition, we suggest the following affective behaviors:
  - Be willing to consider using small-group discussion strategies, where appropriate
  - Value interactive teaching techniques
  - Incorporate flexible group management
  - Appreciate the potential value of cooperative learning

INTRODUCTION AND OBJECTIVES

Using Process Objectives

You have already demonstrated competence in the identifying, writing, and specifying of performance objectives. Now you will find that there is another type of objective that may be of equal, if not greater, importance—the *process objective*. A process objective, as the name implies, is an objective in which the learner is required to participate in some technique, interaction, or strategy.

Consider the following learning activities, and note that the real value of each is in *the process,* or in the *experience:*

- kindergartners having a verbal sharing time
- second graders growing plants
- fourth graders making a time mural

- sixth grade teams doing creative writing
- eighth graders setting up recycle stations as a means of resource conservation
- tenth graders observing a court session
- twelfth graders exploring different ways to apply mathematics to physics problems

When you write process objectives, your goal is to convey explicitly to the students (and others) the importance of the experience per se. "To improve listening skills, speaking skills, and poise by participating in sharing time" could be the process objective for the kindergarten class. An objective for the eighth graders might be "to explore new ideas and to be committed to conserving natural resources." These are examples of process objectives that are often implied in schooling.

A major difference between performance objectives and process objectives concerns learner outcomes. As discussed in Chapter 2, performance objectives require prescribing the exact learner behavior. With process objectives you do not specify a specific learning outcome; in fact, there could be as many final learner behaviors as there are members of the group. What is prescribed is a learning activity, or process. Many of the outcomes may be unanticipated, or "incidental" learning.

Much more subtle than specifying performance objectives, process building requires that the teacher carefully plan *experiences* for the learners. You have heard that the schools should develop student responsibility; yet, the development of learner responsibility is a process that takes years to accomplish, and some teachers never master the process. We submit that a teacher who wishes to develop processes such as writing skills must give students repeated opportunities to practice their writing. The same logic applies to the process building of small-group discussion skills. You need practice, planning, and cumulative experience to gain the skills necessary to be successful in these techniques.

Preparing for Small-Group Discussions: Establishing Goals

The first component of conducting a successful small-group learning activity is the development of a *long-range* set of priorities. Whereas performance objectives are written for immediate achievement, process objectives are usually written for the gradual development of skills, attitudes, and strategies. The process of establishing such long-range objectives is important because it enables you, the planner, to identify the skills that the learners must master before they can achieve the objectives. For example, Figure 7-1 illustrates the skills that *both teachers and students* must develop *prior* to implementing student-led discussion techniques effectively. As Figure 7-1 shows, it takes approximately eight weeks to practice all the discussion elements, but it has been done in four weeks.

"Baking is no accident—it's *Occident*" was an advertising slogan for the Peavey Flour Milling Company's brand "Occident." The slogan implied that one had to select

Figure 7-1   *The Hierarchy of Skill Development Required for Successful Small-Group Discussions.*

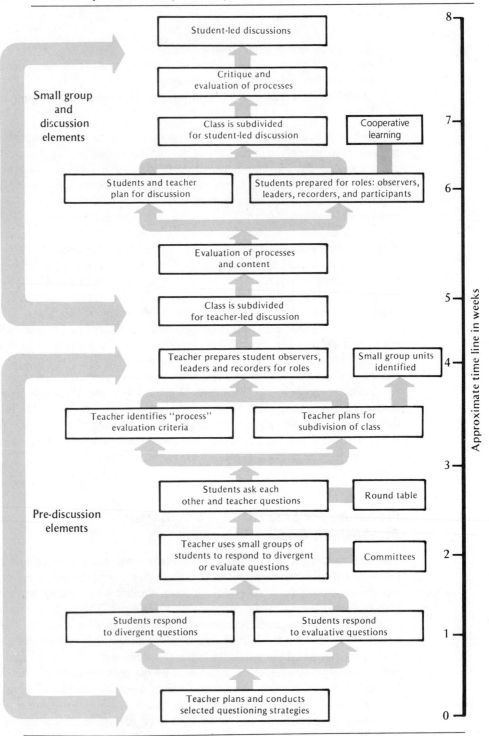

the right brand of flour to succeed at baking. The same logic may be applied to the use of discussions in the classroom.

The teacher who claims that "discussions don't work; I tried one once during the first week of school and my students wouldn't even participate" does not understand small-group discussions. Effective small-group discussions do not take place accidentally: they are learning activities that develop from carefully structured student behaviors. The teacher thus needs to learn what is involved in conducting successful small-group discussions.

Developing Small Groups

Small Group

It is significant that in this chapter we use the term *small-group discussions* rather than *group discussions*. Group size is an important variable that influences learner participation levels. There is no absolute minimum or maximum number of persons that must be included in a small group to ensure a successful discussion. As Dan Pyle Miller (1986) notes, small groups can number anywhere from three to fifteen. Other writers suggest that five is the ideal size (Book and Galvin, 1975). Our own observations suggest an optimal group size ranging between six and eight students. When there are four or fewer individuals involved in a discussion group, the participants tend to pair off rather than to interact with all members.

In our own experiences we have found that when a group consists of twelve or more participants, student interaction begins to diminish. With larger groups—that is, fifteen or more—a few students tend to remain very interactive, a few appear somewhat interactive, and the majority become silent or passive. It may be appropriate to subdivide the class into groups of twelve or less before you initiate a small-group discussion. Size is determined by the topic, the group, and the leader's experience.

Discussion

What is a discussion as it applies to teaching and learning? First, a discussion is *not* merely an informal group chatting in a comfortable corridor. Nor is it a clique-dominated pseudodiscussion conducted by only a few group members. Nor is it the type of activity that is too frequently called a "discussion"; here the teacher tells the class to read certain pages for homework and to be prepared to "discuss" them the following day. Unfortunately, this last situation usually dissolves into a lecture-quiz of textbook facts or into a low-level recitation session. There are times when such recitation of facts formulates a legitimate teaching strategy, but this approach is *not* a discussion and should not be confused with one.

What is the difference, then, between lectures, recitations, and discussions? Obviously, group size is an important distinguishing feature. Lectures can be given to any size group and may be defined as a series of oral *content* or *process* teacher presentations or speeches that do not actively involve student participation. Recitations are more likely to entail one-to-one exchanges; discussions, however, involve high degrees of interaction among all participants.

Discussion denotes, by definition, an exchange of ideas, with active learning and participation by all concerned. A discussion is an active process of student-teacher or student-student interaction in the classroom. Recitation or lecture methods are more passive in terms of student activity. A discussion also allows the student to discover or state personal viewpoints, not merely to repeat those that have already been presented.

For purposes of clarification, and so that the separate parts of the discussion process may be more clearly delineated, a discussion is defined as including the following elements:

1. A small number (preferably four to eight) of students meeting together
2. Recognition of a common topic or problem
3. Introduction, exchange, and evaluation of information and ideas
4. Direction toward some goal or objective (often of the participants' choosing)
5. Verbal interaction—both objective and emotional

We will use this definition to distinguish true *discussions* from recitation periods; however, let us expand the rationale for discussions.

Why Use Discussions?

Discussions and small-group learning units are most appropriate *if* you desire to increase teacher-student and student-student verbal interaction in the classroom. Also, by knowing several different techniques or processes, you are adding flexibility to your professional skills. If you plan to help students adopt a more responsible and independent mode of learning, then small-group discussion strategies will help in attaining this goal.

The discussion method, because it involves the students, requires the teacher to develop a viewpoint and to tolerate and facilitate the exchange of a wide range of ideas. Discussion is an active process of student-teacher involvement in the classroom environment. Discussion allows a student to discover and state a personal opinion and not merely repeat that which the teacher or text has already presented. For example, Steven A. Stahl and Charles H. Clark (1987) reported how fifth graders in discussion-led classes performed better on concept and vocabulary learning than did students who only read the instructional materials and were then tested. The authors observed that in discussions, students are *active learners*.

Why should you bother to learn to use the discussion method? When teachers are shown how to use discussion effectively, they welcome the opportunities it offers for classroom interaction. If you wish to achieve a high degree of student-student-teacher interaction, small-group discussion techniques offer a viable set of alternatives to the usual one-way flow of information.

Another purpose of discussion is to promote meaningful personal interaction and, of course, learning. The learning may be of contents, skills, attitudes, or processes. A widely espoused psychological principle is that people learn best when they are actively involved or participating. Thus, if you want to promote a wide range of interests, opinions, and perspectives, small-group discussion is one way to accomplish that goal. If you wish to improve the speaking-thinking-articulating skills of students, then the discussion technique is appropriate. Michael J. Webb (1985) suggests using discussions as a means of enhancing student conceptualization through analysis of analogies. If you desire to have different students doing different tasks or activities at the same time, all leading to meaningful goals, then discussions are suitable. If you want to practice indirect control of learning, then discussion is the technique to use. If you wish to impart informality to the group, then the use of discussion is a means to that end.

Small-group discussions, moreover, may be a way to "turn on" some of the turned-off students. Being a group member allows a student more options for success because the group requires various kinds of activities and interactions. For example, one may be a flop at initiating but very perceptive at being able to compromise or analyze. The class member who is poor at reading has a chance to be excellent at reporting or visualizing. William Glasser (1986), an advocate of giving students responsibilities, makes a strong case for giving students more control over their learning. Small-group discussions *do* give students some control over their learning and do so in a cooperative manner.

Small-Group Discussions for All Disciplines?

Discussions can be held in any classroom, on any subject matter, and at any age or mental level. Students need to learn how to express their ideas effectively and to incorporate these skills as part of their personalities. This learner goal is appropriate not only in subject areas where discussions are easy to conduct, such as in literature and social studies, but also in other areas such as in physics, chemistry, home economics, art, health, foreign languages, and physical education—in all courses in the school. Discussions need to have meaningful purposes, of course. A discussion about the quadratic equation would surely be inappropriate. But a discussion on the methods of proof or the derivations of the quadratic equation could prove to be mind-stretching for the participants.

Study the following list of *purposes* for small-group discussions and form your own *tentative* opinion about the usefulness of this type of teaching strategy in *your* discipline or teaching area.

1. Interest can be aroused at the introduction or the closing of a new topic.
2. Small groups can identify problems or issues to be studied or can suggest alternatives for pursuing a topic under consideration.

3. Small groups can explore new ideas or ways to solve problems, covering either the entire problem-solving cycle or just a phase of it.
4. Discussions provide the opportunity to evaluate data, opinions, and sources of information, and to structure concepts for future application.
5. Small groups can allow students to demonstrate individual strengths.
6. Students can often learn faster and better from one another.
7. Skills in leadership, organization, interaction, research, and initiative can be learned and improved through discussion techniques.
8. Ideas become more meaningful and personal if a student must defend them. Also, flexibility about understanding other viewpoints may be improved.
9. Discussions can provide the students (and the teacher) with opportunities for learning to accept and value various ethnic and/or cultural backgrounds.

After reading these items, reflect on your own discipline or teaching areas. Ask yourself this question: "Based on the nine elements, how many topics in my subject area lend themselves to a discussion?" If you are uncertain about the answer, select a textbook related to your teaching area and peruse the contents. Undoubtedly, you will identify easily several topics that you can incorporate into a series of small-group discussions. See Table 7-1 for just a few of the hundreds of discussion topics that can be used in schools.

Table 7-1

Sample List of Discussion Topics

Topics	Subject Areas	Grade Levels
Life cycles of cities	Geography; Social studies	4–8
Playground safety	Homeroom	K–3
Community helpers	Social studies	1–4
Ideal office arrangements	Secretarial; Office education	11–12
Effects of colors on moods	Art; Home economics	9–12
Alternative health-care plans	Current issues; Family living	10–12
Place value in mathematics	Mathematics	2–6
Explanations of "electrical charges"	Science; Shop	4–9
Options for cardiovascular conditioning	Physical education; Health; Lifestyles	8–12
Analysis of "popular" advertisements	Speech; General business; Language arts	7–12
Checks and balances in government	Government; History	7–12
Dating etiquette	Family living; Home economics	10–12
Expression, or pizazz in writing	Language arts; English	4–12
Stereotypes and musical preferences	Music; General business	7–12
Successful study habits	All students and teachers	K–12
How to listen	All students and teachers	K–12
Uses of math formulas	Mathematics; Shop	6–12
Impact of science and technology on society	Social problems; Science	8–12

Now ask yourself: "What kinds of sharing experience do I want for my students?" Some of you probably will respond by immediately focusing on the sharing of different cultural experiences such as dress habits, playthings and games, family behaviors, and religious practices. You may have thought about the need for students to display and share their unique talents. No doubt, some of you may have thought about disadvantaged and handicapped students and of their needs.

The two preceding questions are important because most of you will be teaching in mainstreamed classes. Others of you will be involved with gifted and talented classes, and all of you will be faced with the challenge of providing a nonsexist, multiculturally oriented education for your students. Being adept at handling small-group discussions will help you meet the challenge.

Establishment of the Classroom Environment

Possibly the most important criterion for predicting your ability to facilitate small-group discussions is your own set of attitudes and feelings. Mastering small-group discussion methods requires an appreciation of the atmosphere, or emotional setting, of the classroom. As the teacher, you must believe that students can be delegated a degree of responsibility, and that the way the leader (the teacher) acts is closely related to the manner in which the followers (the students) respond.

It is your responsibility as teacher to establish the proper atmosphere in the classroom. You need to develop a "we attitude," an attitude of thinking in terms of "the students and I working together." This "we attitude" will help you in establishing some clear goals that involve teacher-student relationships, student-student relationships, the learning purposes of the classroom, and a supportive emotional climate. The classroom environment needs to be supportive of all persons so that the students will learn to respect all other individuals and their ideas. Such an atmosphere is fostered through small-group learning experiences. But *you* as the teacher must make the decisions that will shape the classroom environment into a supportive learning situation.

Introducing the Concept of Evaluation

The "Discussion Evaluation Form" (Figure 7-2) is designed to provide some feedback to each person who participates in a group activity. Preparing such a form is rather simple. First, you ask what the goals or objectives of the activity are; then, you identify some criteria that would be applicable for judging each component. As this chapter develops, you will observe and then perhaps use many more evaluation forms to judge the value of small-group discussion activities. We feel very strongly that, because small-group discussions are process-oriented, the processes should be continually evaluated so that you and your students will be aware of improvements.

Once the individual has evaluated his or her group activities, it is essential for the group collectively to compile data from each individual so that the group may receive

Figure 7-2   *Discussion Evaluation Form: Individual Participant Rating*

DISCUSSION EVALUATION FORM

Group _____

Participant's name _____

Directions: Rate your own participation in your group by circling one of the numbers in the scales (from 1 to 5) for each of the criteria stated at the left.

Criteria	Very Ineffective	Somewhat Ineffective	Not Sure	Somewhat Effective	Very Effective
1. What overall rating of effectiveness would you give this discussion session?	1	2	3	4	5
2. How effective was the background event in getting you interested in the discussion topic?	1	2	3	4	5
3. How effectively did your group seem to be working together by the conclusion of the discussion?	1	2	3	4	5
4. How well was participation distributed among the group members?	1	2	3	4	5
5. How effective were the decisions your group reached?	1	2	3	4	5
6. How effective was the group in considering every idea that you contributed?	1	2	3	4	5
7. How effective was the leader in making it easier for you to say something?	1	2	3	4	5
8. How effective were you in encouraging others to speak or to become involved?	1	2	3	4	5
9. What were the two main good points and the two main problem areas of your small-group discussion?					

A simple form such as this gives each participant some idea of his or her strengths or weaknesses in the group activity. The recorded information can provide a focus for the improvement of small-group discussion processes. Modifications of the form can be made for specific needs.

cumulative feedback. To accomplish this aim, tally all the individual responses for each item (as marked on forms such as Figure 7-2) and present the sums to the group. This technique allows each individual to compare the self-rating to that of the group.

Figures 7-3 and 7-4 illustrate alternative methods of tabulating group data. We suggest that you file these evaluation forms so that you can determine later the type and direction of growth of each participating individual. Besides, with such baseline and long-range data available, you will be able to help students who have not mastered specific discussion skills. As we previously stated, you may devise shorter discussion evaluation forms. You may decide to help the students become more aware of their own participation by compiling and using very simple evaluation instruments, such as in Figure 7-3.

You may compile group data from such forms to observe the total range of responses. We suggest that a graph be prepared (by a small group, of course) so that the direction of the groups can be graphically portrayed for your instant and easy analysis. It also would give the small groups an idea of how they are progressing.

Because the goal of small-group instruction is to increase the participation of each student, it becomes essential to build simple-to-use evaluative instruments so that the progress can be monitored easily and systematically. An alternative method of gathering information about both the amount of participation of specific individuals and the overall pattern of participation for an entire group is illustrated in Figure 7-4. Figures 7-2 and 7-4 may be held by each student and then be tallied for the entire class so that you can easily and systematically note progress or problems.

Figure 7-3   *A Quick Checklist for Group Discussion*

QUICK CHECK POINTS

Name _____

Directions: To evaluate your group, place an X next to the statement that best describes your reaction to each of the incomplete sentences:

1. I thought that the discussion
   - _____ (a) Gave everyone a chance to participate freely.
   - _____ (b) Allowed nearly everyone a chance to participate freely.
   - _____ (c) Was dominated by only a few.

2. As far as my participation in the discussion is concerned, I
   - _____ (a) Was very involved.
   - _____ (b) Could have been more involved.
   - _____ (c) Was totally uninvolved.

3. The discussion leader
   - _____ (a) Encouraged a wide range of participation.
   - _____ (b) Selected only a few persons to participate.
   - _____ (c) Seemed to dominate the discussion most of the time.

Figure 7-4 *Personal Data Check Instrument*

PERSONAL DATA CHECK

Name _____

Directions: Keep track of the number of times that you participate orally in the small-group activity. Then insert the total number in the place provided in Item 1. After the discussion is over, place an X next to the statement that best describes your reaction to each of the questions.

1. Tally the number of times that you participated verbally in the small-group discussion.
   _____ Your tally.

2. To what extent did you participate in the discussion?
   _____ (a) I really dominated it.
   _____ (b) I participated as much as the others did.
   _____ (c) Not as much as I would have liked to.

3. To what extent would you like to contribute more to the group discussion?
   _____ (a) I'd like to contribute more.
   _____ (b) I'm contributing just about the amount I'd like to.
   _____ (c) I'd like to contribute less.

4. How would you rate the extent to which your group encourages all of its members to participate fully?
   _____ (a) The group encourages everyone to participate fully.
   _____ (b) The group could encourage its members to participate more.
   _____ (c) The group discourages individuals from participating.

Throughout this chapter you are exposed to various kinds of techniques that you can use or adapt for small-group situations. Many of the evaluation instruments can be lengthened or shortened to fit specific circumstances. We have shown some easy-to-use instruments because, as you begin to compile data on process objectives, you will want to keep the systems simple and manageable. After many of the early skills are mastered, more complex forms can be used.

A BRIEF REVIEW OF SMALL-GROUP LEARNING PRINCIPLES

Group development and cohesiveness are attained through an evolutionary process. Everyone has experienced, in either large or small classes, how a lack of respon-siveness and a general climate of anxiety often mark the initial sessions. This phase can be predicted from theories of group development. Effective small-group facilitators (or teachers) understand these theoretical principles and are able to implement the techniques presented in this chapter so as to expedite group development and cohesiveness. Winning coaches have long known and used these principles, often the secret of why they produce winning teams, talent or its lack notwithstanding. So let us proceed to those principles that have stood the test of experience.

Instructional Goals or Rationales for Small-Group Discussions

The question we would like to raise now is as follows: Are educators who suggest the use of discussion justified in making claims that small-group discussions are beneficial? Yes, they are, particularly if the groups are involved in tasks requiring higher levels of thinking, decision-making, problem-solving, or the formulating of positive social behaviors and attitudes. Bruce Joyce, Beverly Showers, and Carol Rolheiser-Bennett (1987) summarize significant gains in group learning when student results are measured by either standardized or criterion-referenced measures.

Studies have shown that small-group methods are superior for *selected purposes when conducted under appropriate conditions.* There is evidence that changes in social adjustment and personality can be best facilitated through small-group instructional methods. Students who work together in a small-group discussion are likely to learn more quickly with more accuracy than are students engaged in other learning methods.

This is not to assert that small-group discussions are always more effective than other methods are. Exhaustive research done by the Human Resources Research Organization (HumRRO) summarized some of the advantages and disadvantages of small-group methods. Olmstead (1970) had these conclusions:

> A review of existing research concerned with small-group methods leads to the conclusions that the techniques are effective for enhancing motivation to learn, developing positive attitudes toward later use of course material, and improving problem-solving skills. The methods are no more effective than lectures for transmitting information, concepts, and doctrines; however, when used in conjuction with lectures, they are helpful for increasing depth of understanding of course content.

The now classic HumRRO study noted five instances in which it is most feasible to use small-group methods (Olmstead, 1970):

1. To increase depth of understanding and grasp of course content
2. To enhance motivation and generate greater involvement of students with the course
3. To develop positive attitudes toward later use of material presented in the course
4. To develop problem-solving skills specific to content of the course
5. To provide practice in the application of concepts and information to practical problems

To increase the effectiveness of the small-group participants, teachers can emphasize two process skills in their classes. These processes are (1) inquiry skills and (2) cooperativeness. Studies have demonstrated the usefulness of inquiry skills; in fact, many of the newly developed curricula now place a heavy emphasis on an inquiry approach to learning.

In groups that have cooperative members, the quality and quantity of learning are often amazingly high. Conversely, if the group members are competing with one another, both the quantity and quality of learning sometimes decrease. Of course, to reach selected instructional goals, intergroup competition may be desirable if it is not carried to an extreme. Again, the decision is yours. The overall success of small groups within your classroom depends on a carefully selected blend of discussion modes, some of which require intragroup cooperation and a few that call for intergroup competition, which may be in the form of games or simulations of some kind.

Concepts Concerning Small-Group Interaction

Studies concerned with selected aspects of small-group interaction have resulted in the development of a number of basic concepts that explain phenomena associated with such groups. These concepts have become components of a set of fundamental assumptions concerning small-group interaction processes; teachers can use these assumptions to facilitate small-group discussions. These concepts are *interaction, process, structure, role, leadership,* and *group cohesion.* Let us examine each in depth.

Interaction

Communication between two or more people is defined as interaction. This communication can, of course, be either verbal or nonverbal or, even more likely, a mixture of both. Astute observation of small-group discussions will reveal both nonverbal and linguistic modes of communication or interaction.

Interaction is the process of persons responding to each other. The essence of the concept is that communication is a reciprocal process between interactors. A group member who says something, but to whom no one listens or responds, is not truly involved in an interaction sequence. Likewise, random body movements are not part of an interaction unless another person notices those movements and verbally or nonverbally responds to them.

Process

Closely associated with interaction is the concept of process. Process may be defined as the aggregate of the interaction. The group facilitator can refer to the interaction process as the communicative actions that occur during the group discussion.

Structure

The interaction process takes place within a structure. Structure can be conceptualized as a pattern of interpersonal relations. Another way to visualize structure is to think in terms of the relative positions of the group members within the framework of the total group. The small-group discussion facilitator will need to remember that the written and unwritten rules of the "school as an institution" may dictate the structure of the group. The institution tends to assign a position or status role to the teacher and different roles to the student. The optimal structure for a small-group discussion in the classroom is one in which the interaction processes are widely and evenly distributed among the members and in which the roles are flexible.

Role

Small-group discussion members can maintain structure because the group members are aware that their particular roles in this setting have certain corresponding expectations. The structure determines the parameters of possible roles. Small-group members can establish expectations that encourage other group members to interact in any given situation. Roles can be associated with sets of expectations. For example, students expect the teacher to give assignments, praise good student efforts, and obey the principal; these functions establish teacher roles.

Group members may be assigned roles, such as teacher or student, or roles may be assumed voluntarily. Each role has specific privileges, obligations, responsibilities, and powers. A role is meaningful only in relation to some other role; thus, roles in such a context are complementary. Although roles are the product of a particular small group's norms, they can be grouped into three general categories. These categories are (1) task roles, (2) maintenance roles, and (3) self-serving roles. In these roles individuals demonstrate a set of behaviors associated with these functions. No one individual always plays one role. It is your responsibility to provide each student with opportunities to participate in a wide spectrum of roles.

Task roles include behaviors such as initiating, providing information, seeking opinions, clarifying, elaborating or interpreting, synthesizing or summarizing, and testing for consensus or group commitment. These roles focus on the task of getting the assignment accomplished.

Maintenance roles tend to be management-oriented. Maintaining group processes requires that participants help the group be cohesive and productive. An encourager role is played by those who are friendly, receptive, and responsive to others. A norm tester notes the relationships in the group and initiates procedures to see whether the group accepts these relationships. A harmonizer works to reconcile differences. A compromiser yields to a more generally accepted position or encourages others to make concessions to maintain group cohesion. A facilitator keeps communication channels open and encourages others to participate. A recognizer keeps the record up-to-date by giving credit for ideas or actions to the appropriate individual. A standard-setter applies criteria when evaluating group functions or productivity.

Self-serving roles are neither as positive nor as constructive as task roles or maintenance roles. Individuals accepting these roles tend to obstruct a true discussion by serving their own interests. The same individual may play the roles of both a dominator and an aggressor.

A dominator may interrupt, monopolize the discussion, embark on a monologue, establish a position early, provoke action, and/or lead by asserting authority. The aggressor struggles for status, boasts, criticizes, and denigrates others.

A blocker interferes with progress by rejecting ideas, by responding pessimistically and negatively, by arguing unduly, and by refusing to cooperate with the group. A deserter withdraws, becomes inattentive, whispers to others to distract them, and wanders away from the subject.

A recognition-seeker is the person who makes exaggerated attempts to get attention. The recognition-seeker may claim to possess great skills, be petty, call for careful examination of all sides of the question, or depend heavily on personal experience as a basis for an opinion.

The playgirl or playboy tends to lack involvement in the group activity and to distract others by the use of horseplay, inappropriate humor, and/or cynical comments.

Leadership

One of the most important roles in small-group discussion is that of the leader. There are several ways to explain leadership and to theorize about the role of the leader. At least two types of leadership roles—status and functional—are evident in the classroom. The *status leadership* role is fulfilled by the person (the leader) having an official or designated title. The title carries an assumption of authority with it—such as teacher, "assigned student" group leader, or spokesperson.

Functional leadership describes the situation in which any group member who performs a function that helps the group move toward accomplishing its task fulfills a leadership role, if only for the duration of the one behavior. Functional leadership is a key concept for those facilitators who subscribe to the "democratic" theory of leadership—that leadership should be shared among the group members.

Group members will be more satisfied with the group if they feel that they have some influence on group decisions. Group facilitators need to be sensitive to the fact that the group members want to feel involved and influential in both the process and product areas. The teacher may be the status leader, but in group work should share the leadership role with the group members. The teacher is also responsible for providing an opportunity for each student to become a leader.

Group Cohesion

The concept of cohesion is best understood if one examines its three crucial elements—unity, attraction, and purpose. The cohesive group displays evidence of the "we attitude" (unity); its members express a strong desire to belong to the group (attraction); and its members can define group goals and activities (purpose). In the vernacular, a cohesive group is one that "has its act together."

Group cohesion is not a desirable end in itself. For instance, the situation in which students are cohesive but rebel against, or exclude, the teacher may make learning impossible. It is crucial that the teacher be a part of the "we"; however, the "we" must not be so strong as to foster too much conformity and ignore the value of individualism.

EIGHT BASIC SMALL-GROUP DISCUSSION TYPES

From among the eight basic discussion techniques that we will present next, our goal is to provide you with at least one discussion type that will fit your teaching style. To be most helpful, the creative teacher must master several teaching styles and techniques, including that of small-group discussions.

If you plan to use a small-group discussion, then you should be able to choose from among many styles. The basic contingency for selection will be the state of preparation of the students. The teacher who knows how to organize and facilitate several different types of discussions can design more varied learning activities than can the teacher who knows only one or two types. To increase your effectiveness as a discussion-oriented teacher, eight kinds of small-group discussions are introduced. As you are exposed to this wide spectrum of small-group methods, you should seek out fellow students with whom to practice each type. In this manner you will acquire first-hand experience.

One method for classifying (and remembering) discussion types is to use the variable of control or domination. When facilitating a small-group discussion, you make decisions regarding the amount of teacher or leader control that you desire. You can dominate almost totally the activities of any group, can act in an egalitarian manner, or can choose not to participate at all. The last situation can be observed in small-group discussions in which interaction is controlled totally by the students. Table 7-2 illustrates the eight basic types of discussions viewed along a control continuum.

Although the element of controlling a discussion is one dimension of planning, there are three other important concepts that you must identify when choosing a discussion type for a particular situation. These are (1) the desired or anticipated process or skill, (2) the desired or anticipated product, and (3) the combination of process and product in a problem-solution type. Group work always has a goal, such as the completion of a given task. This goal is the *product*. How the members interact with one another during the discussion is the *process*. These two objectives must be taught to the students so that they will know how to "play the game." Let us now proceed to those eight basic techniques.

Table 7-2   *A Taxonomy of Discussion Groups*

	Type of Discussion	General Instructional Purposes	Orientation	Knowledge, Skills, and Control Continuum
Skill Building	Brainstorming	Creativity Stimulation Generate ideas	Processes	Lowest need of discussion skills and moderate probability for teacher control
	Phillips 66	Role-building Leadership Responsibility Listening Evaluating	Processes	
Task Building	Tutorial	Individual skills Questioning Basic competencies	Processes and products	
	Task Group	Delegation of responsibility Initiative Achievement Planning skills Group learning	Product and processes	
		Affective consequences Accomplishment Evaluation	Product and processes	
	Role-Playing	Clarifying issues Evaluation	Processes	
	Panel	Debating ideas Reflective thinking Group consensus Values analysis Presenting information	Processes	
Problem-Solution Building	Simulation Inquiry group	Inquiry Evaluation Analysis Synthesis Evaluation Student initiative	Processes and product Processes	Highest need of discussion skills and lowest probability for teacher control

Two Skill-Building Techniques

Brainstorming

A very simple and effective type of technique to use when a high level of creativity is desired is "brainstorming." Any number of students can become involved in a brainstorming activity. The shorter the time for discussion, the fewer should be the number of group participants, so let time dictate the size of the group, which should fall within a five-to-fifteen-person limit.

The brainstorming session is started by the leader, who briefly states the problem under consideration. The problem may be as simple as "What topics would the group like to consider this semester?" or as complex as "How can an office of secretaries and junior executives be arranged to maximize efficiency?" Every school subject has some elements that require students to do some free-wheeling thinking. This is when you want to use a brainstorming group. Refer to Chapter 5 to review the topic of *mapping,* as it is effective when combined with brainstorming.

After the topic is stated and before interaction starts, it is crucial to select a method of recording the discussion. It can be taped, or one or two students who write quickly can serve as recorders. The leader should stress to the group that *all* ideas need to be expressed. All group participants need to realize that *quantity* of suggestions is paramount.

There are some very important rules to follow when using the brainstorming technique. (Different writers have slightly different views on some of the minor techniques. You may want to peruse the chapter's References for these variations.) Although all the students will be oriented to the rules, make sure that the student leader enforces these procedures. The following rules seem to be especially important.

1. All ideas, except for obvious jokes, should be acknowledged.
2. No criticism is to be made of any suggestion.
3. Members should be encouraged to build on one another's ideas. In the final analysis no idea belongs to an individual, so encourage "piggy-backing."
4. Solicit ideas or opinions from silent members; then give them positive reinforcement.
5. Quality is less important than quantity, but this does not relieve the group members of trying to think creatively or intelligently.

An initiating process, brainstorming must be followed up with some other activity. One way would be to use the ideas generated in the brainstorming session as the basis for another type of discussion. *After* the brainstorming session, ideas should be evaluated and as many as possible should be used by students in follow-up activities. Brainstorming can lead to the arranging of the elements in order of priority—for example, when you wish to evaluate a series of suggested topics according to their importance so as to use them for future study.

The evaluation of a brainstorming session should not be lengthy, and it should be nonthreatening for the participants. Remember that you want all to contribute, regardless of their current level of academic capability. Although you may be making some private assessments about academic levels, levels of inhibition, the pecking order, and who is bored in class, all your public evaluations must be highly positive.

Phillips 66

The "Phillips 66" discussion group, which involves exactly six students, was developed by J. Donald Phillips of Michigan State University. Such a group is established quickly and does not require preorientation of students; also, students do not have to be highly skilled in group interaction for this type of discussion to work effectively. In fact, the Phillips 66 technique is most appropriate as an initial mixer activity.

The class is divided into groups of six (by you or on a volunteer basis). The groups then have one minute in which to pick a secretary and a leader. At the end of one minute, give a clear and concise statement of the problem or issue for discussion, worded so as to encourage specific single-statement answers. Then impose the time limit for the discussion: students have exactly six minutes to come to an agreement as to the best solution for the problem. After the discussion is over, you may want to talk with the students about various ways that leaders can keep the group focused on the task. The Phillips 66 method is also a good training technique for future group leaders, recorders, and evaluators.

When using the Phillips 66 group in the primary grades, you may decide to eliminate the role of secretary. We encourage you still to consider the benefits of having one of the students summarize the group's solution. Listening and summarizing are important skills for group work.

The Phillips 66 discussion group can be very useful as the set induction activity for a concept formation-attainment lesson or as the set inducer for a new unit. You should consider using the Phillips 66 technique for some of the times when it would be beneficial to focus the students' attention on, and quickly create interest in, a problem or concept.

Your role is very simple. You decide on the topic, arrange the groups, start the discussion, and then just observe. Figure 7-5 illustrates five spatial arrangements for the Phillips 66 discussion groups. How many other spatial configurations can you suggest?

Four Task-Building Techniques

Tutorial

The tutorial discussion group is most frequently used to help students who have experienced difficulties in learning or in progressing at a satisfactory rate. The group has only a few students (usually less than five) and focuses on a narrow range of materials. Teachers of such subjects as reading, mathematics, home economics, art, and business often use the tutorial group for remediation of basic skills. In the social

Figure 7-5   *Some Configurations for the Phillips 66 Technique*

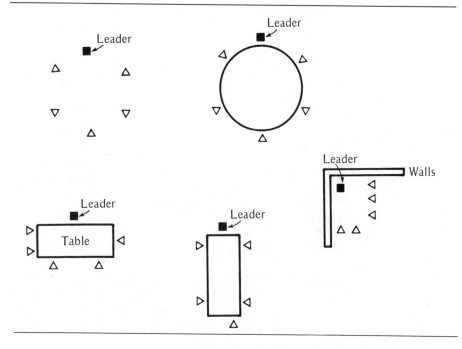

studies, language arts, and sciences, the tutorial group is used to help students grasp a concept, again with the purpose of remedying a learning difficulty. Physical education and primary grade teachers employ a tutorial mode frequently in the area of motor development. It is an excellent way to facilitate the handling of manipulatives, to demonstrate and evaluate motor activities, and to help students understand the relationships between movement-exercise and body function.

The selected discussion leader has three major functions to perform in the tutorial mode: (1) questioning the students to pinpoint the exact problem that has blocked learning, (2) providing the feedback or skills to facilitate learning, and (3) encouraging the students to ask questions and to seek answers among themselves. Lest you have serious reservations about the tutorial technique, it has been demonstrated that students often learn better from one another than from the teacher! We caution, however, that before you use student tutors, you must be satisfied that each potential student tutor has mastered the necessary competencies—such as the skills of questioning, giving positive reinforcement, and analyzing work tasks.

Many school districts currently use student tutors and are finding them to be invaluable resources for the classroom teacher. Although used most often for remedial work, the tutorial discussion group is also an excellent method by which to encourage independent projects or advanced learners. Many gifted students will find it a challenge to try to explain their project to other students.

Figure 7-6   *Spatial Arrangements for Tutorial Groups*

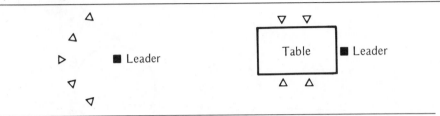

The person who leads the tutorial type of discussion will need to have developed some skills in the area of human relations. Good leadership is patient and provides both feedback and warm encouragement. The leader must also keep the group moving toward its product, accept the inputs from others who learn slowly, and prod those group members who are slow to contribute. (It may even be a good idea to give your student leaders a brief review of those questioning techniques that you studied.)

Figure 7-6 illustrates two excellent spatial arrangements for participants in a tutorial group. Note that in either case the arrangements provide easy "eyeball-to-eyeball" contact. Such visual contact helps facilitate the flow of communication between all persons. Also note that the leader is clearly identified and plays a somewhat dominant role in the group process.

Tutoring that combines feedback and formative evaluation, writes Benjamin S. Bloom (1984), is such a powerful instructional technique that tutored students can gain 98 percent more than students in conventional classes, as measured by achievement tests. This critical finding validates the instructional efficacy of the tutorial. No other instructional variable—homework, advance organizers, conventional classes—surpasses tutoring. Bloom also reports that a tutorial is equally effective with a small group of two or three students participating. Dale H. Schunk's review (1987) also substantiates peer modeling and tutorial techniques as having powerful effects on learning. Improved student behaviors and enhanced social skills are but two. Schunk added that peer instruction increases the self-efficiency of learning-disabled students and those who do not read well.

Task Group

One of the least complex discussion types is that of the task group. As the name implies, students are involved in some kind of work or activity in which each group member can make significant contributions. A prerequisite to using the task group is to specify clearly defined tasks to all group members. The task group is very similar to a committee and probably, under most circumstances, would be classified as a student committee. Like a committee, a task group has clearly defined goals and clearly identified individual assignments and roles. Also, it may be beneficial for you to establish a work schedule and a system for internal monitoring of achievements, and initially even to provide all the learning resources that may be necessary to accomplish the identified tasks.

Task groups tend to be teacher-dominated, in that the teacher usually selects the tasks and assigns each class member to accomplish a specific role. You will find that this is an especially efficient discussion type for helping students learn to interact positively in groups. Furthermore, you may observe how selected students work with one another and how responsibly they tend to accomplish the assigned task.

A cautionary note must be added. Even though you give a specific assignment to each task group member, do *not* assume that the task will be carried out completely. Students must learn how to accept responsibilities, *but* it is your job to provide appropriate goal setting, motivation, and consistent monitoring of each person's activities to help all students achieve their assigned goals.

Role-Playing

Role-playing is a process-oriented group technique that may include almost any number of participants, although seven to ten is ideal. You probably should not use this type of group until you are well acquainted with role-playing techniques. Students also need some coaching in the three aspects of the role-playing group: the briefing, or the establishing of the situation; the drama, or role-playing; and the follow-up discussion. A thorough preparation will help them enjoy the process and experience of the role-playing episode and not be overly concerned about interactions that may, in other situations, be perceived as personal attacks. The role-playing technique should not be employed until all students know one another, because its early use can stereotype certain students unfavorably and thus foster a rigid perspective.

Role-playing can work in almost any situation or subject matter. It is usually the spontaneous acting out of a situation or incident to portray a problem common to group members or to give a common background to all members. The construction is free, with no script, but considerable briefing and planning should precede the role-playing scene. An episode lasts no more than five to ten minutes, and it is important for the activity to approximate reality.

A large-group discussion or debriefing of about fifteen minutes should follow the final scene of any role-playing episode. It is at this point that the class analyzes the group process. During the analysis the leader or teacher should strive to identify the values and behavior of the characters and the consequences of their interactions.

Role-playing is especially beneficial if the participants understand the differences between sociodrama and psychodrama. Role-players and all students who participate in the follow-up discussion should not be allowed to psychoanalyze anyone or to pretend that they are psychologists. Such analytical activities exemplify psychodrama and should be reserved for psychologists and other professionals with considerable expertise in interpersonal relationships. In sociodrama, or role-playing, as we are using the term, the emphasis is not on the psyche of any character, but on reenacting or dramatizing a *real situation* and demonstrating how the different characters react to the situation.

It is difficult to suggest how you should evaluate this type of group discussion because each role-playing group discussion is a unique experience. Some of the elements that you may assess are as follows: Did some of the students who are usually quiet or in the background take a more active part? Did the situation that prompted the discussion seem to be better understood by the participants? Was the situation resolved (if it involved classroom problems)? Did the role-players take their roles seriously? Did the participants avoid self-serving roles during the discussion phase?

Many advocates of role-playing have shown a special concern for low-achieving students or those referred to as educationally "retarded." For these students, role-playing can be the bridge between talking and action. Role-playing provides a safe yet dynamic setting for trying out, or practicing, social skills. In the multiethnic, mainstreamed classroom, the role-playing discussion group can be a powerful teaching tool; however, as with most powerful tools, it must be used wisely.

Role-playing can be applied to all levels of academic achievement and to all levels of school. L. Gerald Buchan (1972), in his book *Roleplaying and the Educable Mentally Retarded,* has suggested role-playing in secondary schools for helping students learn how to interview for a job, how to purchase intangibles such as loans and insurance, and how to establish personal relationships. Teachers in skill areas and vocational areas can easily use role-playing groups to help assess competency levels. An excellent source for additional ideas on how to use role-playing is *Role Playing in the Curriculum* by Fannie M. Shaftel and George Shaftel (1982).

Panel Discussion

The panel discussion is designed to allow students to be productive and to have a meaningful exchange of ideas on *relevant* issues. It is most appropriate when you want students to do high-level thinking and when the discussion topic can be legitimately viewed from different perspectives. Panel discussions are useful in helping students develop tentative or divergent alternatives to controversial issues. We must stress that the group members will not necessarily reach the same solution or conclusion.

The topic for a panel discussion should be identified well in advance. The best topics are obviously oriented to student issues and concerns *relative* to your instructional goals. The topics should involve the students intellectually and emotionally; that is, students should care about the potential solutions. You may want to use a brainstorming session to generate possible topics for the panel discussion groups.

Students need to be well prepared for the panel discussion. Everyone needs to have some basic understandings (knowledge and comprehension) of the topic to be discussed—through lectures, readings, films, or interviews prior to the discussion. In addition, the students who will actually be the panel must conduct more extensive research into the topic.

Probably two or three is the ideal number to be on the panel. A total group of up to fifteen students should listen or interact, although a full class could also listen to the issues and then prepare individual position papers on the topic. At times outsiders may be panel members because of their expertise in a particular area. In these cases, be sure to stress that this will be a *discussion,* not a guest lecture or a debate. It would be helpful to share the following with them.

A moderator begins by introducing the topic and the panel members and by reminding the total group to use their discussion and listening skills. The panel members then present rather short statements of three to five minutes representing various viewpoints. These statements should be provocative and present strong points or arguments. They should *not* be summarizing statements—those can be made at the end of the discussion.

Following the opening statements, the moderator facilitates a free and open discussion. The moderator's goal is to get the total group involved in the give-and-take and yet to give the panel members periodic opportunities to add new information or to clarify previous statements. It is the moderator's responsibility to conduct the discussion so that it does not become an argument between any two people, degenerate to a gab session, or stray to other topics. As you may infer, the panel discussion works much better *after* the students have learned or practiced some discussion skills.

A good way to end the panel discussion is to ask each panelist for some general conclusions or summaries, stated in terms of tentative solutions to the issue being addressed by the panel. The quality of these solutions will aid you in evaluating how well the students have mastered the topic.

The process of the panel discussion should also be evaluated. Students who had special roles, as well as the group as a whole, should receive feedback on how they performed during the discussion. The assessment form shown in Figure 7-7 is suitable for this evaluation. (This form is also appropriate for use with the task group; you may modify any form to fit the particular group and situation.) Figure 7-7 shows a very thorough evaluation of the processes that may have taken place during a small-group discussion. This form would serve as a final or summative process evaluation and would conclude the small-group work or at least one major phase of it. If videotape playbacks are used, then the entire group can evaluate their work as they observe the playback.

Two Problem-Solution Building Techniques

Simulations

Simulation is the presenting of an artificial problem, event, situation, or object that duplicates reality, but removes the possibility of injury or risk to the individuals involved in the activity. It is a model of what exists or might exist in a set of complex physical or social interactions. Simulation is a representation of a manageable real

Figure 7-7   *Comprehensive Evaluation of the Environment in Which a Small-Group Experience*
Took Place

TEST FOR ATMOSPHERE

Using this rating scale, insert a number from 1 to 5 next to each item below to rank
your feelings regarding the atmosphere created during this small-group experience.

Very Low	Low	Needs Improvement	High	Very High
1	2	3	4	5

_____ 1. How free are the participants to state their real opinion?

_____ 2. How free are the participants to choose to work on areas of their own concern?

_____ 3. How free do I feel to interact with the teacher?

_____ 4. How positive do participants feel toward the work in which the group is engaged?

_____ 5. How productive has this small-group experience been?

_____ 6. How well has this learning experience been progressing?

_____ 7. How do you feel about [here you insert some concern]?

_____ 8. How well do you feel this class has used its participant (human) resources?

_____ 9. Do people seem to help one another?

_____ 10. How does this experience compare to the "typical" course activities?

Comments _____

_____

_____

_____

event in which the learner is an active participant engaged in learning a behavior or in applying previously acquired skills or knowledge. Interactive simulations may be special cases of role-playing.

Clark Abt (1966), long associated with the preparation of simulation materials for the private sector, divides simulation into its three major components: (1) models, (2) exercises, and (3) instruction.

Typically, models tend to be *inactive;* that is, they do not interact with the participants. They remain static but do resemble some dimension of reality. Globes of the world, physical models of the solar system, and some case studies are examples of the inactive simulation model. However, computer-controlled models that provide active patterns of interaction with the users are used at various instructional levels. These models are just now becoming available to the public schools, as their costs are now within the schools' budgetary limits. In the not-too-distant future, these models may be commonplace in most schools. Models need not always be physical replicas of the real objects. Pictures, drawings, sketches, and maps can all be classified as models of inactive simulation.

Exercises are activities designed to allow the learner to interact with someone in either a physical or a social manner. Coaches have long utilized exercises as they plan for an upcoming game with the next opponent. Trade and industrial teachers, in setting up equipment that needs to be adjusted or checked (trouble shooting), allow the learners to interact with machines.

Instructional simulations involve the learner in various functions. Cathy Stein Greenblat (1988), a designer and advocate of instructional simulations, suggests that they perform five important functions: (1) stimulate interest, (2) provide information to students, (3) enhance skill development, (4) change attitudes, and (5) assess the performance of the participant by measuring it against an already established standard.

While simulations have long been used in the military, in business, in medicine, and in administrative planning units, their introduction into the schools is a more recent event. But we should remember that teachers have for years used play stores and school councils, as well as other interaction methodologies, as instructional devices to reflect selected dimensions of reality.

Purposes of Simulations   There appear to be at least ten general purposes for simulations and games in education.

1. To develop changes in attitudes
2. To change specific behaviors
3. To prepare participants for assuming new roles in the future
4. To help individuals understand their current roles
5. To increase the student's ability to apply principles
6. To reduce complex problems or situations to manageable elements
7. To illustrate roles that may affect one's life but that one may never assume
8. To motivate learners
9. To develop analytical processes
10. To sensitize individuals to another person's life role

Each of these ten purposes, we must warn, *cannot* be obtained from any one simulation device. You select simulations or games that are appropriate for a specific learning objective. One of the desired results from simulation is that the exercise will stimulate learners to learn additionally through independent study or research. Furthermore, as students engage in relevant simulation exercises, they may begin to perceive that knowledge learned in one context can become valuable in different situations. This is, of course, the well-known concept of "transfer" that keeps psychologists perplexed.

In our own use of simulations, we have observed that students become immersed in the activities almost immediately. Games and simulations are great "icebreakers" for diverse groups of students. There is also an element of risk-taking for all players. Even though there is no penalty for the participants, each individual tends to view the simulation from a serious, personal perspective. We made this observation, especially in case studies that required the participants to make simulated decisions involving critical human values. In the "bomb shelter" simulation (in which you are under nuclear attack, can allow only five persons in your shelter, and must decide who gets in), we observed students who refused to participate because this value decision went too much against their own moral commitments. Of course, we do not suggest that all simulations involve such personal intensity. We cite this example merely to demonstrate the intense personal involvement that can occur with simulations.

Is there a difference between a game and a simulation? One distinction is that games are played to win, while simulations need not have a winner. In some simulations, it is difficult to determine whether or not there are winners and losers and which players belong to which category. For example, in a simulation of a legislature, the issue is whether to raise taxes. Students are provided with character profiles and a scenario describing the various conditions of the issue. After the arguments are made, a vote is taken. In this simulation, it is difficult to say who has won.

Simulations seem to be more easily applied to the study of issues rather than of processes. The principal purpose of a simulation is to encourage students to express, in their own words, the basic arguments for the various sides of an issue. Games, however, try to get students to make more intelligent decisions as they learn the processes represented in the game. Obviously, the distinctions are not clear-cut. Purists may find that any labeling of these activities is a matter of semantics.

Simulations: Examples   Simulation requires the participants to be involved as active players. A book may provide impetus for classroom simulations: take, for example, Joel Garreau's *The Nine Nations of North America* (1981). After analyzing the social, economic, and geographic components of North America, Garreau creatively subdivided the continent into nine new nations, each reflecting a major trait. The nine new nations he designated were New England, The Foundry, Dixie, MexAmerica, The Empty Quarter, Ecotopia, The Breadbasket, The Islands, and Quebec.

Students could use these nine nations as means to simulate national interests, such as a model United Nations, trade, money exchanges, defense, and natural resources. This type of simulator addresses the higher level of Bloom's Taxonomy combined with elements of problem-solving.

Tom G. Denison (1981), concerned about the costs of welding instruction in high schools, devised a simulated arc welder that he calls the "Blue Streak Welding Simulator." Denison's research indicated that students working with the simulator could achieve the needed initial skills in half the time that a real arc welder took. This case illustrates a shop teacher's desire to improve instruction and to decrease costs.

Ronald R. Rosenblatt (1988) described a simulation for that business of businesses—"The Stock Market Game." Schools subscribe to a service that provides the students with general knowledge about the operations of the stock market. When a class understands the operations, they receive a prescribed number of simulated "dollars" to invest. Each week the class receives a printout of their investments. Teachers who participate in these classes find that this simulation generates a great deal of enthusiasm—especially when the class selects winners on the big board. What is more important is that students begin to understand the importance of research, of the monetary system, and of one element of the free enterprise system. With simulation, economics becomes a real issue as opposed to just a subject in the traditionally taught economics class. Students learn how to write reports, to predict costs, and to compute complicated ratios. Application of principles, analysis of trends, synthesis of information, and evaluation of alternatives are all cognitive objectives (remember that these processes are the higher levels of the cognitive domain). Students are involved in the manipulation of data and information. Is the simulation used? Over ten thousand students in the Philadelphia public schools have learned with it.

You can "teach with a newspaper." The local newspaper offers a wealth of information not only for discussions and inquiry but also for simulations, especially for career education. The education, training, or experience needed as entry levels to careers in their community will be eye-opening to most of your students. Also from a newspaper, students can be taught how to proofread, as nearly every local newspaper provides generous numbers of typographical errors. "What's a Headline Have?" is another game that you can devise (in this game, "verbs" are what headlines have). Or newspaper games are an excellent way to reinforce grammar and its impact on communication.

Let us examine other examples of using simulation. Our first is from the area of English or language arts. David Sudol (1983) found that sophomore literature can be a very frustrating experience for teachers and students alike. But Sudol found that literary concepts could be successfully taught by involving the students: having them develop characters and then develop the plot. Such a simulation technique extended students' experiences beyond the usual, confining experience of reading. Similarly, you could select some classic quote, for example, the opening paragraph from *A Tale of Two Cities* by Charles Dickens, "It was the best of times, it was the worst of times," and ask the students to simulate a plot, a story line, characters, and a location. Use the current year. How closely do you think the students might parallel Dickens? After this simulation, *A Tale of Two Cities* could be read both for knowledge and for comparison to the student outlines.

An article on games to be used in foreign language instruction was written by Alice C. Omaggio (1982). Any teacher of foreign languages from kindergarten to graduate school will be intrigued by the wealth of activities, games, simulations, and student involvement technique presented in this one paper. Omaggio clearly illustrates how you can use these techniques to help students master their performance objectives at the knowlege and application levels.

Other Considerations   Our brief introduction to the use of classroom games or simulations must surely have caused you to ask yourself the question: Will they work for my area? The answer depends on what your goals or objectives are. If you want to build processes associated with decision-making, then games and simulations provide alternatives to the usual classroom routines. If you wish to promote human interactions, then simulations and games are appropriate. If you intend to provide experiences that students may not have in the routine application of learning skills or principles, then you should use games or simulations that will achieve this end. With some ingenuity, knowledge of your subject, initiative, and imagination, *you* too can design a simple game or simulation.

Figure 7-8, from Richard Maidment and Russell H. Bronstein (1973) illustrates a general cycle associated with both the design and use of games or simulations in the classroom.

Inquiry Group

If you wish to emphasize problem-solving, or discovery teaching, then you will find the *inquiry discussion group* extremely valuable. Any number of students may be in the discussion group, but we suggest that six students per team would be ideal for this technique.

The purposes of inquiry group discussions are easily identified: (1) the stimulation of scientific thinking, (2) the development of problem-solving skills, and (3) the acquisition of new facts. It is possible that the teacher may be the leader of this type of group. If, however, you have a student who has demonstrated good questioning skills and who understands the concept (facts) under consideration, then allow that student to be the leader.

Teachers establish responsive environments wherein inquiry is used to stimulate students to become *skillful askers of questions.* They also allow students to test the validity of those hypotheses to determine, by direct experiences, whether they are valid. The inquiry group discussion is most appropriate for those disciplines that lend themselves to problem-solving—science and social science.

Before you introduce inquiry discussions, your students should have mastered observing, question-asking, and inferring behaviors. You then encourage these behaviors by having students ask questions based on selected observations of phenomena, by having them collect data, and by having them summarize and draw conclusions. After you and the students have identified the problems, subdivide the class into small groups to complete the investigation of each problem.

The inquiry group can be used most effectively when students are studying about the general subject of "rights" in the social sciences. For example, a group can role-play an episode in which a civil right has been violated and then, through inquiry discussion, isolate the specific aspects of the violation or solve the problem in other ways. To make the inquiry group most meaningful, plan for an activity that has some degree of authenticity. Furthermore, student hypotheses should have a testable quality. Real-life situations are most relevant.

We would even consider the use of inquiry discussions in the field of language

Figure 7-8 *A Design and Use Cycle for Games or Simulations*

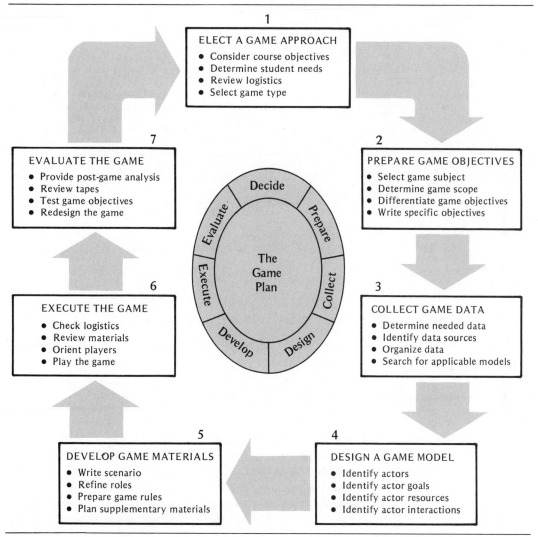

Source: Robert Maidment and Russell H. Bronstein, *Simulation Games: Design and Implementation* (Columbus, Ohio: Charles E. Merrill Publishing Company, 1973), p. 57. Used with the written permission of Charles E. Merrill Publishing Company.

Figure 7-9   *Tabulation Form for Inquiry Discussion Questions*

Observer _____

Teacher _____

Time _____

Type of Question or Statement	Students									
	1	2	3	4	5	6	7	8	9	10
1. Knowledge										
2. Comparison										
3. Cause and effect										
4. Inference										
5. Application										
6. Evaluation										
7. Hypothesis										
8. Other										

Comments _____

_____

_____

arts, especially English. This may be the one opportunity for students to show creativity when posed with a problem, such as an unfamiliar literary device.

The "what" to evaluate concerning the inquiry group is fairly obvious. What you need to know, and what the students need to know, is how well they ask questions. Were they able to ask higher-order questions that could lead to hypothesis-making and testing? Of course, you also will want to know whether they learned the concept being discussed.

The "how" is more difficult to evaluate in the inquiry group. How the students ask questions may be tabulated by using the form in Figure 7-9. Note that there are five categories of higher-order questions, one category of lower-order questions, one category of formal hypothesis-stating, and one category for miscellaneous statements. We suggest that the evaluation be accomplished in one of three ways: (1) Maintain a continuous checklist as each person comments during the discussion. (2) Tape (preferably videotape) the discussion and evaluate the student during the playback. Videotaping has the advantage of allowing you to discuss questioning skills with the students, as well as to point out some academic aspects that they may have overlooked or misunderstood. (3) Have another teacher do the tabulation during the discussion session. This method may be adapted to allow a trained student to perform this task.

We suggest that modifications of this form be made for specific classes or topics. Also, it may be very useful to assign two or more observers to fill out this form to evaluate the discussion. In this manner each observer tabulates certain types of questions or statements, or each observer tabulates all questions or statements. The critique of the group is then made jointly by the committee of reviewers.

More About Inquiry Groups: Buzz Groups

The *buzz* group is a simple variation of an inquiry group. Regardless of the label that you attach to this kind of group, keep two definite guidelines in mind. First, an inquiry group is best suited to a small number of students who are, or can be, fairly self-directed. Second, you will be mainly an outside observer, although you may provide resource help if the group asks for it.

The students in any inquiry discussion group create a free and uninhibited environment in which they can discuss a topic that they select. A buzz group, in particular, is one that is totally student-managed and is oriented to student issues or topics. The major consideration for determining the size of the group is student interest. As many as six students who are interested in the topic can participate in each group. The length of time will also vary with each discussion session, and no absolute time guidelines can be given; however, it is often wise to end the discussion when everyone has expressed a view or the discussion seems to be repeating itself. Relatively short, time-limited problem-solution discussions maintain interest for the next discussion period because students know that they will have another opportunity to express themselves.

The topics are best selected, written, and identified before the discussion begins. The students decide which group to join; then leaders, recorders, and researchers may be assigned their roles in advance. The teacher may wish to meet privately with the leaders to discuss leadership roles and functions. (We strongly recommend all these procedures.) Every student should have an opportunity to be a group leader, but if you attempt to influence the group's selection of leaders, they may feel that you are trying to dominate them. Thus, you may want to point out quietly that "Sally hasn't had an opportunity to lead this year," or you may want to use the other discussion types to provide leadership practice for all students.

The inquiry group is aimed at allowing the students to be productive and to have a meaningful exchange of ideas on *relevant* problems. The student leader should initiate the discussion and should try to keep the group members performing maintenance and task functions. The greatest pitfall of the inquiry group is that it may degenerate into a gab session and lose its intellectual or analytical status. Because each student must be familiar with various group discussion roles before using this technique, problems that arise should be analyzed by their respective group to identify and remedy the role deficiencies. The teacher must not become the arbitrator or the boss of the group. If the group cannot analyze the behavior process that seems to cause the group to degenerate, then the group can be given some additional experiences in role-playing or can be allowed to carry out task and maintenance functions. As an alternative, a videotape may be made for group analysis by using the form shown in Figure 7-9. This additional experience can be teacher-directed; then allow the group to again try an inquiry discussion after they have improved their group skills.

Keep in mind that inquiry groups are designed to produce high-level thinking. They are not spontaneous episodes, nor are they used merely to kill time—for example, on a Friday afternoon, the teacher may be tempted just to let the students discuss anything until the bell rings. Students need time and resources to prepare for inquiry sessions. Group leaders, with your help, should encourage each student to be emotionally and academically equipped for the discussion.

Using an inquiry discussion with physical education, Annemarie Schueler (1979) reports how she effectively incorporates an inquiry model of student-led discussions. Schueler begins the class with a provocative question. For example, the question, "Should girls box?" is one that causes students to probe, clarify, and examine various perspectives. These inquiry discussions integrate six processes: (1) orientating the issue, (2) building a hypothesis, (3) defining terms, (4) exploring alternatives, (5) finding supportive evidence, and (6) generalizing. Schueler finds such discussions to be thought-provoking, stimulating, and student-involving.

We suggest that all evaluation forms be maintained over a long period, so that changes in behavior and growth patterns may be determined by the group.

Summary

There are several questions you can ask yourself that will help you decide which of the eight types of discussion groups is desirable for a given class situation. These are some of the questions:

1. How much control of the group's activities needs to be exerted by the teacher or group leader? Has the group developed its own norms so that little external control is needed? Does the group still need some assistance from the adult leader to function smoothly?
2. Does the objective of the discussion require more emphasis on the *process* or on the *product?*
3. Are the students familiar with the categories of roles and functions, and have they had prediscussion experiences in filling selected roles? Will they receive feedback concerning functions they performed during the current discussion?
4. If skillful leadership qualities and a good academic background are needed for a discussion, is the teacher the only one with these skills or can a student handle the discussion?

Once you have answered these questions, then you can plan meaningful discussion sessions.

FORMATIVE EVALUATION *Small-Group Discussions*

1. Next to each of the following terms, insert the letter of the statement that best defines it.

_____ Task group

_____ Phillips 66

_____ Tutorial group

_____ Inquiry group

_____ Panel discussion

(a) A type of discussion in which the teacher acts as a questioner or responder. The typical way to begin such an activity is to pose a question that is either divergent or evaluative.

(b) Students are involved in some type of activity in which there are clearly defined tasks.

(c) Emphasizes inquiry-to-discovery teaching in which students have to become skillful askers of questions.

(d) Small-group discussion in which the primary purpose is to reach a consensus quickly.

(e) Used to emphasize individualized instruction.

(f) Used to discuss various viewpoints toward a topic. Usually emphasizes higher levels of thinking.

2. Which of the following is true of the brainstorming technique?
   (a) Judgments are made on each idea.
   (b) Notes only practical and logical ideas.
   (c) Piggybacking on someone else's idea is encouraged.
   (d) Quality is the most important feature.

3. Task groups
   (a) Are one of the more complex types of discussion.
   (b) Are similar to a committee.
   (c) Tend to be teacher-dominated.
   (d) Are both (b) and (c).

4. An inquiry group is
   (a) Teacher-dominated.
   (b) A less complex type of discussion.
   (c) A problem-solving approach.
   (d) Appropriate only in science.

5. Panel discussions
   (a) Require previous research or study.
   (b) Are those in which the teacher decides on the topic.
   (c) Are spontaneously generated.
   (d) Require simple skills on the part of the students.

Responses

1. (b) Task group   (d) Phillips 66   (e) Tutorial group   (a),(c) Inquiry group   (f) Panel discussion
2. (c)   4. (c)
3. (d)   5. (a)

COOPERATIVE LEARNING: A SPECIAL APPLICATION

Cooperative learning is one of the more popular, validated small-group teaching strategies. You will certainly recognize that many elements of cooperative learning have been used by master teachers for decades, and that there is overlap with many of the methods already presented. In fact, your ability to use group discussions will be extremely useful when you introduce students to cooperative learning. This technique requires that students work together in mixed ability groups. You will have process objectives for the group and performance objectives for individual *and* group outcomes. But before we describe how to use this technique, a brief rationale is in order.

Rationale for Cooperative Learning

The best argument for cooperative learning is that it increases cognitive achievement. Robert E. Slavin (1987), one of the advocates of this technique, reported that in thirty-five out of forty studies the results favored the cooperative learning methods over traditional methods. Achievement gains can be found across a wide range of subjects and cognitive levels (See *Resource Bulletin,* 1988). Cooperative learning works in music, science, social studies, and language arts in both basic skills and higher-level thinking skills. The Bay Area Writing Project, the Ohio Writing Project, and Cooperative Integrated Reading and Composition are exemplary programs that demonstrate its value. David W. and Roger T. Johnson (1989) conclude that cooperative learning is probably the most defensible new teaching strategy.

Another powerful argument for cooperative learning is that it promotes *affective* achievement. When students begin having success, then they begin to feel more confident; this leads to more satisfaction with self, or self-esteem. In cooperative learning the student has the opportunity for satisfaction by helping others, by being a team player, and by achieving academically (Johnson and Johnson, 1987; Johnson, Johnson, and Stanne, 1986). The need to increase the "affect" is particularly important in classes about which students are phobic, such as advanced mathematics and foreign languages.

Cooperative learning can also be a way to help disadvantaged, or special students. In most regular classes teachers cannot provide constant assistance and feedback to those students who are struggling, and tutoring is out of the question. With this approach disadvantaged or special students receive peer help and encouragement; moreover, they see behaviors and attitudes that they can imitate and eventually internalize.

Organizing for Cooperative Learning

To achieve all they can through cooperative learning, students need to have acquired a satisfactory level of social and verbal skills. We suggest that the students be taught some discussion skills as prerequisites for beginning cooperative learning. They also need to be aware of the reasons for cooperation, group morale, achievement, and motivation. An excellent series of "prerequisite" activities could be taken from a workbook titled *Learning to Achieve*. This booklet is designed to help students learn planning skills necessary for lifetime achievement (Johnson and McClelland, 1984).

The size and composition of the cooperative learning group will vary from activity to activity, with flexibility being a guide. One of the most popular arrangements is the four-person team. This group is usually made up of the highest achiever, the lowest achiever, and two middle achievers. The next team would be composed of the second highest achiever, the next to the lowest, and two in the middle. Even with this method you should vary the groups to get a balance of sexes, races, and backgrounds. When the students are still new at group work, a two-person team is a good starter. Later, a group of three or four could be structured if the task is complicated or large. (Note: These are cooperative working groups, not discussion groups; thus the sizes may vary.)

Cooperative learning groups are appropriate in many situations, but only you can decide if you should use a large group, small group, or an individualized technique for a given learning activity. We encourage you to use cooperative learning regularly, but not necessarily daily. The team approach is an excellent way to review for tests, to explore applications of concepts and theories, to complete laboratory projects, or to practice skills. Base your decision about whether to use cooperative learning for a specific activity on four variables. Is verbal learning needed? Can students learn the content from each other? Would student-to-student sharing be helpful? Are both social and academic outcomes desired?

When you do decide to use cooperative learning, be sure to plan the evaluation procedures carefully. We suggest a three-part scheme. First, make certain that there is individual accountability. Each student should know what he or she must achieve; otherwise, there is a temptation to let the others do the work. You might evaluate on a pre-to-post scheme or on growth from the last unit. Another choice is to set a "reasonable expectation score" based on the student's ability.

Second, establish a procedure for group accountability. The group, or team, should earn points for the group's effort. Remember that you are rewarding *cooperative* learning. They all sink or swim together in regard to their group grade, and it is even expected that the better students will pull that grade up for all the team.

Third, be sure to remember the need for process evaluation. Help all groups analyze their working and learning processes so that they can improve. The evaluation should contribute to the development of social and communication skills. Review some of the process evaluations presented earlier in the chapter as they are most applicable to cooperative learning. Lest you conclude that cooperative learning is a passing fad, we remind you that one national association hailed cooperative learning as the most significant educational technique to be developed in the past twenty years.

ENCOURAGING SMALL-GROUP LEARNING

The preceding text oriented you to the world of small-group learning and urged you to employ small-group discussions for *meaningful* learning experiences. Perhaps at this point you are convinced of the effectiveness of small groups as a distinctive teaching-learning method. But how do you get organized? Throughout this chapter we reiterate that the teacher must systematically build prediscussion skills that culminate in true small-group discussion processes. Let us now address issues related to the building of appropriate small-group environments.

Two major problems encountered during small-group discussions in the schools are these: (1) teachers tend to talk too much, and (2) some students will not talk at all. Pendergrass's study (1973) indicated that teachers made approximately 51 percent of all verbal interactions during small-group discussions. (These were discussions—not lecture presentations.) More than one-half of the students accounted for less than 13 percent of the interactions. Pendergrass also observed that male students were significantly more active in the discussions than were female students. Below are valuable hints to help you avoid the preceding two problems and to increase student participation in small-group discussions.

The concept of the "facilitator" helps explain the role of the teacher in developing and maintaining effective small-group discussions. The kind of development and cohesiveness that we describe in the chapter cannot be "decreed" by the teacher; it must be facilitated. In other words, you enable the students to develop an effective group by making them feel free to express themselves. This occurs most often when you allow for the development (*facilitate* the development) of classroom norms that are conducive to student participation. Such conditions foster the students' belief that *"it is okay for me to express my opinion; it is okay to interact with my peers and with the teacher; my opinion has value."*

Cohesiveness and involvement are enhanced by the development of two specific norms: (1) a norm of self-disclosure (for example, I think or I feel . . .); and (2) a norm of present concrete observations (for example, I like what you're saying . . .). These norms, when created, do help to facilitate cohesiveness and sharing. These qualities are important in some instances, but not in others. A task group, for example, will not, and perhaps should not, have the same cohesiveness as an inquiry group. At some time the facilitator may give way to the more *directive* teacher.

This cautionary note has been added to summarize a very important aspect of small-group discussion behavior. What follows now are some other general suggestions that help to create an atmosphere conducive to student participation.

Developing Listening Skills

Being a good listener is partly a matter of attitude and partly a matter of skill, so you and your students have two things to practice—positive attitudes and listening skills. From our work with students and from the work of Thomas J. Buttery and Patricia J.

Anderson (1980), and Joseph L. McCaleb (1981), we have gathered tips that can help you become systematic and thorough in fostering listening in the classroom.

Begin by modeling excellent listening habits for your students. Pay attention to your nonverbal behaviors, such as eye contact, facial responses, and gestures. Observe yourself: do you lean forward, make eye contact, and seem really interested in the students? Or do you fidget, look away, show boredom, or walk around the classroom? The former behaviors are indicators of listening. You must give the students nonverbal feedback when they talk to you: your nonverbal posture is the only way that they have of determining if you really heard and *understood* what was said. Also observe if you reinforce students for listening to one another.

Follow up the modeling tips with these tips on instructional practices. First, use *short* and *simple* directions. Children in the early grades can usually remember only one or two directions. Even older students forget if you give long directions or a series of directions. (Write detailed sets of directions on paper and hand out to the students.) Second, do not keep repeating and explaining the directions. Expect the students to listen the first time. Three, to help the students develop into listeners, check to see that unnecessary noises, such as teacher talk and equipment noises, are reduced.

Some enjoyable activities can also be meaningful learning activities. One example is to have a discussion in which all classroom managing is done nonverbally; by use of eye contact, hand signals, or passing a small object back and forth to promote student interaction. The object is to get everyone to say something without calling on anyone verbally. Another example is to make up or borrow a page of directions that students must follow exactly. For example, if a classroom microcomputer is available, have the class examine the programming manual, which is usually full of explicit details. The manual conveys the idea of following directions *precisely*.

When students know that there are some purposes for listening, they will improve. If you give them practical listening experience, some of what they learn will show up in their discussion activities. Raising the quality of students' listening skills can affect their learning positively in all subject areas. Yvonne Gold (1981) reminds us that listening is a learned behavior; that is, it helps establish skills that aid in academic achievement, especially in all disciplines that focus on language arts. The teacher's attitude, Gold cautions, is what illustrates to the student that listening is important.

How can you teach attentive listening? We have already presented a few tips. Here is a series of techniques that teachers have told us work.

- Prepare a short, well-organized lecture. Have the class outline the lecture. Then review the lecture to identify main topics and main points.
- Ask a question. Have students paraphrase the question and recite these paraphrases in class.
- Conduct oral tests frequently.
- Limit or avoid repetition of directions, questions, and comments.
- Allow students to conduct some recitations.

- Paraphrase television programs that are observed in the classroom.
- List good speaking habits (at the end of each class, each student could list one good speaking habit).
- Post a bulletin board display relating to listening skills.
- Appoint a class recorder who provides a summary of the day's recitations or discussion activities.
- Appoint one or two students to listen for any grammatical errors spoken in class.
- Ask a student to paraphrase a previous student's response to a question.

As Mortimer J. Adler (1983) observed, speaking and listening are companion skills. Discussions require groups to speak. Listening is a prerequisite skill to discussing. The more effectively you build those skills, the more effective your small-group discussions will be.

Arranging the Room

The best possible spatial arrangement for small-group discussions is a small seminar room in which the participants sit either at round tables or in a circle and have eye contact with one another. While observing classroom discussions, the authors have noticed that, even in this type of room, the teacher often tends to sit several feet away from the group, and group communication basically is limited to teacher-student exchanges initiated by the teacher or to those initiated by the group members. There is very little communication between the students themselves. It is preferable for the teacher or the leader to sit within the boundaries of the group and to encourage interaction between the students.

Probably the second-best room arrangement consists of "discussion centers" within a large room. You can partially isolate the centers from the rest of the room with bookshelves or folding room dividers. Another, simpler way is to turn the seats so that the group participants face one another and are not distracted by activities in the rest of the room. Students will normally block out noise from the other groups if each circle is enclosed so that eye contact is made only with members of the same group. By converting the room into "centers," you can conduct several types of activities simultaneously without disruptions.

Circular or semicircular seating arrangements offer at least four advantages to encourage small-group interaction (Book and Galvin, 1975).

1. They reduce the authority role of the teacher.
2. They provide the ideal that everyone is equal.
3. They reduce the possibility that a student is ignored by the group or withdraws from it.
4. They help create a responsible setting that encourages listening and contributing to the discussion.

Stressing the importance of seating arrangements, personal space, and interaction patterns, Steven A. Beebe and John T. Masterson (1986), reported that if you use a rectangular table there is high probability that students sitting at the corners will contribute the least. They also noted that individuals tend to sit in the same seat or proximity during every class (territoriality).

Knowing these points, you will want to alert all discussion leaders to encourage students sitting in such positions to engage in the discussion. We suggest that you (1) seat students so that they can see everyone in the discussion group, (2) avoid placing students in rows or concentric circles as these configurations inhibit personal interactions, and (3) rotate all small group members to create a climate of cooperation.

Although reported research studies concerning optimal group arrangements have produced conflicting evidence about the superiority of one formation over another, it has been noted that people tend to talk to persons sitting across from, or immediately next to, them rather than to persons sitting at angles to them. Thus, the crucial point for the group leader is to talk to everyone in the group and to encourage other group members to talk to everyone else and to avoid talking only to those across from, or next to, them.

Some persons feel more comfortable when sitting behind an object such as a table or a desk. During the initial phases of discussion-building episodes, therefore, you might encourage the group to sit around tables or to move students' desks into a tablelike arrangement. Once students feel at ease with discussions, they may simply choose to sit in a circle on the floor or in a circular configuration made up of chairs.

Charting Interaction Patterns

You can improve small-group interactions if you have some discrete data about the interaction patterns. These patterns can be determined easily by the use of simply constructed grids. One such grid is illustrated in Figure 7-10. Observe that by

Figure 7-10   *Grid Network to Determine Interaction Patterns*

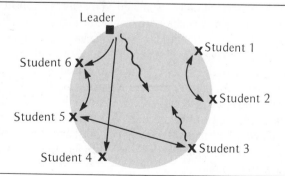

Figure 7-11   *Simple Small-Group Interaction Form*

Date _____

Episode _____

Topic _____

Group _____

Observer _____

Interaction 1: Ann, Al, Ann, Cy, Tom, Ann, Wanda (time: four minutes)
Interaction 2: Ann, . . . Ann [indicates a long response or speech]
Interaction 3: Ann, Tom, Al, Ann, Wanda, Al, Wanda, Al, Wanda, Al (time: four minutes) [Al and Wanda entered into a dialogue that reduced all other inputs]

mapping a discussion configuration and then simply drawing lines with arrows, the directionality of a discussion may be determined. A one-way straight arrow shows that a comment was aimed at one individual. A wiggly arrow indicates that a comment was directed at the entire group. A double arrow shows a dialogue pattern.

Such grid networks can be sketched on a minute-by-minute (or longer) time frame to determine group interaction or the lack of it. In the example given in Figure 7-10, note that nearly all interactions took place between persons seated next to, or directly across from, each other. Knowledge of such spatial interactions allows the leader to keep the discussion less cliquish and more open.

Figure 7-11 illustrates an even simpler adaptation of the grid. For each episode of some specified time frame, an observer lists first the name of the person who initiates an interaction, followed by the names of those who join it. By examining the interaction patterns, a group leader, or the entire small group for that matter, will be able to determine whether the group is being dominated by only a few individuals.

As these two examples of grids show, interaction patterns may be identified easily in an objective and systematic manner. Such tabulations are designed not to chastise the students but to help them to improve in the processes.

You have already examined some forms concerning interaction patterns that small-group participants can complete. Figure 7-12 illustrates just how simple it is to prepare an instrument for checking opinions about the satisfaction gained from participating in a given small group. The type of continuum to be used is contingent on the objectives of the specific discussion episode. By tabulating the group responses, the observer can quickly prepare a master list that will show how each group member feels about his or her respective interactions. Note that we allocated this job to the observer, not to the teacher. You must learn to delegate most of the tasks to the students, because you simply will not have the time to do all the work. Your main role is as the organizer, who will examine the data and then make new decisions on how to continue.

Figure 7-12 *Individual-Response Form*

Date _____

Group _____

Directions: Place an X next to the response that best describes your reaction to each of the following questions.

1. Do you think that your time is being used effectively in the discussion group?
   _____ (a) Not at all
   _____ (b) About right
   _____ (c) Very much

2. Is there sufficient discussion between you and your group members?
   _____ (a) Not at all
   _____ (b) About right
   _____ (c) Very much

3. Is the work being done in your small group informative enough?
   _____ (a) Not at all
   _____ (b) About right
   _____ (c) Very much

Suggestions or comments _____

_____

_____

_____

Selecting a Lively Topic

The topic may be determined by your wish that certain phases of class work be discussed in depth, or it may be generated from the students' responses to, and interest in, a selected area. The usefulness of the discussion depends in large part on the ability and willingness of students to define the nature of the problem. At times even we have been surprised and pleased by the willingness of students to deal realistically with both academic and social problems. (Social problems will be discussed further in Chapter 10.) Examples of such student initiative and ability include (1) a group of "low-ability" third graders successfully handling the topic of uses and misues of drugs; (2) a small group of multihandicapped deaf students discussing Adolf Hitler or John F. Kennedy and the man's influence on society (Pendergrass and Hodges, 1976); or (3) a group of third graders building a thinking machine.

The topic chosen should be dual in nature: it should be pertinent to classroom material and study, and it should be on a subject chosen for maximum interest to the students. Such a discussion topic should be short and worded in a lively manner. If possible, and it usually is, let the students do the wording for the topic they are discussing. We also suggest that the students ultimately take full responsibility for the conduct of the discussion once they have learned the essential skills.

The issue being discussed should be sufficiently difficult to sustain interest and should require serious and creative thinking. In short, the topic must have relevance to those discussing it. The issue also must have sufficient information available to class members if it becomes necessary to research the topic for more meaningful discussion.

Herbert G. Cohen, Willis J. Horak, and Frederick A. Staley (1984) suggest that science classrooms provide a rich arena for lively discussions. They imply using both teacher-initiated and student-initiated topics. Preplanning for the discussion is essential for success.

A beginning teacher or preservice intern can identify those issues that are very likely to become successful discussion topics. One element will be fairly certain: most students do not have the skills that are essential for conducting or participating in true discussions. This should be a challenge to you, and you will experience a feeling of accomplishment as you succeed in helping the students acquire and master these skills. Again, we are not proposing the indiscriminate use of discussion techniques, but we do suggest that these skills be developed systematically.

Encouraging Development of Leadership

When beginning small-group discussions, you may choose the first student leaders on the basis of leadership abilities already observed in class situations. These leadership abilities may include such considerations as personal popularity, academic standing, temperament or sociability, thinking ability, and speaking ability.

Ideally, leadership will develop spontaneously in the groups, but it is wise to discuss with the class early in the semester what qualities a leader must have *to help the group work together.* So that several students may learn and practice leadership, appoint leaders arbitrarily by rotation or select two leaders for each discussion—one a strong leader and the other weaker—until the weaker one shows evidence of growing ability and confidence. It is *your responsibility* to help students develop the desired leadership behaviors and competencies. For example, some time must be scheduled for teaching and learning questioning skills, how to report a summary, how to involve nonvolunteers, and how to restrain the dominating volunteers without using aversive techniques. Ultimately, every class member should have an opportunity to be a leader and to develop the same skills.

An early and leading authority on small-group behavior and organizational development, Matthew B. Miles (1959), emphasizes five main functions of the small-group leader that all students can practice at any time during the discussion, even though the performance burden rests primarily with the leader. These functions are as follows:

1. *Initiating:* keeping the group moving when it is bogged down or off on a dead-end tangent (such as clarifying certain statements or asking questions that call for more than a yes or no answer)
2. *Regulating:* influencing the pace of the discussion (such as summarizing or pointing out time limits)
3. *Informing:* bringing information to the group that no one else may know: never lecturing
4. *Supporting:* making it easier for members to contribute (such as harmonizing opposing viewpoints, voicing group feeling, varying place in group, helping group get acquainted)
5. *Evaluating:* helping the group to evaluate process goals (may test for consensus or note the group progress in some facet)

Not all these functions *must* be performed by one leader, but the person who is leading should provide whatever is missing from the discussion process. Sometimes the teacher may want a leadership team: one student provides the vocal leadership; the other silently records and summarizes, when necessary, the main points made by the group.

A sophisticated discussion group of considerable strength and ability may function well under a nondirective leader. The principal value of this approach is in allowing the group to develop the greatest amount of self-control and self-administration. Such a situation is ideal but extremely difficult to implement—almost impossible with inexperienced leaders and participants in the secondary school classroom. Initial discussions should be conducted with as simple a format as possible. As the students (and you) gain experience, you can add more complex activities.

Providing Positive Feedback

Each of the previous activities in which you participated contained provisions for evaluating the small-group discussion specified in the activity. In addition, several ideas for evaluation formats were presented with the eight types of discussion groups. It will be very beneficial if you think of evaluation as *feedback* and not as *grading*.

Why use positive feedback? First, positive feedback increases responses, and we know that many students do not respond because they are afraid of giving an incorrect reply and then of being subjected to a negative teacher reaction. If they give a partially correct response, some positive feedback from you will usually motivate the student to try again. Peer approval, or feedback, is considered by many students, especially at the secondary level, to be even more important than is teacher approval.

Second, students need to learn to be cooperative and to be supportive of others. Students *can* and *will* learn to give positive feedback to one another, but they probably will not do so if you are always giving feedback. Gradually shift to the group members the responsibility of providing feedback. This helps to promote activity and harmony within the group as well as to give the students practice with the valuable leadership skill of providing feedback to others.

Third, you, or the group leader, and each student need to assess individual progress. At first, this evaluation may be merely a matter of how many responses the student makes during the discussion session, or some general impressions of that person. Later it may focus on specific functions that the student needs to master and, at the highest level, on how the student can get other students to be cohesive group members. Remember that you cannot abdicate the responsibility of helping each student in the class. At times, the group may not be having a positive influence on a particular student. When this occurs, you must bear the responsibility of correcting the student's behavior while working with the group to shape long-term behavior goals.

Evaluation should be nonthreatening and varied, and it should be based on the objective. Students need to know, prior to the discussion, what they are being evaluated on. If you are seeking a variety of ideas, it is totally unfair to put a grade on quality or on any other standard. If students know that evaluation is to be used for diagnostic purposes only, they will feel freer about discussing and participating in the evaluation activities.

In summary, the evaluative processes should accomplish three tasks: (1) provide feedback to the group concerning progress in discussion skills and processes, (2) inform the teacher about how the group is progressing in relation to process objectives and group goals, and (3) allow the teacher and each student to assess individual progress.

All these suggestions have been tested by teachers and have been reported in the literature. To be sure, the use of discussions as a systematic way of learning takes a great deal of planning and encouragement by the teacher. But if you want to promote learning, then we suggest that you try systematic discussions with small groups. The decision is yours.

FORMATIVE EVALUATION *Small-Group Discussions*

1. Place an X next to each statement that would likely increase student participation and make small-group discussions more effective.
   - _____ (a) The teacher models good listening habits.
   - _____ (b) The group leader does not try to get quiet members to talk.
   - _____ (c) Teacher and students determine relevant topics.
   - _____ (d) Feelings or emotions are not permitted in the discussion.
   - _____ (e) Keep students in the same small groups.

_____ (f) Help students learn leadership skills.
_____ (g) Any form of disagreement must be permitted.
_____ (h) Evaluation is nonthreatening and varied.
_____ (i) Students learn to infer, conclude, and summarize.
_____ (j) The teacher encourages direction toward goals.
_____ (k) Develop a plan for getting nonvolunteers to respond.
_____ (l) Repeat directions over and over until everyone listens.

2. There are several ways to evaluate or measure the interaction processes of small-group discussions. Select any two of those presented and test the instruments to observe how they work for you. (We suggest that you work in dyads or pairs to complete this task.)

3. What are some ways that you could initiate cooperative learning into a classroom? Share your ideas with some teachers and analyze their response.

4. Which of the several ways of improving listening skills do you think you might use? Why?

Responses

1. (a) X   (g)
   (b)   (h) X
   (c) X   (i) X
   (d)   (j) X
   (e)   (k) X
   (f) X   (l)

2.-4. These questions require some activity from you. We suggest that you work with a peer or a small group of three or four and discuss these questions.

REFERENCES

Abt, Clark. Address presented at the "Man-Machine Conference" in Portland, Oregon, November 26, 1966.

Abruscato, Joseph. *Children, Computers, and Science Teaching: Butterflies and Bytes.* Englewood Cliffs, New Jersey: Prentice-Hall, 1986.

Adler, Mortimer J. *How to Speak: How to Listen.* New York: Macmillan, 1983.

Beebe, Steven A., and John T. Masterson. *Communicating in Small Groups: Principles and Practices,* 2nd ed. Glenview, Ill.: Scott, Foresman, 120–121.

Bloom, Benjamin S. "The 2 Sigma Problem: The Search for Methods of Group Instruction as Effective as One-to-One Tutoring." *Educational Researcher* 13(6):1984, 4–16.

Book, Cassandra, and Kathleen Galvin. *Instruction In and About Small Group Discussion.* Urbana, Ill.: ERIC/ACS and SCA, ERIC Document Reproduction Service No. ED 113773, 1975.

Buchan, L. Gerald. *Roleplaying and the Educable Mentally Retarded.* Belmont, Calif.: Fearon, 1972.

Buttery, Thomas J., and Patricia J. Anderson. "Listen and Learn!" *Curriculum Review* 19:1980, 319–322.

Cohen, Herbert G., Willis J. Horak, and Frederick A. Staley. *Teaching Science as a Decision Making Process.* Dubuque, Iowa: Kendall/Hunt, 1984.

Denison, Tom G. "The Effectiveness of Simulated Practice for Teaching Welding." Ph.D. diss., Washington State University, Pullman, Washington, 1981.

Garreau, Joel. *The Nine Nations of North America.* Boston: Houghton Mifflin, 1981.

Gold, Yvonne. "Teaching Attentive Listening." *Reading Improvement* 18:1981, 159–164.

Glasser, William. *Control Theory in the Classroom.* New York: Harper & Row, 1986.

Greenblat, Cathy Stein. *Designing Games and Simulations: An Illustrated Handbook.* Beverly Hills, Calif.: SAGE Publications, Inc., 1988.

Johnson, David W., and Roger T. Johnson. *Leading the Cooperative School.* Edina, Minnesota: Interaction Book Company, 1989.

Johnson, Eric W., and David C. McClelland. *Learning to Achieve.* Glenview, Ill.: Scott, Foresman, 1984.

Johnson, Roger T., and David W. Johnson. "How Can We Put Cooperative Learning into Practice?" *Science Teacher* 54:September 1987, 46–48, 50.

Johnson, Roger T., David W. Johnson, and Mary Beth Stanne. "Comparison of Computer-Assisted Cooperative, Competitive, and Individualistic Learning." *American Educational Research Journal* 23:Fall 1986, 382–392.

Joyce, Bruce, Beverly Showers, and Carol Rolhesier-Bennett. "Staff Development and Student Learning: A Synthesis of Research on Models of Teaching." *Educational Leadership,* 45(2):1987, 11–23.

Keltner, John W. *Group Discussion Processes.* New York: Longmans, Green, 1967, p. 113.

Litsey, D. M. "Small-Group Training and the English Classroom." *English Journal* 58:1969, 920–927.

Maidment, Richard, and Russell H. Bronstein. *Simulation Games: Design and Implementation.* Columbus, Ohio: Charles E. Merrill, 1973.

Matheidesy, Maria. "Running Errands: A Communication Board Game." *Simulation/Games for Learning* 17(3):1987, 120–126.

McCaleb, Joseph L. "Indirect Teaching and Listening." *Education* 102:1981, 159–164.

McDonnell, John J., and Robert H. Horner. "Effects of In Vivo Versus Simulation Plus—In Vivo Training on the Acquisition and Generalization of Grocery Items Selection by High School Students with Severe Handicaps." *Analysis and Intervention in Developmental Disabilities* 5(4): 1985, 323–343.

McGinty, Robert L. "Do Our Mathematics Textbooks Reflect What We Preach?" *School Science and Mathematics* 86(7):1986, 591–596.

Miles, Matthew B. *Learning to Work in Groups.* New York: Bureau of Publications, Teachers College, Columbia University, 1959, p. 20.

Miller, Dan Pyle. *Introduction to Small Group Discussion.* Urbana, Ill.: ERIC/RCS and SCA, ERIC Document Reproduction Service No. ED 278037, 1986.

Olmstead, Joseph A. *Theory and State of the Art of Small Group Methods of Instruction.* Alexandria, Va.: Human Resources Research Organization, 1970, pp. vii, 36, and 79.

Omaggio, Alice C. "Using Games and Interaction Activities for the Development of Functions Proficiency in a Second Language." *The Canadian Modern Language Review* 38:1982, 517–546.

Pendergrass, R. A. "An Analysis of the Verbal Interaction of Small Group Discussion Members in Secondary Social Studies Classes." Unpublished diss., Washington State University, Pullman, Washington, 1973.

Pendergrass, R. A., and Marlis Hodges. "Deaf Students in Group Problem Solving Situations: A Study of the Interactive Process." *Annals of the Deaf* 121(3):1976, 327–330.

Plienis, Anthony J., and Raymond G. Romancyzk. "Analysis of Performance, Behavior, and Predictor for Severely Disturbed Children: A Comparison of Adult vs. Computer Instruction." *Analysis and Intervention in Developmental Disabilities* 5(4):1985, 345–356.

Resource Bulletin. National Center on Effective Secondary Schools, School of Education, University of Wisconsin—Madison, No. 4, Spring 1988.

Richman, Gena S., et al. "Simulation Procedures for Teaching Independent Menstrual Care to Mentally Retarded Persons." *Applied Research in Mental Retardation* 7(1):1986, 21–35.

Rosenblatt, Ronald R. Interview, October 22, 1988.

Schueler, Annemarie. "The Inquiry Model in Physical Education." *Physical Educator* 36:1979, 89–92.

Schunk, Dale H. "Peer Models and Children's Behavioral Change." *Review of Educational Research* 57:Summer 1987, 149–174.

Shaftel, Fannie M., and George Shaftel. *Role Playing in the Curriculum,* 2nd ed. Englewood Cliffs, N.J.: Prentice-Hall, 1982.

Slavin, Robert E. "Cooperative Learning and the Cooperative School." *Educational Leadership* 45(3):1987, 7–13.

Stahl, Steven A., and Charles H. Clark. "The Effects of Participatory Expectations in Classroom Discussion on the Learning of Science Vocabulary." *American Educational Research Journal* 24:Winter 1987, 541–556.

Sudol, David. "Creating and Killing Stanley Realbozo or, Teaching Characterization and Plot in English 10." *English Journal* 72:1983, 63–66.

Vincent, Barbara. "Design for Decision Making in the Classroom." *Technological Horizons in Education (T.H.E.) Journal* 14(4):1986, 80–84.

Webb, Michael J. "Analogies and Their Limitations." *School Science and Mathematics* 85(8): 1985, 645–650.

8

Deciding to Use Inquiry

*T*raditionally, teachers at all levels emphasize bodies of knowledge, the content of which becomes both a *means* and an *end* in education. Is it any wonder, then, that hundreds of thousands of students get bored by routine lectures or recitations? We want to offer another teaching technique that is not new but centuries old. The generic term for the technique is *inquiry.* You may find it referred to in the literature as *inquiry, enquiry, discovery, problem-solving, reflective thinking, inductive teaching,* or several other terms. We will discuss these techniques and point out the major differences among them. But, first, what should you learn from this chapter?

Objectives   After completing this chapter, you should be able to:

- Recognize and describe at least five different inquiry techniques
- Observe the role of questioning in inquiry
- Prepare a set of inquiry materials for your own discipline or grade level
- Justify the use of specific inquiry instructional techniques for selected concepts
- Understand that inquiry processes are carefully taught (or learned) by systematic planning and instruction

In addition, the following affective objectives are offered for your own attitude adjustments—as needed. We would like you to

- Appreciate instructional styles or techniques that tend to be "open" rather than closed
- Be willing to incorporate elements of inquiry teaching in your teaching
- Value the goal of "inquiry" by systematically using instructional techniques that will help students learn how to apply the ideals
- Become an advocate for inquiry-related teaching

UNDERSTANDING THE CONCEPT

The concept of inquiry is rather difficult to define in nonoperational terms—that is, without giving precise examples of teacher strategies and the concomitant student behaviors. As we develop a spectrum of inquiry-teaching options, we will demonstrate their operational meanings by example. Inquiry processes require a high degree of interaction among the learner, the teacher, the materials, the content, and the environment. Perhaps the most crucial aspect of inquiry is that, as it is defined in the dictionary, both student and teacher become persistent askers, seekers, interrogators, questioners, and ponderers and ultimately pose the question that every Nobel Prize winner has asked: I wonder what would happen if . . . ?

Of course, we do not expect *all* of you to make internationally significant discoveries, although we would like to see a few of your students do so. What is important is that *you* as the classroom teacher set the stage for the process of inquiry to take place. In short, *you* make the difference. *You* decide how much time will be spent developing the many processes associated with inquiry behaviors. *You* make the decision to try another method of teaching units of instruction that lend themselves to inquiry processes. *You* are the one who systematically will teach *your* students how to ask questions.

Questioning plays a crucial role in both the teaching and learning acts associated with the inquiry mode of learning. Questions lead to investigations that attempt to solve a well-defined aspect of the question. Such investigations are common to *all* areas of human endeavor. The investigative processes of inquiry involve the student not only in questioning but also in formulating the question, in limiting it, in deciding on the best methods to use, and then in conducting the study.

The emphasis on inquiry instruction seems to be a twentieth-century phenomenon. Perhaps the prime advocate for its wide acceptance is none other than John Dewey. This may surprise you, for in most textbooks and lectures and in the common press the late John Dewey seems to be blamed for every conceivable ill that has befallen our society, with the exception of AIDS. We explore the contributions of Dewey as they pertain to problem-solving. You may be surprised to learn that it was Dewey's ideal that became popularized in a conference of scientists, leading to the publication of Jerome S. Bruner's (1960) now classic *The Process of Education*. This brief historical background on the inquiry process is essential to avoid the same fallacious thinking that thousands of teachers have been guilty of because they were not fully aware of the foundations of inquiry.

As we mentioned, inquiry is an old technique. The distinguished trio of ancient Western culture—Socrates, Aristotle, and Plato—were all masters of the inquiry processes. One can argue that the processes they used have since affected the way most people in our Western and technological civilization think. That heritage has given us a mode of teaching in which students are vitally involved in the learning and creating processes. It is through inquiry that new knowledge is discovered. It is by becoming involved in the process that students become historians, scientists, economists, artists, businesspersons, poets, writers, or researchers—even if only for an hour or two in *your* class.

Basic Processes of Inquiry

What, then, are the basic processes of inquiry? Briefly, they are observing, classifying, using numbers, measuring, using space-time relationships, predicting, inferring, defining operationally, formulating hypotheses, interpreting data, controlling variables, experimenting, and communicating.

The above-mentioned basic processes, thirteen in all, are found in every learning episode that involves inquiry—even poets use most of them. The main point that we are developing is that inquiry is not simply the asking of a question; it is a process of conducting a thorough investigation (see Fig. 8-1 on p. 285). A similar chart can be constructed easily for selected aspects of literature, art criticism, homemaking, first aid, and many other nonscience subjects.

It is extremely important that *you* understand that each process associated with inquiry must be carefully developed and practiced in a very systematic manner. This requires you to decide how much *of each* lesson will be devoted to cognitive-skill building and how much to process building—just as with the process of building small-group discussions.

Finally, both you and the students must become aware that the processes must be learned, practiced, demonstrated, and assimilated into the *students'* learning styles. Of course, you must know the processes and how to establish learning situations that will aid in their application. The inquiry processes are most effective when they are internalized by each and every student. We do imply that *every* student can learn the fundamental processes of inquiry, although this does not mean that every student will demonstrate the same quality of inquiry. In our experiences, we have observed that the "slow" and handicapped students enjoy using inquiry processes as much as the very "best" students do. As one more way to learn, inquiry provides a dimension to the classroom environment that no other teaching method can—the excitement of learning something that just might not be regurgitated from a textbook.

Thinking and Inquiry

Before discussing inquiry and its related techniques, we must discuss the topic of thinking. As a nation, we want our schools to teach *thinking*. Nearly every statement on goals has some reference to the "goal of the school is to teach critical thinking." This was articulated forcefully by Ronald S. Brandt (1983), executive editor of *Educational Leadership* and his subsequent work (see Marzano et al., 1988), when he observed that high-technology industrial leaders thought that it was less important to provide a great deal of technical training in the schools than to develop the student's ability to think and solve problems. To develop thinking and problem-solving skills, you must make the decisions to promote thinking; the schools must provide *experiences* in thinking and problem-solving. To think, a student must learn to be actively involved with issues, data, materials, topics, concepts, and problems.

Is there a problem in teaching how to think? Richard C. Remy (1987) certainly provides evidence that there is. He reported data from several different surveys of students aged nine, thirteen, and seventeen that measured *understanding* (there's that "u" word again) about our nation's political system. While these students know the facts about our nation's governmental systems, their written essays illustrate rather simplistic thinking. Most do not recognize the Bill of Rights as belonging to the United States Constitution. A large percentage of high school seniors have little or no *understanding* of basic political liberties as are guaranteed by our Constitution.

You may recall our strong plea in Chapters 4 and 6 for structuring learning to include comprehension, application, analysis, synthesis, and evaluation. These cognitive skills are the traits of thinking. We also report that both textbooks and teachers tend to question predominantly at the Knowledge or lowest cognitive level. Thinking and reflection in most schoolrooms are obviously missing elements of instruction. We would like to change that.

What does it mean to teach thinking? We devote Chapter 9 to that topic, so the points here will be complementary to the extensive treatment there. Lists relating to thinking, plus attendant skills and processes are numerous (see Chapter 9; Gisi and Forbes, 1982; Jones et al., 1988; and Marzano et al., 1988). Nearly all writers agree on the *generic* aspects:

1. Perception of a problem or issue
2. Skill in gathering relevant information
3. Competence in organizing data
4. Analysis of data patterns, inferences, sources of errors
5. Communication of the results

Marzano and colleagues label these as *core* skills. It is obvious that the five do not take place simultaneously. To initiate such skill-building requires careful teacher planning (Chapters 2 and 5), appropriate sequencing (Chapter 3), and a continuous building of cognitive and attitudinal factors (Chapters 1 and 4).

Thomas R. Koballa, Jr., and Lowell J. Bethel (1984) illustrated how teachers of language arts, reading, social studies, health, fine arts, and mathematics can successfully use inquiry-related strategies. From their synthesis it is rather easy to integrate the processes of inquiry incrementally. In summary, students are taught at the *comprehension* level and then learn how to use knowledge. Through inquiry, children learn how to be precise, to interpret situations, to seek underlying ideas, and to feel that moment of personal success. (Note the subtle link between affective and cognitive dimensions of schooling.) Let us now examine the set of processes that your authors consider the epitome of instructional interactions.

INDUCTIVE INQUIRY

We begin with a caveat: There is no pure inductive-inquiry teaching mode. Basically, there are elements of the inductive method that prevail with all inquiry strategies. But note well that inductive teaching methodologies may or may not be true extensions of "discovery." What, then, constitutes inductive inquiry? Induction or inductive logic is a thought process wherein the individual observes or senses *a selected number* of events, processes, or objects, and then constructs a particular pattern of concepts or relationships based on these limited experiences. Inductive inquiry, then, is a method that teachers use when they present sets of data or situations and then ask the students to infer a conclusion, generalization, or a pattern of relationships. It is a process that allows the student to observe specifics and then to infer generalizations about the entire group of particulars.

Inductive inquiry may be approached in at least two different ways: (1) guided, and (2) unguided. Lee S. Shulman and Pinchas Tamir (1973) provided a classic, easy-to-use matrix illustrating that *if* the teacher wishes to provide the basic elements of the lesson—that is, the specifics—but wants the students to make the generalizations, *then* the teacher is conducting a *guided* inductive lesson. If the teacher decides to allow the students to provide the cases and to make the generalizations, the process may be labeled *unguided* inductive inquiry. Such a distinction between guided and unguided inductive inquiry is essential. In most cases, the teacher will begin to build the processes of induction through a set of guided experiences. In this manner, the teacher knows that there is a fixed number of generalizations or conclusions that can be reasonably inferred. The teacher can then go about helping various students to make the observations leading to these conclusions. In our experiences with inductive inquiry, the guided method provides an easy transition from expository teaching to that which is less expository.

Inductive inquiry is appropriate at all levels of instruction, from preschool to university graduate schools. Obviously, the kinds and quality of induction will vary considerably. An important aspect of inductive inquiry is that the *processes* of observation, inference, classification, formulating hypotheses, and predicting are all sharpened (or reinforced) by the experiences.

Guided Inductive Inquiry

Pictures are usually the easiest way to introduce the initial elements of guided inductive inquiry. As one example for younger children, different pictures of the same scene are shown to the class. You selected these because they illustrate some of the differences associated with the seasons. Thus, four typical or even stereotypical pictures show spring, summer, autumn, and winter.

Before beginning the lesson, you arrange to have all of the necessary materials so as to give all the children materials from which they will have similar experiences. In conducting this lesson, you make extensive use of question-asking skills (which you learned in Chapter 6). Ask the children to make observations about what they see in the pictures. As the children venture their responses, be careful to distinguish between statements based on observations and those based on inferences. When an inference is stated, the teacher should simply ask, "Is that an inference or an observation?" (Of course, the lesson should begin with the concepts or processes of observations and inferences presented in the simplest manner.) As the class progresses, prepare a simple chart or list on the blackboard of the actual observations and the accompanying inferences. Each process will be built slowly and carefully with many such examples.

The pattern that the child observes should be stated by the child as some type of generalization that can apply whenever that pattern is repeated. The process of inductive thinking is developed gradually. Each teacher should plan to conduct some guided inductive-inquiry exercises whenever the occasion arises. Ask simple questions such as: "What could cause this type of track in the snow?" and "Where have we seen this before?" These are the kinds of questions that require the child to do the generalizing rather than your simply presenting the generalizations.

In guided inductive inquiry, you cannot expect the students to arrive at particular generalizations unless the learning activities, classroom recitations or discussions, learning materials, and visual aids are all arranged so that everything is available to the learner to make the generalizations. Perhaps these initial experiences can even utilize some small groups, such as task groups. For example, Richard McLeod (1988) developed weather data for computer use. Students use the computer to process weather data and to make generalizations and predictions from the information. In this case the computer program "guides" the learner. Yet, small groups of children can discuss their data and defend their conclusions—based on their weather data, not on intuition or guessing.

At all levels, ask each student to write the observations and, beside them, the inferences. The student will thus gain the habit of becoming systematic. This method also helps you to check the observations that were the bases for any inferences.

Inferences are generalizations about certain objects or events. James G. Womack (1966), a social studies educator, suggests the classic steps to be used in arriving at generalizations through guided inductive inquiry.*

1. Decide on the generalization(s) the students should discover from a particular unit of study.
2. Organize the learning activities and materials in a manner which exposes the strands or parts of the generalization(s) to the students.
3. Ask the students to write a summary of the content which contains the generalization(s).
4. Ask the students to identify the sequence of the pattern of events comprising the content, omitting any reference to any particular people, places, or times.
5. Ask the students to synthesize the various parts of the pattern of events into one complete sentence which purports to be a generalization.
6. Ask the students to offer proof that their statement is, in fact, a generalization by citing examples that it existed and operated in other periods, places, and among other people.

We should note that the sixth step of Womack's process actually approaches the "hypothesis-building" and "testing" stages of the inquiry process. It should be noted that Womack's steps are very similar to those suggested by James A. Banks (1985).

The Time Involved

When you first use any type of inquiry activity in your classes, you must plan to spend at least twice the amount of class time on each lesson than you would normally expect. Any inquiry activity takes much time to initiate and complete. This greater time use is spent on in-depth analysis of the content by the students. Furthermore, inquiry methods demand greater interaction between the learner and the materials used to foster inquiry as well as greater interaction between the teacher and the students. The students are somewhat at risk by not having an authority or book to

---

*From James G. Womack, *Discovering the Structure of the Social Studies* New York: Benziger Brothers Publishing Company, 1966), p. 13. Used with the permission of the Benziger Brothers Publishing Company.

cite; they must rely on their own data or observations. You will find that most children and adults approach inquiry activities with a great deal of caution—if not apprehension. But as the inductive-inquiry activities become a part of the ongoing procedures of the class, learner apprehension diminishes.

Another caveat is required: When you use an inquiry method, the amount of material covered is actually reduced. The reason is that you are using more time to develop process skills and reducing the time spent on memorizing fact or content. You cannot maximize thinking skills and simultaneously maximize content coverage. If you wish to build the so-called higher-order thinking skills, then you must reduce some of the content and substitute processes instead. (See Eylon and Linn, 1988.) In fact, you are not sacrificing anything. You are providing important instruction and experiences that are a part of the function of the structure (epistemology) of the disciplines. Collectively, the processes we label as *inquiry* were studied by Clifford A. Hofwolt (1984). After examining effective science teaching, he concluded that the processes we espouse produced significant learner achievements when they were compared to more traditional or textbook-recitation techniques. It may take more instructional time, but your students will understand better (that "u" word again) what they are studying. The decision to follow this approach is yours. *Your* role is therefore very important.

In lower grades or in initial experiences, the final generalization(s) may involve an oral summary or review of the concepts, a listing of the ideas presented, and finally, the eliciting of the learners' own views as to what constitutes a meaningful generalization. As the learners provide such input, you should use such questioning techniques as probing, concept review, and prompting.

The testing of the generalizations can be accomplished by having the class apply the statement to different times, places, peoples, objects, or events. A major limitation of the testing will be the backgrounds and experiences of the learners.

Another technique with guided inductive inquiry is to write a series of events on cards or on some other manipulative medium. Then ask the learners to place the events in the "proper" sequence, without any reference to the order's being right or wrong. This activity can follow a reading assignment. When the sequence of events is completed, ask the students to observe the pattern of events and to state the pattern in just one sentence. This sentence will be the generalization. Other members of the class can be asked to test the generalization by examining it for significant exceptions.

These suggestions provide some tested models that help students to think inductively—that is, to infer generalizations. Such models are adaptable to all levels of instruction. The learners' efficiency—and your own—will improve with practice.

Analysis of Guided Inductive Inquiry

As you read the previous presentation, you probably noted that we did not have any set prescription or rules to follow. The model illustrated in Figure 8-1 shows six major steps in that inquiry system: (1) identifying the problem, (2) developing tenta-

Figure 8-1   *A General Model of Inquiry*

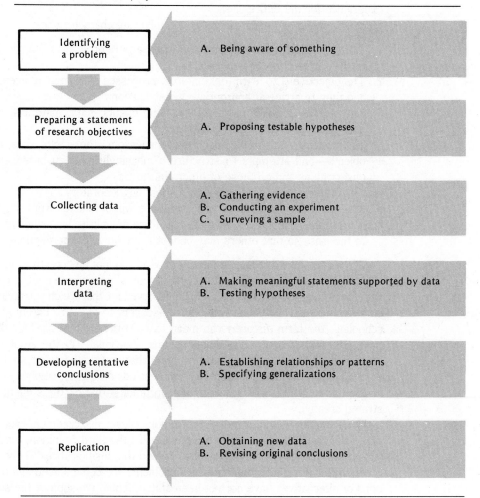

tive research hypotheses or objectives, (3) collecting data and testing the tentative answers, (4) interpreting data, (5) developing tentative conclusions or generalizations, (6) applying or retesting the conclusion; revising original conclusions. Implied in such a model is that the student finds the problem, or at least recognizes it, and then follows the six steps to attempt to resolve it.

These steps usually are needed for introductory guided inductive lessons. Recall that the process objectives are to observe, to infer, and to conclude. The problem, if it can be called one, is to determine a meaningful pattern in an array of events or objects. This process is *not* simply the allowing of wild guesses to take place. All inferences must be supported by some evidence—that is, observations or data. The latter may be obtained from some standard reference source such as the *Statistical Abstract of the United States* or from almanacs, yearbooks, reports, or encyclopedias.

The data become the focal point of the inquiry session and thus serve as a common experience for the entire class.

Guided inductive inquiry includes the following characteristics:

1. The thought processes require that the learners progress from specific observations to inferences or generalizations.
2. The objective is to learn (or reinforce) processes of examining events or objects and then to arrive at appropriate generalizations.
3. The teacher controls the elements—the events, data, materials, or objects—and, as such, acts as the class leader.
4. The student reacts to the specifics of the lesson—the events, data, materials, or objects—and attempts to structure a meaningful pattern based on his or her observations and on those of others in the class.
5. The classroom is to be considered a learning laboratory.
6. *Usually,* a fixed number of generalizations will be elicited from the learners.
7. The teacher encourages each student to communicate his or her generalizations to the class so that others may benefit from individual perceptions.

The use of guided inductive inquiry may or may not be "creative" in the sense of allowing the learners the opportunity to "discover" something new. It can be argued that the process of discovery should be reserved for that which is truly unique in our culture. But such a situation would limit discovery to the U.S. Patent Office only. In schooling, the term *discovery* can mean that (1) the student has, for the very first time, determined something unique to that individual, (2) the student has added something to a discussion about a problem that you or the other students had not known before, or (3) the student has synthesized some information in such a manner as to provide others with a unique interpretation—that is, the student has demonstrated creativity.

Unfortunately, such a variety of definitions causes disagreements about discovery in the schools. Whereas purists tend to support the third definition, teachers usually accept the first definition. We tend to defend the position that discovery should be reserved for those situations in which problems are being solved and possible solutions or alternatives have not yet been stated. Thus, we support the second definition.

Models of Guided Inductive Inquiry

Two models of guided inductive inquiry are presented here. The first model was initially used in Pasco, Washington, when one of the authors was an instructor on a teacher-aide project. The aides were given the challenge of determining the patterns observed when using the compound microscope so that they would be familiar with one of the most commonly used pieces of scientific equipment. This exercise has since been used widely at several grade levels. Note how simple such an exercise can be.

The second model, a clever guided inductive device, allows students to learn about the mixing of colors from their own observations. This model demonstrates how easy it is to adapt elements of guided inductive inquiry to the fine arts. Another aspect of Model 2 is that it readily lends itself to the use of the overhead projector. Later in this chapter, we will discuss the use of transparencies in stimulating group instruction in an inquiry mode.

Although we have made a strong case for individual work during inquiry sessions, there is nothing wrong with the teacher also presenting the stimulus to the entire class. If you decide to use this technique, then you should require that all students write their own observations, inferences, and generalizations, rather than have an oral recitation period. This technique helps learners to become more self-reliant as they develop, individually, their own logical framework, which may not be the case during oral recitations. In a group mode, it may even be wise to prepare a handout for the students so that they may record their observations and opinions in a guided, systematic manner.

After examining the two models of guided inductive inquiry, try to develop a similar lesson for your teaching area or discipline. Do not make the mistake of saying, "It can't be done for my subject." More than three thousand students or teachers in our classes, with majors ranging from art to zoology, have all prepared either a guided or an unguided inductive inquiry lesson.

Model 1 **An Inductive Approach
to the Compound Light Microscope***

Biology and general science students are usually introduced to the compound microscope through a general discussion or lecture on nomenclature, microscope care, proper use of focusing knobs, lens systems, and the like. They are then given a microscope, a set of slides, cover slips, and other materials needed to complete observation exercises, and are expected to prepare suitable drawings for the teacher's examination.

Note: Students are seldom aware that the objects they view are inverted, upside down, or reversed—despite knowledge that movement of the slide causes a reverse action. Furthermore, they are unaware that the focal area is in a plane and that by continual focusing, new planes come into view.

This report describes an exercise needed to give students a better understanding of the compound microscope than they usually acquire through traditional means of presentation. Using an inductive approach, it allows students to make "discoveries" and generalizations about the microscope for themselves. The materials involved are simple and can easily be permanently mounted for classroom use.

---

*From Donald C. Orlich, *Science Teachers' Workshop* (West Nyack, N.J.: Parker Publishing Company, 1970), p. 13. Reprinted with written permission of the Parker Publishing Company.

Figure 8-2   *Slide Used to Determine Field Area of Magnification and Inversion of Objects*

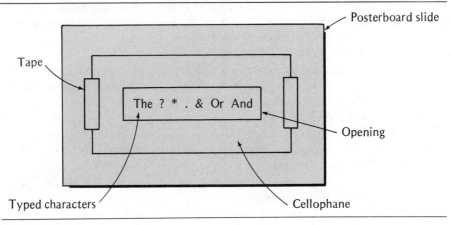

Exploring the Compound Light Microscope

Objectives   The purpose of the exercise is to allow students to arrive inductively at the following three generalizations:

1. Objects appear inverted and reversed left to right.
2. The field of observation is inversely related to the power of the lens being used. As the magnifying power of the lens increases, the area of the observed field decreases.
3. Materials can be viewed as three-dimensional objects and are arranged on distinct planes.

Use   The exercise is presented here as it was developed and used for a class of teacher aides. However, it is readily adaptable for use with high school students.

Part 1   For the first phase of the exercise—to help students realize the inversion of objects under the microscope and their reversal left to right—several words and other symbols were typed on sheets of cellophane paper, using carbon ribbon to make a dark impression. Initially, one line of typed material was mounted on a posterboard slide having a quarter-inch slit to expose the typed line (see Fig. 8-2 above).

Students were asked to observe the line of characters, especially the question mark, and to draw exactly what they observed under low power, medium power, and high power. When all students had completed their drawings, they were asked to state generalizations concerning what they had observed.

Sample Results   Interestingly enough, during the period several students observed that the object being viewed was upside down. However, these students proceeded to reorient the slide on the microscope stage to give them a "cor-

Figure 8-3   *Side View of Slide Illustrating Two Viewing Planes*

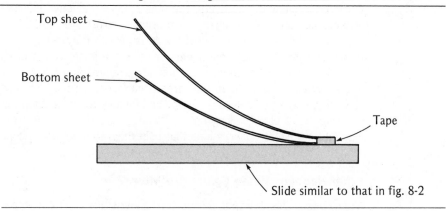

Top sheet

Bottom sheet

Tape

Slide similar to that in fig. 8-2

rected" image! Other students drew the figures as they appeared through the eyepiece—that is, inverted. When asked to make generalizations regarding this phenomenon, all agreed that the objects had been reversed or upside down.

One participant who had recently completed a college biology course was astounded to realize that she had never made this observation in a full quarter of biology lab work. She stated that the slides she had used were either stained or unstained and unprepared but that at no time had she realized inversion took place, and that no one had ever mentioned this in class—including the instructor.

Part 2   The second part of the exercise, seeking generalizations relating field size to the magnifying power of the lens, was difficult for many students to comprehend immediately. However, on repeated observation, without the instructor telling them what they should observe but with leading questions, those who had difficulty were able to state that "you cannot 'see' all of the letter under the highest power that you can see under the lowest power."

Part 3   The third objective—to have students observe that the field is arranged in planes—was achieved by using overlapping pieces of cellophane with type-on letters and other symbols. The letters on one sheet were typed with a red ribbon, those on the other with a black ribbon, so that each plane of focus would be observable even though the planes overlapped (see Fig. 8-3).

Note: While students can obviously be "told" about these phenomena, telling students is not as meaningful as helping them to make the "discoveries" themselves using an inductive method similar to that described here.

Model 2   ***Color Wheeling and Dealing***

The usual approach to teaching the color wheel tends to be rather mechanical, requiring little discovery on the student's part and, most of the time, involving only memorization of concepts and principles. A more inquiry-oriented approach would be to allow the students, through a guided inductive inquiry experience, to observe visually what happens when primary colors are mixed.

This model uses a simple device that is prepared by using three sheets of transparency film. The three sheets are in the primary colors of blue, yellow, and red. They first are identified and then are arranged in a circle so that each third of the circle contains one of the three transparency films. The teacher then displays them on an overhead projector and defines them as the primary colors. A separate set of blue, yellow, and red wedges are prepared so that the teacher may direct student observations that help them to learn about color mixing.

What Happens When Colors Are Mixed?

Objectives   This device is designed to allow students, through observations, to arrive at the following conclusions:

1. Blue + Yellow = Green
2. Blue + Red = Purple
3. Red + Yellow = Orange
4. Orange + Blue = Brown
5. No other color combinations will produce the secondary colors.
6. The lightness of a color is a function of the thickness or concentration of the overhead transparency film.

Procedures   The teacher prepares a color circle that contains the red, yellow, and blue transparency films. These films are then shown to the students so that they will know that they represent the three primary colors. The students are then asked to predict what might happen if the red and yellow films were superimposed on each other and to write down their responses. The teacher then lays the red strip on the yellow strip, or vice versa, and the students observe the resultant orange color.

The teacher next asks the question, "Does it make any difference whether the red or yellow transparency is on top of or under the other?" The students make predictions, and the teacher places the red film on the yellow, and the yellow on the red. The students then generalize that it makes no difference which color is placed on which, since orange is always produced when red and yellow are mixed.

The teacher repeats the procedure using blue and yellow and asks the students to make predictions. The teacher lays a blue strip of overhead transparency film on a yellow strip and, of course, the result is green. The teacher reverses the order, superimposing a yellow strip on a blue strip. The students are again asked to predict the color. Again, it is shown to make no difference which strip is placed on which, for the resultant color is always green. The teacher does the same operation using blue and red transparency film wedges, with the resultant color being purple.

The teacher then displays the orange color, which was made by mixing the red and yellow strips of film, and asks the student to predict what would happen if blue were superimposed on it. After the predictions are made, the teacher lays the blue strip on the orange color, producing a brown color. The teacher then proceeds to mix various transparency colors so that from the primary colors the secondary colors of orange, violet, and green are created. During the entire procedure, the teacher repeatedly asks, "What would happen if we mixed these colors?" The students make predictions, make observations, and then change their predictions based on their observations.

The full color wheel may be impossible to make unless a complete set of overhead transparency films is available. However, a very close approximation of a color wheel can be made to show complementary colors.

The important aspect of this guided inductive device is that students are given an experience that requires them to make observations and to change their predictions based on these observations. Furthermore, the students will observe that the amount of light coming through seems to be reduced as the colors are mixed. The teacher may ask for explanations for this phenomenon (that more light is absorbed with darker mixes). The relationship between the amount of light and the darkness of a mix, as well as the relationship between the amount of light and "concentration," may be discussed.

Another procedure that can be tried is to use solutions of water and food coloring to demonstrate the three primary colors. The water, contained in separate small glass dishes, may be placed on the stage of an overhead projector. The teacher may then drop the food coloring into the water, or the students may be asked to mix the colors. The teacher can set up an experiment in which concentrations of the food coloring may be one variable and the amount of water the other. In this case, sets of identical containers will have varying depths of water but the same number of drops of food coloring. The students are asked to arrange the containers in some type of observable pattern, and then to explain by what variable the containers are arranged. The expected response will be that the darkness or lightness of color is the variable used. The teacher then asks the students to try to match the darkness or lightness of the colors. The students then prepare different sets of solutions with varying color darknesses. In all cases, the students will collect data concerning their observations and the techniques being used.

Depending on how the teacher wants the color-mixing inductive technique to be conducted, students will probably make a chart that will show the following: (1) the number of drops of food coloring in a specific volume of water, and (2) the number of drops of food coloring in different volumes of water. The students will then begin to discover the concept of concentrations being based on the operational definition of lightness.

This model of guided inductive inquiry can be controlled entirely by the teacher, or the students can be involved in conducting all of the trials. The essential elements of inquiry are integrated into the lesson, and the students become more active in a topic that usually does not require involvement. The students can even suggest additional "experiments." However, the teacher has the choice of using either a dry medium (that is, transparency paper) or a solution, depending on the medium being used by the class. But in either case, the students will have learned a useful inquiry technique while "color wheeling and dealing."

Questioning and Guided Inductive Inquiry

We have noted that teacher questioning plays an important role in inquiry, because the purpose of inquiry is to pursue the "search," the "investigation." To accomplish this purpose, the teacher becomes a question-asker, not a question-answerer. Teachers who are masters of guided induction inquiry state that they spend their time interacting with the students but provide very few answers.

What kinds of questions should a teacher ask? Dr. James M. Migaki and one of your authors (Orlich and Migaki, 1981) categorized several "stems" or lead-in questions for teachers who want to have a more inquiry-oriented class environment. What makes the set of stems so interesting is that they are especially suitable for use in social studies, literature, science, and mathematics. But they are usable in *any* class in which the teacher wants to stress the process of inquiry.

If you are conducting an experiment, collecting data, comparing similarities and differences among entities, examining cause-and-effect relationships, searching for errors, verifying the work of others, or analyzing events, then the following set of question stems are very appropriate for challenging the student to think.*

- What is happening?
- What has happened?
- What do you think will happen now?
- How did this happen?
- Why did this happen?
- What caused this to happen?
- What took place before this happened?
- Where have you seen something like this happen?
- When have you seen something like this happen?
- How could we make this happen?
- How does this compare with what we saw or did?
- How can we do this more easily?
- How can you do this more quickly?

Note that this list is oriented to dynamic situations. You may even think of a few more questions to add for your own specialty or grade level. These stems are probably best classified as prompting questions, similar to those described in Chapter 6.

---

*The sets of question stems are reprinted with permission of the National Science Teachers Association.

If you are examining more static living or nonliving objects, the following stems will prove very useful.

- What kind of object is it?
- What is it called?
- Where is it found?
- What does it look like?
- Have you ever seen anything like it? Where? When?
- How is it like other things?
- How can you recognize or identify it?
- How did it get its name?
- What can you do with it?
- What is it made of?
- How was it made?
- What is its purpose?
- How does it work or operate?
- What other names does it have?
- How is it different from other things?

Again, note that these prompting questions help the student to examine all kinds of interrelationships—one of the desired goals of inquiry teaching.

To supplement the role of questioning and process-building, the teacher of younger students can use a series of pictures about where people live. This guided inductive-inquiry project would be ideal in a social studies class. The materials would consist simply of pictures of various "typical" houses of the world, which can be obtained from magazines. If you have no sources of such pictures, just ask the students to bring in old magazines from their homes or from the neighbors. In no time, you will have accumulated a lifetime supply.

There are several ways you can approach this lesson. The first may be to select houses that all have some similar trait—for example, steep roofs, flat roofs, white paint. The objective is to get the students to observe patterns, similarities, and differences.

As a preliminary activity, you can conduct a recitation involving the whole class. (Later, we prefer that you subdivide the class into groups of eight, so that you may practice those discussion skills you learned in Chapter 7.) Have the students observe the pictures while you list their observations on the chalkboard or, better yet, on newsprint. You can tape the newsprint to a wall and place the pictures on a table next to it; this allows the students who did not seem to master the process of inductive logic to practice more on their own. But let us return to the lesson.

You may need to ask a series of questions about the houses, the land, and other observable elements in the pictures. Then you begin to build toward a general statement regarding all the pictures being studied. When this statement is made *by the class,* successful guided inductive inquiry is demonstrated. The lesson can be reinforced by using other objects such as leaves in the fall, old buttons in the winter, mittens, whether or not the children wear mittens, the children's feet, their hands, their earlobes—any objects that can be classified, sorted, counted, or contrasted. It is essential to keep reinforcing the learning wherever possible simply by asking, "What do we observe here?" Or, this situation would be ideal for a cooperative learning episode.

Various documents associated with important historical events are an ideal source for guided inductive inquiry. Patricia Baars, Wynell Burroughs, and Jean Mueller (1986) describe how reproductions of historical documents can be examined by students. For students trying to appreciate the World War II era, they suggest using posters or pamphlets about seldom-discussed topics such as victory gardens, rationing of sugar and meat, press releases, and stated governmental policy statements. These artifacts, which focus on the war's impact on the civilian population of the United States, are rich resources.

Henry F. Billings (1985) suggests that newspaper political cartoons are excellent publications by which to build inquiry skills. He shows how students can be taught to (1) determine main ideas, (2) practice outlining, (3) recognize bias, (4) infer meanings, and (5) construct the context from which to appreciate the cartoon. The movement to use the newspaper in the classroom has similar goals, although on a much broader scale. Students chart news stories (the facts) and show their relationships to editorials (interpretations or opinions). We add that the analysis of political slogans and general advertising, especially on television, would be a "gold mine" for the building of analytic skills.

The teacher with any initiative can apply inquiry lessons at higher grade levels. For example, junior high students can determine the relative standards by which houses are built in different areas of the world and the reasons for the discrepancies. High school students can be challenged to compute the energy costs of heating or cooling systems and the effectiveness of insulation in conserving energy. The teacher is thus the organizer and expediter of guided inductive inquiry, while the students are the active thinkers and doers.

Unguided Inductive Inquiry

In the preceding text concerning *guided* inductive inquiry, you noted that, as teacher, you played the key role in asking the questions, prompting the responses, and structuring the materials and situations; in general, you were the major organizer of the learning. Guided inductive inquiry is an excellent method by which to begin the gradual shift from expository or deductive teaching toward teaching that is less structured and more open to alternative solutions. If you sense that the class has mastered the techniques of guided inductive inquiry, then you ought to introduce situations that are still predicated on inductive logic but are more open-ended in that the students must take more responsibility for examining the data, objects, or events.

The basic processes of observation, inference, classification, communication, prediction, interpretation, formulation of hypotheses, and experimentation are all a part of *unguided* inductive inquiry. Because the teacher's role is minimized, the students' activity increases. Let us briefly summarize the major elements of unguided inductive inquiry.

1. The thought processes require that the learners will progress from specific observations to inferences or generalizations.
2. The objective is to learn (or reinforce) the processes of examining events, objects, and data and then to arrive at appropriate sets of generalizations.
3. The teacher controls only the materials and simply poses a question such as: "What can you generalize from . . . ?" or "Tell me everything that you can about 'X' after examining these. . . ."
4. The students interact with the specifics of the lesson and ask all the questions that come to mind without further teacher guidance.
5. Meaningful patterns are student-generated through individual observations and inferences, as well as those generated by others in the class.
6. The materials are essential to making the classroom a laboratory.
7. Usually, the learners will make an unlimited number of generalizations.
8. The teacher encourages a sharing of the inferences so that all students communicate their generalizations with the class. Thus, others may benefit from one individual's unique perceptions.

Unguided inductive inquiry provides a mechanism for greater learner creativity. Also, the learners begin to approach a genuinely authentic discovery episode. For, as Kenneth A. Strike (1975) argued early on, discovery learning is approached when learners find out something by themselves and come to know that fact. Strike refers to this process as *relative discovery*—that is, the event may have been known to others prior to the time the learner discovered it by himself or herself.

When a teacher begins to use unguided inductive inquiry, a new set of teacher behaviors must come into play. You must now begin to act as the "classroom clarifier." As students start to make their generalizations, there predictably will appear gross errors in student logic, too broadly stated generalizations, too much inference from the data, the assigning of single cause-and-effect relationships where there are several, and the assigning of cause-and-effect relationships where none exists. Then you patiently examine the learner in a *nonthreatening* manner to verify the conclusion or generalizations. If errors exist in the student's logic or inferences, point them out. But you should not tell the student what the correct inference is, for this would defeat the purpose of any inquiry episode.

We suggest that during initial unguided inductive experiences, the students should work alone. In our experiences we have noted that when students work alone, they tend to do most of the work themselves. When they work in pairs or triads, one in the group usually takes the leadership role and dominates the group's thinking, so that there is only one participant and two observers. When students demonstrate the aptitude to use the inductive method successfully in an unguided fashion, then you can assign small groups to work together.

Techniques for Unguided Inductive Inquiry

What are some tested ideas that can be used as prototypes to encourage teachers to incorporate appropriate inductive learning experiences into an ongoing lesson?

Dr. S. Samuel Shermis of Purdue University uses two very inexpensive devices to aid students in understanding the culture of different parts of the United States and of the world. The first device is the telephone directory. Shermis simply gives his students copies of worn-out, discarded, or obsolete telephone directories and then says, "Tell me all you can about Gary"—if the directory happens to be that of Gary, Indiana, of course. The students begin to examine the contents and to jot down notes about the city such as the number of people, industries, services, and organizations. A good problem is to give some members of the class directories from different geographical regions, such as Boston, Tulsa, Nashville, and Salt Lake City, and to ask them to compile a set of generalizations about those cities' religious preferences, by "letting their fingers walk through the Yellow Pages."

To obtain those directories, send a letter to the superintendent of schools in the selected cities to ask for the old editions. Or ask the manager of the directory department of your local telephone company for some of the obsolete volumes. When big business knows that it is helping the schools, it is usually happy to provide materials.

A second Shermis technique for introducing an unguided inductive inquiry is to distribute a set of postcards from any city, state, or country and then to pose the question: "What do you think this city considers to be important?" He does the same thing with travel brochures obtained free from any travel agent.

Use unguided inductive inquiry that combines art, history, and social studies, suggests John Marshall Carter (1986). He distributes pictures of the eleventh-century Bayeux Tapestry. After he makes an introduction, he asks students to list what they know about this unique French pictorial artifact. The inquiry plan allows students to:

1. Infer past events
2. Record their observations of the tapestry
3. Provide some chronological order to the depicted scenes
4. Relate the tapestry to that social and cultural order—roles of women, agricultural techniques, architecture, language, art, astronomy

You may use the local newspaper as an inquiry laboratory. In one such experience you can challenge the students to find examples of bias or news that is slanted. In general, newspaper bias can be classified into eight major types.

1. Bias through selection and omission
2. Bias through placement
3. Bias by headline
4. Bias by photos, captions, and camera angle
5. Bias through use of names and titles
6. Bias through statistics and crowd counts

7. Bias by source control
8. Bias by word selection and connotation

Over time, students will be able to identify these eight sources of bias—by using unguided inductive inquiry techniques. All you have to do is bring in the laboratory materials and provide some time. This laboratory could even take the form of a "learning activity center" located in the corner of the classroom. By establishing a learning activity center, students may work on the material at their own pace and own time.

The important point in these various activities is to require that students analyze and evaluate. Require all students to provide concrete evidence for any generalization; in this manner, their comprehension and analytic skills are reinforced. These techniques help your students progress far beyond simple Knowledge skills.

Note how very much open-ended these experiences are in that there is ample "learning space" allowing everyone in the class to participate. The "slowest" to the smartest students can all make meaningful contributions.

The authors have had fun using data taken from the U.S. Decennial Census. By arranging the census data in five-year increments, by age, for any one or more years, one can build a "population pyramid." The students are asked to discuss in small groups the question "What can you generalize from this figure?" Virtually hundreds of generalizations are offered. Observe the selected pyramids in Figures 8-4 and 8-5 and the data in Table 8-1. How many questions or problems can *you* pose from each of these simple presentations of data. Students always note the "dent" in the pyramid indicating a decrease in the population. Their explanations for the "dent" are interesting. A few examples follow: "The people were killed in World War II"; "they died of starvation during the Depression"; "they died from epidemics"; and "people just had fewer kids."

The advantage of these explanations, or hypotheses, is that they can all be tested. The students are sent to the library to do research to verify their hypotheses. They soon realize that their hypotheses are untenable. The reality dimension of such inquiry exercises helps to develop logical processes in a student's method of looking at numerical displays. (See Frymier, 1989; Census Education Project, 1989; and ZPG Population Education Program, 1989.)

Using data can be a great stimulator of classroom discussions. Data exist for every grade level experience and for every possible subject, ranging from art to zoology. It is also possible to present data in such a way that students must either interpolate (predict what should have come earlier) or extrapolate (predict later outcomes). Teachers can control the flow of data (information) so that predictions may be made and justified. Evidence, facts, and their interpretation all become more meaningful to the students instead of being merely words in a book.

We are suggesting that any teacher at any level has some information that poses questions for which there are no answers. By providing this information to the students, you initiate unguided inductive inquiry. To be sure, you should not assign exercises just for the sake of having the students do them. Exercises must be

Figure 8-4   *U.S. Population by Age and Sex: 1900–1960*

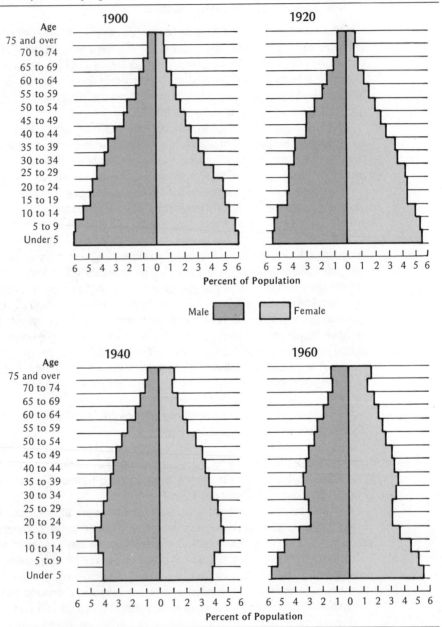

Source: Executive Office of the President: Office of Management and Budget, *Social Indicators, 1973* (Washington, D.C.: U.S. Government Printing Office, 1973), Chart 8/8, p. 250.

Figure 8-5   *U.S. Population by Age and Sex: 1960–1990*

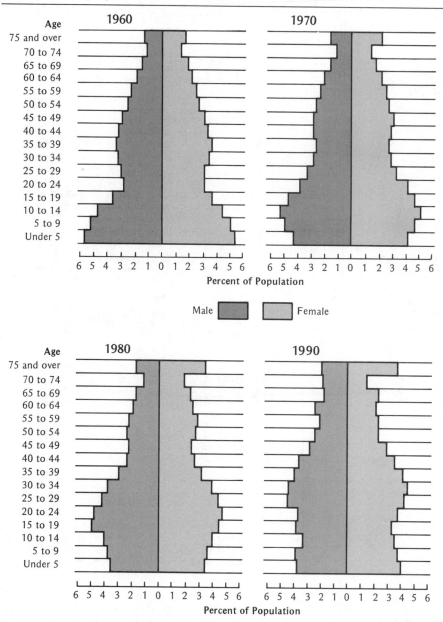

Source: 1980 Pyamid, *Age, Sex, Race, and Spanish Origin of the Population by Regions, Divisions, and States:* 1980, PC80-51-1, Bureau of the Census; 1970 and 1960 Pyramids, Executive Office of the President: Office of Management and Budget, *Social Indicators, 1973* (Washington, D.C.: U.S. Government Printing Office, 1973), Chart 8/8, p. 250. The 1990 estimates are from Bureau of the Census, *Projections of the Population of the United States by Age, Sex, and Race: 1983 to 2080.* Table 6, pp. 53–54, Current Population Reports, Population Estimates and Projections, Series P-25, No. 952.

Table 8-1   U.S. Population, by Age and Sex: 1940–1990

Age	1940 Male	1940 Female	1960 Male	1960 Female	1970 Male	1970 Female	1980 Male	1980 Female	1990 Male	1990 Female
Number of Persons (thousands)										
All ages	66,350	65,815	88,331	90,992	98,912	104,300	110,032	116,473	121,520	128,137
Under 5 years	5,379	5,210	10,330	9,991	8,745	8,409	8,360	7,984	9,827	9,371
5 to 9 years	5,444	5,291	9,504	9,187	10,168	9,788	8,538	8,159	9,511	9,080
10 to 14 years	5,980	5,820	8,524	8,249	10,591	10,199	9,315	8,926	8,586	8,207
15 to 19 years	6,209	6,178	6,634	6,586	9,634	9,437	10,752	10,410	8,670	8,299
20 to 24 years	5,728	5,917	5,272	5,528	7,917	8,454	10,660	10,652	9,443	9,137
25 to 29 years	5,482	5,664	5,333	5,536	6,622	6,855	9,703	9,814	10,878	10,645
30 to 34 years	5,095	5,186	5,846	6,103	5,596	5,835	8,676	8,882	11,014	10,992
35 to 39 years	4,767	4,813	6,080	6,402	5,412	5,694	6,860	7,103	9,933	10,068
40 to 44 years	4,435	4,379	5,676	5,924	5,819	6,162	5,708	5,961	8,799	9,048
45 to 49 years	4,221	4,055	5,358	5,522	5,851	6,265	5,388	5,701	6,831	7,148
50 to 54 years	3,765	3,511	4,735	4,871	5,348	5,756	5,620	6,089	5,519	5,903
55 to 59 years	3,021	2,838	4,127	4,303	4,766	5,207	5,481	6,133	4,954	5,479
60 to 64 years	2,406	2,335	3,409	3,733	4,027	4,590	4,669	5,416	4,917	5,701
65 to 69 years	1,902	1,913	2,931	3,327	3,122	3,870	3,902	4,878	4,458	5,538
70 to 74 years	1,274	1,300	2,185	2,554	2,315	3,129	2,853	3,944	3,405	4,634
75 years and over	1,242	1,405	2,387	3,176	2,979	4,651	3,546	6,419	4,775	8,887

Table 8-1 Continued

Age	1940		1960		1970		1980		1990	
	Male	Female	Male	Female	Male	Female	Male	Female	Male	Female
Percent of Total Population										
All ages	50.2	49.8	49.3	50.7	48.7	51.3	48.58	51.42	48.7	51.3
Under 5 years	4.1	3.9	5.8	5.6	4.3	4.1	3.7	3.5	3.9	3.8
5 to 9 years	4.1	4.0	5.3	5.1	5.0	4.8	3.8	3.6	3.8	3.6
10 to 14 years	4.5	4.4	4.8	4.6	5.2	5.0	4.1	3.9	3.4	3.3
15 to 19 years	4.7	4.7	3.7	3.7	4.7	4.6	4.7	4.6	3.5	3.3
20 to 24 years	4.3	4.5	2.9	3.1	3.9	4.2	4.7	4.7	3.8	3.7
25 to 29 years	4.1	4.3	3.0	3.1	3.3	3.4	4.3	4.3	4.4	4.3
30 to 34 years	3.9	3.9	3.3	3.4	2.8	2.9	3.8	3.9	4.4	4.4
35 to 39 years	3.6	3.6	3.4	3.6	2.7	2.8	3.0	3.1	3.9	4.0
40 to 44 years	3.4	3.3	3.2	3.3	2.9	3.0	2.5	2.6	3.5	3.6
45 to 49 years	3.2	3.1	3.0	3.1	2.9	3.1	2.4	2.5	2.7	2.9
50 to 54 years	2.8	2.7	2.6	2.7	2.6	2.8	2.5	2.7	2.2	2.4
55 to 59 years	2.3	2.1	2.3	2.4	2.3	2.6	2.4	2.7	1.9	2.2
60 to 64 years	1.8	1.8	1.9	2.1	2.0	2.3	2.1	2.4	1.9	2.3
65 to 69 years	1.4	1.4	1.6	1.9	1.5	1.9	1.7	2.2	1.8	2.2
70 to 74 years	1.0	1.0	1.2	1.4	1.1	1.5	1.2	1.7	1.4	1.9
75 years and over	0.9	1.1	1.3	1.7	1.5	2.3	1.5	2.8	1.9	3.6

Note: Data do not include Armed Forces overseas.

Sources: Bureau of the Census, 1940 Census of Population, Vol. IV, Part 1; 1960 Census of Population, Vol. I, Part 1; 1970 Census of Population, Vol. II, Part 1; and unpublished data. Executive Office of the President: Office of Management and Budget, Social Indicators, 1973. Washington, D.C.: U.S. Government Printing Office, 1973, p. 255; and Bureau of the Census, 1980 Census of Population, Supplementary Reports, "Age, Sex, Race, and Spanish Origin of the Population by Regions, Divisions, and States: 1980," PC80-S1-1, p. 3. The 1990 estimates are from Bureau of the Census, Projections of the Population of the United States by Age, Sex, and Race: 1983 to 2080. Table 6, pp. 53–54, Current Population Reports, Population Estimates and Projections, Series P-25, No. 952. The authors thank Annabelle Kirschner Cook, Department of Sociology, Washington State University, for her help in supplying the 1980 and 1990 data.

correlated with the learning objectives or goals that *you* have selected for the unit, chapter, or module. Some topics lend themselves easily to inductive inquiry, whereas others do not. *You* must decide on these topics.

In the humanities and the arts, the teacher is the *only* limiting factor. If you really know your discipline, you also know its "structure"—that is, its epistemological basis. By collecting materials from your area of expertise, you can build a file of appropriate items, objects, events, or artifacts with which to supplement the usual classroom instruction.

Using Inquiry

Again, a word of caution to future teachers: You do not suddenly begin to use inquiry without preparation. You plan for experiences that are meaningful and relevant. For language arts classes, the local newspaper is one of the finest and cheapest resources for raw data (see Orlich, 1989). Have the students examine the editorial pages and the front-page news stories of the local "scandal sheet" as well as those of various cities around the state or country. Let them make generalizations about such matters as editorial positions, the use of propaganda and persuasive techniques, and the ways of slanting (or biasing) stories.

Weekly, biweekly, and monthly magazines are gold mines of inquiry activities. Junior high school teachers in the language arts have long used advertisements in magazines to illustrate various communication principles. Art classes also can use these materials to illustrate communication techniques as well as to examine the artistic principles.

Even physical educators can use inductive inquiry techniques with selected skill-building activities. Students can be allowed to determine various moves, stances, balance points, and the like through guided inductive inquiry.

Poets use inductive logic to a great extent, especially when developing such elements as characters, images, and themes. The readers must infer the meaning or determine the pattern being built. It can be fun when poetry is employed—if it is appropriate to the objectives of the lesson—to teach students how to use inductive logic while attempting to analyze meanings. (Of course, the authors are well aware of John Ciardi's [1979] criticism that teachers tend to overanalyze poetry to the point of *reductio ad absurdum.*)

Along the guidelines suggested, the history program for eighth grade in Northampton, Massachusetts, was totally restructured to incorporate historical interpretation, analysis, and evaluation as basic skills—along with knowledge of history. Provided with materials and reprints from early newspapers dating back to 1754, students determined the effects of selected governmental decisions on the merchants, landowners, and other groups. Students also created a play about one of the periods in the town's growth; they did the research, wrote the script, and made the costumes.

As they studied local history, they created storyboards and time lines so as to gain a historical perspective. Incidents were linked to other historical events. And they examined social concepts such as justice, prejudice, development of laws, government, politics, and group dynamics. Compare this exciting course with the one you had in eighth grade.

If you want to develop some initial inductive skills, offer the class a challenge: how is the national zip code organized? One of the authors of this text has developed a "zip code game" that uses inductive and unguided inquiry techniques (Orlich, 1986). Students receive the challenge and a blank map of the United States. Cards with state capitals and their zip codes are distributed; and, as the exercise progresses, patterns of zip codes begin to emerge. The national areas are identified and zip codes are predicted for states, territories, and islands in the Atlantic and Pacific Oceans. This experience helps develop pattern-building, inference, prediction, and classification skills. Further, it reinforces geographic areas, names and locations of states, and knowledge of the zip code.

Students are then challenged to compare the zip codes of the United States with the postal codes of Canada and other countries. Similarities and differences are then identified. The processes of inquiry are nicely reinforced with the content (Orlich, 1986).

Although we have not emphasized the process of classification in the inquiry modes, we wish to mention that, as human beings, we constantly classify everything in our lives—such as people, objects, baseball games, suits, houses, cars, movies, and TV shows. One of the generalizations that will quickly emerge as you use inductive modes is that there is no one way to classify anything. Your students will arrive at usable classification schemes that you may not have thought existed.

One of our favorite classification exercises involves the "old button box" device. Obtain as many buttons as you can from a scavenger hunt and place them in a bag. Then ask each class member to establish a classification scheme for the buttons that he or she has. We guarantee that you will be surprised at the number of characteristics that the students will observe as being useful in classifying their buttons.

Classification exercises can lead to some elements of evaluation as we know it in Bloom's Taxonomy. Evaluation, as you recall, is conducted using explicitly stated criteria. But how does one classify or evaluate the criteria? Utility has to be one consideration. There are others, but allow the students to determine them for themselves. Table 8-2 presents some topics appropriate for inquiry.

About the Inductive Method

Perhaps you have been taught that the inductive method of inquiry is "the method of science." If so, you have been led astray. To be sure, scientists use inductive methodologies. But detailed analyses of scientific thought by Karl R. Popper (1959; originally published in 1934) and by Thomas S. Kuhn (1962) show that modern science is characterized more by *hypothetico-deductive* reasoning than by pure inductive logic. However, inductive logic is a basis for inference building, and scientists typically rely on theories or working hypotheses on which to base their "inductive

Table 8-2   *Topics Appropriate to Inquiry by Discipline*

Discipline	Topics
Art	Color wheels
	Drawing: what happens to movement
English	Symbols in a masterpiece
	Mapping for writing
History	Bias in recorded history
	Life in the Great Depression
Family living	Properties of different textiles
	Family interactions
Industrial arts	Commonalities of period design
	Hardware choices
Languages	Cultural differences in prefixes
	Comparing similar objects, such as tickets, maps, advertisements
Music	Infer style and moods
	Establish patterns from different composers
Physical education	Disease control
	Athletic injuries
Science	Animal communications
	Chemical reactions
Social studies	Demographic trends
	Cultural geographical similarities and differences
Theater arts	Social impact of playwrights
	Symbolism in set design

experiments." This means that modern-day empiricism is undergirded by theoretical propositions. Actually, Popper argues that there is no such thing as theory; there are only testable hypotheses. The longer a hypothesis stands the tests of experimentation and predictability, the more it gains "respect" in the scientific community. Emerging social science fields such as sociology, psychology, and anthropology, to list three, are now developing substantial bodies of tenable theory—that is, working hypotheses. The worth of any theory or hypothesis is its ability to predict future events. The so-called hard sciences—chemistry and physics—have had a long tradition of hypotheses that have stood the rigors of experimentation and prediction. Physicists and chemists proudly state that without the strong theoretical commitment those disciplines have, they would be unable to function in the laboratory to conduct systematic research.

Compare this position to teaching or education. Our field has few tenable hypotheses for helping the teacher to teach better. Thus, the state of the art for education is far behind that of the other social sciences. Perhaps you have complained that education courses "have too much theory." We argue that you have been exposed to too many classroom anecdotes, without the necessary theoretical structure.

PROBLEM-SOLVING

A curricular model that should have had a greater impact on the schools than it has was one advocated by John Dewey, a major writer who published extensively from 1884 to 1948. Among his major educational contributions was his advocacy of a curriculum *based on problems*. He defined a problem as anything that gives rise to doubt and uncertainty. This theory is not to be confused with the "needs" or "interest" theories of curriculum. Dewey did have a definite idea of the types of problems that are suitable for inclusion in the curriculum. The problems that Dewey promoted had to meet two rigorous criteria: (1) the problems to be studied had to be important to the culture, and (2) the problems had to be important and relevant to the student.

It is very apparent that many curriculum projects developed between 1958 and 1970 in science, mathematics, and social studies tended to be based on Dewey's problem-solving approach. Most contemporary curricula and a large majority of textbooks suggest "problems" to be solved by students. Some of the curricula that you may encounter will stress elements of inquiry, discovery, or problem-solving. Contemporary curricula, especially interdisciplinary ones such as environmental studies, rely heavily on the two criteria that were first suggested by Dewey. If you assign "research reports" to be prepared by your students, you will be using elements of problem-solving. Again, we caution that this technique, like any inquiry method, requires careful planning and systematic skill-building.

Implicit within the framework of problem-solving is the concept of "experience." This concept assumes that activities of students under the school's direction will produce certain desirable traits (or behaviors) in those individuals, so that they will be better able to function in our culture. Furthermore, the experiences provided by the schools should articulate the *content* and the *process* of knowing. Both knowing what is known and knowing how to know are important objectives for the learner.

The Teacher's Role

When using problem-solving with learners, you must constantly play the "great clarifier" role. Always help the learners to define precisely what it is that is being studied or solved. Problem-solving methodologies focus on the systematic investigation of the students' problems. The students set up the problem, clarify the issues, propose ways of obtaining the needed information or data to help resolve the problem, and then test or evaluate the conclusions. In most cases the learners will establish written hypotheses for testing. We cannot overemphasize the fact that students need your continual monitoring. Problem-solving demands that you continually receive "progress reports" from those students engaged in the investigative process.

Students are not simply allowed to follow their whims. Problem-solving requires the building of close relationships between students and teacher. It also involves a systematic investigation of the problem and the proposing of concrete solutions. Let us present two case histories of real problems that took place in Washington, D.C., and Massachusetts elementary schools.

Examples of Real Problem-Solving

Our first example is taken from one man's efforts to help break the poverty cycle and to instill an appreciation for basic school subjects that can ultimately improve economic well-being. Recall that in Chapter 7 we discussed the national stock market simulation. Well, Robert Radford (not Redford) of Washington, D.C., wanted to help the children attending the Amidon Elementary School.

General goals of the project are to assist inner-city children:

1. Gain insights into the American economic system
2. Understand the concepts of compounding, the time-value of money, and capital appreciation
3. Practice the concept of delayed gratification (to break the poverty cycle)

No question about it, this is *real problem-solving.*

Children in the intermediate grades are introduced to economics and business principles in practical ways. Each child must provide an example of the topics or concepts being discussed. This instructional strategy leads to *understanding* (that word again). Next, stock market activities are introduced. Children examine the *Investor's Daily, Value Line Survey,* and *Barron's Financial Weekly.* (We must insert that there is good chance most seniors in high school will never have read these financial tools, nor will they comprehend the various business and financial transactions that "Wall Street" provides.) Yes, the children read and reported on findings and even computed the Dow Jones Industrial Average.

Through hands-on experiences they studied and discussed business cycles. They tracked selected stocks and graphed fluctuations in prices and compared industrial stock profiles to that of the market as a whole. Through this real-life activity, children vividly realize the need to master arithmetic, reading, social studies, and language arts.

A decision was made to purchase Philadelphia Electric Company common stock. Money to purchase the shares came from Radford's solicitation of funds and gifts from seventy-five individuals who wanted to help in this project, plus the support of seventeen companies and corporations. The investments are such that each graduating class receives a proratio number of shares of common stock of Philadelphia Electric, which is then placed into custodial account trusts for each child.

Accompanying the real-life component to this project is a stock simulation project. Each child receives a hypothetical $50,000 account in which ten different stocks are purchased. Students track their "portfolios" each week so that additional drill and practice in arithmetic and decision-making take place.

To add the reality dimension one step further, thirty-one students attended the

1987 annual stockholders' meeting of Philadelphia Electric. With their peers' proxies in hand the delegates cast their votes and presented issues to the stockholders at large.

Is this real problem-solving? John Dewey would applaud it. The Amidon project illustrates how children who, through no cause of their own, live in an economically deprived environment can be exposed to an *experientially* rich curriculum that helps them understand how to better themselves in *their own immediate future.* Having a trust fund will undoubtedly encourage these children to pursue socially valued occupations and professions.

Finally, the Amidon project illustrates how *affective* objectives may be integrated in the schools. Every kid is a winner: intellectually and financially. Those feelings have a carry-over effect on student behaviors, and ultimately on positive student. actions.

You don't have to lecture or give stern warnings that "this stuff will be good for you in fifteen years!" (The classic lecture No. 101 that falls on deaf ears.) Children can't wait two or three lifetime equivalencies to understand concepts. They need appropriately structured experiences and activities that allow them to apply knowledge and then figure out what it all means. And we suggest this strategy for all levels—grade five, grade nine, grade twelve! Inquiry teaching is a technique that allows a teacher to build and integrate a holistic structure gradually to schooling. This is a way of intentionally inviting learning.

In our second example, children in a Massachusetts elementary school collected data and presented it to their local school board showing that a major intersection was a grievous safety problem. The students then showed how an overpass walk could be constructed and even contacted architects to obtain estimates of the cost of such a structure. The school board was impressed and so was the city council, for the walk was constructed later just as the elementary school children had proposed.

These are just a sample of case studies of teachers and students using problem-solving in the real world. Such examples are a bit dramatic, although they do not all have to be. For instance, a class may observe problems in the immediate school environment—parking, lunch lines, locker rooms, dropouts, or noise—and may begin to investigate these problems with the idea of creating alternatives to the existing situations. Examples from the social sciences are especially appropriate. Judith Brenneke and John C. Soper (1985) provide a common problem to be solved: *airport noise.* Their activity has several elements: (1) applying the concepts of cost/benefit analysis, (2) understanding concepts of economic trade-offs, equity, growth, and efficiency, and (3) establishing alternatives and priorities. In part, their problem resembles a simulation exercise in which different students may play different roles. The airport noise problem has such wide-spread applicability that it can be used as a long-term class project in virtually any major city.

Similarly, Mark C. Shug and Stephen Haessler (1985) provide a real problem associated with the rise and decline of the Harley-Davidson Motor Company. (The name needs no introduction to "real bikers.") The market share of Harley-Davidson motorcycle sales declined from a near monopoly for most of the twentieth century to its current share of about 15 percent. The problem provides data illustrating that Harley is *the lone* survivor of 143 motorcycle companies in the United States. A case study-problem approach is developed. Students can be assembled into several different cooperative learning groups. Each group can explore data relative to the problem of foreign competition to domestic manufacturers. Research problems and investigative questions can be developed to guide each team's efforts. Various solutions and alternatives—all data-based—can be proposed. Your group might even send the results of their investigation to the chief executive officer of the company.

Some Steps in Solving Problems

Problem-solving implies a degree of freedom and responsibility to explore the problem and to arrive at a possible solution. One tackles a problem to achieve objectives and not simply to use the process of inquiry per se. The following steps are associated with the problem-solving technique:

1. Becoming aware of a situation or event that is labeled a "problem"
2. Identifying the problem in exact terms
3. Defining all terms
4. Establishing the limits of the problem
5. Conducting a task analysis so that the problem may be subdivided into discrete elements for investigation
6. Collecting data that are relevant to each task
7. Evaluating the data for apparent biases or errors
8. Synthesizing the data for meaningful relationships
9. Making generalizations and suggesting alternatives to rectify the problem
10. Publishing the results of the investigation

Obviously, if *you* decide to use a problem-solving episode in your classes, you must realize that it will last for days or even weeks. During that time, other learnings may be accomplished as well—for example, using reference books, writing for unavailable information or data, interpreting data, presenting progress reports to the class, and taking responsibility for the conduct of a task.

If the problem allows for other independent study, that also may be arranged. You may be able to conduct both the problem-solving episodes and the elements of the "regular" class lessons. In many cases, there are time lapses between phases of the problem-solving procedures; make appropriate use of such time so that it will not be wasted.

The students will experience a sense of accomplishment in problem-solving. We suggest that you plan for a systematic evaluation of the episode. You can do so by adapting the evaluation forms presented in Chapter 7's treatment of discussions. In this manner both you and the learners will be able to benefit from the experience. Problem-solving, then, is one more inquiry technique available for making schooling a more memorable experience.

DISCOVERY LEARNING

Who really discovered America? Although Leif Ericson seems to have been the first European to visit our shores, Christopher Columbus gets the credit for the discovery simply because he announced it first. But the territory is named for Amerigo Vespucci because he knew he had landed on a brand-new continent and not in India. Thus the defining of *discovery* is difficult.*

Dictionary definitions of *discover* carry connotations that go beyond the denotations. For example, examine the following definition quoted from *Webster's New Collegiate Dictionary*:**

> **dis·cov·er** . . . **1 a:** to make known or visible; EXPOSE   **b** *archaic:* DISPLAY
> **2:** to obtain sight or knowledge of for the first time: FIND ⟨~ the solution of a puzzle⟩ ~ *vi:* to make a discovery— . . .
> **syn 1** see REVEAL
> **2** DISCOVER, ASCERTAIN, DETERMINE, UNEARTH, LEARN *shared meaning element:* to find out something not previously known to one
> **3** see INVENT

With all these connotations for one term, it is not surprising to observe so much confusion in the use of the word in the field of education. This is not to be construed as derogating the technique of discovery; it is meant merely to show the possibilities attending the state of the art.

The terms *discovery learning* and *inductive methods* often appear in place of the same generic term of *inquiry*. We will differentiate among these so that each method will be better understood. Induction is a method of logic, whereas discovery is a method by which thoughts are synthesized to perceive something that an individual has not known before. In this vein, Kenneth A. Strike's (1975) comprehensive analysis of methods associated with discovery learning may be of immediate use. Strike establishes two categories of discovery: *absolute* discovery and *relative* discovery. Absolute discovery is that attributed to those classic firsts—the discovery of the DNA molecule's reproduction mechanism, America, new planets, theories, or synthetic materials. Relative discovery means that an individual has learned or found out something for the first time.

Strike also presents four modes of discovery: (1) knowing that, (2) knowing how, (3) discovering that, and (4) discovering how. Finally, he provides a basic criterion that is essential for any act to be labeled a discovery. The discoverer must communicate both the *what* and the *how* to others. Thus, if you discover the Lost Dutchman Mine in Arizona but do not tell a single individual, you have not made a discovery.

The four modes of discovery that Strike presents are very consistent with the thirteen major processes described early in this chapter (see the section "Basic Processes of Inquiry"). Communicating is a major inquiry process and is very much a

---

*We thank Kenneth A. Strike (1975) for the idea about Christopher Columbus.
**By permission. From *Webster's New Collegiate Dictionary* © 1979 by G. & C. Merriam Co., Publishers of the Merriam-Webster Dictionaries.

part of discovery. Also, the model that Strike describes implies that learners must "know" something before they can "discover" something. Content, knowledge, fact, and processes are all very much a part of the discovery strategy.

Although there is much luck involved in discovery, Louis Pasteur's statement that "chance favors the prepared mind" is yet very valid. Even though there is a trial-and-error element associated with discovery, the most important discoveries made by scientists—including social and behavioral scientists—are the result of careful observation and systematic research. Discovery makes use of the same processes and skills that were described for inductive inquiry and problem-solving. This should come as no surprise because we have already emphasized the idea that inquiry, by its very epistemological nature, requires systematic conduct, not haphazard bungling. (Note: The method by which knowledge of a field is determined, as well as the limits and validity of that knowledge, constitute the science of epistemology. Inquiry-related techniques are based on the epistemology of empiricism. Observations, experiences, experiments, and replications are the techniques of empiricism—and of inquiry.)

Classic Examples of Discovery Learning

The Black Widow Spider and Other Insects

Judith Miles of Lexington, Massachusetts, wondered how spiders would spin webs under the effects of weightlessness. The subject of her curiosity was one of nineteen Skylab Student Projects conducted in the National Aeronautics and Space Administration (NASA) earth-orbiting space station in 1973. The Skylab Project placed three astronauts above the earth for twenty-eight days. Judith's experiment demonstrated that a black widow spider was initially "confused" and did not spin the appropriate web pattern. But within a relatively short time, the spider did, in fact, spin the appropriate web!

Is this an example of problem-solving or discovery? We think that it fits in the category of *absolute* discovery because it was the first time that anyone had communicated the problem and had completed the research. Her science teacher, J. Michael Conley, had encouraged Judith to submit her idea in a contest sponsored by the National Science Teachers Association in conjunction with NASA. This demonstrates the partnership that develops when learners and teachers share in the excitement of inquiry.

Similarly, Todd Nelson, a student from Adams, Minnesota, designed an experiment for the third mission, March 1982, of the space shuttle Columbia. Nelson suggested that Columbia's crew videotape the behavior of selected flying insects—velvetbean caterpillar moths, honey bees, and common houseflies—to determine the effects of a gravity-free environment. Todd's experiment was selected along with those of Ph.D. research botanists to determine the same effect on pine tree, oat, and Chinese bean sprouts. Again, this experiment demonstrates absolute discovery—

and by high school students, too. And recall John Vellinger's egg embryo experiment that was conducted on the Discovery shuttle flight of March, 1989. John designed the experiment when he was a high school student in West Lafayette, Indiana. The NASA researchers were so impressed with the soundness of his project that they originally placed it on the ill-fated Challenger shuttle; then rescheduled it. The results showed negative effects on chick embryos during the first two days, but chicks that hatched appeared to be normal: Absolute Discovery on the Discovery mission!

Mystery Island

Not all discovery learning needs to be as dramatic as the NASA experiment. One common technique to generate the fun and discipline accompanying the conduct of inquiry or discovery is to utilize the overhead projector for presenting an event that requires student analysis. Jack Zevin (1969) reported on how to make use of a set of overlays that depict an unnamed island. The stimulus—the overhead projector—is presented to the entire class. The initial projectile shows the outline of an island. The map contains some standard clues to the island's general world location such as topographical symbols, rivers, and latitude and longitude symbols. This device is used primarily to focus the learner's attention on the event or to motivate inquiry.

The episode usually begins with the students being told that the island is uninhabited and that they are going to be the first persons to land on it. Their task is to choose where they will settle and to justify their choices. Ultimately, they are given other tasks such as to find the places that may be the best for farming, industries, railroads, harbors, airports, resorts, and the like. Inferences concerning rainfall, winds, deserts, and other natural phenomena can all be generalized by the students.

One can argue that mystery island is simply an inductive exercise. To be sure, induction is used; so is problem-solving and the application of previously learned skills and content. This stimulus does allow children to know "that" and "how" and to discover "that" and "how." This device has unlimited opportunity for student inquiry.

Assumptions About Inquiry

Perhaps this topic should have been the very first in the chapter. However, if we gave the rules first, followed by the activities, we would be using a deductive approach rather than an inductive one. But it must be thoroughly understood that all inquiry exercises are predicated on selected assumptions about both learning and learners.

Several writers who have addressed the assumptions about inquiry learning include Joseph Abruscato (1986), Arthur Carin and Robert Sund (1985), Peter C. Gega (1986), Willard J. Jacobson and Abby B. Bergman (1987), Vincent N. Lunetta and Shimshon Novick (1981), and Leslie W. Trowbridge and Rodger Bybee (1986). The following list is a synthesis of their collective views as well as of those of the present authors.

1. Inquiry requires that *the learner* develop the various processes associated with inquiry, which include those basic thirteen processes that were presented earlier in this chapter (p. 279).
2. Teachers and principals must be supportive of the concept of inquiry teaching and must *learn* how to adapt their own teaching and administrative styles to the concept.
3. Students at all ages and levels have a genuine interest in discovering something new or in providing solutions or alternatives to unsolved questions or problems.
4. The solutions, alternatives, or responses provided by the learners are *not* readily located in a textbook. Reference materials and textbooks are surely used during inquiry lessons, just as real scientists use books, articles, and references to conduct their work.
5. The content of inquiry is often *process*. In many instances, the product or solution will be relatively unimportant compared to the processes that were used to arrive at it.
6. All conclusions must be considered relative or tentative, but not final. Since inquiry depends mainly on empirical epistemology, the students must also learn that, as new data are discovered, conclusions tend to be modified.
7. Inquiry learning cannot be gauged by the clock. In the real world, when people think or create, it is not usually done in fifty-minute increments.
8. The learners are responsible for planning, conducting, and evaluating their own efforts. It is essential that the teacher play a supportive role, but not the active role of doing the work.
9. Students have to be taught the processes associated with inquiry in a systematic manner. Every time that a "teachable moment" arrives while the class is being conducted, the teacher should immediately capitalize on it to further the building of inquiry processes.
10. The work of the teacher is usually increased owing to the many interactions that may emanate from inquiry teaching/learning.

This set of assumptions is presented so that you will understand better the theoretical bases on which inquiry rests. The more of these assumptions that your classes measure up to, the closer will your classes approach becoming learning laboratories in the truest sense of the term.

Other Uses of Inquiry

Sandra Salo Deutchman (1988) described the use of pictures of childrens' art juxtaposed with examples of adult art. Her model consists of sixteen basic picturing techniques that become an analytic tool for observing art. Deutchman's "universal picturing techniques" cause children to identify approaches to pictorial organization that constantly appear in all art works. Recurring visual structures define spatial orientation, placement, scale, or point of view. By applying distinct terms for describing pictorial organization, the viewer learns to perceive a wide array of recurring structures. Deutchman's work as an artist illustrates how inquiry may be applied to the cognitive domain of analysis and evaluation. However, as one applies the picturing techniques, an affective dimension emerges—art appreciation. Thus, the artist combines two of the taxonomies with this model. And the psychomotor domain is added when children create their own art pieces. The final product relates to all four domains, including the perceptual.

The "California Raisins" have won the hearts of television viewers, but Marilyn Burns (1987) prefers non-dancing ones to stimulate inquiry in the third grade. She uses small boxes of the fruit to develop process skills such as estimating, measuring, and using proportional reasoning. Her students receive experiential learning which is the hallmark for any inquiry strategy.

Don't get mad at textbooks that slight important social issues—put them on trial. That is the adaptation of inquiry used by Rob Berry (1985). He establishes a "court of inquiry" that places a geography textbook on trial concerning its treatment of apartheid in South Africa. All students become involved as they seek evidence supporting or refuting the textual coverage. You could use this method on most controversial issues such as elections, wars, or treatment of labor movements compared to corporate growth. For example, Frances A. Maher (1987) described an inquiry unit that uses the feminist movement as its focus. Her strategy is to list researchable questions about the roles of women in our society. Specific issues such as suffrage, the Great Depression, World War II, and current social themes direct the high school students' inquiry efforts.

It takes between ten and forty hours to complete an analytical reasoning course that stresses thinking, analyzing, and solving problems, reported Nancy J. Vye and John D. Bransford (1981). What is novel about their approach is that the skills are focused on adolescents who have been labeled retarded or learning disabled.

To make social studies more exciting, Barry K. Beyer (1982) integrates writing and five inquiry processes. He has his students applying social studies content by (1) inventing testable hypotheses, (2) generating new knowledge of the content being studied, (3) developing concepts and generalizations from the content, (4) reinforcing previously studied materials, and (5) developing empathy for the group. Observe the mixing of cognitive, affective, and process skills.

Robert F. Bibens (1980) provides an excellent set of tips for those who desire to "experiment" with inquiry techniques. As a teacher, you should

1. Focus on the students and the content.
2. Pace the instruction, but do not expect to have students master any set number of concepts on a specific schedule.
3. Accept student responses; if responses are off the track, guide the students back through questioning.
4. Be sure that all steps of inquiry are conducted by each student, even if a solution has been formulated early on.
5. Encourage every student to search for implications beyond the immediate solution.

6. Respond to student solutions with the question "Why?" In this manner the student must review all the steps used to determine a solution.

Finally, Bibens agrees with our position: inquiry teaching takes time and much teacher energy. In our collective experiences, we have never seen teachers sitting at their desks when teaching through inquiry—they are on the go, and so are their students.

We close this section with examples of historical inquiry suggested for high school students by the College Entrance Examination Board (1986). The board illustrates how selected major historical topics focusing on inquiry skills can be expanded. One topic is the theme of *migration*. That theme can be explored locally (new migrants to some area), nationally (migrations to the country), or globally. The methods used by historians and their means of interpreting historical events are all taught to the class.

By focusing on selected historical themes, students began to recognize:

1. Relationships between the present and past
2. Contrasts between institutions and culture values
3. Major historical turning point
4. Historical cause and effect
5. Different historical interpretations

You will not find the above five points in those traditional, bland history textbooks that must pass *censors* in Texas, California, and several other states. There is some evidence that over 90 percent of all secondary teachers rely on adopted textbooks as their primary source for the curriculum. Because very, very few textbooks provide inquiry (or thinking) experiences, you will need to gather appropriate data, material, and resources from the school's library for class study. Inquiry techniques can transform a history class into a lively and contemporary course that imparts real meaning to students.

And that is exactly what is supported by the prestigious Bradley Commission on History in Schools report, *Building A History Curriculum: Guidelines for Teaching History in Schools* (1988). The report, prepared by some of the most prominent historians and social science educators in the United States, calls for an *actively learned* history in grades K–12. *Verbs* used by the writers to describe how history should be taught include:

1. understand
2. distinguish between
3. perceive
4. comprehend
5. contrast
6. compare

These are the transitive verbs so often associated with inquiry and critical thinking.

To break the pattern of insipid social studies textbooks, the commission members recommend the creation of *real history* books that stress topics in depth. Vital themes would include:

1. Civilization, cultural diffusion, and innovation
2. Human interaction with the environment
3. Values, beliefs, political ideas, and institutions
4. Conflict and cooperation
5. Comparative history of major developments
6. Patterns of social and political interactions

Obviously, this report will begin having impact on the curriculum during the last decade of the twentieth century. What we applaud is the implied stress on inquiry-related skills and history that is as contemporary as history can be. To be sure, we cannot rip out the Union Pacific tracks to replay the Westward Movement. But students who apply discussion, inquiry, and critical thinking processes will better understand the past.

In summary, our main intent has been to illustrate a general technique that has long been considered the exclusive domain of science teachers. We wish to clarify this false assumption; inquiry strategies, in fact, belong to all disciplines and to all grade levels. And, we must note, the use of inquiry, especially problem-solving, meets the criteria established by Eliot W. Eisner (1988) for *creative education*. You are being challenged to ask new questions and raise the consciousness of both students and fellow teachers. The only real limitation to the technique is your initiative.

Complete the formative evaluation and proceed to Chapter 9, where the topic of critical thinking is expanded further.

FORMATIVE EVALUATION *Inquiry*

A. Identify the response that *most* correctly completes the statement or answers the question.

_____ 1. An inquiry technique on the use of some instruments would help to bring out the idea that
 (a) A lecture demonstration should always be given before students touch the instruments.
 (b) Students should memorize the rules for handling the instruments before using them.
 (c) An inductive approach helps the students to make discoveries and generalizations that can be remembered.
 (d) The instruments are so complex that extensive lesson plans and learning techniques must be prepared.

_____ 2. To stress thinking skills properly, the teacher should emphasize which of the following:

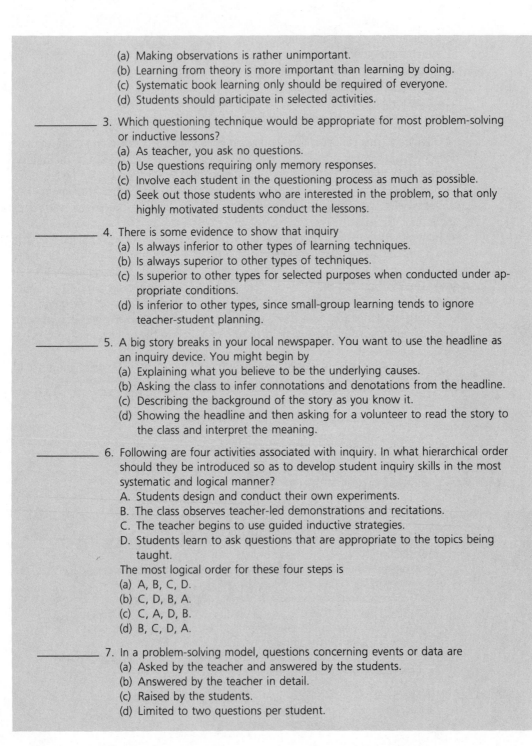

(a) Making observations is rather unimportant.
(b) Learning from theory is more important than learning by doing.
(c) Systematic book learning only should be required of everyone.
(d) Students should participate in selected activities.

_____ 3. Which questioning technique would be appropriate for most problem-solving or inductive lessons?
(a) As teacher, you ask no questions.
(b) Use questions requiring only memory responses.
(c) Involve each student in the questioning process as much as possible.
(d) Seek out those students who are interested in the problem, so that only highly motivated students conduct the lessons.

_____ 4. There is some evidence to show that inquiry
(a) Is always inferior to other types of learning techniques.
(b) Is always superior to other types of techniques.
(c) Is superior to other types for selected purposes when conducted under appropriate conditions.
(d) Is inferior to other types, since small-group learning tends to ignore teacher-student planning.

_____ 5. A big story breaks in your local newspaper. You want to use the headline as an inquiry device. You might begin by
(a) Explaining what you believe to be the underlying causes.
(b) Asking the class to infer connotations and denotations from the headline.
(c) Describing the background of the story as you know it.
(d) Showing the headline and then asking for a volunteer to read the story to the class and interpret the meaning.

_____ 6. Following are four activities associated with inquiry. In what hierarchical order should they be introduced so as to develop student inquiry skills in the most systematic and logical manner?
A. Students design and conduct their own experiments.
B. The class observes teacher-led demonstrations and recitations.
C. The teacher begins to use guided inductive strategies.
D. Students learn to ask questions that are appropriate to the topics being taught.
The most logical order for these four steps is
(a) A, B, C, D.
(b) C, D, B, A.
(c) C, A, D, B.
(d) B, C, D, A.

_____ 7. In a problem-solving model, questions concerning events or data are
(a) Asked by the teacher and answered by the students.
(b) Answered by the teacher in detail.
(c) Raised by the students.
(d) Limited to two questions per student.

_____ 8. If you decide to use inquiry strategies in your teaching, you will assume that
   (a) Inquiry teaching will require less time to achieve the instructional objective than does expository teaching.
   (b) Inquiry teaching requires about the same amount of time to achieve the instructional objective as does expository teaching.
   (c) Inquiry teaching requires a greater amount of time to achieve the instructional objective than does expository teaching.
   (d) None of the above.

_____ 9. When using *unguided inductive inquiry*
   (a) The objective is to arrive at one generalization.
   (b) There is usually a limited number of generalizations.
   (c) Materials are not essential to the success of the experience.
   (d) There is usually an unlimited number of generalizations proposed by the learners.

B. How would you use the following or similar short statement as an inquiry stimulus?

Agent Orange

Agent Orange is the U.S. military name for a mixture of two chemicals: 50% 2,4-dichlorophenoxyacetic acid and 50% 2,4,5-trichlorophenoxyacetic acid. These chemicals are defoliants, meaning that they cause trees and bushes to lose their leaves. A by-product formed when the chemicals are synthesized is "dioxin," which has been shown to cause cancer and birth defects.

During the Vietnam War, from 1965 to 1971, approximately 12 million gallons of Agent Orange with its dioxin contaminant were sprayed in South Vietnamese jungles to expose Viet Cong troops. The U.S. says this made our troops less vulnerable to ambush. Some 2.5 million U.S. servicemen in South Vietnam were exposed to Agent Orange, as well as much of the indigenous population of South Vietnam.

Following the Vietnam War many veterans have complained that exposure to Agent Orange has caused birth defects in their children. The Veteran's Administration's stand on the issue is that "There is no medical evidence to establish that exposure to Agent Orange has caused birth defects in the children of Vietnam veterans."

Now a recently released study of 40,000 Vietnamese families shows a high correlation between a man's exposure to Agent Orange and birth abnormalities in his children. A U.S. government study of Vietnam veterans is "years away from completion," according to the National Veteran's Law Center.

RESPONSES

A. 1. (c). The emphasis is on participation.
2. (d). Thinking strongly stresses activity.
3. (c). The technique requires much student interaction.
4. (c). As with any technique, inquiry must be used under the appropriate conditions.
5. (b). It is preferable to get the entire class involved.
6. (b). This is the most logical order, as it progresses from a simple pattern to a more complex one.

7. (c). This technique is described in the text.
8. (c). Undoubtedly, inquiry techniques require great amounts of time.
9. (d). With unguided inquiry, there is a tendency for an unlimited number of generalizations to be proposed.
  B. The essence would be to locate *evidence* to support or refute any statement.

REFERENCES

Abruscato, Joseph. *Children, Computers and Science Teaching: Butterflies and Bytes.* Englewood Cliffs, N.J.: Prentice-Hall, 1986.

Academic Preparation in Social Studies. New York: College Entrance Examination Board, 1986.

Baars, Patricia, Wynell Burroughs, and Jean Mueller. "Teaching with Documents." *Social Education* 50:1986, 317–318.

Banks, James A. *Teaching Strategies for the Social Studies: Inquiry, Valuing, and Decision-Making,* 3rd ed. New York: Longman, 1985.

Beyer, Barry K. "Using Writing to Learn Social Studies." *The Social Studies* 18:1982, 100–105.

Bibens, Robert F. "Using Inquiry Effectively." *Theory Into Practice* 19:1980, 87–92.

Billings, Henry F. *Skill Builders in Social Studies.* Portland, Maine: J. Weston Walch, 1985.

Birckbichler, Diane W., and Judith A. Muyskens. "A Personalized Approach to the Teaching of Literature at the Elementary and Intermediate Levels of Instruction." *Foreign Language Annuals* 13:1980, 23–27.

Brandt, Ronald S. "Teaching for Thinking." *Educational Leadership* 40:1983, 3, 80.

Brenneke, Judith, and John C. Soper. "Economics in the Secondary Classroom." In *Economics in the School Curriculum, K–12.* Mark C. Schug, ed. Washington, D.C.: National Education Association of the United States, 1985, pp. 60–73.

Bruner, Jerome S. *The Process of Education.* Cambridge: Harvard University Press, 1960.

Building a History Curriculum: Guidelines for Teaching History in Schools. The Bradley Commission on History in Schools. Washington, D.C.: Educational Excellence Network, 1988.

Carin, Arthur, and Robert Sund. *Teaching Modern Science,* 4th ed. Columbus, Ohio: Charles E. Merrill, 1985.

Carter, John Marshall. "The Bayeux Tapestry in the Social Studies Class." *Social Education* 50:1986, 314–315.

Census Education Project: 1990. Washington, D.C.: U.S. Bureau of the Census, Department of Commerce, 1989.

Ciardi, John. "Manner of Speaking." *Saturday Review,* passim; and telephone interview, April 27, 1979.

Deutchman, Sandra Salo. "Children's Art as an Entry to Art Criticism and History." Abstract in the *Proceedings of the International Society for Education Through Art.* European Congress, Stockholm, Sweden, August 14–18, 1988.

Dewey, John. *Democracy and Education.* New York: Macmillan, 1916.

———. *Experience and Education.* New York: Macmillan, 1938.

Eisner, Elliot W. "Qualitative Aspects of Evaluating Teaching." Tacoma, Wash.: Presentation at University of Puget Sound, March 10, 1988.

Eylon, Bat-Sheva and Marcia C. Linn. "Learning and Instruction: An Examination of Four Research Perspectives in Science Education." *Review of Educational Research* 58:1988, 251–301.

Frymier, Jack. *Graphs of America.* Bloomington, In: Phi Delta Kappa, 1989.

Gega, Peter C. *Science in Elementary Education,* 5th ed. New York: John Wiley, 1986.

Gisi, Lynn Grover, and Roy H. Forbes. *The Information Society: Are High School Graduates Ready?* Denver: Education Commission of the States, 1982.

Hofwolt, Clifford A. "Instructional Strategies in the

Science Classroom." In *Research Within Reach: Science Education.* David Holdzkom and Pamela B. Lutz, eds. Washington, D.C.: National Science Teachers Association, 1984, pp. 41–58.

Jacobson, Willard J., and Abby B. Bergman. *Science for Children: A Book for Teachers.* Englewood Cliffs, N.J.: Prentice-Hall, 1987.

Jones, Beau Fly, Annemarie Palincsar, Donna Ogle, and Eileen Carr. *Strategic Teaching and Learning: Cognitive Instruction in the Content Areas.* Alexandria, Va.: Association for Supervision and Curriculum Development, 1988.

Koballa, Thomas R., Jr., and Lowell J. Bethel. "Integration of Science and Other School Subjects." In *Research Within Reach: Science Education.* David Holdzkom and Pamela B. Lutz, eds. Washington, D.C.: National Teachers Association, 1984, pp. 79–107.

Kuhn, Thomas S. *The Structure of Scientific Revolutions.* Chicago: University of Chicago Press, 1962.

Lunetta, Vincent N., and Shimshon Novick. *Inquiring and Problem Solving in the Physical Sciences: A Source Book.* Dubuque, Iowa: Kendall/Hunt, 1981.

Marzano, Robert J., Ronald S. Brandt, Carolyn Sue Hughes, Beau Fly Jones, Barbara Z. Presseisen, Stuart C. Rankin, and Charles Sukov. *Dimensions of Thinking.* Alexandria, Va.: Association for Supervision and Curriculum Development, 1988.

McLeod, Richard J. "Teaching Problem-Solving Skills with a Weather and Climate Control Database." Presentation at the National Convention, National Science Teachers Association, St. Louis, Missouri, April 8, 1988.

Orlich, Donald C. "Science Inquiry and the Commonplace." *Science and Children* 26:March 1989, 22–24.

———. "The Zip Code Game." *Science and Children* 23:February 1986, 18–19.

Orlich, Donald C., and James M. Migaki. "What Is Your IQQ—Individual Questioning Quotient?" *Science and Children* 48:May 1981, 20–21.

Popper, Karl R. *The Logic of Scientific Discovery.* New York: Harper & Row, 1959.

Remy, Richard C. "The Constitution in Citizen Education." *Social Education* 5:1987, 331–335.

Schug, Mark C., and Stephen Haessler. "Teaching Economics Using the Local Community." In *Economics in the School Curriculum, K–12.* Mark C. Schug, ed. Washington, D.C.: National Education Association of the United States, 1985, pp. 92–106.

Shulman, Lee S., and Pinchas Tamir. "Research on Teaching in the Natural Sciences." In *Second Handbook of Research on Teaching.* Robert M. W. Travers, ed. Chicago: Rand McNally, 1973, pp. 1098–1148.

Strike, Kenneth A. "The Logic of Learning by Discovery." *Review of Educational Research* 45: 1975, 461–483.

Trowbridge, Leslie W., and Rodger Bybee. *Becoming a Secondary School Science Teacher,* 4th ed. Columbus, Ohio: Charles E. Merrill, 1986.

Vye, Nancy J., and John D. Bransford. "Programs for Teaching Thinking." *Educational Leadership* 26:1981, 26–28.

Webster's New Collegiate Dictionary, 8th ed. Springfield, Mass.: G. & C. Merriam, 1979, p. 326.

Whimbey, Arthur. "Teaching Sequential Thought: The Cognitive-Skills Approach." *Phi Delta Kappa* 58:1977, 255–259.

Womack, James G. *Discovering the Structure of the Social Studies.* New York: Benziger Brothers, 1966, p. 13.

Zevin, Jack. "Mystery Island: A Lesson in Inquiry." *Today's Education* 58:1969, 42–43.

ZPG Population Education Program. Washington, D.C.: Zero Population Growth, 1400 16th Street, N.W., 1989.

9

Decisions to Encourage Critical Thinking

*A*rthur Whimbey (1977) will ask you, "What day follows the day before yesterday if two days from now will be Sunday?" How would you answer his question? Most likely, you would "think" about the given information and try to arrange it in a way to determine the answer. However, when Whimbey asked this and similar questions of numerous college classes, many students did not know how to proceed. They either guessed an answer or gave up on the question.

The above example tends to validate conclusions from the National Assessment of Education Progress (NAEP) and the National Commission on Excellence in Education that students at all levels make no improvement in thinking processes as a result of schooling. In fact, the NAEP registered a decline of inferential thinking skills from thirteen-year olds to seventeen-year olds. Such data underscore the efforts of educational commentators such as John I. Goodlad (1984), Richard W. Paul (1984), and Barry K. Beyer (1988) to have schools take greater responsibility for teaching students to think more effectively. Indeed, John E. McPeck (1984) argues that such instruction is the primary purpose of schooling.

What do we mean when we say, "We will help students to become more thoughtful, to be better problem-solvers, or to become more effective thinkers?" Will we add a new course to the curriculum? Will we teach a new content area or a new group of process skills? Must we learn new methods of instruction and evaluation? These concerns and more will be addressed in this chapter. If your goal is to help students become better thinkers, then you must systematically and continually instruct in ways to think more effectively. You and every teacher have this responsibility. (See Marzano et al., 1988, for a major statement.) In addition, this chapter will show you several methods for including thinking instruction within the context of your teaching area.

Objectives   After completing this chapter, you should be able to:

- Identify several broad areas of thinking
- Identify particular skills related to thinking
- Plan instruction to include thinking skills among your objectives
- Prepare "thinking" lessons from knowledge-based texts
- Create and sustain an atmosphere supportive of thoughtful behavior in your classroom
- Understand the meaning of learning styles
- Reflect on ways to integrate learning styles and thinking

DEFINING THE TOPIC

First, it is necessary to specify what we mean by "thinking." The word is a construct, a label we apply to processes we cannot see but can only observe indirectly through actions or products. That is, when someone behaves in a careful, prudent manner, we infer the behavior to result from deliberate thought. When we observe an example of complex problem-solving—space flight, for instance—we infer the incredible amounts of reasoning that were necessary.

Attempts to define thinking—beyond the circularity of such synonyms as "reasoning" or "forming an idea"—become clouded by differences of psychological positions. Despite lack of consensus on definition, we can still characterize the concept of thinking and suggest methods to make its practice more effective.

We propose that "thinking" is a combination of knowledge, skills or processes, and attitudes. Knowledge is involved, of course, because thinking requires an object. One must think about *something*. The more knowledge one has in any area, the more effectively one can think about it. As Louis Pasteur commented, "Chance favors the prepared mind."

Specifically, subject-matter knowledge allows experts to recognize patterns and principles in a problem. In contrast, the novice focuses upon surface characteristics. The opening moves of chess, for example, are seen in terms of long-range strategy by the experienced player; the novice tends to concentrate on randomly selected short-term alternatives. In essence, there is a *qualitative* difference between the two players' thought patterns (Nickerson, 1985b).

Further, broad content knowledge increases your potential for helping students understand. Their understanding depends upon your expressing what they don't know in language they do know. Explanation is best done through analogies; for example, comparing molecular movement to the movements of guests in a several-tiered apartment building. Using imagery in comparisons is often a key to understanding, but only a deep knowledge of content can help us to recognize and use them (Marzano and Arredondo, 1986).

But we also recognize thinking to be comprised of several processes; that is, particular steps and techniques can be identified and shown to be more effective than other methods in particular circumstances. The opening problem of this chapter, concerning the day before yesterday, is most readily solved by a systematic, linear arrangement of the information, but such a method is not appropriate for all problems.

Figure 9-1 lists some of the skills associated with thinking. Systematic practice in helping students to identify and to use these skills must be a basic part of instruction in *all* classes if students are to benefit from schooling.

Thinking also contains attitudes or dispositions to perceive and relate to one's surroundings in particular ways. One can, for instance, be basically curious about one's environment, or one can be indifferent. Whichever choice (or, more likely, position along a continuum), the attitude determines in part *what* we think about and in *what ways* we think about it. But, because attitudes tend to be learned responses, we *can* help students adopt appropriate ones for effective thinking. Such attitudes include the following:

- A willingness to suspend judgment until sufficient evidence is presented
- A tolerance for ambiguity
- A willingness to question rather than simply to accept authority
- A willingness to believe as evidence dictates

Figure 9-1   *Skills Associated with Effective Thinking*

General Skills	Skills to Identify Examples of	Skills to Distinguish
Observe	Patterns	Relevant from irrelevant data
Compare/contrast	Relationships	Verifiable from nonverifiable
Classify	Cause/effect	data
Infer	Assumptions	Problems from irrelevant
Interpret	Reasoning errors	statements
Summarize	Logical fallacies	
Analyze	Bias	
Synthesize		
Generalize		
Hypothesize		
Imagine		
Establish criteria		

As an educator you will find useful the following characterization of thinking: *Thinking is a complex act composed of attitudes, knowledge, and skills by which the individual can relate to and shape the environment more effectively than intuition alone would allow.* (See especially Ennis, 1979; Smith, 1975; Paul, 1984; McPeck, 1981; Ennis, 1985; and Beyer, 1987, for more detailed discussions of the elements basic to thinking.)

The above statement focuses our attention upon those aspects of thinking that can be identified and taught to students—namely, knowledge, skills, and attitudes. The assumption is, of course, that students will think more effectively as a result; that they will be able to relate to and alter their environment better than they otherwise would. While such a result seems intuitively reasonable, considerable empirical evidence also supports it. Of many studies, the following are particularly applicable: Arthur N. Applebee (1984), "Writing and Reasoning"; Benjamin S. Bloom (1984), "The 2 Sigma Problem"; Arthur L. Costa (1984), "Mediating the Metacognitive"; and Raymond S. Nickerson (1984), "Kinds of Thinking Taught in Current Programs."

REVIEW QUESTIONS FOR DISCUSSION

In keeping with the chapter topic, we have appropriately altered the Formative Evaluations. Work alone or in small groups to solve the exercises.

1. Identify the steps by which you answered the opening question.

2. What factors in schooling might be related to a reported decline in thinking skills between ages thirteen and seventeen?

3. What reasons can you suggest for urging schools to improve students' thinking processes?

4. What behaviors seem to be associated with thinking?

5. In what ways might knowledge in such fields as chemistry, ecology, or teaching be related to productive thinking in that field?

6. Can you identify additional skills and attitudes that seem relevant to effective thinking?

7. List the ways that you can associate Bloom's Cognitive Taxonomy with this description of thinking.

CATEGORIES OF THINKING

Within the framework of the characterization presented above about the thinking process, we can identify several varieties of thinking for instructional purposes. It must be understood, however, that such a division is artificial, for thinking itself is a *whole* act, greater than the sum of its parts.

There may be many other ways to subdivide and categorize the processes. Moreover, the categories are not discrete; each overlaps the other, with influence extending in both directions. Thus, upon the basis of current knowledge, and to be of most value for instructional purposes, we can characterize thought as being a nebulously bounded aggregate of processes, with each process exercising some influence on all others.

Critical Thinking

The three varieties of thought (or categories of processes) that can be isolated for instructional purposes are (1) critical thinking, (2) problem-solving, and (3) creative thought. Each has distinguishing as well as shared characteristics. Critical thought is distinguished by being essentially evaluative. It answers the questions "what shall I believe?" or "which alternative shall I select?" Such thought is characterized by establishing criteria for belief and action and by maintaining an attitude of "reflective skepticism" and suspended judgment until all relevant data have been considered. Formal logic and the analysis of evidence are among the tools by which the critical thinker determines what can reasonably be believed. (See especially Ennis, 1985, and McPeck, 1981, for discussions of critical thinking, and Chapter 4 to review the evaluation category of the cognitive taxonomy.)

Problem-Solving

Problem-solving thought tends to be a systematic, analytical process by which we use what is known to discover what is not known. The steps for solving a linear equation in algebra are an example; when we arrange and manipulate the symbols in a particular way, we can determine the unknown values. Such thought processes are usually based upon the empirical acts of observing, inferring, generalizing or predicting, and testing of the predictions, as stressed in Chapter 8. The "scientific method" is an example of this process. It should be noted, however, that the most productive problem-solving is often accompanied by creative insight. (Discussion of problem-solving can be found in Whimbey, 1984; Tuma and Reif, 1980; and Wells and Wells, 1984.)

Creative Thought

Creative thinking, of course, focuses upon developing original solutions, products, or processes. Although often considered the particular province of writer, musician, or artist, creativity is part of each person's "universe" of thinking skills; it can be developed as readily as the other types of thinking are. Creative thinking is marked by imaginative, divergent approaches to problems. At least initially, quantity, variety, and diversity of thought are most important; and intuition (or a "hunch") is a useful knowledge source. As an introductory process to approaching any problem, creative thought is a most useful tool. (Refer to Chapter 4 again to review the discussion of synthesis in the cognitive domain and to Chapter 6 to review divergent and evaluative questions.)

Figure 9-2 uses a Venn diagram (a useful thinking tool) to illustrate a relationship among the several categories of thinking. Current knowledge does not tell us how large the inner circles should be, either in relation to one another or to the entirety of thinking skills. Thus, no inferences should be drawn other than that the areas are part of thinking and are interrelated.

Figure 9-3 lists essential elements associated with the three types of thinking. Since the types are not mutually exclusive, some characteristics can appear in all categories. The chart points out those which make each type distinctive.

An example may illustrate the relationships among the several varieties of thought. The state of South Carolina, since the 1940s, has had an atomic/nuclear research facility operated by the federal government through private contractors. Recently, the disposal of radioactive waste from the facility has become controversial among the state's residents. Resolution of the controversy might involve all the above processes in the following way.

The empirical analytical techniques of problem-solving would gather data to determine if, indeed, a problem exists and, if so, its extent and possible solutions. The assembled data would be tested for credibility by the methods of critical thinking. If problems were found, the divergent, imaginative approaches of creative thought

Figure 9-2   *Relationship Among Three Types of Thinking*

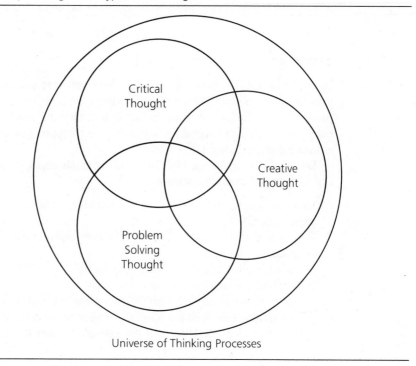

Universe of Thinking Processes

Figure 9-3
Characteristics of Three Types of Thought

Critical Thought	Problem Solving Thought	Creative Thought
* Evaluative by stated criteria	• Analytical	! Intuitive
* Reflective skepticism	• Empirical	! Speculative
* Suspended judgment	• Systematic	! Questioning
* Use of logical analysis	• Uses heuristics	! Synthesizes experiences
* Systematic	• Uses algorithms	
	• Convergent	
	• Linear	

would be applicable in determining possible solutions. Finally, establishing criteria for an acceptable solution and making a decision would be the function of critical thought.

Summary

In brief, this introduction has asserted that improving students' thought processes must be a responsibility of schooling. Further, we have examined the nature of those processes and defined thinking in terms that indicate instructional boundaries. Finally, we have characterized three types of thinking processes that we can artificially isolate for instructional purposes.

Before you examine methods for teaching and learning these processes, consider the following discussion questions.

1. Can you identify additional types of thinking? What would be characteristic of these types?
2. How would the three categories described be useful, if at all, in the following situations:
   a. A judge presiding over a homicide trial
   b. The defense attorney in the same trial
   c. An engineer designing a bridge to replace the Golden Gate Bridge
   d. An architect designing a shopping mall in an expanding urban area.
3. What other characteristics can you assign to each of the three thinking categories?

INSTRUCTIONAL ASSUMPTIONS

What can you, as a teacher, do to help your students improve their thinking processes? Begin with the following assumption: All subjects in the school curriculum can be taught and learned in ways that will not only transmit information but will also enhance thinking abilities. Thus, the problem is not to determine which subject or grade should teach "thinking skills," nor is it to structure a separate class for teaching of thought processes. The problem is for you and every other teacher to determine how you can most effectively present your subject to use students' present base of skills, knowledge, and attitudes for further development (see Tiedt et al., 1988).

Second, accept Robert H. Ennis's assertion (1985) that the teacher is the most important factor in thinking instruction. Prepared texts, workbooks, preplanned programs, and drill exercises may be useful instructional aids, but of themselves they are insufficient to induce thinking abilities. The most effective instruction emanates from a teacher who is knowledgeable about both subject matter and thinking processes; who demonstrates continually the skills and attitudes previously listed; and who demands systematic, rigorous thought from students—both in speaking and in writing.

Finally, determine to increase your own knowledge systematically, both in subject matter areas and in learning about thought processes. As you learn more of both, only your imagination can limit the methods by which you can present your subjects in ways to encourage and improve thought processes. This chapter, its review exercises, and the suggested reading are a beginning to a long intellectual journey.

ORGANIZING THINKING INSTRUCTION

Arthur L. Costa (1985) suggests that much thinking instruction can be organized around three concepts: teaching "for" thinking, teaching "of" thinking, and teaching "about" thinking. These useful concepts for shaping all instruction will be explored in detail to help you plan thinking skills into your lesson.

Teaching "for" Thinking

Teaching "for" thinking means creating and sustaining a learning environment that promotes and rewards disciplined, reasoned, and/or creative thought. A basic question always before the class should be: "For what reasons—or based on what evidence—do you believe, think, or act in that way?" "Reasons" and "evidence," of course, are the key words. A thought-provoking environment places value on knowledge, opinion, and authority only to the extent that each is supported. You and the students are encouraged to question yourselves, one another, and your texts to determine the evidence on which belief and opinion rest. Naturally, you should execute such a questioning process carefully (as with any instructional method) to avoid embarrassing or discouraging students. If tactfully and skillfully maintained, the freedom to question—and particularly an insistence upon reasoned, well-supported answers—can create an environment encouraging to the development of thought processes.

A "thinking" atmosphere can also be enhanced by systematically promoting both creative and divergent thought as students discuss their assignments. The following suggestions should help you think of others applicable to your teaching area. You might review techniques for questioning (Chapter 6) and small-group discussions (Chapter 7).

Multiple Answers   Ask for "an" answer rather than "the" answer. This promotes multiple answers and provides a less threatening atmosphere for a student's reply by making almost any relevant answer at least partially acceptable. Also, the "guess what the teacher is thinking" problem is avoided. Note the following four examples:

a. What was a reason the Puritans came to America?
b. What is one argument opposing a sales tax?

c. Given these data (an algebra story problem), how might we proceed?

d. What is one way we might improve the election of the President?

Summaries   Summarize (or have a student summarize) discussion answers on the chalkboard or an overhead transparency. Data are thus before the students at all times, reinforced visually rather than simply being heard and (perhaps) remembered. Building arguments, noting strengths or weaknesses of evidence, and accepting or rejecting statements then becomes a more logical, systematic process.

Brainstorming   Use brainstorming frequently to generate numerous and perhaps creative possible solutions in a nonjudgmental atmosphere. Again, use the chalkboard, newsprint, or a transparency to keep data visible. For example:

a. What verbs describe how John crossed the room?

b. What *might* happen if we inflate the balloon in a vacuum?

c. What *could* result from increasing the average lifespan to ninety years?

Small Groups   Use small groups of six to eight students frequently to encourage a thinking atmosphere and to reinforce skills and attitudes. Two methods below have proven useful to one of your authors in secondary English and history classes.

First, divide a problem or area of instruction into several parts. Each group works on one part; then each brings its solution or information to the class for large-group consideration. Examples of suitable problems include political, social, and economic causes of the American Civil War, or influences of French, Latin, and German words on English vocabulary.

Second, allow each small group to consider the same problem; then present *its solutions and reasoning* to the class. The whole class then determines the best solution based on the *evidence presented*. Current social and political issues—particularly those affecting young people—are sources for such problems. Consider the following examples:

a. In what ways is a sales tax discriminatory?

b. What can *our school* do to decrease drug use?

Questioning   Use specific questioning techniques (see Chapter 6) to maintain a thinking atmosphere while helping students become accustomed to supporting their opinions with reasons. Probing, clarifying, and multiple-response questions are particularly effective. Consider how the following questioning sequence might help to sustain a thoughtful atmosphere.

a. Give one example of poverty as a cause of social revolution? (*Pause.*) John?

b. Support John's reply. (*Pause.*) Carol, Bart?

c. What *reasons* suggest a disagreement with Carol's and Bart's replies? (*Pause.*) Mike, Connie?

d. Suggest another example of poverty as a cause of social revolution. (*Pause.*) Laura, Ann?

In summary, you teach "for" thinking by deliberately creating a classroom atmosphere that encourages thoughtful, reasoned, and critical approaches to learning. You do this by your behavior as a teacher, by the tasks you ask of your students, and by the questioning and discussion strategies you use in conducting your classes.

REVIEW QUESTIONS FOR DISCUSSION

1. What are several characteristics of a "thinking atmosphere" in a classroom?

2. Suggest additional techniques for establishing and maintaining a thinking atmosphere.

3. What specific steps might encourage a thinking atmosphere in the following subjects?
   (a) Home economics
   (b) Physical education
   (c) Keyboarding (typing or computing)
   (d) Art
   (e) Music

4. How can the presence or absence of a thinking atmosphere be noted by the following?
   (a) A pupil
   (b) A teacher from another class
   (c) A parent

5. Use the following question in a small-group activity: "What would be the effects upon the following areas of society if the schools succeed in significantly improving thinking abilities?"
   (a) Schools
   (b) Colleges
   (c) Government
   (d) Business
   (e) Entertainment, especially television

Teaching "of" Thinking

Refer again to Figure 9-1 on p. 324. These are the skills generally considered essential for effective, purposeful thinking. Teaching "of" thinking means to instruct your students directly in these skills. Such instruction includes identifying individual skills, providing examples of their use, demonstrating, and providing guided practice for the students. To the degree that discrete skills are part of thought processes, it makes intuitive sense that such instruction is beneficial. Additionally, there is considerable empirical evidence suggesting that (1) such instruction does indeed improve thinking ability, and (2) without such instruction, most students are not likely to develop thought processes as effectively. (See particularly Gibson, 1985; Bredderman, 1983; Costa, 1985.)

When included at all in the curriculum, thinking skills instruction is usually organized in one of two ways: either as a separate course based on packaged learning materials or as an integration or "infusion" of thinking skills within one or more content areas of instruction. Both methods have advocates who urge that their way is the most effective. Many of their differences, however, reflect differing concepts of what constitutes thinking, its processes, and its improvement. The following discussion will indicate strengths and weaknesses of both approaches, give examples, and conclude that either method, effectively taught, can help students improve their thinking. (See Ennis, 1989, for extended discussion.)

Thinking Skills Program

Numerous programs intended to improve thinking skills have been published in recent years. Each defines "thinking," "skills," and "improvement" in a particular way, then provides instructional materials and suggestions for teaching.

Figure 9-4 illustrates one program, "Strategic Reasoning," developed by John Glade and based on research by Albert Upton of Whittier College. This program,

Figure 9-4   *"Strategic Reasoning"*

The Four Instructional Stages of the Strategic Reasoning™ Program

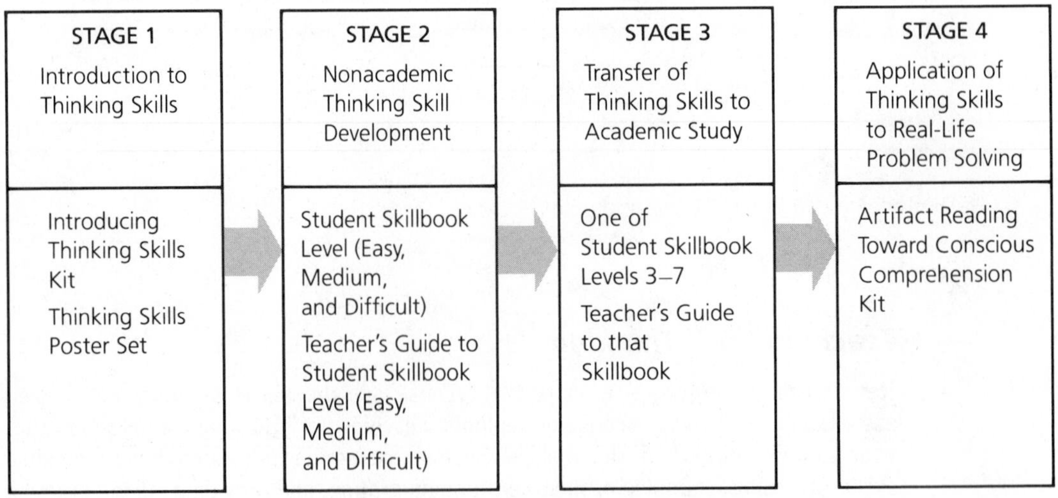

STAGE 1	STAGE 2	STAGE 3	STAGE 4
Introduction to Thinking Skills	Nonacademic Thinking Skill Development	Transfer of Thinking Skills to Academic Study	Application of Thinking Skills to Real-Life Problem Solving
Introducing Thinking Skills Kit Thinking Skills Poster Set	Student Skillbook Level (Easy, Medium, and Difficult) Teacher's Guide to Student Skillbook Level (Easy, Medium, and Difficult)	One of Student Skillbook Levels 3–7 Teacher's Guide to that Skillbook	Artifact Reading Toward Conscious Comprehension Kit

Source: John J. Glade and Howard Citron, "Strategic Reasoning." In Arthur L. Costa, ed., *Developing Minds*. Alexandria, Va.: Association for Supervision and Curriculum Development, 1985, pp. 198–200. Used with permission of ASCD and Innovative Science, Inc. Copyright 1985, ASCD.

Figure 9-5   *Sample from the Expanded Solution Key*

To academic curriculum to increase content mastery

EASY

Study the example. Then choose from the numbered items and write your answer.

Ex: ___ fa ___ as ___ moth ___   A. ___ bat ___ as ___ sit ___
       father   (mother)   batter   (   )

    (1) moth   (1) site
    (2) mother   (2) down
    (3) mole   (3) sitter

MODERATE

Read and explain this analogy.

| brain |
| nervous system |
| electricity |

as

| computer |
| wiring system |
| electricity |

DIFFICULT

Complete the statements below by selecting words selected from the following: *necessity, necessary, state, achievement, achieve*

Independence is a _____ for a nation to   (_____) as (_____)
achieve _____ admission at the United Nations.   (_____) as (_____)
In the same way, confidence is a _____ in
order for a man to _____ success at home and
on the job.

Write an analogy that will express the ideas in the   (_____) as (_____)
above statements.

Source: John J. Glade and Howard Citron, "Strategic Reasoning." In Arthur L. Costa, ed., *Developing Minds*. Alexandria, Va.: Association for Supervision and Curriculum Development, 1985, pp. 198–200. Used with permission of ASCD and Innovative Science, Inc. Copyright 1985, ASCD.

which identifies six thinking skills as the basis of all thinking, provides instruction in three areas: nonacademic, academic, and "real-life performance and success" (Costa, 1985, p. 201). Figure 9-4 shows the overall program; Figure 9-5 shows increasingly difficult levels of verbal analogies (academic curriculum), and Figure 9-6 is an example of a nonverbal analogy from the nonacademic curriculum. Table 9-1 highlights several other programs. Review of those programs and numerous others

Figure 9-6   *Sample Applications of the Seeing Analogies Thinking Skill*

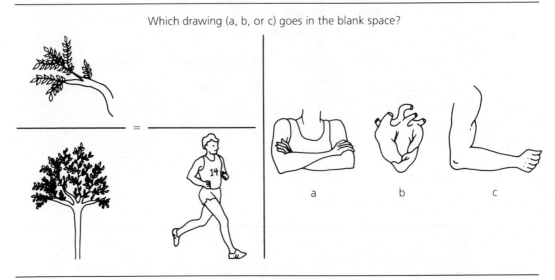

Source: John J. Glade and Howard Citron, "Strategic Reasoning." In Arthur L. Costa, ed., *Developing Minds.* Alexandria, Va.: Association for Supervision and Curriculum Development, 1985, pp. 198–200. Used with permission of ASCD and Innovative Science, Inc. Copyright 1985, ASCD.

Table 9-1   *A Sample of Thinking Skills Programs*

Program	Author	Goal or Emphasis
Higher-Order Thinking Skills (HOTS)	Stanley Pogrow	Compensatory program, basic learning and problem-solving skills, grades 3–6.
Instrumental Enrichment	Reuven Feuerstein	Overall cognitive performance of low-achieving adolescents; produce autonomous learner.
Cognitive Research Trust (CORT)	Edward de Bono	Cognitive skills for daily living; creative problem-solving.
Philosophy for Children	Matthew Lipman	Think about thinking; excellence in all aspects of thinking.
Strategic Reasoning	Albert Upton, John Glade	Conscious use of six basic thinking skills for effective living.
Structure of the Intellect (SOI)	Mary Meeker, J. P. Guilford	Basic and higher-level critical thinking abilities.
Synectics	William Gordon	Creative problem-solving.

Source: Arthur L. Costa, ed., *Developing Minds.* Alexandria, Va.: Association for Supervision and Curriculum Development, 1985, pp. 187–243.

can be found in *Developing Minds,* edited by Arthur L. Costa and published by the Association for Supervision and Curriculum Development, 1985.

Two major strengths are associated with the separate programs approach. First, a standard, uniform curriculum is provided, as the teacher has no problems of materials development and use. Freed from finding materials and developing lesson plans, you can concentrate just on delivering instruction. To use the program effectively, you need only to be trained adequately (a critical factor in all instructional changes) and to follow the program as described.

Second, separate programs are often assumed to be more effective because the student's entire attention is focused upon skills, rather than being partly distracted by subject matter. Edward de Bono, developer of the Cognitive Research Trust (CoRT) Program, summarized this position by concluding that emphasis on content distracts from attending to the thinking processes being used. He cautioned against trying to think thought patterns while actually experiencing the thoughts (Costa, 1985, p. 206).

Opponents of thinking skills programs raise several issues. Some (Snook, 1974; Berlak, 1965; McPeck, 1984) assert that there are no "general reasoning skills" except in a superficial way. Certainly one observes, infers, and hypothesizes in thinking, but the nature of these activities is fundamentally different in each subject. Observation in history, opponents maintain, is a different process from observation in physics—a difference determined by the nature of what is observed and the uses to be made of the data. Such objections are said to apply to any list of general thinking skills.

Other opponents to thinking skills programs (Paul, 1984; Scriven, 1985; McPeck, 1984; Glaser, 1985) argue that, although skills such as logical analysis may be involved, effective thinking is primarily a matter of having accurate information. The kinds of issues requiring the most serious thought—how to direct one's personal or professional life, how ecology and economy should be balanced, how society can survive in a nuclear age—are primarily dependent upon precise, specific information. Voting to approve or oppose a nuclear waste site, for instance, raises many complex issues—issues centering on technical details of radiation and its long-term effects on the environment. For example, Faith Hickman (1985) presents an excellent example of the asbestos problem by creating a case study of the Johns Manville Corporation decision to file for bankruptcy. For important, "real life" issues, then, marketed thinking skills programs can be opposed as insufficient and perhaps even irrelevant.

Finally, specific programs are often opposed as being extremely difficult to incorporate into an already crowded curriculum. Particularly is this true of most middle and secondary schools where, if one class is added, another must be dropped or else the entire curriculum be reorganized. Most schools have not, and probably will not, reorganize their schedules to accommodate one class.

Many programs are available that claim to enhance thinking skills. Diversity among the programs, and opposition to them, is evidence of the diversity of what constitutes "thinking" and "skills." A decision to use such a program must be based on careful matching between student needs and the programs being used in the classroom (see Feldhusen and Clinkenbeard, 1986).

REVIEW QUESTIONS FOR DISCUSSION

1. Examine the thinking skills listed in Figure 9-1. Selecting three, show how they are generic; that is, how they are essentially the same skill regardless of subject matter.

2. Again from Figure 9-1, select three skills and show how they would differ across academic disciplines. Is evaluation, for example, the same process in literature as in chemistry? If not, what differences do you note?

3. Explain at least one advantage each of the following groups might find in having thinking skills taught from a prepared program:
   a. Parents   d. Students
   b. Principals   e. Teachers
   c. School board

4. Using the same groups as in question 3, explain at least one disadvantage.

5. Describe ways a teacher might model or demonstrate particular thinking skills, both orally and in writing. Especially consider observing, inferring, analyzing.

Infused or Integrated Instruction

In contrast to a separate program approach, an infusion method teaches "of" thinking by including skills instruction within the subject matter taught. Earlier in the chapter we noted the essence of this approach: all subjects can be taught and learned in ways that will not only transmit information but will also enhance thinking abilities.

An example best illustrates this approach. Consider a high school class in United States history focusing on the colonial period. One way to combine thinking skills and content coverage would be to have students prepare a large wall chart of specific characteristics from several colonies. These might be geographic features, economic characteristics, or social backgrounds and attitudes. From these data, students could infer and hypothesize colonists' possible attitudes toward future events such as declaring independence, free public education, or eliminating slavery. Similarly, science teachers could help students create a periodic chart of the elements through observing, inferring, and generalizing rather than simply trying to understand a given example.

Note how many of the skills listed in Figure 9-1 (p. 324) could be reinforced in examples. Depending upon instructional emphasis, students could be involved with virtually all thinking processes, from low-order observing and classifying to the highest levels of distinguishing relevant and irrelevant statements. Proponents of this approach (Beyer, 1985; Solomon, 1987; and Parker, 1987) assert that such flexibility—the applicability of virtually any subject matter to teach a full range of thought processes—is the primary strength of the infused approach.

Other strengths, as well, are often attributed to an infused approach. Some proponents assert that content and thought are inseparable: we must think about *something.* Jerome W. Bruner (1960) used this position to launch the curriculum reform programs of the 1960s and 1970s by asserting that understanding of a subject means thinking like a practitioner of that subject. Thus, major curriculum efforts such as Man: A Course of Study (MACOS), Biological Science Curriculum Study (BSCS), School of Mathematics Study Group (SMSG), and Science: A Process Approach (SAPA) were essentially inductively oriented programs to teach content by helping students to think like anthropologists, biologists, mathematicians, and scientists, respectively.

Finally, some urge an integrated approach on the basis of efficient transfer of learning. *Teach for transfer* has long been an instructional truism that is supported by learning theorists (Hilgard and Bower, 1966). Robert Sternberg (Baron and Sternberg, 1987, p. 258) asserts that specific teaching to promote transfer is equally true of thinking skills. Maximum transfer results only from a close correlation between classroom-taught processes and thinking processes necessary beyond the skill.

Criticism of the infused approach centers on two areas—uniformity of program and reduced content coverage. Critics note that leaving each teacher responsible to incorporate skills into content gives no assurances of what skills, if any, will be learned. Further, detractors argue that even if all teachers are conscientious in such instruction, they may not be either consistent or systematic; they may needlessly repeat some skills while overlooking others. At the same time, critics argue, content coverage is diminished when thinking skills are stressed. Replies to these criticisms note that thinking skills instruction should be systematically woven into the K–12 curriculum to assure adequate coverage, *assigning particular skills at appropriate grades and classes.* Since content and thinking skills are not easily separated in any subject, the loss of "coverage" time is often regarded as an irrelevant issue.

Teaching "of" thinking, then, means deliberately instructing in the skills and techniques of effective thought. Such instruction tends to follow one of two patterns. The first creates a separate program or class for this subject. The second integrates the relevant skills within all classes. Both methods have strengths and weaknesses. It seems more likely, though, that the infused approach will predominate, since most schools are not likely to revise their curricula to accommodate a new program—at least, not without considerable evidence that it is the better alternative. Moreover, the infused approach also seems reasonably the better way. Careful, effective thinking is as much an attitude as a set of skills; it is a way of approaching life as well as school. Thinking belongs in every class, every day, modeled and encouraged by teachers who themselves are dedicated to the pursuit of intellectual excellence.

Instructional Strategies

As noted previously, teaching "of" thinking is as much an attitude and way of life in the classroom as it is a set of teaching behaviors. But you can strengthen these attitudes with several techniques and strategies that have proven effective across

Figure 9-7   *Instructional Assumptions for Teaching "of" Thinking*

- There are many possible instructional objectives and many teaching methods to achieve them.

    Therefore,

- Teachers should select methods to match objectives,

    realizing that

- No single learning experience, of itself, has a very profound effect upon the learner;

    therefore,

- Educational experiences must reinforce one another,

    through

- Systematically and continually reinforcing and building upon what students already know,

    in order to

- Help students create meaning and develop understanding of what they need to know

    which are

- The primary goals of schooling.

many subject areas. Figure 9-7 states assumptions that underlie these methods. Table 9-2 and Figure 9-8 outline several relevant strategies. Explanations supplement each figure.

Implicit in Figure 9-7 is the assumption that *information processing psychology* and *schema theory* are the most useful explanations of how students learn. Information processing psychology asserts that learning is an interactive process between the learner and the environment, with both contributing; that is, the learner is not just a passive receiver of stimuli. (See Woolfolk, 1987, for discussion.) Schema theory asserts that we organize what we learn according to patterns or *schema,* which help us *make sense* of the multiple stimuli we constantly receive. Learning becomes an *individual meaning-building process,* by which the student either relates new data to existing patterns or must create new schema in order to understand. (See Smith, 1975, for discussion.)

From this base of instructional assumptions, then, the techniques in Table 9-2 are reasonable and empirically verified ways to help students improve their thinking processes. The table illustrates an instructional process to keep thinking skills constantly before your students. These techniques have proven useful across a broad range of subjects, from primary grades to graduate school.

The first strategy, and of primary importance, is to plan your instruction to emphasize thought processes. This planning usually results in a different organization

Figure 9-8

Structuring of Knowledge for Thinking

	Examples
Facts: Items of specific information at the lowest available level of abstraction. Facts have no transfer value and no predictive value.	Commodore Perry visited Japan in 1853 Rainfall 80 inches last year 82 percent urbanization 11,000,000 tons of coal 18 percent arable land Abraham Lincoln elected President in 1860
Concepts: A word or phrase that denotes a category of information. Concepts may range from high-level abstractions that encompass numerous specifics to a lower-order abstraction near a concrete base. They are the understandings each of us has about the discrete items that make up our world; from simple, concrete examples such as dogs to the abstract idea of democracy. Basic concepts have the power to organize and symbolize vast amounts of information. Any one concept can be illustrated at different levels of complexity, abstraction, generality.	Scarcity Interdependence Power Interaction Raw materials Division of labor Culture Relative location Conflict Comparative advantage Social control
Generalizations: A broad inclusive statement of relationships among concepts. Generalizations have degrees of complexity and completeness and can be the essence of the principle. Generalizations are derived from social studies content, but they are not content themselves. They have content as their source, and their substantiation and proof comes from content. Although generalizations may vary in their inclusiveness, the most useful one should have universal application and contain no references to any particular peoples, places, or times. Often, they have predictive value.	Since natural resources are limited and human wants unlimited, every society has developed a method for allocating its scarce resources. Every society has had rules, written or unwritten, by which social control over the people's conduct is maintained.

Used with permission of Thomas P. Ruff.

from that of a textbook. History texts, for instance, nearly all organize facts chronologically; yet, such a structure may have little relationship to thinking about history. A more effective organizer is to arrange historical facts around selected basic concepts and generalizations of that subject.

Definitions and examples of the key organizational terms (facts, concepts, and generalizations) are summarized in Figure 9-8. Notice from this illustration that a fact—"Rainfall was 80 inches last year"—is of little importance in isolation. Facts

Table 9-2   *Ten Teacher Behaviors That Encourage Thinking Skills*

1. *Plan* for thinking. Develop units and lessons based on concepts and generalizations.

2. *Teach* for meaning. Connect each lesson to the student's experience.

3. *Ask* thought-provoking questions. "How do you know?" "What is the main idea?" "What alternatives can we think of?"

4. *Make* students aware of their mental processes. "From your observations about prices in this chart, what might we infer about supply and demand?"

5. *Explain* your thought processes frequently. "On this tape I recorded my thought as I planned today's lesson. As you listen, identify examples of the following thinking skills."

6. *Keep* data before students. Summarize and record student answers on the board or a transparency.

7. *Call* on students to explain. Give students frequent opportunities to explain what they do or don't understand.

8. *Encourage* credibility as a criterion. "Does this make sense?" "Why not?"

9. *Be consistent.* Thinking instruction should be part of each lesson, each day.

10. *Be patient.* Significant change requires at least a semester.

must be related to broader terms such as the concept of "geographic regions" or the generalization that "amount of rainfall determines building construction methods" before they have significance. Effective instructional planning first determines the primary generalizations relevant to a unit or a course. The key concepts essential to understanding each generalization are determined, and they become the subjects of individual lessons. Finally, facts needed to understand each concept are selected and the lesson is planned. If you do the above process carefully and consistently, with an emphasis upon students' understanding rather than simply memorizing material, you will be developing thinking skills effectively, and your content coverage will have a meaningful pattern to the student.

"Thinking aloud" is a second technique for keeping thought processes before your students. The rationale for this technique is that by stating your own thinking steps in problem-solving, you become aware of the steps and perhaps may verbally create alternative methods. In this example, a listener is included to note confusions and ask for clarifications (see Whimbey, 1977). One way to introduce students to the method is to have them read aloud a sample problem from one of the textbooks being studied.

Another think-aloud method is to use your own thought processes as examples. Share with students the thinking steps you follow in planning a lesson, making a conclusion, or working any other activity relevant to them. Have your students identify particular skills and suggest other strategies you might have followed. Such examples can take the forms of printed handouts, audiotapes, or perhaps an unrehearsed problem-solving exploration of a student's question or of a problem being studied.

Once students understand the think-aloud process, they can pair up and practice by using selected topics related to classroom issues and subject-matter content. A useful exercise is for pairs of students to explain to each other their understanding of an assignment and the steps they will follow in completing it. This exercise discovers ambiguities in assignments and helps students identify productive thinking and study strategies. Two considerations, though, are paramount in all thinking-aloud exercises: (1) *each* student must have as much practice as possible, and (2) *process* of thinking (in this instance) is more important than product—the objective is to identify effective steps, not necessarily to find a solution. This technique is ideal for open-ended science activities.

The final technique that has been found generally useful for implementing the methods shown in Table 9-2 is the summarizing of main ideas. Sources of such summaries abound in all subjects and within many routine classroom activities. Basically, a summary exercise takes the form of "Tell me, in your own words. . . ." The reference may be to outlining the steps in a math solution, to listing causes of a social condition, or to giving reactions to an assembly speaker. Your imagination is the only limit to the choices.

The summary can be made in writing or orally. Considerable evidence (see Gibson, 1985, for a summary) suggests that the act of writing is itself both an exercise of thinking skills and a generator of those skills. We must think to write, but frequently when writing we make statements we had not thought of before beginning. Thus, *any* writing associated with learning is probably useful. Writing summaries, however, is even more effective, since it forces the student to develop criteria for rating some ideas more important than others. Such activity stimulates and reinforces the highest-levels of thinking skills.

Gordon Wells and Joan Wells (1984) assert that oral summaries are also effective in helping students develop speaking skills that will readily transfer beyond school. Moreover, oral summaries can be part of the dialogue that is an essential in developing student critical reasoning.

When you assign a summarizing activity to a student, observe the following four precautions:

- Insist upon students' own words, not quotations, to stimulate understanding of the material summarized.
- Limit the length, whether written or oral, to assure that students have judged the relative importance of ideas.
- Have students discuss the summaries, especially the establishment of criteria for including and excluding information.
- Have students discuss the summarizing process: what steps were followed, what *dead ends* were reached, what problems developed, what the final conclusion is.

Summary

Procedures for *teaching of thinking* require instruction in specific skills that focus on thinking. First, including thinking skills within unit and lesson planning is basic. Such instruction will not occur unless you deliberately arrange it. Second, you need to base your instruction on a reasonable theory of how students learn. Information processing and schema theory are suggested as initial steps. Finally, you need to emphasize teaching techniques that have been shown to improve thinking processes. Students must be directly involved in explaining, oral problem-solving, and summary writing. Intentionally invite students to evaluate their own thinking and that of others.

REVIEW QUESTIONS FOR DISCUSSION

1. Referring to Figure 9-7 (p. 338), list at least five subjects, each matched to a "best" method of instruction. Use at least three different methods.

2. Using text references for sources, write a brief summary of schema theory.

3. Within your teaching area, write three generalizations, each of which could serve as the focus of an instructional unit. For each generalization, identify the concepts and explain their relationships.

4. Examine a chapter in any elementary or secondary textbook in your teaching area. How many concepts do you find? Selecting three of the concepts, explain what students could *do* to demonstrate understanding.

5. Use the oral problem-solving method described, with a partner, to explain the process you would follow in preparing a lesson plan.

Thinking "About" Thinking

To teach "about" thinking is based on the assumption that the more students know about thinking as *content,* the more effective their own thinking becomes. The previous concepts provided an atmosphere *for* thinking and began teaching skills *of* thinking. When you also instruct *about* thinking, you help students gain a knowledge and theory base for improving their mental skills and processes.

Several instructional areas are relevant. The brain and its functioning are, of course, basic. You must be acquainted with the biological bases of thought, developmental theories such as Jean Piaget's, and learning theories such as information processing. And you need to understand the concepts of hemisphericity, memory, and brain damage. Then begin to help students become aware of human thought processes as you ask questions about that process and encourage students to learn how and where to search for answers. Obviously, age and grade level must be taken into consideration.

A second instructional area focuses upon *metacognition*—being conscious of our thought processes while we are thinking. Thinking aloud is one example. Research (Whimbey and Lockhead, 1982, pp. 137, 227) indicates that effective problem-solvers subvocalize; that is, they talk to themselves frequently. This subvocalizing includes constantly restating the situation, rechecking progress, and evaluating if one's thinking is moving in an appropriate direction. Consider the oral account shown in Figure 9-9 (Whimbey and Lockhead, 1982, p. 200) of a solver's method for finding the next three numbers in a sequence.

Notice that the solver proceeded systematically, restating the problem and noting possible trends. Then a plan was developed to test for a pattern. The solver executed the plan, monitoring constantly to be sure that *the strategy fit the data.* Finally, the thinking was evaluated in the closing pattern description, which was a valid solution. Emphasize for students that having more than one valid explanation is a common situation. Encourage them to discover as many explanations as possible. *Performed consciously,* the above steps are the essence of metacognition.

Several techniques have been found useful for helping students become accustomed to thinking about and stating their thoughts. Perhaps the most effective is simply to have students describe what is going on in their mind while thinking, as in the earlier discussion of thinking aloud. Dividing the class into pairs for fifteen to twenty minutes several times a week would provide them the necessary initial practice to overcome awkwardness with the method (and even to practice cooperative learning). Once accustomed to the process, students could recall their thinking processes in larger groups or before the entire class to maintain the skill. The teacher, of course, should model this behavior as often as possible.

Another approach to metacognitive instruction is to have students identify what is known in a situation or problem. From this, they can suggest what needs to be known and, finally, what steps are required to obtain the information. For example, the question might be asked in history class, "How would President Reagan really know of the arms sales to Iran and channeling of the money to Nicaragua at the time of the events?" Initial student responses are listed on the board and constitute what is known. In small groups, students then could generate what else would need to be known and how to obtain the information to determine possible answers. Such exercises, done frequently and with attention to identifying relevant processes, will help students to use similar steps in their own thinking.

You can improve students' metacognition by having them study how others think, particularly those who have become famous for their achievements. Students may be surprised to discover, for instance, that a high I.Q. is not necessarily associated with achievement; the application of intellect is what matters. Thus, they can explore and discuss how Einstein or Mozart worked, what steps they took, and what things were

Figure 9-9 *An Example of Metacognition*

| *Original Problem* | 2 7 4 9 6 11 8 13 ___ ___ ___ |

Problem Solution

The Problem Solver read and thought aloud, pointing to the numbers with his pen.	2 7 4 9 6. The numbers seem to be going up and down. Let's see the rest. 11 8 13 Yes, they're going up and down.
	I'll look at the differences between the numbers to see if there is a pattern.
	2 to 7 is up 5. 7 to 4 is down 3. 4 to 9 is up 5. 9 to 6 is down 3. 6 to 11 is up 5.
The Problem Solver wrote each of these differences as he computed.	$\begin{array}{ccccccc} +5 & -3 & +5 & -3 & +5 & -3 & +5 \end{array}$ 2 7 4 9 6 11 8 13 __ __ __ __ __
	It seems to be going up 5, down 3, up 5, down 3. I'll check the rest.
	11 to 8 is down 3. 8 to 13 is up 5.
	I'll fill in the blanks. The last pair of numbers were 8 to 13, which is up 5. So the next should go down 3. 13 minus 3 is 10. I'll write that in the first blank.
	$\begin{array}{ccccccc} +5 & -3 & +5 & -3 & +5 & -3 & +5 \end{array}$ 2 7 4 9 6 11 8 13 10 15 __ __
	Next, the numbers should go up 5. 10 plus 5 is 15. I'll write that.
	$\begin{array}{ccccccc} +5 & -3 & +5 & -3 & +5 & -3 & +5 \end{array}$ 2 7 4 9 6 11 8 13 10 15 __
	Then they should go down 3. 15 minus 3 is 12
	$\begin{array}{ccccccc} +5 & -3 & +5 & -3 & +5 & -3 & +5 \end{array}$ 2 7 4 9 6 11 8 13 10 15
	Pattern description: The pattern is add 5, subtract 3, add 5, subtract 3, etc.

Source: Arthur Whimbey and Jack Lockhead, *Problem Solving and Comprehension,* 3rd ed. Hillsdale, N.J.: Lawrence Erlbaum Associates, Inc., 1982. Used with permission.

important to them in achieving. Students can interview accomplished people from their own community, or such individuals can visit class to discuss what thoughts go through their head while painting a picture, running a race, or writing a newspaper article.

Metacognition can also include teaching students to monitor their own academic behavior. Do they have test-taking strategies? Are the strategies effective? Might they be improved? What about learning strategies? Do they know if they learn better visually, auditorily, or kinesthetically? Do they have strategies to help in each area? All the above questions are relevant to students' school experience. All are areas that you can explore with students as you help them share with one another and provide useful information. The result will be improved metacognition and application of selected thinking processes.

This final area of thinking instruction has focused upon knowledge about thinking. Two topics were relevant: (1) teaching students knowledge of human thought processes in general, and (2) teaching them to be aware of, to monitor, and to evaluate their own thinking strategies. Both intuitively and empirically we know that some people are more effective thinkers than others. By helping your students identify their own weak and strong areas, you help them to achieve all their academic and personal potential.

Evaluation of Thinking Skills

As educators have focused more intently upon thinking skills in recent years, evaluation of those skills has become increasingly important. In fact, the states of California and New Jersey have already created their own tests of critical thinking to evaluate mandated instruction in that area. Other states can be expected to follow. We will conclude this section with a discussion of evaluating thinking skills. Please note, however, that we are not presenting a comprehensive summary of standardized tests or their construction. (Refer to Ennis et al., 1983.) We are simply suggesting ways that you might achieve your evaluational needs. In general, you will undertake evaluation to determine if particular needs and/or objectives are being met.

Teacher-Made Evaluations

Are our students becoming more effective thinkers? Can they recognize and use particular skills? Is our instructional environment becoming more "thinking-oriented?" Answers to these and related questions are best found through tests, observations, and checklists devised for the particular skills and circumstances in question. The following suggestions will help you determine applicable methods for your teaching areas and classroom environment.

Effective evaluation depends upon carefully planning for intended thinking skills outcomes in your unit and lesson plans. These clearly stated process objectives are an important prerequisite to useful evaluations. Useful aids within your text for such planning include Kaplan's Matrix and Bloom's Taxonomy, questioning strategies, learning hierarchies, and concept analyses. (See also Bloom et al., 1971.)

Student thinking skills such as observing, classifying, and summarizing can be evaluated with textbook material. For example, a social studies class might group a series of states in any way they think relevant. Given a dozen or more states, categories might include size, population, sources of state name, amount of federal land (notice how many classifications come to mind). A similar exercise can be developed in science class, asking students to arrange fifteen to twenty chemical elements into classes. Categories might include the obvious solid-liquid-gas, but some students might also note active-inert, or electron donor–electron receiver categories. Such evaluations can be done individually or by groups and, if results are discussed in class, can be a valuable learning as well as evaluation method.

Other basic problem-solving skills such as pattern finding, following directions, solving analogies can also be evaluated with additional practice material. For example, one of the authors created a zip code game. This exercise stresses classification, pattern building, analyzing data, testing hypotheses, and synthesizing the information. The game is ideal for a cooperative learning strategy that engages students in thinking (see Orlich, 1986).

You have several ways of determining student understanding of concepts and generalizations—again, either individually or in groups. Concept understanding is perhaps most effectively evaluated by having students either identify or create examples. To do this, students must understand the characteristics for inclusion within that category. For instance, the concept "living being" might be part of life science. Students could be given a list of objects to classify as living or not, stating for each decision the relevant characteristics of the concept. In social studies class, "justice" could be a concept to study. Understanding of the concept might be determined by the teacher providing examples to be included or excluded, based upon concept characteristics developed in class. Again, students must state the characteristics.

A less-effective but more common way you could evaluate concept understanding is to have students state or recognize definitions. However, as Chapter 2 pointed out, their knowing the words doesn't necessarily assure their full understanding; they need practice with examples, nonexamples, and identifying characteristics. Such is equally true of the many concepts you teach. Stating a definition demonstrates recall, but the important issue is comprehension. (Review Chapter 4 for our novel interpretation of the comprehension level of the cognitive taxonomy.)

You evaluate generalizations the way you evaluate concepts except that generalizations also have predictive ability; therefore, you should also measure understanding on the application level. Consider the following generalization: Poverty breeds crime. Students' understanding of the two concepts can be measured by their providing or recognizing examples of each. However, a higher-level evaluation would have students find additional examples from local sources to support the generalization. Alternatively, you might provide several scenarios, asking the students which are examples of the generalization and why.

Evaluation of higher-level skills such as noting assumptions, evaluating arguments, and analysis can be done with standardized tests. Checklists, however, are particularly useful and more practical for giving day-to-day feedback to students and for measuring effectiveness of instruction. For example, as you read your students' written summaries, you can indicate with symbols where they have overlooked an assumption, asserted without evidence, made an error of logic, or fallen short in any other categories you establish. The following categories and abbreviations are illustrative.

E = Use of extremes or either-or thinking

- This is the *only* way to do it.
- She is *either* right *or* wrong.

S = Stereotyping and overgeneralizing

- If they (any group) *weren't so lazy,* they might get somewhere.

U = Unsupported generalizations, likes, and dislikes

- That was a *bad* play; I didn't *like* it.
- His ideas are *ridiculous.*

The list of symbols can be as long or short as necessary, but consider three points: (1) be certain that students understand the meaning of each category, (2) use only a few categories; that is, do not overwhelm students, and (3) be persistent, as developing thinking skills requires consistent, continual feedback.

There are also ways to assess students' change in thinking behaviors, extending from informal conversations to nationally normed standardized tests. However, because of the ambiguities present in defining and measuring thinking processes, use a variety of methods—checklists of students' classroom responses, journals of student behaviors, individual and group projects, and participation checklists (see examples in Chapter 7) that provide data about students' thinking habits. Do not place too much weight on any single evaluation; thinking is much too complex a behavior to be quickly or easily assessed. You will recognize the ways to help your students become more effective thinkers as you show them where they have improved and indicate areas needing further attention.

Closing Statement on Thinking

Chapter 9 has provided a basis for you to make decisions about including thinking skills within your instructional program. We established a need for such instruction, and began with one conception that thinking is a complex act composed of skills, attitudes, and knowledge by which individuals relate to their environment. For instructional purposes, it is useful to subdivide thinking into critical, creative, and problem-solving thought, and we identified particular skills and attitudes characteristic of each area.

Thinking skills instruction can be organized around three major concepts:

1. *Teaching "for" thinking* by maintaining an environment in which you encourage students to question and in which you reward them for demonstrating effective thinking techniques.
2. *Teaching "of" thinking* by directly instructing in skills associated with thinking.
3. *Teaching "about" thinking* by increasing students' knowledge of mental skills and processes.

Each concept was explored in detail, with skills instruction receiving the most attention. We tend to support the instructional method of infusing thinking skills into subject-matter areas and of organizing instruction around major concepts and generalizations of the subject. Thus, students learn by relating what they do not know to what they already understand.

Using a variety of indicators of thinking behaviors—both written and nonwritten—is recommended for evaluating students because thinking cannot be described, defined, or measured with precision.

In closing this section, your authors ask you to consider that improved thinking is what education should be about—and this chapter is simply an outline of a challenge we urge you to accept. We now focus on the associated concepts of *learning styles*.

INDIVIDUAL DIFFERENCES AND LEARNING STYLES

No two people think alike, and it is safe to say that no two people learn in exactly the same way. Teachers respond to this diversity in a number of ways, one of the most prevalent being grouping. Grouping at the elementary level often results in students' being divided into subgroups in math and reading on the basis of skills and abilities. Grouping at the high school level often results in tracks, with the curriculum in each track being aimed at different educational and vocational goals. But there are other more subtle ways than in aptitude and ability that students differ.

Dimensions of Human Diversity

The cultural and background experiences of students influence how they understand new material and how they respond to, and benefit from, instruction. For example, teachers who move from a rural setting to a big city will attest to the need of adapting how they teach to the types of students being taught. Differences in background experience as well as in socioeconomic status, culture, and language all influence learning. A simple question to the first graders about where milk comes from will elicit one response from farm kids (cows) and a completely different one from inner-city kids (the store).

In a formal study of the effect of cultural differences on school learning, researchers noted an incongruence between Hawaiian culture and Hawaiian schools (Au and Mason, 1981). When members of the Hawaiian families interacted with one another, there was a casual give-and-take with considerable overlap in terms of conversations; one person would begin talking while others were still speaking. The schools, however, were characterized by very formal patterns of discourse, with one person waiting until the other finished. Hawaiian children didn't feel comfortable with this interaction pattern. When researchers changed the classroom to better fit the backgrounds of students, achievement improved.

Educators have recognized the importance of cultural differences on school success for some time (Sleeter and Grant, 1987), and most teacher education programs contain multicultural components for helping teachers become sensitive to the powerful effect of background experiences. But, more recently, considerable attention has focused on other less apparent dimensions of individual differences called field dependence, field independence, and learning styles. These are the topics of the next section.

Field Dependence/Field Independence

Perception is the first step in processing information and in solving problems. The type of information we focus on influences what information we encode and how we will use it. Researchers have identified two distinct groups of people in terms of perceptual tendencies (Woolfolk, 1987). *Field dependent* children perceive whole patterns rather than parts. Because of the tendency toward the big picture, they have difficulty in reducing larger situations into component parts. Field dependent people tend to be people-oriented; because social relationships are important to them, they work well in groups.

Field independent children, by contrast, are more analytical, perceiving separate parts of a whole and are more inclined to analyze a problem (à la Bloom's Taxonomy) into its component parts. They are often task-oriented and enjoy working with unstructured material to solve problems, such as those found in math and science. They tend not to be socially oriented, often preferring to work alone rather than in groups.

Do these patterns sound familiar to you? Do you know anyone that fits into either pattern? What about yourself? Perhaps what is more important, how can you as a teacher use this information to improve instruction?

Let us answer that last question in several ways. One adaptation would be to plan to those strengths and tendencies with appropriate learning experiences. For example, you might use a deductive approach with field dependent learners, providing advance organizers and outlines to help this type of student see the big picture. In addition, you might assign this type of student to work on projects in groups.

The opposite would be true for the field independent student. Because this type of student likes to work alone and is good at analytical problem-solving, you might structure significant segments of the curriculum around individual, long-term projects that emphasize problem-solving.

Learning Styles: What Are They?

We asserted earlier that no two people learn exactly alike, but are students completely dissimilar in the ways they approach learning? Or, asked another way, are there any similarities in terms of how different groups of students learn, and what can teachers do about these similarities and differences? Researchers in this area have termed these similarities "learning styles" and have developed instructional programs to meet the needs of different groups of students. Learning styles are usually defined as cognitive affective and physiological traits of learners as they interact in the classroom environment.

Students with different learning styles understand educational problems in different ways, and they try to solve them in different ways. These characteristic approaches to solving problems are relatively stable. The stability of learning styles is important. Because they remain relatively constant over time, they not only influence learning but also allow the teacher to identify them and adapt instruction accordingly.

For some time now, psychologists have used I.Q. and aptitude tests to differentiate people in terms of mental abilities; personality researchers have used concepts like introvert and extrovert to describe different personality types. Researchers in the area of learning styles think of these styles as on the borderline between mental abilities and personality. Learning styles fall between these two areas and are the "preferred ways that different individuals have for processing and organizing information and for responding to environmental stimuli" (Shuell, 1981, p. 46). Let us illustrate these ideas by examining several ways that several researchers have approached learning styles.

Dunn and Dunn: A School-Based Approach

One of the oldest and most widely used approaches to learning styles is that proposed by Rita and Kenneth Dunn (1978; Rita Dunn, 1982). Through their work in curriculum development, they observed distinct differences in the ways students responded to instructional materials. Some liked to learn alone, while others preferred learning in groups or from a teacher. Out of this preliminary work, they identified four key dimensions on which learning styles differed: (1) the environment, (2) emotional support, (3) sociological composition, and (4) personal/physical elements. The separate elements within each dimension are found in Table 9-3 and summarized below.

In terms of the environment, the Dunns noted that students differed in terms of their definition of an ideal place to learn. Some wanted a warm, brightly lit niche with desks, many people, and much verbal interaction, while others preferred cooler, more subdued lighting with a quieter, more informal environment. Though many teachers believe that they have little control over these elements, Dunn and Dunn describe how the standard square box of a classroom can be partitioned into separate areas with different environmental climates.

The emotional dimension centers around the extent to which students are self-directed learners. At one end of the continuum are self-starters who can be given a long-term project and who monitor and pace themselves until finishing the job. At the

Table 9-3   *Dunn and Dunn's Learning Styles*

Dimension	Elements
Environment	Sound; Light; Temperature; Seating Design
Emotional Support	Motivational Support; Persistence; Individual Responsibility; Structure
Sociological Support	Individual; Pairs or Teams; Adult; Varied
Personal/Physical	Modality; Time; Mobility

Adapted from Dunn and Dunn, 1978.

other end are students who need much support and to have their assignments in small chunks with periodic due dates. Semester-long projects without periodic checks would be disastrous with these students. Understanding your students' apparent needs for support allows you to design learning experiences that help students learn more effectively.

Students also differ in how they react to peer interaction. Some dislike group projects, preferring instead to learn by themselves; others thrive on the companionship and support provided by group work. Still others prefer the more traditional approach of learning from an adult. You can capitalize on these preferences by varying your teaching techniques based on different student configurations. (We note that our entire book stresses variety and decision-making in all instructional strategies.)

The final dimension identified by the Dunns relates to individual differences in terms of personal/physical preferences. Probably the most important element here is learning modality; some of us are visual; others prefer auditory channels. Mobility, or the ability to periodically move around, is another element here. Another important element in this dimension is time. Some of us are morning people, while others don't function fully until later in the day. Teachers accommodate this dimension when they set up learning centers that allow student movement. This dimension may be one of the hardest for teachers to accommodate. What do you do if you teach a class of afternoon people at 7:45 in the morning?

One reason for the popularity of Dunn and Dunn's categorization system is that it was generated by classroom experience and therefore has considerable ecological validity. Other approaches to learning styles come to us from psychological explanations that describe individual differences in terms of how people look at the world.

Gregorc Style Delineator

Another approach to learning styles is Gregorc's (1985) Style Delineator. Based on research on the different functions that left and right hemispheres of the brain perform, Gregorc's system focuses on the implications of these functions on perceiving and ordering. Perceptual preferences refer to ways students like to gain information. *Concrete-oriented* students prefer input through the physical senses. *Abstract-oriented* students prefer more logical, deductive modes of learning. Ordering abilities refer to the ways in which students arrange, systematize, and dispose of new information. Some students, called sequential, prefer a systematic step-by-step presentation. Others, called random, find the linear approach boring; they would rather have an unorganized, simultaneous display of information. Random-oriented students prefer to do their own ordering, making sense of new information as a presentation proceeds.

On the basis of these two dimensions, Gregorc has developed a self-report instrument that classifies children into one of four categories: concrete sequential, abstract sequential, abstract random, and concrete random. This is done by asking people to describe themselves in terms of a number of descriptors. For example, rank-order the following list of words in terms of how well they decribe the "real you."

1. thorough, logical, spontaneous, trouble-shooter
2. practical, rational, lively, perceptive

On the basis of these rankings, people are placed into one of four cluster areas (no one is described entirely in terms of one dimension). Like the concepts of field dependence and independence, these clusters describe students' preferred ways of processing information. These cluster areas and preferred learning environments are shown in Table 9-4. From the table's descriptions, you can see several implications for instruction. The concrete sequential person would respond best to a deductive sequence that has many concrete examples. A science demonstration in which the teacher first explains a concept or principle and then illustrates it with real-world phenomena would be an example here. The concrete random, by contrast, still needs an abundance of concrete examples, but would prefer to deal with these in inductive or inquiry-oriented activities. An abstract random student might respond to more

Table 9-4   *Gregorc Learning Styles*

Cluster	Thinking Patterns	Preferred Learning Environment
Concrete sequential	Linear, sequential processing of concrete world	Ordered, linear, and stable
Abstract sequential	Abstract, analytical thinking	Mentally stimulating but ordered
Abstract random	Emotional, imaginative	Active, colorful, and free
Concrete random	Concrete world of activity; nonlinear and intuitive	Stimulus-rich problem-solving

open-ended activities like role-playing, group problem-solving, or cooperative learning. Abstract sequential students, with their preference for abstract and analytical thought, might prefer discussions.

Learning Styles: Practical and Instructional Considerations

In our discussion of learning styles, then, we have defined the concept and illustrated it with three different approaches, one empirically grounded in education and two originating from the field of psychology. We are now at a point to ask two interrelated questions: Should we adapt our instruction to individual learning styles, and—perhaps as importantly—can we? Let us consider the instructional question first.

One way to respond to the "should we" question is a glib "Of course, we should do everything we can to accommodate student preferences." But, in doing so, are we short-changing our students, nurturing only narrow ways of learning at the expense of other ways? Should we not expose our students to a broad array of teaching strategies, in so doing making the students flexible and adaptive? An interesting idea.

The second, more practical question relates to the "can we" issues; that is, to what extent are teachers able to adapt all their instruction to individual learning. Research shows, and teachers verify, that classrooms are extremely busy places and that teachers currently have considerable loads with existing group-based approaches. To ask teachers to individualize in terms of learning styles may be impractical as well as philosophically unsound.

A compromise position has emerged from the work of people working in the area of teacher effectiveness. In reviewing studies attempting to link teacher behaviors to student achievement, Barak Rosenshine (1971) found that variety of teaching methods is positively correlated with achievement. Teachers who had more teaching strategies in their repertoire—and used them—produced more student learning. When explaining an idea, teachers are advised to use different modalities to accommodate individual differences. One systematic way of accomplishing this is described by Bernice McCarthy.

McCarthy's 4MAT System

The previous approaches categorize students in terms of distinctive learning styles and then worry about the educational implications later. Bernice McCarthy's (1987) 4MAT system is different in that it integrates the learning styles research into a comprehensive instructional strategy that accommodates several different learning styles.

McCarthy's system, like Gregorc's, is based on the premise that education should stress not only the logical, analytical dimensions of the left brain but also the more creative, imaginative aspects of the right brain. McCarthy identifies four learning styles based again on those dimensions of perceiving (thinking/analyzing versus sensing/feeling) and how people prefer to process information (active doing verus more reflective watching).

On the basis of these four dimensions, McCarthy has developed a four-step sequential teaching process that integrates right- and left-brain functions, or experiencing and thinking. In step one, the teacher creates an experience that causes students to think or reflect. This might be a discrepant event in science or a problem in social studies. The key here is to present something concrete and real that makes connections with the student's world. For example, an elementary lesson on the American flag might begin with the presentation and discussion of familiar symbols such as Smokey the Bear or McDonald's arches.

Step 2 emphasizes concept formation to accommodate both left and right hemispheres. Teaching in this stage must emphasize both examples and real-world problems and analytical talk. In this phase, characterized by both concrete experiences and abstract thought, the teacher extends the information base established in step 1 through information and applied activities. For example, in extending the flag topic, you might lecture or have students read about flags and symbols; and you might have students make their own flags.

In step 3 the teacher carries students one step further by providing more information and asking them to apply these ideas. Sometimes, information is gained through standard drill and exercise with workbook pages and worksheets; at other times, more creative approaches like individual research are used. In the flag example, you might introduce the idea that the American flag corresponds to the number of states and has changed over time. Then you might ask each student to construct a flag corresponding to a particular time in U.S. history.

Step 4 of the model focuses on evaluation and refinement of ideas. In the final stage of the strategy, the teacher asks students to analyze and evaluate their application for relevance and usefulness and to extend it to new areas. Pursuing the flag idea further, the class could compare the constructed flags to the actual ones, discussing similarities and differences.

In analyzing this four-step model, you will see a number of similarities to Bloom's Taxonomy discussed in Chapter 4. There is a hierarchy of steps beginning with concrete knowing and proceeding through comprehension, application, analysis, synthesis, and evaluation. What is distinctive about McCarthy's approach is the importance it places on linking real-world problems to the background experiences of students.

IMPLICATIONS

We have combined two major instructional topics: teaching thinking skills and adapting to student learning styles. The two models have different foci, but we have tried to merge the distinct ideas into a meaningful synthesis. One teaches thinking skills in a systematic manner, just as one adapts to the apparent styles of learners. The techniques described in Chapter 9 would utilize virtually every preactive planning device and all the interactive strategies described in Chapters 6, 7, and 8. In short, you must master a wide spectrum of teaching skills to achieve excellence in teaching and to be able to apply emergent instructional designs.

Critical thinking is in short supply worldwide. Our plea is for all educators to integrate the best of teaching and thinking strategies systematically and diligently so as to make all schools truly effective. Obviously, you begin slowly, gradually, and thoughtfully. The challenge is yours. We have confidence that you will address the challenge as one that is intentionally inviting.

REVIEW QUESTIONS FOR DISCUSSION

1. What similarities and what differences are there among the discussed systems of learning styles?

2. Reflect on your class or grade level. How could you use a specific learning style to improve instruction?

3. Create a model lesson that would integrate teaching thinking skills with one of the learning styles.

4. How can you determine a student's attitude toward thinking?

5. *In 1956,* Myron Lieberman cautioned (with some irony) that it was in vogue to teach critical thinking. But, he warned, don't criticize anything important. Think about that statement and discuss it with three other colleagues.

REFERENCES

Applebee, Arthur N. "Writing and Reasoning." *Review of Educational Research* 54:1984, 577–596.

Au, Katherine, and Jana M. Mason. "Social Organizational Factors in Learning to Read: The Balance of Rights Hypothesis." *Reading Research Quarterly* 17:1981, 115–152.

Baron, Joan B., and Robert J. Sternberg, eds. *Teaching Thinking Skills: Theory and Practice.* New York: W. H. Freeman, 1987.

Berlak, Harold. "The Teaching of Thinking." *The School Review* 73(1):1965, 1–13.

Beyer, Barry K. *Developing a Thinking Skills Program.* Boston: Allyn and Bacon, 1988.

———. *Practical Strategies for the Teaching of Thinking.* Boston: Allyn and Bacon, 1987.

———. "Teaching Thinking Skills: How the Principal Can Know They Are Being Taught." *NASSP Bulletin* 69(477):1985, 70–83.

Bloom, Benjamin S. "The 2 Sigma Problem: The Search for Methods of Group Instruction as Effective as One-to-One Tutoring." *Educational Researcher* 13(6):1984, 4–16.

Bloom, Benjamin S., et al. *Taxonomy of Educational Objectives: The Classification of Educational Goals. Handbook I: Cognitive Domain.* New York: David McKay, 1956.

Bloom, Benjamin S., J. Thomas Hastings, and George F. Madaus. *Handbook on Formative and Summative Evaluation of Student Learning.* New York: McGraw-Hill, 1971.

Bredderman, Ted. "The Effects of Activity-Based Elementary Science on Student Outcomes: A Quantitative Synthesis." *Review of Educational Research* 53:1983, 499–518.

Bruner, Jerome W. *The Process of Education.* New York: Vintage Books, 1960.

Costa, Arthur L. "Mediating the Metacognitive." *Educational Leadership* 42(3):1984, 57–62.

Costa, Arthur L., ed. *Developing Minds: A Resource Book for Teaching Thinking.* Association for Supervision and Curriculum Development, 1985.

de Bono, Edward. *CORT Thinking Program,* 2nd ed. Elmsford, N.Y.: Pergamon, 1987.

Dunn, Rita. "Teaching Students Through Their Individual Learning Styles: A Research Report." In *Student Learning Styles and Brain Behavior.* Reston, Va.: National Association of Secondary School Principals, 1982, pp. 142–151.

Dunn, Rita, and Kenneth Dunn. *Teaching Students Through Their Individual Learning Styles.* Reston, Va.: Reston Publications, 1978.

Ennis, Robert H. "A Concept of Critical Thinking." *Harvard Educational Review* 32(1):1979, 81–111.

———. "Critical Thinking and the Curriculum." *National Forum* 65(1):1985, 28–31.

———. "Critical Thinking and Subject Specificity: Clarification and Needed Research." *Educational Researcher* 18(3):1989, 4–10.

Ennis, Robert H., J. Millman, and T. Tomko. *Manual for Two Tests: Cornell Critical Thinking Test, Level X and Cornell Critical Thinking Test, Level Z,* 3rd ed. Champaign, Ill.: University of Illinois, 1983.

Feldhusen, John F., and Pamela A. Clinkenbeard. "Creativity Instructional Materials: A Review of Research." *Journal of Creative Behavior* 20(3):1986, 153–182.

Gibson, Harry W. "Critical Thinking: A Communication Model." Unpublished doctoral diss., Washington State University, 1985.

Glaser, Edward M. "Critical Thinking: Educating for Responsible Citizenship in a Democracy." *National Forum* 65(1):1985, 24–27.

Goodlad, John. *A Place Called School.* New York: McGraw-Hill, 1984.

Gregorc, Anthony. *Gregorc Style Delineator.* Maynard, Mass.: Gabriel Systems, 1985.

Hickman, Faith. "A Case Study of Innovation." In *Redesigning Science and Technology Education.* Rodger W. Bybee, Janet Carlson, and Alan J. McCormack, eds. Washington, D.C.: National Science Teachers Association, 1984.

Hilgard, Ernest R., and Gordon H. Bower. *Theories of Learning,* 3rd ed. New York: Appleton-Century-Crofts, 1966.

Lieberman, Myron. *Education as a Profession.* Englewood Cliffs, N.J.: Prentice-Hall, 1956.

Marzano, Robert J., and Daisy Arredando. "A Framework for Teaching Thinking." *Educational Leadership* 43:May 1986, 20–27.

Marzano, Robert, Ron Brandt, Carolyn Hughes, Beau Fly Jones, Barbara Presseisen, Stuart Rankin, and Charles Suhor. *Dimensions for Thinking: A Framework for Curriculum and Instruction.* Alexandria, Va.: Association for Supervision and Curriculum Development, 1988.

McCarthy, Bernice. "The 4MAT System." *Teaching to Learning Styles.* Barrington, Ill.: Excel, 1987.

McPeck, John E. *Critical Thinking and Education.* New York: St. Martin's Press, 1981.

———. "Stalking Beasts But Swatting Flies: The Teaching of Critical Thinking." *Canadian Journal of Education* 9(1):1984, 28–44.

Nickerson, Raymond S. "Kinds of Thinking Taught in Current Programs." *Educational Leadership* 42(10):1984, 26–36.

———. *Teaching Thinking.* Hillsdale, N.J.: L. Earlbaum Associates, 1985. (a)

———. "Understanding Understanding." *American Journal of Education,* February 1985, 201–239. (b)

Orlich, Donald C. "The Zip Code Game." *Science and Children* 23:February 1986, 18–19.

Parker, Walter C. "Teaching Thinking: The Pervasive Approach." *Journal of Teacher Education,* 37:May-June 1987, 50–56.

Paul, Richard W. "Critical Thinking: Fundamental to Education for a Free Society." *Educational Leadership* 42(1):1984, 5–14.

Rosenshine, Barak. *Teaching Behaviors and Student Achievement.* London: National Foundation for Educational Research, 1971.

Shuell, Thomas J. "Dimensions of Individual Differences." In *Psychology and Education.* F. Farley and N. Gordon, eds. Berkeley, Calif.: McCutchan, 1981, pp. 32–59.

Scriven, Michael. "Critical for Survival." *National Forum* 65(1):1985, 9–19.

Sleeter, C., and C. Grant. "An Analysis of Multicultural Education in the United States." *Harvard Educational Review* 57:1987, 421–444.

Smith, Frank. *Comprehension and Learning: A Conceptual Framework for Teachers.* New York: Holt, Rinehart, & Winston, 1975.

Snook, I. A. "Teaching Pupils to Think." *Studies in Philosophy and Education* 8(3):1974.

Solomon, Warren. "Improving Students' Thinking Skills Through Social Studies Instruction." *Elementary School Journal* 87(5):1987, 557–568.

Tiedt, Iris McClellan, Jo Ellen Carlson, Bert D. Howard, and Kathleen S. Oda Watanabe. *Teaching Thinking in K–12 Classrooms: Ideas, Activities and Resources.* Boston: Allyn and Bacon, 1988.

Tuma, David T., and Frederick Reif. *Problem Solving and Education: Issues in Teaching and Research.* New York: John Wiley, 1980.

Wells, Gordon, and Jon Wells. "Learning to Talk and Talking to Learn." *Theory into Practice.* 33:1984, 190–197.

Whimbey, Arthur. "The Key to Higher Order Thinking Is Precise Processing." *Educational Leadership* 42(1):1984, 66–70.

———. "Teaching Sequential Thought: The Cognitive-Skills Approach." *Phi Delta Kappa* 59:1977, 255–259.

Whimbey, Arthur, and Jack Lockhead. *Problem Solving and Comprehension,* 3rd ed. Hillsdale, N.J.: Lawrence Erlbaum Associates, Inc., 1982.

Woolfolk, Anita E. *Educational Psychology,* 3rd ed. Englewood Cliffs, N.J.: Prentice-Hall, 1987.

10

Deciding How to Manage a Class

*T*he classroom is a center for a dynamic system of interactions. Hundreds, if not thousands, of individual verbal and nonverbal behaviors and a multiplicity of possible combinations occur in every classroom. The more enthusiastic the teacher is, the greater is the likelihood that the number of interactions will increase. Enthusiasm and interaction are essential to the learning process. However, while enthusiasm and interaction can promote learning, if not carefully managed, they also can sabotage and ultimately destroy the fragile balance between them, causing students to move from productive to nonproductive behaviors. The management of the classroom and the balancing of the interactions within it will be the focus of this chapter.

Objectives   After completing this chapter, you should be able to:

- Comprehend the concept of "classroom management"
- Analyze the use of "norms," "power," and "teacher awareness" in the classroom
- Evaluate the applicability of self-discipline systems
- Analyze the uses of imposed-discipline systems
- Evaluate the effective use of referral resources
- Develop a rationale toward corporal punishment, suspension, and drug or alcohol abuse management
- Evaluate classroom management systems and to be able to select appropriate options to fit specific situations
- Be aware of issues affecting your behavior in the classroom

Additionally, we would like to encourage you to incorporate the following attitudes:

- Perceive the role of classroom management as enhancing the potential of *all* students
- Analyze any classroom management system for its value to student learning
- Realize that there is no one best system for all classes

THE ROLE OF DISCIPLINE

The *Phi Delta Kappan* has reported in annual polls of public attitudes on education that, for eighteen of the last twenty years, discipline is viewed as a major problem for the schools (Gallup and Elam, 1988). With or without data from national polls, teachers, administrators, parents, school patrons, and students know that there are many discipline problems in the schools. And it comes as no surprise that the students cause most of the behavioral problems; however, some discipline problems are caused by teachers themselves.

Why are management issues of such concern? First, most persons have never been charged with establishing and enforcing guidelines for behavior. Until faced with classroom management, the vast majority of college students have had responsibility for only themselves. A teacher is asked to become responsible for the management of others, namely a group of precocious and energetic students.

Discipline is usually perceived as the preservation of order and the maintenance of control. These are traditionally the outcomes of classroom management techniques; however, we feel that this view of discipline is far too simplistic. Teachers make on-the-spot, split-second decisions and must react spontaneously when using management techniques to solve problems that arise in the classroom. Classroom management is determined by *teacher-student-situation* factors. The attitudes that students develop in formal classroom situations are influenced by the classroom management skills of a teacher. Your ideas about what the classroom should look like and how it should function will determine classroom atmosphere.

Most individuals focus their primary attention on subject-matter preparation. Precious little time is left to think consciously about management. This chapter, though, will provide you with a variety of management strategies for your review. Your task will be to read and understand them, sample their ideas in classroom practice, and measure your classroom observations of teachers against the strategies detailed here. You will need to prepare yourself for a successful classroom experience by formulating a management program. We want you to succeed where many others have failed because they were not prepared for classroom management. You are responsible for your own success. The knowledge and background are available; you need to think and respond adequately and systematically to the task ahead.

A Few Historical Insights

Prior to the late 1950s and early 1960s, the major emphasis in teacher preparation involved classroom control. The theory of "mental discipline," physical punishment, order, and obedience all tended to provide educators with a rather consistent frame of reference. Later schools began to shift more of the burden for classroom climate and conduct to the teacher. While this shift in responsibility was occurring, the results of relevant studies of discipline by social and behavioral scientists began to be applied in the schools. The shift to teacher responsibility, combined with social and behavioral research, set the stage for "democratic discipline." At least two teaching principles emerged from democratic discipline that could be applied to classroom management.

1. As the adult member of the class, the teacher must add the rational dimension to the rule-making capacities of the group.
2. Rules administered by the teacher should reflect the wisdom and fairness of a judge who participates in a trial as an impartial observer and arbiter.

No longer would the teacher be described in terms that implied superior or subordinate status. Thus, such words as *facilitator* and *learner* emerged in the jargon of educational practitioners.

Classrooms began to change even more dramatically during the 1970s and 1980s. Four changes can be isolated. First, families have become very mobile. It is not uncommon for even a rather stable school to show 25 percent student turnover and for others to range between 35 and 70 percent. The mobility factor simply means that classrooms tend to be relatively unstable social systems.

The second phenomenon focuses on the so-called breakup of the family. More students now live with single parents than at any other time in our educational history and this number is increasing. Only about 6 percent of all families now resemble the classic "Dick and Jane" model: father as primary breadwinner, mother at home, and two children in school.

Third, there tends to be a prevailing student ethos that school is a place to "get through." Motivating students has become more difficult.

Finally, urban schools have different problems than do suburban or nonurban schools. One simply cannot compile a list and expect it to apply to all schools. Julie P. Sanford and Edmund T. Emmer (1988) note that a productive working environment in which students know what is expected of them is a trait of successful classroom management. Another of those traits is providing a safe and positive school climate. Teaching during the 1990s will be affected by classroom management problems never encountered in previous decades.

Concepts behind Classroom Management

Our definition of classroom management implies a humanistic orientation toward the classroom environment. Young minds and attitudes are being shaped by overt and covert teacher behaviors. The most successful teachers are those who knowingly make decisions based on sound principles. A discussion follows of three concepts that are central to the principles of classroom management: norms, power, and awareness.

Norms

A norm is usually defined as a behavioral rule accepted to some degree by most members of a group. The members feel some obligation to adhere to the behavioral rule, as it introduces a high degree of regularity or predictability into their social interaction. Norms are not recorded like the laws of a country. However, there exists in the minds of the group members an ideal standard for how each member ought to behave under specific conditions. Deviation from the norm usually results in some kind of punishment by the group.

Norms are functionally valuable to social relationships because they reduce the necessity for exercising direct, informal, and personal influence. Adherence to norms provides for the control of individual and group behavior without any one individual overtly exerting power.

Power

By virtue of role position in the classroom, the teacher has superior power. Unrestrained use of that power creates insecurities and resistance among the class members, adversely affecting the attainment of learning objectives. While the administrative organization of schools keeps students in a relatively powerless position, students can nonetheless retaliate against the teacher who overuses power by forming coalitions, by creating irritating disturbances, and by intellectual sit-down strikes. In order to be an effective classroom manager, the teacher should learn to exercise the least amount of power necessary to accomplish the desired result (Wolfgang and Glickman, 1986).

Awareness

Teacher attention and insight toward the classroom environment is awareness. A class is constantly giving the teacher verbal and nonverbal cues. This communication occurs between the teacher and individual students and between the teacher and the class as a whole (Hawley and Rosenholtz, 1984). How does the teacher *read* this network of communication?

Initially, the teacher must determine how the class is presenting these cues. The teacher who complains, "My class was particularly lousy today," says nothing in terms of effectively dealing with the input received. This teacher must define with some precision what is meant by the term *lousy*. What behaviors did the class exhibit that led to the inference that the class was "lousy"? Have the students recited inappropriately, not paid attention, or not accomplished the work requested? Whatever the reason, the teacher must know how to specify what behaviors are being alluded to when the class is identified as "lousy" and how the students can model the appropriate behaviors (Evertson et al., 1989).

A Continuum of Management Systems

As a teacher you need to understand the consequences of any classroom management systems you intend to implement. You cannot implement a system on "the spur of the moment." Systems can be studied and analyzed. Yet, whatever the circumstances, you are faced with choosing along a continuum of management strategies between self-discipline and imposed discipline. Self-discipline implies a system of organized behavior designed to promote self-interest while contributing to the welfare of others. Imposed discipline suggests a code of conduct prescribed for the best interests of the individual and of the classroom or the society in which he or she lives. Between self-discipline and imposed discipline are numerous choices.

To provide you with an overview of selected classroom management systems, we will discuss four strategies that lean toward self-discipline, with a special focus on

Figure 10-1   A Continuum of Classroom Management Systems

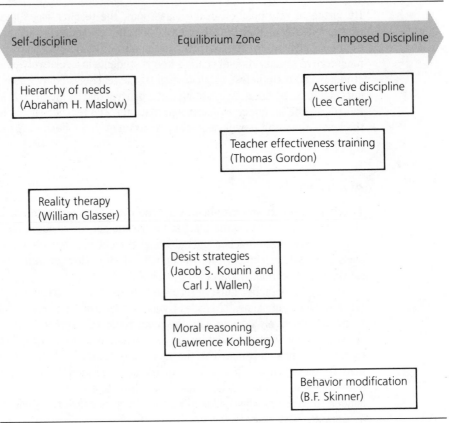

reality therapy. On the imposed-discipline side, we will present three strategies, focusing in depth on desist strategies and behavior modification. We selected reality therapy, desist strategies and behavior modifications to highlight because they tend to be "generic" (that is, other systems have been initiated or developed from them). Figure 10-1 shows the array of classroom management systems we present.

SELF-DISCIPLINE SYSTEMS

Self-discipline strategies are built on the premise that effective classroom management is a function of effective teacher-student and student-student relationships. Advocates argue that teachers need to recognize that facilitating learning rests upon the following attitudinal qualities in their personal relationship with the learner: (1) realness in the teacher, (2) teacher acceptance and trust of the student, and

(3) teacher empathy regarding the student. With these attitudinal qualities in mind, let us examine classroom management strategies that focus on self-discipline.

Hierarchy of Needs

Abraham H. Maslow (1968) has had a major impact on educational theory and classroom management for decades. He is best known for establishing his hierarchy of basic needs. In brief, they are (1) the need of the individual to fulfill physiological requirements, (2) the need to safeguard one's existence, (3) the need to build personal affiliations, (4) the need to find self-esteem, and, finally, (5) the need for self-actualization or personal fulfillment.

Maslow's hierarchy is applied to classroom management by assuming that an individual's behavior at any time is determined by the strongest need. For example, a hungry student will have a hard time focusing on learning skills. An effective teacher tries to determine what "need" might be causing a behavior problem, then addresses that need. Naturally, teachers and schools would like their students to achieve at the personal-esteem and self-actualization levels, for such students would be truly self-disciplined.

To use Maslow's ideas, you must truly *believe in* your students. Students need to be shown that they are loved and are really important in the class. Structure, routines, and consistency are all hallmarks of this strategy. You help all students to develop a positive and constructive self-image. The classroom environment must be structured to be supportive. Even when someone is "in trouble," it is always *the act, not the person* that is criticized. Teachers stress the intrinsic value of each student and attempt to motivate every student to do the best possible. This is a long-term system.

Moral Reasoning

Lawrence Kohlberg (1981) has argued that the schools should focus more on moral development. He reasons that highly moral citizens can maximize their contributions to society and manage their personal and professional lives from a highly ethical perspective.

Kohlberg's work led to the development of a six-stage moral development hierarchy. He advocates presenting "moral dilemmas" in which students are faced with a moral choice. For example, twelve individuals must leave a sinking ship and the available life raft can survive with seven. How do you choose which seven are allowed to leave the sinking ship in the life raft?

In such an exercise, the class is subdivided for the discussion. Kohlberg believes that such discussions will help the students raise their consciousness and come to understand the motivation of others better. He stresses that the classroom must establish a "just community" in which the essence of a democratic society is the model. Obviously, the dilemmas selected for discussion are fluid and must match the maturity and instructional goals of the class. To use this model, the class needs mastery of some discussion processes as described in Chapter 7. Further, each student would complete some written evaluation form similar to Figures 7-2, 7-4, and 7-7. In this manner you evaluate each student for individual growth.

Advocates note that Kohlberg's model improves listening, speaking, and resolving of conflicts. Of course, reasoning, sharing, and applying principles of justice are concepts that find operational meaning when the class uses moral reasoning. Again, this is a time-consuming model that requires honest involvement, trust, frankness, and—overriding all—individual uniqueness. You need extensive preparation to apply the model appropriately.

Teacher Effectiveness Training

Positive relationships between teachers and students are the basis for Thomas Gordon's (1974) well-known teacher effectiveness training movement of the 1970s. His "no lose" strategy was one of his most successful contributions to the conflict resolution literature.

This "no lose" strategy follows a six-step problem-solving method. First, the students define a conflict or apparent behavioral problem. Second, they brainstorm ideas to resolve the conflict. It is important not to eliminate any ideas, no matter how crazy, during this step. All ideas are equal. Third, the potential solutions are discussed, with pros and cons listed. Fourth, after ranking the solutions, both teacher and students select one. The fifth step involves the designing of an implementation strategy with which all class members can live. The plan is then implemented and evaluated during step six. Although teacher effectiveness training is very systematic, the motivation remains oriented toward group participation and decision-making.

Explicit to this model is the concept of *communication*. Everyone in the classroom is expected to communicate by stating points clearly, by having the opportunity of being uninterrupted, and by feeling that everyone has certain rights. The latter is critical, for everyone must respect one another's rights in the spirit of justice and democratic ideals.

Nonverbal language is stressed. Maintaining eye contact, the teacher faces the students and gestures supporting "body language." Smiles, open eyes, and positive regard are ultimately incorporated in one's nonverbal repertoire. Openness and trust are essential for using this model.

Reality Therapy

Reality Therapy is *an approach that helps individuals to take responsibility* for solving their own problems. As humans, we have the ability to determine our own personal destinies. We are not uncontrolled victims of circumstances. William Glasser (1965) wrote that Reality Therapy is a "therapy that leads all patients toward reality, toward grappling successfully with the tangible and intangible aspects of the real world." As a technique, reality therapy requires positive, genuine, human involvement in which persons recognize their own realities and begin to reshape their own behaviors to meet selected needs.

Basic Principles

Let us turn to the principles of the technique as they apply to classroom management. A basic tenet is that teachers must avoid labeling inappropriate behaviors with some interesting-sounding tag—for example, paranoia, schizophrenia, or character behavior disorders. Also, examination of family history or of past case histories is unessential. The main premise is that an individual must perceive his or her own failures and must be personally responsible for becoming successful. Glasser (1986) expands these ideas in his extensive work *Control Theory in the Classroom,* which is must-reading for those employing his model.

Principle 1   The first principle of Reality Therapy is human involvement. All the other principles of reality therapy are derived from the basic concept of involvement. Essentially, Glasser (1986) notes that we are always involved with other people—at the very minimum, one and, ideally, with many more. The teacher's objective is to be involved enough to give the pupil the confidence needed to make new and lasting self-involvements both with the teacher and with others.

In the classroom setting, the strategy involves devising a structure that facilitates teacher-student and student-student involvement. Management problems can then be resolved in ways that express care and concern, primarily on the part of the teacher, with direct student involvement.

Principle 2   The next step is to examine current behaviors. While Reality Therapy does not deny emotions and their importance, successful use depends on focussing on current behaviors—on what the student *is doing now.* To apply the second principle, the teacher should ask a misbehaving student what he or she is doing. Typically, teachers tend to recapitulate previous activities, such as in the comment: "Well, that is the seventh time today that you've interrupted without raising your hand." Rather, the teacher should ask, "What are you doing?" Note that the emphasis is on the *you,* so that there can be no misinterpretations as to who is responsible for the misbehavior.

Principle 3   Reality Therapy requires the student to examine his or her current behavior, to evaluate it, and to make a determination that the current behavior is not beneficial or appropriate. In terms of classroom management problems, this means that the student who is constantly misbehaving must be made to discuss the current behavior and to come to the conclusion that another type of behavior would be more appropriate. Also, the student is simply labeled as responsibile or irresponsible if not coming to grips with inappropriate behavior. This point is very important. The teacher does not evaluate or label the behaviors as good or bad but, without moralizing, simply indicates whether they are appropriate or inappropriate.

Principle 4   Once a student makes a self-judgment about his or her behavior, the teacher must assist that student in making realistic plans to change that behavior. A failing person in need of success must take small, individually positive steps to attain success.

For example, a student who never studies should not be expected to study two hours a night. Realistically, fifteen-minute sessions a few times a week are more appropriate. Be certain that the remedial plans are realistic in terms of the individual who makes and must implement them. This is a particularly important principle for teachers, because Reality Therapy, as applied to the classroom situation, emphasizes student contracting. The student, with the help of the teacher, develops a plan to help meet personal or educational goals; the student individually and responsibly implements this plan under the teacher's guidance. It is essential that the teacher take great care in helping the student to develop realistic plans for small, individual steps that can be successfully completed.

Principle 5   Reality Therapy demands a commitment from the student. After a reasonable plan has been devised, it must be carried out. In terms of the classroom setting, Glasser's Reality Therapy most frequently requires that the student prepare a plan in writing and sign it as a means of increasing personal motivation to maintain and fulfill the plan. This kind of commitment intensifies and accelerates the behavior of the student, and it offers the student a concrete way of demonstrating commitment to a change in behavior. It also helps to provide a means of measuring success and individual responsibility.

Principle 6   There are no excuses when the student fails to change in behavior. The student has expressed a commitment in the form of a written plan and cannot be excused for not fulfilling the plan. However, it is essential that both the teacher and the student be willing to reexamine the plan constantly and to renew or change the commitment if the original plan is in some way inadequate. This does not mean that the teacher excuses the failure of the student. When failure occurs, it must be mutually recognized that the responsibility lies with the student either for not having fulfilled the plan or for not having planned appropriately in the first place.

Note well that this technique places the onus of responsibility on the student and not on the teacher. Too often, we believe that it is the teacher's responsibility to make students "behave." The tenets of Reality Therapy reverse this role. The teacher must be a helper to the student; the teacher's praise of student success increases the involvement between the teacher and the student and leads to more responsible student behaviors (William Glasser, *Impact,* 1972).

Principle 7   The final principle of Reality Therapy is the absence of punishment. Glasser believes that punishment hinders the personal involvement that is essential between the teacher and the student. The purpose of punishment is to change an individual's behavior through fear or pain. Glasser observes that punishment has proved ineffective; if it had been effective, we would not have so many failures in our present society.

Reality Therapy and the Entire Class

Thus far, the emphasis has been on Reality Therapy as an individually oriented management technique. However, Reality Therapy also may be applied to an entire class through the use of classroom meetings. These are discussed so that you may observe a logical extension of the technique to large groups.

Social Problem-Solving Meeting   As the name implies, this is a meeting that basically is concerned with the students' social school behaviors. To implement this type of meeting, the teacher should observe the following guidelines:

1. All group and individual problems in the class are eligible for discussion.
2. The session focuses on solving the problem, not on finding faults or specifying punishment.
3. Meetings are conducted with all individuals positioned in a tight circle to foster interaction.

Glasser (1969) provides the following illustration of such a social problem-solving meeting. Students in an eighth grade class were truant at an increasing rate as the warm days came in the spring term. A social problem-solving meeting was called and the teacher asked if everyone was there. In discussion, the class admitted that eight of thirty-five were absent. The class was then asked why the others were absent. Most student responses included terms such as *dull* and *boring*. With the "problem" exposed, the teacher then pressed for a solution. The students were asked to make value judgments on the worthiness of school. They were asked to sign a statement promising to come to school the next day. Only one-third of the class would sign. Next, they were asked to sign a paper stating that they would not sign the promise. This was to cause the students to make some type of commitment. Once again, one-third of the students would sign, leaving one-third who would sign nothing. This last group was then asked to allow their names to be placed on a paper stating that they would not sign anything, and to this they agreed.

There was little improvement in truant behavior as a result of this meeting; however, the problem became a principal topic of general class discussion and set the stage for additional meetings that eventually resolved the problem. In this particular case, the general class discussion eventually may focus on the teacher's responsibility for stimulating student interest through a variety of teaching strategies and materials. Would a written promise or contract on the teacher's part be appropriate according to the principles of Reality Therapy?

There are many individual and group techniques that teachers can use in implementing a program of Reality Therapy. However, there is one requirement that is essential to all of these techniques: being involved to the degree demanded by

Reality Therapy. Although it is not easy to function according to the principles of Reality Therapy, it can be done. It takes training, patience, and, above all, perseverance on the part of teachers.

Teacher Involvement and Individual Strategies   As Glasser (*Impact,* 1972) wrote, "We begin and end with involvement."* Most teachers would immediately retort, "We're involved up to our ears." The problem with the latter type of involvement is that the teachers really mean that they interact with the class members but usually do not get involved. This is because it is generally much easier to send a student who appears to need help to a counselor or to the vice-principal. In this manner, the teacher avoids involvement as it applies to Reality Therapy.

What, then, is teacher involvement? First, it is the teacher's wanting to work in a personal manner with the individual on behavioral or academic problems. Second, it requires that the teacher remain in a "teacher role," for the teacher is not the student's peer, but a mature and responsible adult. The teacher helps the student to make plans, to carry them out, to revise them, and to strive continually for success. Third, involvement means that the teacher helps the student to become more responsible for individual behavior by having the student constantly state what he or she is doing.

Involvement also means meeting with parents, if possible, and seeking their cooperation. Furthermore, teachers can set up short interviews with other teachers in the school to discuss the welfare of certain students. How many teachers have ever gone to the locker room to talk with the coaches about helping a young man or woman to become more responsible? Involvement means helping the student in every possible way. Does it require too much effort? The answer lies with the teacher, who must decide whether to tolerate inappropriate student behaviors or to try to improve them in a systematic manner.

In conclusion, the basic principle of Reality Therapy is that each individual is personally responsible for his or her own behavior and improvement. If student behavior is to change, the seven principles of Reality Therapy, which require positive human involvement by both teachers and students, should be followed. As with any management plan, the success or failure of the outcome rests with the teacher's willingness to become involved.

Self-Discipline: A Final Word

Positive teacher expectations are essential for self-discipline strategies to be effective. In far too many classrooms, teachers are not fully aware that students must experience early success before attaining further success. Not expecting their students to succeed, some teachers express negative feelings toward them. And, true

---

*Used with written permission of William Glasser.

to expectations, their students do not succeed. Self-discipline requires a positive perspective, even though some techniques may fail (McDaniel, 1987).

IMPOSED-DISCIPLINE SYSTEMS

The application of imposed-discipline strategies is related to the teacher's power and authority. The teacher's power resides in the definition of the role of teacher, which is traditionally determined by the expectations of various segments of society. Accordingly, the teacher's authority is defined as the legitimate use of power as recognized by society, that is, by parents, school administration, courts, legislatures, and students. Not everyone, though, will recognize the teacher's authority all the time; there will be occasional instances when it is not respected. When this happens, the teacher's authority can become characterized by the power to reward and punish.

The following discussion of imposed-discipline strategies examines three strategies that use a variety of methods to impose the teacher's authority within the classroom learning environment. Let us begin with desist strategies.

Desist Strategies

Of the classroom management techniques we discuss, the desist strategy is the most traditional. The term is derived from "desist techniques" suggested by Jacob S. Kounin and Paul V. Gump (1959). The technique of desist strategies is a means of systematically communicating the teacher's desire to stop or alter the behavior of a student. The communication may be accomplished by a command such as "Stop that!" or by a glance or by a movement made near the student.

Desist strategies offer a systematic framework for applying the teacher's authority to maintain group norms. The technique of desist strategies involves two basic concepts. First, there are three levels of force dimension—low, moderate, and high. Second, there are two types of communication-of-force dimension—public and private. Desist strategies require almost immediate decision-making.

In dealing with classroom management problems, it is usually best to use a low rather than a high level of force, and it is always better to use a private rather than a public form of communication. Occasionally, however, a situation may call for a high-level, public dimension. A classroom fight would be an example. In the vast majority of cases, though, you will find it best to use *low-level, private* forms of desist strategies to handle the "normal" classroom management problems. Desist strategies are further explained in Tables 10-1 and 10-2, which present sets of operationally defined terms and their appropriate teacher behaviors.

The concept of "desist strategy" is summarized in two principles that were first described by Carl J. Wallen in 1968. They are as follows.

Table 10-1 *Examples of Desist Strategies*

	Level of Force	Definition	Desist Strategy
Level of Force Dimension	Low	Nonverbal, a signal or movement	A glance, shaking of head, moving over to child unobtrusively in the instructional activity
	Moderate	Verbal, conversational, no coercion	Appeal to child to act reasonably, remove disturbing objects, command the child to stop
	High	Verbal and nonverbal, changed voice pitch, may use coercion	Raise voice and command child to stop, remove the child from group, threaten, punish, physically restrain
	Type	*Definition*	*Desist Strategy*
Public-Private Dimension	Public	Intended to be noticed by most of the children in a class	Acting and/or speaking in a way which commands attention
	Private	Intended to be noticed only by small groups of children	Using unobstrusive actions or moving close to a child when speaking

From Carl J. Wallen, *Establishing Teaching Principles in the Area of Classroom Management* (Interim Report, Project No. 5-0916). Monmouth, Oregon, Teaching Research, January, 1968. Appendix A, p. 15.

Table 10-2 *Desist Strategies in Combination*

Level	Private	Public
1. Glance Low Level	Teacher shakes head so only one or two other children notice the action.	Teacher shakes head dramatically so most of class notices the action.
2. Appeal Moderate Level	Teacher moves close to child, asks child to act reasonably, and uses voice and manner so only one or two other children notice the action.	Teacher asks children to act reasonably in a manner which most of the class notices.
3. Threat High Level	Teacher moves close to child, tells what will happen if misbehavior continues, and uses voice and manner so only one or two other children notice the action.	Teacher tells what will happen if misbehavior continues, uses a loud and commanding voice which most of the class notices.

From Carl J. Wallen, *Establishing Teaching Principles in the Area of Classroom Management* (Interim Report, Project No. 5-0916). Monmouth, Oregon, Teaching Research, January, 1968. Appendix A, pp. 15–16.

Principle 1

If a classroom activity is about to occur and you have not previously established standards of student behavior and your expectations, specify these expectations and behavioral standards before you begin the activity.

Principle 2

If in a continuing activity a student or group of students behave in a manner contrary to specific expectations, use a desist strategy aimed at reaching the level of expectations while causing the least possible disruption to the classroom setting.

It is important that you specify the appropriate behavior for a particular activity. During a test, for example, you may decide that the students should not speak out if they raise their hands and are called on. During a construction period, the students may be permitted to speak quietly. Your verbal statement of the appropriate social behavior is the social standard or norm. You may establish this standard directly by telling the students what you expect of them, or you may establish it indirectly by leading a discussion on the appropriate behavior for a specified activity. Providing appropriate behavioral cues and clearly stated classroom standards will improve classroom climate and learning (Brophy, 1986).

Classroom Regulations

When you use desist strategy in establishing classroom regulations, keep five important elements in mind. First, students are, for the most part, reasonable human beings who are anxious to make their classrooms cooperative and pleasant places in which to learn. By enlisting student aid in the formulation of classroom regulations, you help prevent classroom management problems in two ways: (1) students tend to have a greater interest in the maintenance of these regulations when they have had a part in generating them, and (2) they have a greater understanding of the need for, and the meaning of, regulations when they help to develop them.

Second, you must state classroom regulations as clearly as possible so that the students are not confused about what the regulations are or what they mean.

Third, maintain classroom regulations with justice. If the regulation was worth establishing, it should be worth maintaining with consistency for each student throughout the school year.

Fourth, use classroom regulations to establish a classroom routine. When you state regulations with clarity and maintain them with fairness, students soon realize what is expected of them in the classroom without being constantly reminded and nagged. When a routine is established in the classroom, deviations from the routine are more obvious and, therefore, more controllable in terms of classroom management techniques.

Fifth, and finally, the teacher and the class should make as few regulations as possible.

Desist Strategies: Observations

We should not leave the topic of desist strategies without including a short summary of one of the more important works on the topic. Jacob S. Kounin (1970) reported that over half (55.2 percent) of the teachers' perceived student "misbehaviors" could be categorized as talking or noise behaviors. In addition, nontask misbehaviors—for example, gum chewing—accounted for 17.2 percent of the total; and all other deviations—being late, not having homework, moving about the room without permission—accounted for the remainder of the misbehaviors (27.6 percent). According to Kounin's categories, the bulk of student misbehaviors would be rated as "low" level in significance.

Yet, when teachers were given the options of punishing, providing a suitable desist, or prescribing another form of productive activity in reaction to these misbehaviors, over half of the teachers' reactions were classified as high-level, public-dimension desists (see Table 10-2). The interesting, or perhaps sad, finding in Kounin's study is that in 92 percent of the cases, the teachers could give *no reasons* why the student misbehavior was perceived as being bad. Furthermore, in 95.6 percent of the cases, the teacher never provided the class with any knowledge of the expected standards. This, of course, is an indictment of the teacher, not of the students.

The "Ripple Effect"   In another study Kounin noted the effects on the class of the way in which teachers either punished students or provided desists when a student or group misbehaved. After observing students in kindergarten through college, he collected data based on experimental conditions to show that the way the teacher provided a desist had, in fact, an accompanying effect on all of the class members. This Kounin called the "ripple effect." As students observe the teacher confronting a student for apparent misbehavior, all other class members tend to be adversely affected as well. Kounin reported that the nature of the angry desist did not motivate the other students to behave better or to attend to the task; rather, they became anxious, restless, and uninvolved.

Lest it seem that all is lost because of teacher insensitivity, Marvin L. Grantham and Clifton S. Harris, Jr. (1976) reported that an entire elementary school faculty in Dallas decided to improve student discipline by determining that they, the faculty, were part of the problem. Taking action, the faculty decided on a course of inservice education. Within one year, a marked *decrease* in discipline problems resulted, along with some student gains in standardized tests.

The use of desist strategies is predicated on prudence and wisdom. When dealing with classroom management problems, it is usually best to use a low rather than a high level of force, and it is generally better to use a private rather than a public form of communication. However, there will be occasional situations in which a high-level, public dimension is the most appropriate. A classroom fight or other life-threatening situations are examples of such a use. In the vast majority of cases, the teacher's use of low-level, private desists will handle the classroom problem. The indiscriminate use of power will render any classroom management technique ineffectual.

Assertive Discipline

As the name implies, "assertive discipline" is a no-nonsense approach to student-teacher and student-student behavior in the classroom. It has obviously caught the attention of the educational community. Lee and Marlene Canter (1988) claim they have trained over 300,000 teachers in assertive discipline techniques.

In brief, an assertive teacher will not tolerate behaviors that interrupt learning in the classroom. After establishing positive expectations early in the school year, the teacher practices consistent reinforcement of these established procedures. When a student behaves inappropriately, the teacher promptly provides feedback to limit the behavior. If the behavior persists, the teacher clearly and publicly defines the undesirable behavior to the student and suggests the desirable behavior. Rewards to the class, as well as to the individual, are provided if the class meets identified behavioral and learning objectives. Punishment to individuals in the assertive discipline classroom often takes the form of "time-out" sessions, removal of preferred activities, parent conferences, and detention.

Assertive discipline requires more than one teacher's use. Our experience leads us to conclude that this strategy needs school implementation. The principal and other teachers must subscribe to the idea to make it effective. Further, parents must be fully oriented to its use. Edmund T. Emmer and Amy Aussiker (1988) caution that some teachers abuse the processes associated with assertive discipline, thus reducing its efficacy. As with any management system, teachers must be alert to problems caused by the imposed management system. Assertive discipline is no exception. Thomas McDaniel (*Educational Leadership,* March, 1989) followed up a series of articles debating the value of assertive discipline with these cautionary notes. Any school contemplating any model of discipline ought to measure the program on the following criteria:

1. It should be philosophically sound.
2. It should be pedagogically defensible.
3. It should be psychologically appropriate.
4. It should be pragmatically feasible.
5. It should be professionally evaluated.

Meaning? Read the research, consider the principles espoused by the model, and then determine its appropriateness for your students, learning objectives, and environment.

Behavior Modification

Behavior modification is an imposed-discipline approach to managing both individual and classroom behaviors. Technically, behavior modification refers to the use of modern learning principles in the design and improvement of educational practice. For our purposes, behavior modification means that instructional procedures are planned, implemented, and modified according to the student's progress toward identified educational or behavioral goals.

Two issues should be clarified before we address the principles behind behavior modification. First, behavior modification, with all its formats, procedures, and contingencies, is often attacked because of its "excess baggage." As teachers often state, "It's just not realistic; it asks too much of the teacher." Indeed, teachers, without help, will not be able to implement the extensive charting and interventions that we detail in this chapter. However, *experienced* teachers will adapt many of the procedures listed here to suit the conditions and constraints of their situations. In other words, if this approach works for you, use it; if parts of it work for you, adapt it; and if none of it works for you, drop it.

Second, the neophyte teacher who goes into the teachers' lounge and announces that he or she is trying behavior modification on a particular student will quickly learn that *all* good teachers have been using this approach for years without benefit of the label. With these ideas in mind, we will move on to the procedures and principles of behavior modification.

Basic Principles

The use of behavioral principles necessitates that a rather well-prescribed format be defined (Strother, 1985). Generally, this involves four phases: (Phase 1) charting baseline information, (Phase 2) using an intervention phase when the contingencies are changed or manipulated, (Phase 3) conducting a reversal state when the original contingencies are reinstated, and (Phase 4) returning finally to the intervention condition.

Phase 1: Charting Baseline Behaviors   During the baseline period, observations and tabulations of the target behavior (the behavior to be changed) are recorded. Information is provided on how often the target behavior occurs and when and under which classroom conditions it occurs. This phase provides evidence whether or not the problem actually exists. Many times systematic observation reveals that a student who has been labeled as "disruptive" does not exhibit the disruptive behavior more often than do his or her peers. All data are identified and tallied so that an established "rate" may be determined. (See Figure 10-2, which illustrates one example of charting.)

In collecting these data, use units of time. The units that you choose depend on the frequency of behavior. For example, if a response occurs very infrequently, it is not worthwhile to use very short time intervals when determining the frequency of its occurrence. For behaviors that occur frequently, you can use a time sampling of a few minutes. The time intervals depend on the situation. A code system can be utilized so that the recordings can be listed rapidly. For example, you can use codes such as Ti (talking at inappropriate times) and At (attention from the teacher). This type of systematic data collection provides you with information about the frequency of the behavior and the contingencies that produce or maintain it.

By the end of three or four days, the chart should show a pattern of when the defined behavior occurs. Study the chart carefully because the behavior may be

Figure 10-2   *Typical Chart Illustrating Student's "Turning in Homework" Behaviors During Four Phases of Behavior Modification Paradigm*

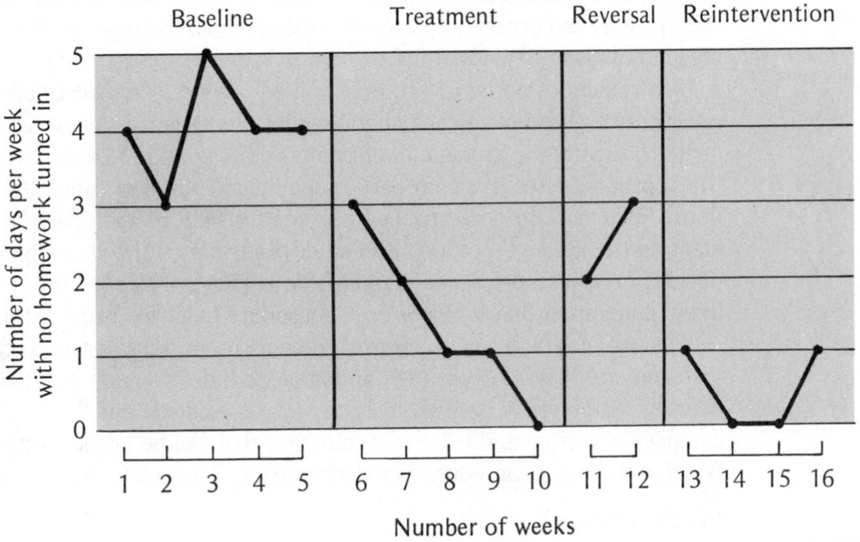

demonstrated only at specific times during the day. The problem, then, is limited to a specific behavior at a specific time and is now much more readily corrected by various behavior modification strategies.

The chart also serves as a baseline that will help you to choose an appropriate strategy and to determine the effectiveness of the strategy chosen. If the behavior occurs only two or three times during silent reading, you may select ways to increase the student's ability to read silently. Structure the day so that during these periods you are positioned near the student to administer verbal praise when the appropriate behavior (silent reading) occurs. During this time, continue to record the student's behavior to determine whether or not the intervention is effective. If, after a few days of your increased attention, there is a decrease in the number of times the student talks to neighbors during a silent reading period, you can assume that the strategy is having a positive effect.

Phase 2: Intervention or Experimental Phase   Once the specific behaviors have been identified and their frequency charted, a plan is then devised for changing the behaviors in some desired direction. In most cases, you will try to reinforce an appropriate behavior while ignoring or not responding to the inappropriate ones.

Often, student problem behaviors are followed by more attention than usual from the teacher or peers; if a student shows isolate behavior, for example, cajole or persuade that student to cooperate with other class members. During the intervention phase, you can test the reliability of the strategy by reversing the contingencies. This means that the student will no longer receive attention for working in isolation but will be given attention only when there is observable interaction with others. If the strategy is correct, the student will show an increase in interaction and a decrease in isolate behavior.

The results of an initial strategy will be shown to be valid or invalid during the intervention phase of the behavioral model. Sometimes, verbal reinforcers are adequate to modify the student's behavior. You may need to experiment to determine the appropriate set of reinforcers that requires the least effort to change the student's behavior. In some cases, you need visible or material reinforcers such as stars on the student's papers, the student's name on the class "honor list," tokens, pencils, or special privileges given to the student. Whatever the reward, it is absolutely imperative that it follow the appropriate behavior immediately.

The use of *reinforcers* is a critical component for behavior modification. If you use the same set of reinforcers over an extended time, you may find that they lose their efficacy. After studying this problem, Roger Addison and Donald T. Tosti (1979) compiled a system and a list of reinforcers that can be applied with various motivational strategies in an education environment. The reinforcers are these:

1. recognition
2. tangible rewards
3. classroom learning activities
4. classroom and school responsibilities
5. status indicators
6. incentive feedback
7. personal activities
8. social activities
9. relief from aversive policies or procedures
10. relief from aversive classroom environments

Addison and Tosti caution that reinforcers are very personal, and a teacher may have to try various reinforcers with a specific student before finding the most powerful one. Obviously, there is no one universal reinforcer. Anne Turnbaugh Lockwood (1988) classifies several of the above activities as being aspects of *student recognition programs*. She stresses that such programs emphasize student success. In this regard, Lockwood reinforces worthy student achievements. Recognition helps create a positive climate and makes schooling *intentionally inviting*.

Charles B. Schultz and Roger H. Sherman (1976) also warn teachers that the preference for a reinforcer should be made "separately for each individual rather than by the a priori judgments of the experimenter." Schultz and Sherman analyzed studies that concerned the selection of student reinforcers by persons who used the social class status of the student as the primary criterion. Teachers, they caution, tend to think that lower socio-economic class students need material things as reinforcers, while middle and upper class students respond better to nonmaterial reinforcers. Their study showed this generalization to be erroneous!

Phase 3: Reversal Phase   For most teachers, there is no further class manipulation once the appropriate reward or reinforcer is determined. However, following the behavior modification paradigm completely, you should revert from phase 2 conditions to those that took place during original baseline conditions. This requirement is often resisted by teachers, since it means returning to the original undesirable condition. But how else will one know whether or not the condition instituted in phase 2 is really effective? By reverting to the previous phase, you obtain data to demonstrate whether or not the change in behavior is due to your intervening action.

As with phases 1 and 2, in phase 3 data are consistently tabulated so that the behavioral patterns are quickly discernible. Phase 3 usually is conducted only long enough to effect a reversal of behavior to the baseline type. When you have observed such behavior, go on to phase 4.

Phase 4: Reinstating the Intervention Conditions   The final stage reinstates the conditions used during phase 2. If the intervention caused a change in behaviors during the second phase, it should do so again during this final phase. But if there is no change toward the desired behaviors, then you were just lucky in phase 2, and you will have to start all over again.

One variation that may be applied in lieu of moving to phases 3 and 4 (reversal and reinstatement) is to use a multiple series of baselines. This technique follows the same format as noted above, but does not use the reversal and reinstatement components. Instead the student is "charted" in several or possibly all classes, for example, math, science, physical education, art. The intervention or reinforcement is applied in only one of the classes while baseline data collection is maintained in the remaining classes. If a change in behavior takes place in the reinforced, but not in other, classes, then the other teachers might begin that intervention to change behavior in their classes also. However, if there is a change (in the direction desired by the teachers) in behavior in all classes, reinforcement in the one class was probably adequate to alter the student's behavior.

Intervention may also be applied to other inappropriate behaviors. The math teacher might reinforce the completing of assignments; the science teacher might simultaneously reinforce "attending" behaviors. With the participation of the key people with whom the student interacts (other teachers, counselor, parents), the identification and implementation of a plan of reinforcement is assured.

Principles for Effective Classroom Management

There are several general principles that can help the teacher to apply behavior modification in a classroom situation.

Accentuate the Positive   Schools have been criticized for being too "unpleasant" and teachers for being far too negative toward students. To change this image, the teacher must praise students, even if it is for the most inconsequential matter.

Admittedly, it may be very difficult to be supportive of a student who continually disrupts the classroom, but it has been frequently demonstrated that simply admonishing a student will not reduce the inappropriate behavior. Praising some positive aspect of the student's behavior is more likely to bring about change (Cochran, 1983).

How does the teacher use different forms of praise or social reinforcement? There are verbal, nonverbal, and tactile reinforcers. For example, there are positive verbal praise terms such as:

All right	Fantastic	Mighty fine	Splendid
Awesome	Fine	Neat	Super
Beautiful	Great	Nice work	Terrific
Clever	Ideal	Oh, boy	Unreal
Darn good	Just great	Pleasurable	Very interesting
Dynamite	Keep it up	Quite nice	A winner
Excellent	Lovely	Really great	Wonderful
Fabulous	Marvelous	Royal	Wow

Nonverbal praise can be provided by the following actions:

Laughing	Pointing with a smile	Smiling
Looking with interest	Raising the eyebrows	Thumb-up signal
Moving toward student	Signaling by	Winking
Nodding approval	lifting palms	

Identify Productive Behavior for the Class   Praise is a reinforcement not only for the student to whom it is directed but also for the entire class. You are providing them an explicit model of what is expected. To be sure, public praise can be embarrassing as well as reinforcing; therefore, you must learn what technique works best for each student—and hence, for the whole class.

Start Small   In most cases, students view major changes in behavior as being unachievable. If a student hands in about 25 percent of the required homework, there is little chance that reinforcement will result in 100 percent production of the work right away. Given this situation, establish a definite contingency schedule and make a behavior contract with the student. The student may complete two of five assignments in the first week. If so, move up the requirement to three of five assignments for the next week. In terms of successive approximations to the desired behavior, it is important to remember that the student probably did not reach the present level of academic deficiency in just one giant step. Therefore, do not expect to remedy the problem in one great leap. Follow small initial steps by increasing the quantity or the quality until the student reaches the criterion measure agreed on. This requires you to be patient and to give constant positive feedback to the student.

Be Consistent As you begin to use some form of behavior modification in the classroom, whether on an individual or group basis, modify your behaviors so as to keep them consistent and predictable. If you remain consistent in your responses to student stimuli, then you can better predict the reactions of class members.

Summary

Behavior modification is a viable alternative with a set of strategies that you can use in establishing effective classroom management. Many teachers, principals, and counselors are outwardly hostile to the behavior modification model because it is allegedly "unhumanistic." To be sure, there is behaviorism and there are behaviorists. They are not one and the same. The classroom teacher may select components of the behavioral approach and yet retain a humanistic approach to learning and students. If the ultimate goal of classroom management is to change behavior and if behavior modification will accomplish the goal with the least amount of effort, then behavior modification is a very humane contribution to the mental health of all concerned.

We conclude this section with that classic story told by Albert Rosenfeld (1974) about a junior high school in Visalia, California. The teachers were complimenting one of the special education teachers on doing a great job in improving the behavior and scholarship of the problem students. Finally, the special education teacher confessed that he had taught his charges to use behavior modification on their teachers. Using positive reinforcement to shape teacher behaviors, the students received higher-quality teaching and better treatment from the teaching staff. Maybe that is the answer—teach the students how to apply behavior modification.

CLASSROOM ROUTINES

This section will apply the previous theories to fit the classroom culture. Through experience, you will discover that many issues falling clearly into classroom management do not fall clearly into the constructs of any management strategies. We present several of those issues now because they are issues every teacher faces: (1) classroom routines, (2) management style diversity, and (3) interactions, reactions, distractions.

There are common elements in any management system that suggest routine ways of dealing with instructional and behavioral interactions in the classroom (see Table 10-3). The research on teacher effectiveness gives us a perspective through which to synthesize the strategies that we already presented. We will focus on five elements of effective teaching: (1) planning, (2) establishing usable rules, (3) getting off to a good start, (4) monitoring of the environment, and (5) providing clear directions (see Rutter, 1983, for detailed discussion).

Table 10-3   *Selected Problems Associated with Classroom Management*

Problems of Motivation	Instructional Problems
Lack of activity for students	A need for variety of instructional techniques
Apathetic student attitudes	Goals or objectives not clearly communicated to students
Getting all students involved in activities	Pace too fast or too slow
Uninvolved students	Students who missed the orientation or prerequisite skills
Daydreaming	Necessary prerequisite entry skills not developed; thus, students fail to achieve stated objectives
Lack of success	Students who are upset over their evaluation
Teacher's negative attitude	Students not following directions
	Failure to complete all assignments

Procedural Problems	Disruptive Problems
Unclear assignments given by teacher	Excessive talking at beginning of class
Moving the class to a different room	Note passing
Establishing a systematic routine for procedural activities	Cheating
Teacher did not reserve a special room or space for the activity	Stealing
	Vandalism
Projector or A-V equipment not previously checked out	Students seeking attention
	Students arriving late for class
Films not previewed by teacher; thus, inappropriate material presented	Teacher making unenforceable threats
	Racial tensions
Necessary materials not available in the room	Teacher making value judgments about student's dress, home life, or parents
Discussion groups not planned in advance	Obscene verbal or nonverbal gestures

Planning

Detailed planning is initially time-consuming, but teachers who make explicit plans are better organized and see the worth of these plans (Worsham and Emmer, 1983). Studies by Carolyn M. Evertson (1986) and by Andrew C. Porter and Jere Brophy (1988) illustrate that teachers who plan and communicate their expectations to their students promote academic achievement. For example, effective teachers know what, whom, and how they will teach; they have materials ready for students; they plan for smooth transitions between classes or activities; and they have activities ready for students who finish early.

The well-prepared teacher keeps the lesson moving at a brisk pace but does not ignore any student having some learning difficulty. These teachers do not allow interruptions during the lesson, and they stress the importance of every lesson. Our observations show that good teachers are efficient in their planning time and do critique the day's work. They jot a few notes into their lesson-planning books to act as tips for future lessons. We also observed that their lesson plans are very brief and are conceptual in nature. But they do formal planning.

Establishing Usable Rules

Effective managers teach students how to follow the rules and procedures and begin with the rules that are of the most immediate importance (How do I get permission to go to the bathroom? How do I ask a question?) Clear rules should also be consistently enforced. On-again, off-again enforcement muddles clarity and contributes to student behavior problems (Frieberg, 1983). Rules are made to emphasize academic and social achievement.

Effective teachers also make rules not related to discipline. These cover classroom systems for distributing materials, for making smooth transitions, for starting and ending class on time, and for accomplishing such routines as pencil sharpening and using the bathroom (Doyle, 1985). Simplicity is the hallmark of establishing rules. If the rules are not used or enforced, students become confused; thus, consistency is a trait that we all strongly endorse.

Getting Off to a Good Start

Effective classroom managers discuss classroom procedures with their students at the beginning of the school year and provide opportunities for practice to ensure understanding (Swick, 1985). During the first few days of the school, much feedback is needed. State your expectations frequently and give students positive or corrective feedback. By the end of the third or fourth week of school, you can anticipate that transitions will be smoother and shorter and that reminders to your students on class routines can be greatly reduced (Evertson et al., 1989).

Effective teachers hold students accountable for their behavior and for learning. They monitor student behavior in the classroom, and they return completed papers and homework with feedback. Effective teachers make each student responsible for some work during the learning activity and then monitor to see that it was actually accomplished. These teachers are also strong student motivators (Gage and Berliner, 1984).

Continuous Monitoring

Room arrangement is an important part of classroom management strategies. The orderly arrangement of desks and tables in a classroom contributes to a smooth, businesslike atmosphere that promotes effective use of instructional time (Brophy, 1983). Two aspects of room arrangement are critical: (1) your ability to see all students at all times, and (2) the traffic patterns that you establish. It is important to be able to monitor all students from your desk and from all other areas where you are likely to be. Simply being visually close to a student can prevent many problems.

Moreover, J. T. Dillon (1988) found questioning to be an effective monitoring strategy. During questioning activities, effective teachers ask questions, then look around the room before calling on a student. They call on volunteers as well as nonvolunteers and seem to get around to everyone, but not in a predictable manner. Effective teachers interspersed group answers with individual responses and occasionally threw out challenging statements such as: "I don't think anyone can get this!" Finally, effective teachers monitored the class by asking students to react to the answers of others. Such monitoring strategies as questioning techniques and classroom arrangements will promote a smooth-flowing, highly interactive learning environment with a high percentage of on-task student behavior.

Providing Clear Directions

The giving of directions is a critical part of a teacher's function (Long, 1985). Whether the directions concern instruction or classroom procedures, they must be given clearly and succinctly and, most importantly, their orientation must be positive. Directions given to disruptive students, such as "stop that" or "cut that out" omit the most important part of the teacher's objective: *What is the student to do after he or she "stops" or "cuts out" the disruptive behaviors?* It is much more accurate and meaningful to give directions to students in a positive form. Provide the student with a constructive alternative. For example, you may suggest that the student return to work, or you may provide some instructionally related activity that replaces the disruptive behavior. This approach both changes behaviors and directs students to a *positive activity*.

Effective teachers prepare students for transitions (Evertson, 1986) between activities and at the end of activities. Besides making transitions from one activity to the next quickly, they are especially careful not to end one activity and begin a second, then return to the first. Effective teachers prepare their classes for transition between lessons. Abrupt endings set the stage for numerous behavior problems. Paul V. Gump (1982), for example, computed that 21 percent of student time is spent in *transition*. This is the time needed to end one lesson or activity and begin another. To become more efficient, Gump suggests, give signals, set time limits, and provide very clear instructions—even modeling as needed.

Summary

In conclusion, the research on effective teacher practices presented here can apply to both elementary and secondary classrooms. The specific ways in which you approach planning will obviously vary according to student maturity and achievement

Table 10-4   *Examples of Discipline and Classroom Management Teacher Behaviors*

Discipline

In-school suspension
Sending misbehaving student to the office
Parent contacted regarding misbehaving student
Use of check or demerit system
Student's grade is lowered as a consequence of behavior
Public humiliation of misbehaving student
Loss of privilege for misbehaving student

Classroom Management

Teacher emphasizes rules at start of school year
Teacher plans for smooth transitions, having minimal loss of time between activities.
Teacher pays attention to entire class; continuous scanning of group
Well-paced activities
Teacher gives clear and concise instructions
Classroom environment is carefully designed
Activities are organized in advance

Used with permission of Rita Seedorf.

levels. While the five areas of effective teacher practices detailed above are especially helpful during the first few weeks of school, they are also useful for targeting or diagnosing classroom management problems throughout the year.

Elementary teachers may spend much time during the first few weeks of school teaching students rules and procedures, while in secondary schools, less time may be applied. The research at both levels remains quite clear: *teachers who do not actively teach the rules and routines have less time available for instruction and, consequently, less sustained learning.*

We use the terms *discipline* and *classroom management* throughout Chapter 10. Table 10-4 illustrates how the two concepts differ operationally. The list for discipline may be summarized as showing *reactive* teacher behaviors. The classroom management behaviors illustrate *proactive* teacher actions. This comparison shows how much management differs from discipline. Being proactive reduces the need to be reactive.

MANAGEMENT STYLE DIVERSITY

When behavior problems arise, you may wonder which classroom management strategy is the most effective or whether or not you can combine several strategies successfully. Generally, the strategy that most often produces the desired results with the lowest expenditure of your time and effort is the most effective. *Effective* is a relative term and implies a continuum of qualities that approximate effectiveness. The term also must be understood as being "situational". In specific situations with a specific student, Reality Therapy may be completely successful, while with other individuals, desist strategies may be more effective. You need to make these observations and to decide on the most suitable course of action.

Classroom management strategies often can be mixed successfully. Although all techniques are based on different theoretical premises, they are all oriented toward improving behavior in a positive, productive manner. In any one classroom, the teacher may find that there are individuals who have experiences that require many diverse management responses. In no case do we imply that the teacher should resort to negative behaviors such as sarcasm or ridicule, which, in our professional opinion, are never appropriate strategies for classroom management.

One last caution should be given on the eclectic approach. The effectiveness of any strategy often depends on how much time, energy, and confidence you invest in the technique. A possible pitfall is moving quickly from one technique to another without expending the necessary time and energy. Such efforts are likely to be counterproductive, thus confusing the student and making management problems more severe.

Every teacher must use some type of classroom management system or systems. We have introduced three such systems, all of which tend to be humane. The final selection and implementation of any one strategy or combination of strategies rest solely with you. But the ultimate criterion is student success.

INTERACTIONS, REACTIONS, DISTRACTIONS

Gender and Equity Issues

Teachers are often unaware that they may be biased toward or against some group of students because of sex, ethnic background, or intelligence level. This bias is most obvious in science classes. As a consequence, Dale Baker (1988) reported, females were more negative toward high school sciences than were males. Thomas L. Good and Jere E. Brophy (1987) provide examples from several studies showing that (1) teachers rewarded boys more than girls in secondary science classes, (2) girl-initiated science interactions *declined* during middle school years, (3) teacher expectations favored boys, and (4) racial minorities tend to be rejected more by teachers than majority students are. These traits are all *intentionally disinviting* to learners.

What can you do to be an unbiased teacher? First, you can tabulate, or have a designated tabulator chart, your student interactions. Positive and negative feedback, nonverbal cues, use of male pronouns, and male bias can be tabulated. If bias is apparent, use a list of student names to conduct recitations on a regular schedule. Change your verbal and written communication patterns to use inclusionary language. (In case you need a model, this textbook is written with inclusionary language.) Provide an equitable number of leadership positions to males, females, minority, and handicapped students. In short, you become proactive by making the classroom environment equitable to all.

To enhance greater equity for achievement, Sam Kerman (1979) perfected a series of fifteen strategies that are collectively labeled TESA, "Teacher Expectations and Student Achievement." The program has three strands. The first is *response opportunities,* which has five specific points: (1) equitable distribution of participation, (2) individual help, (3) latency or wait-time, (4) delving, and (5) higher-level questions. The second strand focuses on *feedback:* (1) affirmation for correct responses, (2) praise, (3) reasons for praise, (4) listening, and (5) accepting feelings. The third strand refers to *personal regard:* (1) proximity of teacher to student, (2) courtesy, (3) personal interest and compliments, (4) touching (as a positive gesture), and (5) desist strategies.

As you examine these fifteen elements, you will conclude that we have stressed all but touch. Very young pupils do touch their teachers and vice versa; but we suggest that, beginning at middle school, do *not* touch students, especially members of the opposite sex. The best intentions may be misinterpreted and lead to charges of sexual harassment.

The critical point is to be fair, impartial, and *intentionally inviting* to every student.

Complex Instructional Environments

Much of this book is devoted to interactive teaching strategies—discussions, inquiry, simulation, and classroom management. As you incorporate the various interactive techniques, be aware that they tend to be complex methods and, as such, the classroom routine changes quite drastically. For example, when using any inquiry strategy, you will find students working on tasks. Some students will be working in pairs, others in small groups, and yet others individually. This format requires far more teacher energy to manage than does the class with every student in place. As you use more materials, integrate microcomputers into the program, and establish a complex learning environment, you must also adapt your management styles.

Complex instructional environments require some student autonomy and self-direction. Without these traits the classroom would be chaotic. The complex instructional condition was examined by Elizabeth G. Cohen, JoAnn K. Intili, and Susan Hurevitz Robbins (1979). In their analysis, the role of the teacher as classroom manager changes as one evolves from large groups to complex designs. For example, in large groups or with teacher-directed instruction, student supervision tends to be routine with an authority figure (teacher) using rules or desist strategies. However, with complex designs (e.g., inquiry, discussions, or laboratories), the teacher must delegate authority and establish constructive behavior norms. Students are managed through extensive feedback, student-teacher communications, and systematic record-keeping. Student cooperation and commitment are essential. Teachers work much harder, plan more thoroughly, and demonstrate greater numbers of interactions when using complex classroom designs.

In addition, we have observed that teachers can establish a positive classroom climate by (1) enriching the room with books, magazines, and wall charts, (2) ordering materials that are durable, (3) allowing some time for student-initiated learning, (4) making efficient transitions between activities, and (5) establishing procedures for classroom routines.

Tracking

Teachers enjoy working with the top 10 percent. And why not? After all, the academic elite virtually teach themselves. So, some schools have resorted to tracking. As a result, those who are labeled as, say, Cayuses are not expected to amount to much. And once put in the Cayuse pack, they will probably stay there for all twelve years of their education. Teachers expect them to do poorly there. (What an example of being *intentionally disinviting!*)

The most compelling evidence against tracking comes from a 1988 study by Adam Gamoran and Mark Berends. They concluded that tracking:

1. Favors students in the high-track
2. Accounts for disparities in student achievement
3. Produces a cycle of low expectations for low-track students
4. Creates poor morale among other teachers and students

In their review of tracking, Good and Brophy (1987) note inconclusive findings on the benefit of tracking at both elementary and secondary levels, especially over long periods of time. However, they did report that *teachers* dislike teaching low-ability classes, spend less time preparing for them, and schedule less interesting or less challenging activities for them. As a matter of note, students in low-track classes are merely kept busy with mundane, irrelevant work. Conversely, students in high-track classes have better attitudes toward school, better work norms, and assume greater leadership positions.

And, as we stated above, the evidence is that there is little movement among tracked students (Cayuses) with one exception: movement tends to be downward. Many problems of tracking reflect poor placement. For example, one middle school girl was placed in the school's slow reading track for three years. The teachers and principal were quite unaware that during these years this young adolescent on her own had read *every* Nancy Drew mystery book that had been published! So much for objective placement.

We recognize that specific classes will automatically draw the top academic students in high school, for example, advanced mathematics, physics and chemistry, advanced foreign language study. Of course, many of these teachers will discourage girls, the handicapped, or minority students from entering or worse advise them *not* to enroll in the early prerequisite classes. Such incidents are commonly reported by university undergraduate students. Gender bias is closely related to tracking and, in our opinion, is extremely unprofessional teacher behavior.

In middle and elementary schools, tracking has no professional defense (see Becker, 1988). Review Chapter 7 for several tested strategies that will have a far more effective impact on student achievement, attitude and quality of work in these grades. These include cross-age peer tutoring, cooperative learning, feedback, reinforcement, and mastery learning. To be sure, there are gifted and talented programs in most schools. Several use the "pull-out" model; that is, they pull these students out of regular classes for enrichment experiences. That such a model disrupts the regular class is often ignored. After all, wouldn't you want your children to get the gifted treatment? The real challenge is how to provide *all* children with that elusive "best of educations."

Punishment

Sometimes the school climate is not positive and some form of punishment must be administered. *Loss of privilege* is the most common form, for example, loss of recess, sports pass, or an assembly. *Corporal punishment* is generally lawful, but it must be administered cautiously. All school districts have a policy on this matter. Generally, *suspensions* are handled by the school principal. *In-school suspensions* are currently very common. This technique removes disruptive students or chronic mischief makers from a class and places them in a special isolated area when they must do their school work.

Expulsions are so serious that they are reserved to the local school board. Expulsion is the "court of last resort" and is administered most prudently.

Referral Agencies

A new teacher must know the school's policy on referral agencies. These include welfare organizations, youth advocacy groups, mental health clinics, juvenile court counselors, and ministers. It is common for teachers to use school-supported services such as counselors, social workers, coaches, special service personnel, and administrators.

All schools have policies relating to the role of the police in the schools and court referral systems. Teachers are not usually associated with these agencies.

Alcohol and Drug Management

In today's classroom you will almost certainly come in contact with drug and alcohol abuse among your students. This is an especially difficult issue for the new teacher because of the widespread use of alcohol and drugs on college campuses. For many new teachers, alcohol and drug use is considered to be a question of personal choice and parental responsibility and not community-based law.

As a teacher, though, you are responsible for developing and encouraging student understanding and value for our system of government and laws. Your role demands a high set of ethical standards because the community has given you charge of its youth. Further, professional ethics preclude your support of *student use* of alcohol or illegal drugs. Watch for these early warning signs of alcohol and drug abuse:

- Sudden behavioral changes—classwork is lost, is not turned in, is copied, or declines in quality
- Attitudinal changes—comments are made to hurt others' feelings, or an "I don't care" demeanor emerges
- School problems—grades decline, difficulties with other teachers and school personnel appear, fights and arguments occur
- Changes in social relationships—new friends are involved in a different social scene
- Self-destructive behavior—student has injuries from falls or fights that he or she has difficulty recounting
- Avoidance—student withdraws or refuses to communicate, spends an inappropriate amount of time in isolated behavior

All teachers must be cautious in handling students suspected of drug or alcohol abuse. An accusation may lead to a lawsuit by the student or the parents of the student. Our advice is to check with school administrators on the accepted protocol for dealing with such problems. The alcohol and drug problem is not simply critical—it is pandemic!

Records Management

Every teacher faces the task of recording grades, attendance, absences, tardiness, homework assignments, class participation, disciplinary actions, and other acts of classroom life. For legality, fairness, consistency, and documentation, you need a comprehensive and systematic approach to keeping records.

A major facet of records management is the establishment of a fair and equitable grading policy. You must establish guidelines for standards, quality, late work, missed assignments, bonus work, make-up tests, and class participation. Consistency and reasonableness are two criteria that will help you construct an appropriate grading policy.

Lastly, anecdotal records should be objectively maintained to document classroom incidents such as fights, inappropriate behavior, and cheating. Of course, you should also record student acts of courage, ingenuity, or creativity. Record these acts when they happen. This record provides you with a chronicle of highlights that may provide evidence to support or oppose a student.

Your understanding of these issues and your prompt decision when a problem arises help to develop teacher-student rapport and cooperation and to provide a role model for students. Collectively, classroom management considerations are often critical to the lives and safety of youngsters. Your ability to fulfill these conditions is acquired by on-the-job training. Perhaps this is the only way the concepts of classroom management truly can be mastered—in a classroom with real students, and a teacher who understands the theories and knows how to apply them.

Conclusion

We will close this book somewhat as we began: teachers make the difference in effective schools. Schooling is a mandatory legal requirement in nearly all states and provinces. Those who attend are not there of free will. Of course, there are some people in the schools who ought not to be there, but well over 95 percent of the population between ages six and eighteen can enjoy school and they can benefit to a maximum from those experiences.

Schooling does not have to reflect *flatness* or *mindlessness*. If you make a commitment to be *intentionally inviting* to all students—and we know that this is a tough goal—then you will have both learner and teacher success. Nobody said that you cannot love your work and impart some of that love to your students. You can model love of work; love of learning; love of sharing a newfound fact, concept, or principle. Only you can transform the classroom into a lively, interesting, and positive environment.

You control the classroom learning environment. Structure that environment so that everyone in it is highly motivated and successful in learning. It is the least you can do or, perhaps, the most!

FORMATIVE EVALUATION

Choose the best response to each statement below.

_____ 1. Ms. Anderson has been teaching a difficult concept in chemistry, and one student has disrupted the class. What type of meeting would Glasser recommend?
   (a) Social problem-solving
   (b) Educational diagnostic
   (c) Open-ended
   (d) Task-oriented

_____ 2. Behavior modification will be effective if the following guideline is followed:
   (a) Work on one behavior at a time.
   (b) Use the same reinforcer for each class member.
   (c) Do not use group pressure.
   (d) Never use negative reinforcement.

3. Regarding discipline or classroom management, the text supports the position that:
   (a) There is one good, acceptable method of maintaining classroom discipline, and teachers should use it.
   (b) Most teachers tend to contribute to the problem.
   (c) There are several techniques that can be appropriately applied.
   (d) Most techniques are not based on any theory; you find out what works for you in practice.

4. Democratic discipline implies that:
   (a) No rules are permissible, for they imply authority; authority has no place in a democratic classroom.
   (b) Rule-making should be limited to items that hinge on the state laws.
   (c) Rule-making should reflect rational explanations of behavior.
   (d) Because the teacher realizes that the students are mere juveniles, he or she makes the rules, which the students must endorse.

5. Teachers are most resistant to what phase of the behavior modification design?
   (a) Intervention phase
   (b) Reinstatement phase
   (c) Baseline phase
   (d) Reversal phase

6. Research on Teacher Effectiveness Practices has shown the following:
   (a) Directions should be few and best delivered in a casual manner.
   (b) Planning has little impact on student learning.
   (c) Questioning strategies are ineffective monitoring techniques.
   (d) Teaching procedures on classroom routines early in the school year are essential.

7. The concept behind desist strategies is
   (a) Characterized by the teacher's power to reward and punish.
   (b) That a teacher's authority is never challenged.
   (c) One of student self-responsibility.
   (d) Essential to the collection of baseline data for a teacher intervention.

8. According to Wallen's level of force dimension, a "threat" is categorized as
   (a) Low level of force.
   (b) High level of force.
   (c) Moderate level of force.
   (d) None of the above.

9. Which of the following is not an important element in establishing classroom regulations?
   (a) Enlist student aid in formulating classroom regulations.
   (b) Clearly and repeatedly state classroom regulations.
   (c) Provide variety in the classroom by frequent changes in expectations.
   (d) Maintain regulations with justice.

10. We could argue that classroom management is really school management. Discuss the implications of that assertion.

11. How can you implement a classroom management system to the concept you have not experienced in operation?

12. From a classroom management perspective, what are some indicators of a successful school climate?

13. How do you counter the tendency to seek only *one best* classroom management system?

14. Formulate a personal rationale for classroom management.

Responses

1. (a) 6. (d)
2. (a) 7. (c)
3. (c) 8. (c)
4. (c) 9. (c)
5. (d) 10.–14. These questions require some activity from you. We suggest that you work with a peer or a small group of three or four and discuss these questions.

REFERENCES

Addison, Roger, and Donald T. Tosti. "Taxonomy of Educational Reinforcement." *Educational Technology* 19:1979, 24–25.

Baker, Dale. "Teaching for Gender Differences." *NARST News* 30(1):April 1988.

Becker, Henry J. *Addressing the Needs of Different Groups of Early Adolescents.* Baltimore, Md.: Center for Research on Elementary and Middle Schools, Johns Hopkins University, 1988.

Brophy, Jere. "Classroom Management Techniques." *Education and Urban Society* 18:1986, 182–194.

———. "Improving Instruction: Effective Classroom Management." *School Administrator* 40:1983, 33–36.

Canter, Lee, and Marlene Canter. *Assertive Discipline: A Take-Charge Approach for Today's Educator.* Los Angeles: Lee Canter and Associates. Display at National Convention of National Staff Development Council, Chicago, December 11–14, 1988.

Cochran, Kathy H. "Prescription for Discipline." *Music Educators Journal* 70:1983, 32–36.

Cohen, Elizabeth G., JoAnn K. Intili, and Susan Hurevitz Robbins. "Task and Authority: A Sociological View of Classroom Management." In *Classroom Management,* the Seventy-eighth Yearbook of the National Society for the Study of Education. Daniel L. Duke, ed. Chicago: University of Chicago Press, 1979.

Dillon, J. T. *Questioning and Discussion: A Multidisciplinary Study.* Norwood, N.J.: Ablex Publishing, 1988.

Doyle, Walter. "Recent Research on Classroom Management: Implications for Teacher Preparation." *Journal of Teacher Education* 36:1985, 31–35.

Emmer, Edmund, and Amy Aussiker. "Assertive Discipline Ineffective." *Classroom Management SIG Newsletter,* American Educational Research Association, June 1988, 1–2.

Evertson, Carolyn M. "Do Teachers Make A Difference?: Issues for the Eighties." *Education and Urban Society* 18:1986, 195–210.

Evertson, Carolyn M., Edmund T. Emmer, Barbara S. Clements, Julie P. Sanford, and Murray E. Worsham. *Classroom Management for Elementary Teachers,* 2nd ed. Englewood Cliffs, N.J.: Prentice-Hall, 1989.

Frieberg, H. Jerome. "Consistency: The Key to Classroom Management." *Journal of Education for Teaching* 9:1983, 1–15.

Gage, N. L., and David C. Berliner. "Classroom Teaching: Planning and Management." *Educational Psychology,* 3rd ed. Boston: Houghton Mifflin, 1984.

Gallup, Alec M., and Stanley M. Elam. "The Annual Gallup Poll of the Public's Attitude Toward the Public Schools." *Phi Delta Kappan* 70(1):1988, 33–46.

Gamoran, Adam, and Mark Berends. *The Effects of Stratification in Secondary Schools: Synthesis of Survey and Ethnographic Research.* Madison, Wisc.: National Center of Effective Secondary Schools, University of Wisconsin at Madison, 1988.

Glasser, William. *Control Therapy in the Classroom.* New York: Harper & Row, 1986.

———. *The Identity Society.* New York: Harper & Row, 1972.

———. *Reality Therapy.* New York: Harper & Row, 1965, p. 6.

———. "Reality Therapy: An Anti-Failure Approach." *Impact* 2:1972, 6–9.

———. *Schools Without Failure.* New York: Harper & Row, 1969.

Good, Thomas L. "Recent Classroom Research: Implications for Teacher Education." In *Essential Knowledge for Beginning Educators.* David C. Smith, ed. American Association of Colleges for Teacher Education, Washington, D.C., 1983.

Good, Thomas L., and Jere E. Brophy. *Looking in Classrooms,* 4th ed. New York: Harper & Row, 1987.

Gordon, Thomas. *Teacher Effectiveness Training.* New York: Peter H. Wyden, 1974.

Grantham, Marvin L., and Clifton S. Harris, Jr. "A Faculty Trains Itself to Improve Student Discipline." *Phi Delta Kappan* 57:1976, 661–664.

Gump, Paul V. "School Settings and Their Keeping." In *Helping Teachers Manage Classrooms.* Daniel Duke, ed. Alexandria, Va.: Association for Supervision and Curriculum Development, 1982.

Hawley, Willis D., and Susan J. Rosenholtz. "Good Schools: What Research Says About Improving Student Achievement." *Peabody Journal of Education* 61:Summer 1984, 15–52.

Kerman, Sam. "Teacher Expectations and Student Achievement." *Phi Delta Kappan* 60:June 1979, No. 10, 716–718.

Koenig, Peter. "Glasser the Logician." *Psychology Today* 7:1974, 66–67.

Kohlberg, Lawrence. "The Cognitive-Developmental Approach to Moral Education." *Phi Delta Kappan* 56:1975, 670–677.

———. *Essays on Moral Development. Vol. 1: The Philosophy of Moral Development.* New York: Harper & Row, 1981.

Kounin, Jacob S. *Discipline and Group Management in Classrooms.* New York: Holt, Rinehart and Winston, 1970, pp. 22–25.

Kounin, Jacob S., and Paul V. Gump. "The Ripple Effect in Discipline." *Educational Digest* 24: 1959, 43–45.

Lockwood, Anne Turnbaugh. "Student Recognition Programs." *Resource Bulletin* 5:Fall 1988, National Center on Effective Secondary Schools, University of Wisconsin—Madison.

Long, James D. "Troubleshooters' Guide to Classroom Discipline." *Instructor* 95:1985, 122–124.

Maslow, Abraham H. *Motivation and Personality.* New York: D. Van Nostrand, 1968.

McDaniel, Thomas R. "Practicing Positive Reinforcement: Ten Behavior Management Techniques." *Clearing House* 60:1987, 389–392.

———. "The Discipline Debate: A Road through the Thicket." *Educational Leadership* 46:1989, 81–82.

Porter, Andrew C., and Jere Brophy. "Synthesis of Research on Good Teaching: Insights from the Work of the Institute for Research on Teaching." *Educational Leadership* 45:May 1988, 74–83.

Rosenfeld, Albert. "The Behavior Mod Squad." *Saturday Review of the World* 2:1974, 49.

Rutter, Michael. "School Effects on Pupil Progress:

Research Findings and Policy Implications." In *Handbook of Teaching and Policy.* Lee S. Shulman and Gary Sykes, eds. New York: Longman, 1983, pp. 3–41.

Sanford, Julie P. "Management of Science Classroom Tasks and Effects on Students' Learning Opportunities." *Journal of Research in Science Teaching* 24:1987, 249–265.

Sanford, Julie P., and Edmund T. Emmer. *Understanding Classroom Management: An Observation Guide.* Englewood Cliffs, N.J.: Prentice-Hall, 1988.

Sanford, Julie P., Edmund T. Emmer, and Barbara S. Clements. "Improving Classroom Management." *Educational Leadership* 40:1983, 56–60.

Schultz, Charles B., and Roger H. Sherman. "Social Class, Development, and Differences in Reinforcer Effectiveness." *Review of Educational Research* 46:1976, 25–59.

Skinner, B. F. *Science and Human Behavior.* New York: Macmillan, 1953.

Strother, Deborah B. "Classroom Management." *Phi Delta Kappan* 66:1985, 725–728.

Swick, Kevin J. *A Proactive Approach to Discipline: Six Professional Development Modules for Educators.* Washington, D.C.: National Education Association, 1985.

Wallen, Carl J. "Establishing Teaching Principles in the Area of Classroom Management." In *Low Cost Instruction Simulation Materials for Teacher Education.* Monmouth, Oreg.: Teaching Research, 1968. (U.S. Department of Health, Education and Welfare, Office of Education, Bureau of Research.)

Wolfgang, Charles H., and Carl D. Glickman. *Solving Discipline Problems: Strategies for Classroom Teachers,* 2nd ed. Boston: Allyn and Bacon, 1986.

Worsham, Murray E., and Edmund T. Emmer. *Teachers' Planning Decisions for the Beginning of School.* R&D Report No. 6152. Austin: Texas University, Research and Development Center for Teacher Education, 1983.

Index